OXFORD READINGS IN FEMINISM

FEMINISM AND THEOLOGY

PUBLISHED IN THIS SERIES:

Feminism and Renaissance Studies
edited by Lorna Hutson

Feminism and Science
edited by Evelyn Fox Keller and Helen E. Longino

Feminism, the Public and the Private
edited by Joan B. Landes

Feminism and Politics
edited by Anne Phillips

Feminism and History
edited by Joan Wallach Scott

Feminism and Cultural Studies
edited by Morag Shiach

Feminism and Pornography
edited by Drucilla Cornell

Feminism and the Body
edited by Londa Schiebinger

Feminism and History of Philosophy
edited by Genevieve Lloyd

OXFORD READINGS IN FEMINISM

Feminism and Theology

Edited by
Janet Martin Soskice
and
Diana Lipton

OXFORD
UNIVERSITY PRESS

OXFORD
UNIVERSITY PRESS

Great Clarendon Street, Oxford OX2 6DP

Oxford University Press is a department of the University of Oxford.
It furthers the University's objective of excellence in research, scholarship,
and education by publishing worldwide in

Oxford New York

Auckland Bangkok Buenos Aires Cape Town Chennai
Dar es Salaam Delhi Hong Kong Istanbul Karachi Kolkata
Kuala Lumpur Madrid Melbourne Mexico City Mumbai Nairobi
São Paulo Shanghai Taipei Tokyo Toronto

Oxford is a registered trade mark of Oxford University Press
in the UK and in certain other countries

Published in the United States
by Oxford University Press Inc., New York

Introduction, Notes, and Selection © Janet Martin Soskice
and Diana Lipton 2003

The moral rights of the authors have been asserted

Database right Oxford University Press (maker)

First published 2003

British Library Cataloguing in Publication Data

Data available

Library of Congress Cataloging in Publication Data

(Data applied for)

ISBN 0–19–878246–2

1 3 5 7 9 10 8 6 4 2

Typeset in Minion
by RefineCatch Limited, Bungay, Suffolk
Printed in Great Britain by
T.J. International Ltd., Padstow, Cornwall

Contents

Notes on Contributors

RACHEL ADLER is an Associate Professor at Hebrew Union College, Los Angeles, USA. She was a pioneer in the tasks of integrating feminist perspectives into the interpretation of Jewish texts and the renewal of Jewish law and ethics. She is the author of many articles on feminist philosophy, liturgy, and Jewish feminism.

SHARON A. BONG received her Ph.D. from the Department of Religious Studies at Lancaster University, England. Her research draws on her exposure to and involvement with women's non-governmental organizations at regional, national, and international levels, and considers the impact of cultures and religions on women's human rights in Malaysia. She is currently lecturing in Communication at Monash University, Malaysia.

ATHALYA BRENNER is Professor of Hebrew Bible/Old Testament at the University of Amsterdam, The Netherlands, and Distinguished Professor in the Rosenthal Chair in Hebrew Bible at Brite Divinity School, Fort Worth, Texas, USA. Her main interests are feminist criticism of the Hebrew Bible and early Judaisms; transdisciplinary approaches; Semitic philology; and computer applications in the humanities. She is the editor of the *Feminist Companion to the Bible* series (20 vols., 1993–2001) and is on the editorial board of the New Dutch Translation of the Bible, the *Journal of Biblical Literature*, *Biblical Interpretation*, the Brown Judaic Studies series, and the *Journal for the Study of the Old Testament*.

ELIZABETH A. CASTELLI is Associate Professor of Religion at Barnard College in New York, USA. She is the author of *Imitating Paul: A Discourse of Power* (1991), co-author of *The Postmodern Bible* (1995), and editor of several volumes, including *Women, Gender, Religion: A Reader* (2001). Her forthcoming book is *Martyrdom and Memory: Early Christian Culture-Making*.

ELIZABETH CLARK is the John Carlisle Kilgo Professor of Religion at Duke University, USA. She is the author/editor of eleven books on early Christianity, and is co-editor of the *Journal of Early Christian Studies*. She has been president of the American Academy of Religion, the American Society of Church History, and the North American Patristics Society.

SARAH COAKLEY is the Mallinckrodt Professor at Harvard Divinity School, USA. Her most recent book is *Powers and Submissions: Spirituality, Philosophy and Gender* (2002). Her published work moves between studies of modern theory (*Christ Without Absolutes*, 1994), comparative religion (*Religion and the Body*, 1997), patristic theory (articles on Gregory of Nyssa, especially), and feminist theology (*God, Sexuality and the Self: On the Trinity*, forthcoming). She is an ordained priest in the Church of England.

MARY DALY has lectured at over 300 colleges and universities in the United States and Canada, as well as at many international gatherings. She is the author of important books on feminist theology, philosophy, and ecology which include: *The Church and the Second Sex* (1968), *Beyond God the Father: Toward a Philosophy of Women's Liberation* (1973); *Gyn/Ecology: The Metaethics of Radical Feminism* (1978*); Pure Lust: The Elemental Feminist Philosophy* (1984); and *Quintessence . . . Realizing the Archaic Future: A Radical Elemental Feminist Manifesto* (1998).

JANE DEMPSEY DOUGLASS is Hazel Thompson McCord Professor of Historical Theology Emerita of Princeton Theological Seminary, USA. She is an ordained ruling elder in the Presbyterian Church (USA), and from 1990 to 1997 was president of the World Alliance of Reformed Churches. Her books include *Women, Freedom, and Calvin: The 1983 Annie Kinkead Warfield Lectures* (1985); *Justification in Late Medieval Preaching: A Study of John Geiler of Keisersberg* (1989); and (co-edited with J. F. Kay) *Women, Gender, and Christian Community* (1997).

ANITA DIAMANT is a freelance writer living in the area of Boston, USA. Since 1985 she has written on contemporary Jewish practice and the Jewish community, publishing articles in such magazines as *Reform Judaism* and *Hadassah*, and handbooks to Jewish life and lifecycle events that include *The New Jewish Wedding* (Simon & Schuster, 1985/2001), *The New Jewish Baby Book* (Jewish Lights, 1988/1994), and *Choosing a Jewish Life: A Handbook for People Converting to Judaism and for their Family and Friends* (Schocken, 1997). *The Red Tent* (St. Martin's Press, 1997) was her first work of fiction, and she has since written *Good Harbor* (Scribner's, 2001/2002). *Pitching my Tent*, a non-fiction collection of writings, is forthcoming in 2003.

J. CHERYL EXUM is Professor of Biblical Studies at the University of Sheffield, England. She is the author of numerous studies in the areas of biblical literary and feminist criticism; her books include *Tragedy and Biblical Narrative: Arrows of the Almighty* (1996), *Fragmented Women: Feminist (Sub)versions of Biblical Narratives* (1993), and *Plotted, Shot, and Painted: Cultural Representations of Biblical Women* (1997). She is Executive Editor of *Biblical Interpretation* and editor of the Sheffield Academic Press series Gender, Culture, Theory.

JACQUELYN GRANT is Callaway Professor of Systematic Theology at the Interdenominational Theological Center in Atlanta, Georgia, USA, and Director of Black Women in Church and Society.

BLU GREENBERG is the author of *On Women and Judaism: A View From Tradition, How to Run a Traditional Jewish Household*, and *Black Bread: Poems*

After the Holocaust. Since 1973 she has been active in the movement to bridge feminism and Orthodox Judaism. She chaired the first International Conference on Feminism and Orthodoxy in 1997, and is the co-founder and first president of the Jewish Orthodox Feminist Alliance. She is a former President of the Jewish Book Council of America and serves on the advisory boards of *Lilith*, the Jewish Student Press Service, and the International Research Institute on Jewish Women.

DAPHNE HAMPSON is Professor of Post-Christian Thought in the School of Divinity at the University of St Andrews, Scotland. She is the author of *Theology and Feminism* (1990), *After Christianity* (1996, 2002), and *Christian Contradictions: The Structures of Lutheran and Catholic Thought* (2001), and the editor of *Swallowing a Fishbone? Feminist Theologians Debate Christianity* (1996). She is at present working on *Theology, Feminism and Continental Philosophy*. She has broadcast and lectured widely on the implications of feminism for theology, in the United States, Canada, Germany, and the Netherlands as well as in Britain.

VERNA HARRISON is a monastic of the Orthodox Church of America and lives in Berkeley, California, USA. She is the author of *Grace and Human Freedom According to St Gregory of Nyssa* (1992) and many articles on topics in patristics and contemporary Orthodox theology. Her major research interests include the Cappadocian fathers, theological anthropology, and gender studies.

ADA MARÍA ISASI-DIAZ was born and raised in Havana, Cuba, and is now Professor of Ethics and Theology at Drew University in New Jersey, USA. Over the past twenty years she has worked at elaborating a *Mujerista* theology, a liberation theology from the perspective of grass-root Latinas/Hispanas living in the USA. She is the author of four books, and has edited and contributed to many other books and journals. She has lectured widely in the USA and has taught in the Philippines and in Cuba.

GRACE M. JANTZEN is Research Professor of Religion, Culture and Gender at the University of Manchester, England. She is centrally concerned with the ways in which mortality and violence are taken as natural and crucial to the human condition, while natality and flourishing are under-theorized, and sees these preoccupations as always shaped in constellations of gender, 'race', and power. These concerns are reflected in her books and articles, especially *Julian of Norwich: Mystic and Theologian* (2000); *Power, Gender and Christian Mysticism* (1995); and *Becoming Divine: Towards a Feminist Philosophy of Religion* (1998).

DIANA LIPTON read English at the University of Oxford, England, and did her doctoral research at the University of Cambridge, England. She has been a Fellow of Newnham College, Cambridge, since 1997, and is an Affiliated Lecturer in the Cambridge Divinity School and a part-time Lecturer at Leo

Baeck College–Centre for Jewish Education, London. She is the author of *Revisions of the Night: Politics and Promises in the Patriarchal Dreams of Genesis* (Sheffield Academic Press, 1999), and is working on a book on kings (divine and human), writing, and prophetic intercession in the Hebrew Bible.

BENJAPORN MOCHAI is from Thailand. She works on development projects with the poor, especially women, in the north-eastern regions of her country.

RACHEL MUERS is Margaret Smith Research Fellow in Religious Studies at Girton College, Cambridge, England. Her doctoral work on silence and the theological ethics of communication was completed in 2001. Her published articles include 'Silence and the Patience of God' in *Modern Theology*.

HAVIVA NER-DAVID is a writer, student, teacher, and activist living in Jerusalem, Israel, with her husband and four young children. She is completing her doctorate in Jewish Law at Bar Ilan University while studying for Orthodox rabbinical ordination. Her book *Life on the Fringes: A Feminist Journey Toward Traditional Rabbinic Ordination* weaves her personal experiences as a Jewish feminist with Jewish legal analysis on issues pertaining to women.

TERESA OKURE, SHCJ, a well-known Nigerian biblical scholar, teaches Scripture at the Catholic Institute of West Africa, Port Harcourt, Nigeria. She has lectured worldwide and published extensively on contextual and inculturated readings of the Bible. She has a special interest in mission, Africa, and women's issues.

SISTER CAROLYN OSIEK, RSCJ, is Professor of New Testament Studies at Catholic Theological Union, Chicago, USA, and a regular faculty member of the school's Israel Studies Program. She holds a doctorate in New Testament and Christian Origins from Harvard University, and is a past President of the Catholic Bible Association. She is editor of the fifteen-volume *Message of Biblical Spirituality* and the author of *Beyond Anger: On Being a Feminist in the Church* (1986) and *What Are They Saying About the Social Setting of the New Testament?* (revised 1992). Recent publications include *The Shepherd of Hermas* (1999) and *Philippians and Philemon* (2000).

ALICIA OSTRIKER has published ten volumes of poetry, most recently *The Little Space; Poems Selected and New* (2000) and *The Volcano Sequence* (2002), as well as several volumes of criticism and midrash, including *Feminist Revision and the Bible* (1992) and *The Nakedness of the Fathers: Biblical Visions and Revisions* (1994). She is a Professor of English at Rutgers University, New Jersey, USA.

PHEME PERKINS was born in Louisville, Kentucky, USA, and has been a Professor in the Theology Department at Boston College since 1972. She is the author of many books, including *Gnosticism and the New Testament* (1993), *Peter, Apostle for the Whole Church* (1994/2000) (winner of the Choice award for distinguished academic books), *Ephesians* (1997), and *Abraham's Divided Children: Galatians and the Politics of Faith* (2001). She has contributed in various voluntary ways to her Roman Catholic parish, and her interests include adult education.

ROSEMARY RADFORD RUETHER is the author or editor of thirty-five books on feminist and liberation theologies. From 1976 to 2002 she was the Georgia Harkness Professor of Applied Theology at the Garrett-Evangelical Theological Seminary and a member of the graduate faculty of Northwestern University in Evanston, Illinois, USA. She is currently the Carpenter Professor of Feminist Theology at the Graduate Theological Union in Berkeley, California, USA.

ELISABETH SCHÜSSLER FIORENZA is Krister Stendahl Professor of Divinity at Harvard Divinity School, USA. She combines her pioneering work in biblical interpretation and feminist theology. She is a co-founder and editor of the *Journal of Feminist Studies in Religion* and a co-editor of *Concilium*. She was the first woman President of the Society of Biblical Literature, and was elected to the American Academy of Arts and Sciences in 2001. Her published works include *In Memory of Her; Bread Not Stone; But She Said; Discipleship of Equals; Revelation: Vision of a Just World; The Power of Naming; Jesus: Miriam's Child; Sharing Her Word; Jesus and the Politics of Interpretation;* and *Wisdom Ways: Introducing Feminist Biblical Interpretation.*

JANET MARTIN SOSKICE was born in western Canada and has lived for some years in Britain, where she is the Reader in Philosophical Theology at the University of Cambridge, England. She is the author of *Metaphor and Religious Language* and editor of several volumes on feminism and ethics. Her main areas of research are in philosophy of religion (especially religious language), modern theology, and ethics, and her feminist interests overlap all these. She is a member of the editorial board of *Concilium* and a past President of the Catholic Theological Association of Great Britain.

ELSA TAMEZ is a Mexican living in Costa Rica, where she is Professor of Biblical Studies in the Latin American Biblical University. She studied for her doctoral degree at the University of Lausanne, Switzerland, and her books include *The Bible of the Oppressed* (1982), *The Amnesty of Grace* (1983), and *When the Horizons Close: A Reading of Ecclesiastes* (2000). She is married and has two children.

PHYLLIS TRIBLE is Baldwin Professor of Sacred Literature Emerita, Union Theological Seminary in New York City, and University Professor at Wake Forest University in North Carolina, USA. Her academic interests include biblical theory, feminist interpretation, and literary criticism.

KARI VOGT is Associate Professor at the Department of Cultural Studies, University of Oslo, Norway. She has written widely on Christian and Islamic issues.

LINDA WALTER lives in Melbourne, Australia, and works within the disciplines of psychotherapy and spiritual direction. Strengthened by Christian feminism, she has recently returned to the Anglican Church, where the acts of putting out hands for bread and wine, singing hymns, and hearing the Scriptures read aloud in the company of others have regained for her their fresh and powerful simplicity.

AVIVAH GOTTLIEB ZORNBERG gained a Ph.D. in English Literature from the University of Cambridge, England, and worked as a lecturer in the English Department at the Hebrew University in Israel before turning to the teaching of religion. She has conducted classes in Torah for thousands of students at several different institutions in Israel. She also lectures widely in the USA, Canada, and the UK, and holds a visiting lectureship at the London School of Jewish Studies, an affiliate of the University of London. Her first book, *The Beginning of Desire: Reflections on Genesis*, won the National Jewish Book Award in 1995.

Acknowledgements

Many people have helped us with advice and suggestions for this volume, and we would like to thank especially Susan James, Margie Tolstoy, Namsoon Kang, Tina Beattie, Cathy Wardle, Melissa Lane, Carrie Pemberton, Melissa Raphael, and Morny Joy.

During the preparation of this volume Teresa Brennan, co-editor with Susan James of the series, was the victim of a hit-and-run driver. Teresa was especially keen to have a volume on theology in the series and was helpful and generous in her oversight of its production. Her Catholic faith was increasingly important to her in recent years, although never unproblematic. She will be much missed. Requiescat in Pace.

JMS

General Introduction

Janet Martin Soskice

This collection has been assembled with two readerships especially in mind: first, those with a prior interest in theology and in feminist theology and, second, those interested in feminism who, seeing a book in this series on *Feminism and Theology*, may wish to pause to make themselves better acquainted. Since we have presumed little previous acquaintance with the literature, this collection can serve as an introduction for those in search of one; we hope, though, that even veterans in the field will find something new here.

WHY SHOULD THEOLOGY MATTER TO FEMINISTS?

European feminists know little of his [Jesus'] life. They hope to be done with these religious traditions without having gauged their impact on the societies in which they live . . . an ingenuous error . . . (Luce Irigaray)[1]

It is no secret that some feminists regard the term 'feminist theology' as an oxymoron. Moreover, the two religions addressed in this volume, Judaism and Christianity, are often cast as prime villains in the Western history of the subordination and oppression of women. Their ideologies, their symbolism, and, above all, their established institutions stand accused of putting a stranglehold on women's aspirations. Asked recently whether feminism had 'succeeded' in the decades since the 1960s, Gloria Steinem replied that it would take more than forty years to overcome 5,000 years of 'racism, sexism, nationalism and *monotheism*'![2]

We need not look far for apparent confirmation. Here is Scottish theologian John Knox in his evocatively named tract of 1588, 'The First Blast of the Trumpet against the Monstrous Regiment of Women':

1

To promote a woman to bear rule, superiority, dominion or empire above any realm, nation or city is repugnant to nature, contumely to God, a thing most contrarious to His revealed will and approved ordinance, and finally it is the subversion of good order, of all equity and justice. . . . Nature, I say, doth paint them forth to be weak, frail, impatient, feeble and foolish; and experience hath declared them to be inconstant, variable, cruel and lacking the spirit of counsel and regiment. . . . As St Paul doth reason in these words: 'man is not of the woman but the woman of the man. And man was not created for the woman, but the woman for the cause of man . . .' (1 Cor. 11:8) . . . and therefore that she should never have pretended any kind of superiority above him, no more than do the angels above God the creator or above Christ Jesus their head. So I say that in her greatest perfection woman was created to be subject to man.

Knox brings together scripture, nature, the revealed will of God, the Holy Spirit, and all past authorities whose validity he recognizes to reinforce his assertion that no woman should be sovereign over any man, whether in public office or the home.[3]

Yet must women be preoccupied even now with the ill-effects of monotheism? Surely religion in the twenty-first century is no longer a force to be reckoned with? French Enlightenment *philosophes* and Marxists predicted that religion, along with other superstitions and 'mere' tradition, would be on the scrap heap of history. In fact, they have not proved so easy to discard. Not only have Christianity and Judaism continued to exist and to exert their historical influence, but women have become ever more actively involved with them. In modern Britain, sociologists find that Christian women, at least, are, by any determining variable, more religious than men. More Christian women than men belong to churches, more attend public acts of worship, more say they pray, and more work for religious charities. If men have, in the past, been responsible for most of the writing of theology, women have done at least their share of the acting. Now, it seems, women are both writing and acting. The possible social and psychological explanations are familiar: if religion is the opium of the people, then women are most in need of doping. Yet this is a harsh call, both on women in former generations where piety held sway and on contemporary women. It is all too easy in the West to forget that over three billion of the world's people belong to one of the major faith traditions.[4] It is also the case that some women, even feminist women, come to religion (to Judaism, Christianity, or Islam, as well as to seemingly more hospitable Eastern religions) without dropping their feminist concerns. Teresa Brennan, our series editor, whose tragic death occurred while this volume was being compiled, was one such woman.

Feminists must surely be willing to concern themselves with the curious interaction of women, theology, and God.

FEMINISM AND THEOLOGY OR FEMINISM AND RELIGION?

But why *Feminism and Theology*? Why not *Feminism and Religion*? This is in part a matter of reasonable breadth. An attempt to give an account of feminism in relation to Hinduism or Buddhism, Sikhism or Taoism, even if that task were within our editorial competence, would mean thin fare for all and risk oversimplification of the diversity of feminist perspectives within any one tradition. Is this to imply there is no 'theology' in Hinduism or Taoism? In a sense yes, or rather—caution should be taken in assuming that there is. All key terms carry a freight of cultural meaning, and 'theology' is no exception. The word betrays its Greek ancestry and etymological kinship with the other 'ologies' in the modern university. 'Theology', as discourse about God or the gods, antedates both Christian and Jewish use; in this sense, both Aristotle and Plato wrote theology. Jews have traditionally rejected the term as overly Christian, reflecting a concern with doctrine over and above practice. Yet even if theology did not emerge organically as a Jewish enterprise, the long history of interaction between Judaism, Christianity, and Islam resulted in a body of Jewish literature that is inherently theological. In more recent times, many Jewish scholars have come to define theology as a sustained examination of the categories of a religious tradition, and of the world as seen by that tradition. For them, at least, there is no better word than 'theology' to sum up much Jewish scholarly literature.[5] Theology, for all its mildewed, medieval connotations, is at least frank in its bias.

Even the seemingly neutral terms 'religion' and the 'study of religion' are arguably the offspring of the Enlightenment, when Europeans discovered and denominated religions with the same aplomb they showed in categorizing new varieties of rhododendron or gazelle. Inevitably, the patterns of culture identified as religions, rather than folklore or superstitions, were those that best matched Western expectations of what a religion should be and do. The very neutrality of the term is, paradoxically, something that modern students of religion have come to question. It now appears we cannot force all faith traditions onto the Procrustean bed of Western religion. It is two religions of Middle Eastern origin, Judaism and Christianity, which

3

have been woven, warp and woof, into the fabric of Western intellectual history. By the first century CE an extensive Jewish diaspora, much of it Greek-speaking, had already spread through North Africa, the Middle East, and the Mediterranean basin. Christianity, originally a sect of first-century Judaism, spread rapidly in these regions and, following the favour it found with Emperor Constantine in the fourth century CE, to the tribes of northern Europe. In the sixth and seventh centuries Islam, a new faith from the same biblical stock, spread rapidly across the southern Mediterranean and Middle Eastern regions. In the twelfth and thirteenth centuries Islamic philosophers, who had retained texts of Aristotle lost to the West, had a considerable impact on Jewish and Christian thought, as well as on medicine, mathematics, and philosophy. When peaceful interests were eclipsed by later struggles, the paths of Islam and Western culture began to diverge.[6] Despite persistent Christian persecution of Jews, there was more or less continuous interaction between Jewish and Christian thought in their wider cultural setting. From this fruitful, if inevitably fraught, interaction emerged many concepts that have shaped the Western world. There is almost no aspect of Western life—its laws, ceremonies, music, medicine, literature—unaffected by this religious legacy, however slight its apparent contemporary presence.

WHAT IS THEOLOGY AND WHAT IS FEMINIST THEOLOGY?

In countries where separation of church and state excludes theology from state universities—and even in countries with a state religion and no such exclusions—it is easy to form the impression that religious studies is the scholarly study of belief systems while theology (or divinity) is oriented solely to devotion or sectarianism. This distinction is neither just nor accurate. The difference is largely in the matter of engagement. Religious studies is concerned with the phenomena of religiosity, while theology is a first-order engagement with a community of faith. Whereas the feminist sociologist of religion looks at changing patterns of worship, the feminist theologian asks about the pain or exasperation that excludes women from organized religion and asks if it need be so. Needless to say, there is an important overlap, with theologians drawing on the insights of social scientists, but the theologian retains her engagement with the faith community, even where she finds herself operating at a critical distance.

Early theological writing usually took the form of commentaries on scripture, sermons, letters, spiritual guides, and, later, catechisms and *summae* for the teaching of students. With the rise of the modern university in early nineteenth-century Germany, a professionalization occurred. Theology became formalized as a discipline, with standard sub-disciplines including church history, doctrine, patristics, ecclesiology, pastoral theology, and Old and New Testament studies. By the late nineteenth century, under pressure to be 'scientific', many of these sub-disciplines assumed the nature of academic guilds. Women were barred from universities in this period, and theological colleges and rabbinical seminaries were remarkably slow to open their doors. Since these were precisely the contexts in which sacred texts and teachings were studied, women's access to these disciplines was necessarily restricted. In the case of institutions for the training of clergy, this access was related to presumed professional suitability. Most Christian and Jewish denominations found women to be unsuitable until well into the twentieth century. Resistance to women as holders of religious offices merged with a more general resistance to the idea of women theologians.

None of this means, of course, that women did not read or, in their own way, write theology; Christina Rossetti and Emily Dickinson are good examples. Nor were women ignorant of the challenges posed to religious faith by new textual critical methods and the developing geological and biological sciences. George Eliot's Mr Casaubon (*Middlemarch*), a figure representative of the insularity of English theology in the nineteenth century, labours through his books quite ignorant of the radical German scholarship with which his creator, as translator of Ludwig Feuerbach's *The Essence of Religion* and David Strauss's revolutionary *Life of Jesus*, was well acquainted.

Despite all the obstacles, women were engaging with works of theology and producing their own. Why, then, was there a need for feminist theologians? In 1960, in the vanguard of what is now known as feminist theology, Valerie Saiving Goldstein wrote an article called 'The Human Situation. A Feminine View'.[7] Her modest suggestion was that, within a theological work, soteriology (doctrine of salvation) was dependent on anthropology (understanding of the human condition), and that the analysis of 'the human condition' given by modern male theologians was specifically from a man's point of view. Reinhold Niebuhr, Anders Nygren, and other influential Protestant theologians of the time saw sin in terms of self-assertion, self-centredness, and pride. Yet these, asserted Saiving Goldstein, are not necessarily the

temptations of women. The sins of women might be better represented by such terms as triviality, diffuseness, and dependence on
others for a sense of self. (Saiving Goldstein called this an 'under-
development or negation of self'.) Her article had a significant impact
on male theologians, as well as on the women who were just beginning
to study theology in significant numbers. Saiving Goldstein's observation was not that women did not sin, nor is it tied to a conception of
distinctive male and female essences. Her point works just as well for
those who believe that women and men have different, culturally
formed experiences of the world. What men read in a particular way,
women may read quite differently. Liberation theology was producing
a similar kind of observation with respect to the world's poor. The
surge of interest in feminist theology had begun.

But what is feminist theology? In this volume, we distinguish 'feminist theology' from 'theology influenced by feminism', giving (we
hope) representative examples of both, along with some pieces that fall
somewhere in between. We reserve the label 'feminist theology' for
work emerging from the movement that flowered in the 1970s and
1980s, an advocacy theology concerned with correcting the unjustness
of sexism and closely related by many practitioners to liberation theology. Elizabeth Johnson's definition of a Christian feminist theology
is helpful:

By Christian feminist theology I mean a reflection on God and all things in
the light of God that stands consciously in the company of all the world's
women, explicitly prizing their genuine humanity while uncovering and
criticizing its persistent violation in sexism, itself an omnipresent paradigm of unjust relationships. In terms of Christian doctrine, this perspective claims the fullness of the religious heritage for women precisely as
human, in their own right and independent from personal identification
with men.[8]

As feminist theology developed as a distinctive specialist area, feminism and gender theory were having the deepest impact across traditional theological subject divisions such as biblical studies, church
history, rabbinics, spirituality, and doctrine. Historians of religion
were especially quick to embrace the feminist insight, as expressed by
Caroline Walker Bynum, that

all human beings are 'gendered'—that is, there is no such thing as a generic
homo religiosus. No scholar studying religion, no participant in ritual, is ever
neuter. Religious experience is the experience of men and women, and in no
known society is this experience the same.[9]

This observation had interesting consequences for the histories of doctrine and scriptural interpretation. Some contributors to this volume would not consider themselves to be doing feminist theology as understood by Elizabeth Johnson, but they might well describe themselves as theologians, text scholars, or historians of doctrine whose work has been influenced by feminist theory or a feminist agenda. The boundary between feminist theology and theology influenced by feminism is fluid, and the same writer may cross to and fro many times.

We have been determined here to resist the temptation to play off feminist theology against theology informed by feminism. The former can be dismissed as transient and polemical, the latter as colluding and complacent, but nothing is gained by such caricatures. The pungency of Mary Daly's writings was required to waken theologians from centuries of slumber. Subtle exegesis by women scholars of texts previously analysed only by men is quite another project. The impact of this quieter work is sometimes less obvious in the short term. Sister Nonna (Verna) Harrison, for instance, has worked quietly for many years on gender issues in the formative writings of her Christian Orthodox tradition. Her work, well within the canons of traditional patristic theology, is not evidently revolutionary, but her 1990 essay, 'Male and Female in Cappadocian Theology', an examination of the writings of Gregory of Nyssa, Gregory Nazianzen, and Basil the Great, contains this bombshell in a footnote: 'the thesis of Thomas Hopko ... that there is a basis in Greek patristic theology for regarding gender as a fundamental ontological structure, is not confirmed by the Cappadocian material examined in this paper.'[10] Readers may judge for themselves the significance to a tradition of taking gender to be a 'fundamental ontological structure'. In the context of her Orthodox tradition, Nonna Harrison's work is quite as challenging as anything else in this volume.

Feminist writings present a challenge to traditional theology, transgressing its disciplinary boundaries, questioning its neutrality, and deliberately combining advocacy with scholarship. They raise the question as to whether all theology does not involve advocacy, with feminist practitioners simply being honest about it. Feminist theology is sometimes attacked by others in feminist fields as a theoretical backwater. If this is true, it may be part of the price paid for keeping an ear to the ground. 'A theologian', goes a Christian Orthodox adage, 'is one who prays'—and on this reckoning there are many theologians who have minimal access to education of any sort, much less to theological education. Feminism in theology may lack the theoretical fireworks of some of its sister subjects, but its prospect for reaching millions of lives, including those of the world's poorest women, is immense.

THE ORGANIZATION OF THIS VOLUME

We have divided this book into five sections, each with introductory comments, and provided a brief introduction to each selection. Classification is always awkward. Our search for categories shared (for the most part) by Jews and Christians led us away from the familiar New Testament, Old Testament, church history, doctrine, and so forth to a thematic schema: sources; identity; sacred texts; practice; and Incarnation and embodiment. Christianity, in comparison to Judaism, is disproportionately interested in questions of doctrine. Rather than omit doctrine entirely, though, we have devoted a whole section to one central Christian doctrine, the Incarnation, and tried to provide a diversity of views within it. To balance this in the whole, we have weighted the Sacred Text section towards the Hebrew Bible, somewhat at the expense of New Testament writings. The select bibliography is limited to edited volumes that might complement this one.

Both editors are active members of religious communities and committed to working within them, Jewish in Diana Lipton's case and Christian in that of Janet Martin Soskice. We have tried hard not to overemphasize our own positions. While all the works selected here are notable pieces, they represent a range of critical perspective and religious adherence, and by no means serve as summations of their authors' views. It should be noted that authors have in some cases moved far from positions expressed in the selections in this volume (see especially Daphne Hampson and Elisabeth Schüssler Fiorenza).

It is impossible to be truly representative in a book of this size. We were thus unable to include works from all the theological suburbs— or to represent all major thematic concentrations. We have focused instead on a few areas in an exemplary way and tried to create clusters. For instance there are five or more essays, across the collection, which touch on early Christianity (formerly patristics). We might easily have clustered around work on medieval texts, or those from the early modern period. Similarly, we have not been able to represent all regions of the world, and those represented are distributed throughout the volume. (We wished to avoid the suggestion that geographical origin trumps all other aspects of a theological contribution.) While some selections reflect our assessment of their contribution at their time of writing, we make only passing reference to movements that were significant at the time, yet seem to have peaked and passed on their way—the goddess movement (see Ruether) is a good example. We have also felt constrained to exclude subjects which, however important, have generated little to date that can properly be described as feminist theological writing.[11]

What of the future of feminism and theology? We believe it should be both critical and constructive. Pain, abuse, oppression, and silencing cannot be ignored, but neither can they provide the sole *raison d'être* for women's theological writing. Even theology written by women in the harshest circumstances must hold potential for joy. For us, this wider enterprise must look back as well as forwards, precisely because it concerns traditions we love as well as criticize. Return to scripture, whether through feminist midrash or Christian exegesis, is not archaism, but attests to the belief that scripture may speak newly today.[12] As with the writings of the prophets, criticizing the ills of the present is a sign of hope for the future.

JMS
Passover and Easter 2003

Notes

1. 'Equal to Whom?', *differences* 1(2) (1989), 70.
2. BBC Radio 4, 2 Aug. 1999 (emphasis added).
3. Repr. in Richard A. Mason (ed.), *On Rebellion* (Cambridge: Cambridge University Press, 1994), 8–12. Admittedly, Knox's target was the Catholic regent of Scotland, Mary of Guise; and Knox's co-religionists (if not Knox himself) found themselves greatly embarrassed by his tract when the Protestant Queen Elizabeth came to the English throne shortly after its publication. Knox never recanted.
4. Christianity is the largest of these, at an estimated 33%. Jews make up less than 1% of the global figure, but have had a disproportionate impact on Western culture.
5. See Judith Plaskow, 'Jewish Theology in Feminist Perspective', in *Feminist Perspectives on Jewish Studies* (New Haven, Conn.: Yale University Press, 1994).
6. For example, Islam was not affected by the textual criticism which so rocked Christianity and Judaism in the nineteenth and twentieth centuries. This does not mean that Islam is not modern, but simply that its relationship to Western modernity differs significantly from the relationships of Christianity and Judaism.

7. *Journal of Religion* 40 (1960), 100–12.
8. Elizabeth A. Johnson, *She Who Is: The Mystery of God in Feminist Theological Discourse* (New York: Crossroad, 1994), 8.
9. 'Introduction: The Complexity of Symbols', in Caroline Walker Bynum, Steven Harrell, and Paul Richman (eds.), *Gender and Religion: On the Complexity of Symbols* (Boston: Beacon Press, 1986), 2.
10. Nonna Verna Harrison, 'Male and Female in Cappadocian Theology,' *Journal of Theological Studies* 41 (1990), 469. Another important Orthodox theologian, working with Syriac texts, is Susan Ashbrook Harvey. See e.g. 'Feminine Imagery for the Divine: The Holy Spirit, the Odes of Solomon and Early Syriac Tradition', *St Vladimir's Theological Quarterly* 37(1) (1993).
11. For instance, although many women have written on the Holocaust, their approach is seldom theological. See, however, Melissa Raphael, 'When God Beheld God: Notes Towards a Jewish Feminist Theology of the Holocaust', *Feminist Theology* 21 (May 1999).
12. See Judith Plaskow and Carol P. Christ, *Weaving the Visions: New Patterns in Feminist Spirituality* (San Francisco: Harper & Row, 1989), 46.

Part I. Sources: In the Beginning God . . .

The selections in this section were chosen for those tempted to ask: why feminism and theology? The title recalls the opening verse of Genesis, the biblical book of beginnings, but it is not historical development that concerns us here. We hope rather to point to sources from which feminist reflection on religion continues to flow.

The distinctive cluster of concerns known as feminist theology can be given a simplified chronology. It emerged in the academy of the 1960s in association with the second-wave feminism that generated feminist literary criticism, feminist anthropology, and feminist philosophy. Yet we can discern precedents for feminist theology in *The Women's Bible*, compiled in the 1890s by Elizabeth Cady Stanton and friends, or in any number of the writings of nineteenth-century women novelists, poets, and social reformers. Only in the nineteenth century, as feminism became identified with the rights of women, do we see the beginning of anything like a movement; but of course thoughtful women have always pondered their religious lives from a female perspective.

Prior to the twentieth century, women had limited educational opportunities and virtually no chance of university education (this is still the case for many women). Apart from a few missionary and Bible colleges, seminaries and religious colleges for the training of ministers, priests, and rabbis were closed to women until well into the second half of the twentieth century. Partly as a consequence, much important theological reflection by women is not to be found in academic journals and books but in verse, fiction (see below the contributions of Anita Diamant and Alicia Ostriker), and, especially, in occasional writing for community newsletters and women's gatherings. This type of literature, represented here by Linda Walter's 'Canterbury Tale', is often evanescent, lost as soon as it has served its immediate purpose. Feminist reflections often come from hard-pressed women working with the poor, with little experience in public speaking or writing for publication (see Benjaporn Mochai). Such simple stories of faith in action are the life-blood, not just of feminist theology, but of theology

11

itself. We cannot dismiss them for lack of theological superstructure or feminist critical theory.

We have mentioned a few of the ways and means of feminist theology, but a question remains: why is it written? An important motivation has been academic dissatisfaction. Distressed by the way their academic discipline has limped along, one-legged and one-eyed for so many years, some scholars have tried to improve their situation. Yet even within the academy, many (perhaps most) writers of feminist theology are nourished by the vitality of their religious grassroots. These are women responding to the events of their daily lives: loyalty to and frustrations with churches and synagogues; love for the traditions that have formed them; anger with the people and institutions that constrain them; the pain of giving birth, of failing to give birth, of choosing not to give birth. The writings in this section articulate rejection, silencing, and loss, but there is more. The feminist path has led some women (Mary Daly) away from religion altogether. Other feminists (Rosemary Radford Ruether) find much in need of revision yet look to religion as a powerful tool against the violence that corrupts our lives and our world.

JMS

1 A Canterbury Tale

Linda Walter*

Throughout the 1970s and 1980s debates on the ordination of women absorbed the mainstream Christian denominations. They rumble on today. Objections to women in ministry, other than lack of historical precedent, have been of two basic kinds: the more Protestant that St Paul forbade women to teach, and the more Catholic that women could not signify a male Christ, the true high priest. For many women, and not a few men, these debates were the first occasion for thinking that anything might be amiss vis-à-vis women and Christianity. In 1986, Linda Walter was attending a conference of the Movement for the Ordination of Women in Canterbury, England. Participants were divided into small groups and asked to write briefly on what had brought them this far on their way. Linda Walter had come all the way from Australia. Her response, especially as I first saw it, handwritten and with crossings out, has all the pulse of life and pain of exclusion of the moment, and a fine sacramental sense. The saying that the best theology is written on your knees is doubly exemplified by this previously unpublished piece.   JMS

There are two quotations which have helped me perhaps more than any others in my life as a Christian.

The first is from Harry Williams' book, *True Wilderness*, in which, amongst other wonderfully useful things, he writes—'Refuse to be satisfied with anything less than what is totally satisfying—not what should satisfy, but what in fact *does.*' *These* words stood by me when traditional worship and formula for prayer have left me cold.

The second quotation is from Teilhard de Chardin: 'by virtue of the Creation and still more of the Incarnation nothing here below is profane for those who know how to see.' These words comforted me even though I hardly dared believe they might be true.

* Linda Walter, 'Telling Tales', from the Movement for Ordination of Women Conference (Canterbury, 1986). Previously unpublished.

So these men have helped to equip me for the journey which has brought me to this point in my life. I sometimes wonder if they would be glad to hear where this journey has led me.

I am 39 years old. I trained as a nurse and now I work as a lay chaplain in a cancer hospital in Melbourne. [. . .] I have had a good Anglican upbringing in the faith. It showed me something of Jesus in the Gospels. It taught me how to be present at the Eucharist. It gave me a framework—a liturgical calendar of powerful events and underlying themes—into which I was drawn with a sense of mystery. It did sustain me for an important stage of my life. *But it was as if the body simply didn't exist*—or worse: it was an unclean impediment. And when my body took over—as it does in menstruation and passion and pregnancy and childbirth and breastfeeding—my faith had nothing positive to say. In the intensive years of motherhood the God who was reached by dutiful prayer and regular attendance at the Eucharist was far away. And in this I felt myself both guilty and abandoned.

The year is 1976. It is the time of my third child's birth. A difficult pregnancy, and anxious delivery of a tiny but healthy girl and then massive hemorrhaging. A curette, more voluminous bleeding—a close call necessitating an emergency hysterectomy. I found out about blood then. Blood is not unclean. Blood is precious. Blood from a pierced side, blood from a womb—it doesn't make much difference to me. Blood is the life of the body. Women know about blood. We do not faint at the sight of it. Month by month we see it and know it as part of the gift of our fertility. Yes it is a nuisance—a costly gift. But why has it been called 'the curse'? [. . .]

The weakness and utter vulnerability of this time for me put me right inside my body. I was like an animal who knows she must turn in on herself and lick her wounds and heal herself. The God out there did not know me then. Nor I him. I could not pray the way I'd been taught. I was at home in my body but God did not come to visit. The loss of my womb coincided with a spiritual barrenness.

The year is 1977. The charismatic movement is making itself felt. My beloved 65-year-old parish priest opens himself to these promises held out and blossoms like a late flower. 'Linda,' he says, with tears in his eyes, 'now I *know* my Redeemer liveth.' With trepidation I ask for his laying on of hands. Will it work? Will I be me any more? Will I be purified out of existence? In my spiritual barrenness I have little to lose. So I ask [. . .] and the difference it makes is as ordinary and as profoundly simple as the difference between clenched fists and open hands. Now I begin to recognize what has always been within. I am surprised at every turn. By virtue of the creation and still more of the Incarnation nothing here below is profane for those who know how to see. In the most ordinary things and moments the Word is made flesh. Now I begin to know that my Redeemer liveth, and, better still, *that in my flesh shall I see God.* The body does exist—our bodies are wonderfully and marvelously made—every bit of them hidden and seen, above, below—nothing profane.

Now the year is 1980. Our parish licenses its first women ministers of the chalice and I am one of them.

I stand in the sanctuary with a brimming chalice of red fragrant wine in my hands. I go from face to well-known face. I know how to put this cup to these lips. I am mother. I stoop and rise. I am nurse. I am woman who knows about blood. The blood of Christ keep you in eternal life. No one has to show me how to do this. I have been doing it all my life it seems. I am at home in the sanctuary in this supremely ordinary act—this sacrament which focuses all our acts of feeding, all our meals, all our ordinary day to day relating and depending on one another.

And finally the year is 1986. In my work as chaplain in the gynecology cancer ward I listen to women's stories and encourage them to trust the profound spirituality of their own experiences of their bodies and of the truth behind the circumstances of their lives. The life within me greets the life within them. Once we say Yes to the life of the Spirit of God within us it is not only good news for us. We will call it forth in one another. We will find ourselves saying as Elizabeth said to Mary, 'As soon as I heard your greeting the baby within my womb leapt with gladness.'

2 Selection from *The Red Tent*

Anita Diamant*

A central task of feminist Bible scholars is to raise the profile of biblical women, but few can compete in this regard with Anita Diamant. *The Red Tent*, Genesis according to Jacob's silent daughter Dinah, has been translated into dozens of languages and has inspired hundreds of websites. As my mother-in-law discovered when she read her copy in a New York City hospital waiting room, to read *The Red Tent* is to join a community whose membership, though primarily female, spans all ages and backgrounds. It is no surprise that this community played a major role in the book's commercial success. Faced with a pile of remainders, Diamant, by then a well-known author of books on conversion to Judaism and Jewish lifecycle events, sent free copies of her novel to every Reform rabbi in the USA. Word of mouth and the internet did the rest. The eponymous red tent is a menstrual tent, and the excerpt reproduced here is an account of Dinah's first period. DL

When the air was sweet with spring and the ewes heavy with lambs, my month arrived. As evening gathered on the first night of darkness, I was squatting to relieve myself when I noticed the smear on my thigh. It took me several moments before I understood what I saw. It was brown rather than red. Wasn't it supposed to be red? Shouldn't I feel some ache in my belly? Perhaps I was mistaken and bled from my leg, yet I could find no scrape or scratch.

It seemed I had been waiting forever for womanhood, and yet I did not jump up to tell my mothers. I stayed where I was, on my haunches, hidden by branches, thinking: My childhood is over. I will wear an apron and cover my head. I will not have to carry and fetch during the new moon anymore, but will sit with the rest of the women until I am pregnant. I will idle with my mothers and my sisters in the ruddy

* Anita Diamant, extract from *The Red Tent*. Copyright © 1997 by Anita Diamant. Reprinted by permission of Macmillan Publishers Ltd and St. Martin's Press, LLC.

shade of the red tent for three days and three nights, until first sight of the crescent goddess. My blood will flow into the fresh straw, filling the air with the salt smell of women.

For a moment I weighed the idea of keeping my secret and remaining a girl, but the thought passed quickly. I could only be what I was. And I was a woman.

I raised myself up, my fingers stained with the first signs of my maturity, and realized that there was indeed a dull ache in my bowels. With new pride, I carried myself into the tent, knowing that my swelling breasts would no longer be a joke among the women. Now I would be welcome inside any tent when Rachel and Inna attended at a birth. Now I could pour out the wine and make bread offerings at the new moon, and soon I would learn the secrets that pass between men and women.

I walked into the red tent without the water I'd been sent for. But before my mother could open her mouth to scold me, I held up my soiled fingers. "I am not permitted to carry anything either, Mother."

"Oh, oh, oh!" said Leah, who for once had no words. She kissed me on both cheeks, and my aunts gathered around and took turns greeting me with more kisses. My sisters-in-law clapped their hands and everyone began talking at once. Inna ran in to find out what the noise was about, and I was surrounded by smiling faces.

It was nearly dark, and my ceremony began almost before I realized what was happening. Inna brought a polished metal cup filled with fortified wine, so dark and sweet I barely tasted its power. But my head soon floated while my mothers prepared me with henna on the bottoms of my feet and on my palms. Unlike a bride, they painted a line of red from my feet up to my sex, and from my hands they made a pattern of spots that led to my navel.

They put kohl on my eyes ("So you will be far-seeing," said Leah) and perfumed my forehead and my armpits ("So you will walk among flowers," said Rachel). They removed my bracelets and took my robe from me. It must have been the wine that prevented me from asking why they took such care with paint and scent yet dressed me in the rough homespun gown used for women in childbirth and as a shroud for the afterbirth after the baby came.

They were so kind to me, so funny, so sweet. They would not let me feed myself but used their fingers to fill my mouth with the choicest morsels. They massaged my neck and back until I was as supple as a cat. They sang every song known among us. My mother kept my wine cup filled and brought it to my lips so often that soon I found it

17

difficult to speak, and the voices around me melted into a loud happy hum.

Zebulun's wife, Ahavah, danced with her pregnant belly to the clapping of hands. I laughed until my sides ached. I smiled until my face hurt. It was good to be a woman!

Then Rachel brought out the teraphim, and everyone fell silent. The household gods had remained hidden until that moment. Although I had been a little girl when I'd seen them last, I remembered them like old friends: the pregnant mother, the goddess wearing snakes in her hair, the one that was both male and female, the stern little ram. Rachel laid them out carefully and chose the goddess wearing the shape of a grinning frog. Her wide mouth held her own eggs for safekeeping, while her legs were splayed in a dagger-shaped triangle, ready to lay a thousand more. Rachel rubbed the obsidian figure with oil until the creature gleamed and dripped in the light of the lamps. I stared at the frog's silly face and giggled, but no one laughed with me.

In the next moment, I found myself outside with my mother and my aunts. We were in the wheat patch in the heart of the garden—a hidden place where grain dedicated to sacrifice was grown. The soil had been tilled in preparation for planting after the moon's return, and I was naked, lying facedown on the cool soil. I shivered. My mother put my cheek to the ground and loosened my hair around me. She arranged my arms wide, "to embrace the earth," she whispered. She bent my knees and pulled the soles of my feet together until they touched, "to give the first blood back to the land," said Leah. I could feel the night air on my sex, and it was strange and wonderful to be so open under the sky.

My mothers gathered around: Leah above me, Bilhah at my left hand, Zilpah's hand on the back of my legs. I was grinning like the frog, half asleep, in love with them all. Rachel's voice behind me broke the silence. "Mother! Innana! Queen of the Night! Accept the blood offering of your daughter, in her mother's name, in your name. In her blood may she live, in her blood may she give life."

It did not hurt. The oil eased the entry, and the narrow triangle fit perfectly as it entered me. I faced the west while the little goddess faced east as she broke the lock on my womb. When I cried out, it was not so much pain but surprise and perhaps even pleasure, for it seemed to me that the Queen herself was lying on top of me, with Dumuzi her consort beneath me. I was like a slip of cloth, caught between their lovemaking, warmed by the great passion.

My mothers moaned softly in sympathy. If I could have spoken I would have reassured them that I was perfectly happy. For all the stars of the night sky had entered my womb behind the legs of the smiling little frog goddess. On the softest, wildest night since the separation of land and water, earth and sky, I lay panting like a dog and felt myself spinning through the heavens. And when I began to fall, I had no fear.

The sky was pink when I opened my eyes. Inna was crouched beside me, watching my face. I was lying on my back, my arms and legs wide like the spokes of the wheel, my nakedness covered by my mother's best blanket. The midwife helped me to my feet and led me back to a soft corner in the red tent, where the other women still slept. "Did you dream?" she asked me. When I nodded that I had, she drew close and said, "What shape did she take?"

Oddly, I knew what she wanted to know, but I didn't know what to call the creature that had smiled at me. I had never seen anything like her—huge, black, a toothy grin, skin like leather. I tried to describe the animal to Inna, who seemed puzzled. Then she asked, "Was she in the water?"

I said yes and Inna smiled. "I told you that water was your destiny. That is a very old one, Taweret, an Egyptian goddess who lives in the river and laughs with a great mouth. She gives mothers their milk and protects all children." My old friend kissed my cheeks and then pinched them gently. "That is all I know of Taweret, but in all my years, I never knew a woman who dreamed of her. It must be a sign of luck, little one. Now sleep."

My eyes did not open until evening, and I dreamed all day about a golden moon growing between my legs. And in the morning, I was given the honor of being the first one outside, to greet the first daylight of the new moon.

On Being a Woman: Thailand

Benjaporn Mochai*

What is theology and who writes it? This short piece was delivered at a meeting where Asian women (not necessarily theologians) were invited to do theology together by sharing their stories and ideas on the theme of 'women's empowerment in Asia: Celebration and Lamentation'. Benjaporn Mochai's is amongst the stories of celebration, but not without its dark side. The introduction to the papers cites Teresa Okure (see her essay elsewhere in this volume): 'There is a way of doing theology that starts with shared experience from oral transmission, from the simple fact of sharing life.'   JMS

Thank you very much for the opportunity to speak to you. I am afraid I am a bit nervous. I think that it is very hard to communicate with the English language—at least we can communicate that we care and love. This meeting has already given me a lot of inspiration to go back to work with the poor women in my region.

First, let me tell you something about myself. I was born to a poor family in Isan (Northeast Thailand). My family was not happy when I was born because, not unlike to many families in the Northeast, a baby girl is not welcome. As someone told my mother: "To have a daughter is like having a toilet in front of your house." A girl leaves and "destroys" her family. Eventually, when she gets married, she loses her last name. When I was a little girl, I wanted to be a real woman because as a child I was a tomboy. When I was 15 or 16 years old, I came to study the Bible. Then I realized that human dignity is not from being a man or a woman. What is important is how you respond to God's blessing to you. I want to celebrate my being a woman. And if I were to be physically born again, I want to be a woman! There are things that women can do that men couldn't. The most important one is that

* Benjaporn Mochai, 'On Being a Woman: Thailand' from *PTCA Bulletin* 12 (1 and 2), edited by Salvador T. Martinez (1999).

women can bear children! I am married and have two daughters. My husband and I work together on development projects with the poor and marginalized people. I work especially with women in the mountains of the Northeast. That region in Thailand has many problems: it has a large population, the land is not very fertile, the people are poor and literacy is not very high.

During the past two decades, Thailand developed very fast, but the Northeast was left behind. Because work is hard to find in the region, many families send one of their members, including the women, to work in Bangkok or other countries. Many of them, however, are cheated by the employment agencies. They pay a huge amount of money but end up with no work. Many of the women become sex workers to support their families. Thailand had an agricultural economy, but now it has become industrialized. People were not quite ready for this. The economic meltdown in Thailand had a disastrous effect on many poor families. Many families allow their daughters to become sex workers in some of the rich Asian countries. Some could not bear the loss. They simply commit suicide. They have no one to talk to about their problems.

I am happy that God had allowed me to have a ministry with the poor and suffering women in our community, both Christians and Buddhist. In my community the women have become united, and they help each other. This is something to celebrate about.

Not everything is fine, however. I would like to tell you the story of one woman under the care of our ministry. Her name is Duang. She comes from Laos. She is only 16 years old but has to migrate to Thailand with her mother and father because of the war. She went to Bangkok, and there she met a man from the Northeast. People from the Northeast also call themselves Lao, because they speak the same language as the Laotians. Duang and the Lao man fell in love and soon she got pregnant. When she was 4 months pregnant, her boyfriend took her home to the Northeast. The boy's mother did not like Duang because she is a foreigner and she does not have an identity card. She wanted her son to go south to work and not to come back. In the meanwhile, the mother beats Duang almost everyday and makes her work hard. On the last month of her pregnancy, she was driven out of the house. She had no food and no bed. A widow in a little church helped her. Even the church members were afraid to help her lest they be arrested for harboring an illegal alien. Duang planned to have her baby in the hospital and run away after she delivers the baby. When the time has come for her to deliver, the town hospital refused to admit her because of its limited facilities. She needed to go to another hospital in the city but no one was willing to take her there. I was also afraid, like the other people. I consulted my husband and daughter, and they told no one to go with Duang to the hospital.

No one visited Duang in the hospital. She was alone. My husband and I went to see her. When I walked into her room, I was so ashamed of myself for not being there with her. The baby was naked and had nothing, not even a piece of cloth. The baby reminded me of Jesus. Duang didn't want to leave the baby in the hospital. She wanted to take her home and care for her. "Even a dog would take care of its puppy, I should also care for my baby," Duang insisted. So I brought her home with the baby and we went to the police and her employer to explain what had happened. The police and her employer helped Duang.

4 Ecofeminism

Rosemary Radford Ruether*

Acts of violence against women and attempts to dominate them, especially where mandated by culture or cult, have long been targets of feminist criticism. Ecofeminism extends this critique to include the despoliation of nature. Since ancient times, nature has been identified as female (Mother Nature). This gave rise to some problematic images; the sixteenth-century philosopher Francis Bacon famously described the natural realm as woman in need of subduing. In this essay, Rosemary Radford Ruether charts Christian complicity with the ideology of domination. She sketches the alternative offered by 'Goddess' movements, before suggesting that the older faith traditions may have resources to bring to bear on the ecological crisis that is destroying the earth and impinging so harshly on the lives of the poor.   JMS

What is Ecofeminism? Ecofeminism represents a union of two concerns: ecology and feminism. The word "ecology" emerges from the biological science of natural environmental systems. Ecology examines how these natural communities function to sustain a healthy web of life and how they become disrupted, causing death of plant and animal life. Human intervention is the main cause of such disruption as it occurs today. Thus ecology was popularized as a combined socioeconomic and biological study in the sixties to examine how the human use of nature is causing pollution of soil, air, and water, the destruction of the natural life systems of plants and animals, and threatening the base of life upon which the human community depends.

Deep ecologists have insisted that it is not enough to analyze this devastation of the earth in terms of human social and technological

* Rosemary Radford Ruether, 'Ecofeminism: First and Third World Women', from *Women Resisting Violence: Spirituality for Life*, edited by Mary John Mananzan *et al.* (Orbis Books, 1996).

use. We have to examine the symbolic, psychological, and cultural patterns by which humans have distanced themselves from nature, denied their reality as a part of nature, and claimed to rule over it from outside. Ecological healing demands a psycho-cultural conversion from this anthropocentric stance of separation and domination. We have to recover the experience of communion in nature and rebuild a new culture based on the affirmation of being one interconnected community of life.[1]

Feminism is also a complex movement with many layers. It can be defined as a movement within liberal democratic societies for full inclusion of women in political rights and access to equal employment. It can be defined more radically in socialist and liberationist feminism as a transformation of the patriarchal socioeconomic system in which male domination of women is the foundation of all social hierarchies. Feminism can also be studied in terms of culture and consciousness, charting the symbolic, psychological, and cultural connection between the definition of women as inferior mentally, morally, and physically, and male monopolization of knowledge and power.

This third type of feminist analysis has affinities with deep ecology, although many ecofeminists have faulted deep ecologists for their lack of gender analysis and their failure to see the relations between anthropocentrism and androcentrism.[2] Ecofeminism is founded on the basic intuition that there is a fundamental connection in Western culture, and in patriarchal cultures generally, between the domination of women and the domination of nature. What does this mean?

Among Western ecofeminists this connection between domination of women and domination of nature is generally made, first, on the cultural-symbolic level. One charts the way in which patriarchal culture has defined women as being "closer to nature," or as being on the nature side of the nature-culture split. This is shown in the way in which women have been identified with the body, earth, sex, the flesh in its mortality and weakness, vis à vis a construction of masculinity identified with spirit, mind, and sovereign power over both women and nature.[3]

A second level of ecofeminist analysis goes beneath the cultural-symbolic level and explores the socioeconomic underpinnings of how the domination of women's bodies and women's work interconnects with the exploitation of land, water, and animals. How have women as a gender group been colonized by patriarchy as a legal, economic, social, and political system? How does this colonization of women's bodies and work function as the invisible substructure for the extraction of natural resources? How does the positioning of women as the caretakers of children, the gardeners, weavers, cookers, cleaners, and waste managers for men in the family both inferiorize this work and identify women with a subhuman world likewise inferiorized?

This socioeconomic form of ecofeminist analysis then sees the cultural-symbolic patterns by which both women and nature are inferiorized and identified with each other as an ideological superstructure by which the system of economic and legal domination of women, land, and animals is justified and made to appear "natural" and inevitable within a total patriarchal cosmo-vision. Ecofeminists who stress this socioeconomic analysis underlying the patriarchal ideology of subordination of women and nature also wish to include race and class hierarchy as well.

It is not enough simply to talk of domination of women as if women were a homogenous group. We have to look at the total class structure of the society, fused with racial hierarchy, and see how gender hierarchy falls within race–class hierarchy. This means that women within the ruling class have vastly different privileges and comforts than women in the lowest class, even though both may be defined in a general sense as mothers, child raisers, and sex objects. It also means that there are different ideologies about upper-class and lower-class women, exacerbated when racial ideologies are also present. Thus in American society, the images of the white woman as sheltered leisure-class Lady, and the Black woman as strong Mammy or sexually available tart, shaped by slavery, still informs cultural patterns, despite the much greater complexity of actual class–race patterns affecting real African-American and Euro-American women today.

How does religion come into this mix of ecofeminist cultural-symbolic and socioeconomic analysis? Religion, specifically the Christian tradition with its roots in the Hebrew and Greco-Roman worlds, has been faulted as a prime source of the cultural-symbolic patterns which have inferiorized women and nature. The patriarchal God of the Hebrew Bible, outside and over against the material world as its Creator and Lord, fused with Greek philosophical dualism of spirit and matter, is seen as the prime identity myth of the Western ruling-class male. He has made this God in the image of his own aspiration to be both separate from and ruling over the material world, such as land and animals or non-human "resources" and subjugated groups of humans.

The denunciation of Christianity and scientific ideology as the main sources and enforcers of the domination of women and nature is often connected with what might be called an ecofeminist "fall from paradise" story. In this story, humans in the hunter-gatherer and hunter-gardener stages lived in egalitarian classless societies in a benign nurturing relation to the rest of nature. The social system of war, violence, and male domination came in with a series of invasions by patriarchal pastoralists from the northern steppes sometime in the sixth to third millennia b.c.e., reshaping earlier egalitarian societies into societies of militarized domination. This view has been popularized in Riane Eisler's book, *The Chalice and the Blade.*[4]

Key to this shift is a religious revolution from the worship of a Goddess, who represents the immanent life force within nature, to a patriarchal sun God positioned outside and ruling over nature as warrior Lord. The implication of this ecofeminist "fall from paradise" story is that recovery of a partnership relation between men and women and a life-sustaining relation with nature demands a rejection of all forms of patriarchal religion and the return to, or re-invention in some way of, the worship of the ancient nature Goddess. This viewpoint is expressed by groups of women and some men, not simply as a theory, but as a practice of creating worship groups that have developed ritual practices that they see as reviving the ancient worship of the Goddess. Perhaps the best-known theologian and liturgist of this neo-pagan or Wiccan movement is Starhawk, author of books such as *The Spiral Dance: A Rebirth of the Ancient Religion of the Great Goddess.*[5]

My own view is that this "fall from paradise" story is a myth, a powerful contemporary myth. By myth, I do not mean that it is "untrue," but that it is a vastly simplified and selective story that contains elements of truth about the actual shaping of Western history in the last 6000–8000 years. It charts a process that led from the invention of agriculture and the domestication of animals to the shaping of early urban cultures and empires in the ancient Middle East in the third millennium, with their patterns of patriarchy, slavery, temple and palace aristocracies controlling the land and labor of peasants and slaves, and the subjugation of women. It re-imagines a lost alternative that lay behind and was covered over by this process of shaping the system of domination.

This story, as told by its contemporary myth-makers, however, also tends to take for granted certain gender stereotypes about masculinity and femininity and the connection of women and nature with nurture that have more to do with certain lines of American Victorian culture than with ancient Anatolia or Crete. This is why the story "rings true" to many contemporary American women and some men. Like all good myths, this story should be taken seriously, but not literally. We should ask what it tells us about ourselves and our histories, but also how it may mislead us about ourselves and our histories and particularly about what is to be done to heal ourselves, our relations to each other and to the earth.

Here I see a sharp distinction between two lines of thought among ecofeminists, even though they may share many common values. One line of thought sees the woman–nature connection as a social ideology constructed by patriarchal culture to justify the ownership of and use of both women and the natural world as property. In reality women are no more like nature than men, or, to put it another way, men are as much like nature as women.

This critique of the woman–nature connection as a patriarchal cultural construction can be used to separate both men and women as humans, who are much like each other, from the rest of nature. Or it can be used to insist that men as much as women need to overcome the myth of separation and learn to commune with nature as our common biotic community, while respecting trees, lakes, wolves, birds, and insects as beings with their own distinct modes of life and raison d'être apart from our use of them. Ecofeminists see the separation of women from men by patterns of cultural dualism of mind–body, dominant–subordinant, and thinking–feeling—and by the identification of the lower half of these dualisms with both women and nature—as a victimology. These dualisms falsify who women and men (and also nature) really are in their wholeness and complexity, and justify the treatment of both women and nature as property of men, to be used as they wish. Ecofeminism is about deconstructing these dualisms, both in regard to women and in regard to nature.

A second line of ecofeminism agrees that this patriarchal woman–nature connection justifies their domination and abuse, but also believes that there is a deeper truth that has been distorted by it. There is some deep positive connection between women and nature. Women are the life-givers, the nurturers, the ones in whom the seed of life grows. Women were the primary food gatherers, the inventors of agriculture. Their bodies are in mysterious tune with the cycles of the moon and the tides of the sea. It was by experiencing women as life-givers, both food providers and birthers of children, that early humans made the female the first image of worship, the Goddess, source of all life. Women need to reclaim this affinity between the sacrality of nature and the sacrality of their own sexuality and life-powers. To

27

return to worship the Goddess as the sacred female is to reconnect with our own deep powers.[6]

I find this exaltation of woman and nature as Great Goddess exciting, but also potentially dangerous and misleading. First of all, this religion either excludes men altogether or else allows them in as "sons" of the great Mother, which means not only that men can't be dominators, but also that they cannot be adult peers of women. Some men will be content in this role (i.e. to be taken care of all their lives), but most men will be turned off. Some will be filled with vehement outrage that demands retaliatory vengeance.[7]

We have seen such outrage and self-righteous retaliatory backlash in much of the anti-feminist New Right today. Such backlash also tells us something about where we are and have come from, but in a way that reduplicates the old patterns that have long underlain and reproduced patriarchy. We are still far from the kind of transformed story that will break the cycle of both female maternalism and submission, of both male insecurity and retaliatory dominance, and find real partnership.

Much of Western essentialist or matricentric ecofeminism (as distinct from social ecofeminism) fails to make real connections between the domination of women and classism, racism, and poverty. Relation with nature is thought of in psycho-cultural terms; rituals of self-blessing of the body, dancing on the beach, chanting to the moon, etc. I do not disvalue such ceremonial reconnecting with our bodies and nature. I think they have a place in our healing of our consciousness from patterns of alienation.

But I believe they become recreational self-indulgence for a privileged counter-cultural elite, if our cultural expressions of healing of our bodies and our imaginations as white Americans are not connected concretely with the realities of over-consumerism and waste by which the top 20% of the world enjoys 82% of the wealth while the other 80% of the world scrapes along with 18%, and the lowest 80% of the world's population, disproportionately female and young, starves and dies early from poisoned waters, soil, and air.

An ecofeminism which is not primarily a mystical (mystified) and recreational escapism for a privileged Western female elite must make concrete connections with women at the bottom of the socioeconomic system. It must recognize the devastation of the earth as an integral part of the appropriation of the goods of the earth by a wealthy minority who can enjoy strawberries in winter winged to their glittering supermarkets by a global food procurement system while those who pick and pack the strawberries lack the money for bread and are dying from pesticide poisoning.

I remember standing in a market in Mexico in December looking hungrily at boxes of beautiful strawberries and wondering how I might sneak some back on the airplane through customs into the United States. A friend of mine, Gary McEoin, a longtime Latin American journalist standing next to me, said softly, "Beautiful, aren't they, . . . and they are covered with blood." To be an ecofeminist in my social context is to cultivate that kind of awareness about all the goods and services readily available to me.

I look for an important corrective to the myopias of the white affluent context from dialogue with ecofeminists from Asian, Africa, and Latin America, as well as from the struggles of racial-ethnic peoples against environmental racism in the United States and other industrialized countries. I find that ecofeminism sounds very different when it comes from women in these class, racial, and cultural contexts. Ecofeminists in the United States could profit from reading how these women see the women–nature connection.

While there are also many differences among women of these many non-white and non-affluent contexts, what seems to me basic is that women in Latin America, Asia, and Africa never forget that the baseline of domination of women and of nature is poverty—the impoverishment of the majority of local people, particularly women and children, and the impoverishment of the land. This connection of women and nature in impoverishment is present in everyday concrete realities. Deforestation means women walk twice and three times as long each day gathering wood; it means drought, which means women walk twice and three times farther each day to find and carry water back to their huts.

When these women talk about how to heal their people and their land from this impoverishment and poisoning, they talk about how to take back control over their resources from the World Bank and the wealthy nations. They critique the global system of economic power. They also envision ways of reclaiming some traditional patterns of care for the earth and indigenous forms of spirituality, but in a flexible, pragmatic way. For example, women from Zimbabwe and Malawi point to local territorial cults in their traditions where women were the spirit mediums and guardians of the land. Women led ceremonies calling for rain and giving thanks for harvests, kept sacred forests from being cut down, and guarded sacred pools.[8]

But these traditions are not romanticized. These African women

29

also know how women were limited by pollution taboos that forbade them access to forests and kept them from growing their own trees. They want to combine pragmatically some of the old customs that cared for the water, trees, and animals with modern understandings—of conservation and the legal right of women to own land and have equal access to agricultural credit—that have come to them from Western liberalism. If they are Christians, they don't mind citing some good stories from the Bible, side by side with good stories from their indigenous traditions. In short, they are practical ecumenists who know how to cross cultures, to speak Shona and also English, to use whatever comes from these many cultures to enhance life for all, particularly for women at the bottom of society.

I believe Western feminists of Christian background need to be similarly ecumenical and similarly clear-sighted about the economic system in which we stand. I don't believe there is a readymade feminist ecological culture that can be resurrected from prehistoric cultures, although we can catch glimpses of alternatives in ancient pasts that might help midwife new futures. We also need to mine our Greek, Hebrew, and Christian heritages, as well as modern emancipatory traditions, for useable insights.

Catherine Keller has suggested that feminist theologians are the great recyclers of culture, just as women have always been the recyclers of the waste products of human productions.[9] In constructing an ecofeminist culture and spirituality, we are the cultural equivalent of the many marginalized people around the world who pick through garbage heaps seeking for useable bits and pieces from which to construct a new habitation. While this is a grim picture of our relation to the past, it does highlight two important aspects of our task. First, that there is much of our Christian and Western past which is useable, but only by being reconstructed in new forms, as material reorganized by a new vision, as compost for a new organism. Second, it is we who must be artisans of this new culture. It will not come to us readymade, either from Christianity or science, or from Asian or Indigenous peoples.

We are facing a new situation which humans have never faced before—namely, that the human species' power, actualized by a dominant class, has grown so great that it may destroy the planetary basis of life for all other humans, as well as the non-human biosphere. Past cultures, whether they sought to harmonize humans with each other and with nature in the name of immanent deities or to subdue nature in the name of a transcendent God, did not imagine that such power was ours to possess. Most accessible cultures, including indigenous ones, had some patterns of subordination of women, and many tied this to serf, slave, or worker populations. Their cosmologies and ethical codes reflect and justify these social patterns.

But religious cultures have not only mandated the social patterns of their societies. They have also, in various ways, sought harmony and justice, overcoming enmity and alienation, reconciling humans and humans, humans and animals, humans and the ultimate Source of life. It is these many quests for harmony, reconciliation, and justice which we can assemble as the gold in the trash heaps of past cultures. Our legacy will doubtless need to be reconstructed by our children and grandchildren. At best we may construct a new foundation that is more sustainable as the base for their rebuilding.

Many cultures can provide us with clues to a healing culture. The great Asian spiritualities of Taoism and Buddhism, Hinduism and Confucianism have possibilities to be explored, particularly in their vision of letting go of overweening individualism, which releases an outflowing compassion for all sentient beings, the harmonization of the dialectical forces at work in society and the cosmos.[10]

The many cultures of indigenous peoples of the Americas, Asia, Africa, and the Pacific islands, long scorned as "pagans," have begun to be accorded more respect as we recognize how each of these peoples created its own bio-regional culture that sustained the local human group as part of a community of animals and plants, earth and sky, past ancestors and future descendants. Euro-Americans can also look for hints of such indigenous spiritualities in our pre-Christian pasts in the Celtic, Germanic, and Slavic worlds, careful to separate these roots from their misuse by fascist racist ideologies.

But we Western Christians also need to free ourselves from both our chauvinism and our escapism to be able to play with the insightful aspects of our Jewish, Greek, and Christian legacies, as well as critically appraising their problems, letting go of both the need to inflate them as the one true way, or repudiate them as total toxic waste. In my book *Gaia and God* I suggest two patterns of biblical thought that are important resources for ecological theology and ethics: covenantal ethics and sacramental cosmology.[11]

Covenantal ethics gives us a vision of an integrated community of humans, animals, and land that seeks to live by a spirituality and code of continual rest, renewal, and the restoration of just, sustainable relations between humans and other humans, and between humans and the land, in one covenant under a caretaking God. We need to reject the patriarchal aspects of this covenantal tradition, while reclaiming

31

the vision of community sustained by processes which continually righted the distorted relationships created by unjust domination and exploitation: the fertility of the land renewed by letting it lie fallow, the human and animal workers given rest, the debts forgiven, those in servitude emancipated, and land restored to those who had become landless.

Covenant ethics can be complemented by the Jewish and Christian heritages of sacramental cosmology. Here we have a sense of the whole cosmos come alive, as the bodying forth of the Holy Spirit, the Word and Wisdom of God, which is its source and renewal of life. In God we live and move and have our being, not as some detached male ego beyond the universe, but as the Holy One who is in and through and under the whole life process.

Covenantal ethics and sacramental cosmology are profound resources from our biblical and Christian heritage, but we Christians also have to let go of the illusion that there is one right way to create the new ecological world culture and that we can and should do it all. We need to see ourselves as part of a converging dialogue, as ecofeminists in many regions make their distinctive cultural syntheses; as Zimbabwe ecofeminists interconnect spirit mediums and kinship with animals with themes of just self-government that came to them from the British; as Indian ecofeminists, such as Vandana Shiva, connect the pre-Hindu understanding of Shakti, the feminine cosmic life principle, with the critique of Western science and development;[12] and as Korean ecofeminists, such as Chung Hyun Kyung, integrate a Buddhist woman Bottisatva and shaman dance with Christian emancipatory visions.[13]

But white affluent Western Christian feminists must not only shape cultural syntheses from the best of their traditions, in dialogue with those of others; we also need to know who we are. We are those who profit from the most rapacious system of colonial and neo-colonial appropriation of the land and labor of the earth ever created. We need to repudiate this system and its benefits to ourselves in order truly to stand in solidarity with poor women.

We need to keep their reality firmly in our mind's eye, as they hold the child dying of dehydration from polluted water and trek long hours to fetch basic necessities, and also as they continue to struggle to defend life with a tenacity that refuses to be defeated. Only as we learn to connect both our stories and also our struggles in a concrete and authentic way can we begin to glimpse what an ecofeminist theology and ethic might really be all about.

Notes

1. Cf. Bill Devall and George Sessions, *Deep Ecology: Living as if Nature Mattered* (Salt Lake City: Peregrine Smith Books, 1985).
2. Cf. Marti Kheel, 'Ecofeminism and Deep Ecology: Reflections on Identity and Difference', in Irene Diamond and Gloria F. Orenstein (eds.), *Reweaving the World: The Emergence of Ecofeminism* (San Francisco, Calif.: Sierra Club Books, 1990), 128–37.
3. Cf. Ynestra King, 'Healing the Wounds: Feminism, Ecology, and the Nature/ Culture Dualism', in Diamond and Orenstein, *Reweaving the World*, 106–21.
4. Riane Eisler, *The Chalice and the Blade* (San Francisco, Calif.: Harper & Row, 1987).
5. Starhawk, *The Spiral Dance: The Rebirth of the Ancient Religion of the Great Goddess* (New York: Harper & Row, 1979).
6. Charlene Spretnak, 'Ecofeminism: Our Roots and Flowering', in Diamond and Orenstein, *Reweaving the World*, 1–14.
7. Cf. e.g. the column by Jon Margolis, 'Gyno-supremacism Engenders a Political Revolt', *Chicago Tribune*, editorial page, 30 Jan. 1995, and reply by Rosemary Ruether, 'Letters to the Editor', 18 Feb. 1995.
8. These essays from African, Asian, and Latin American women appear in Rosemary Ruether (ed.), *Women Healing Earth: Third World Women on Ecology, Feminism, and Religion* (Maryknoll, NY: Orbis Books, 1996).
9. Oral remarks by Catherine Keller in a workshop on Buddhist–Christian Dialogue, Berkeley, Calif., Aug. 1991. Cf. her article, 'Talk about the Weather: The Greening of Eschatology', in Carol J. Adams (ed.), *Ecofeminism and the Sacred* (New York: Continuum, 1993), 43.
10. Cf. Mary E. Tucker and John A. Grim (eds.), *World Views and Ecology: Religion, Philosophy, and the Environment* (Maryknoll, NY: Orbis Books, 1994).
11. Rosemary Ruether, *Gaia and God: An Ecofeminist Theology of Earth Healing* (San Francisco: Harper, 1992), chs. 8 and 9.
12. Vandana Shiva, *Staying Alive: Women, Ecology, and Development in India* (New Delhi: Kali for Women, 1989).
13. Chung Hyun Kyung, 'Come Holy Spirit: Renew the Whole Creation', address at the World Council of Churches conference in Canberra, Australia, Feb. 1991. Published in Michael Kinnamon (ed.), *Signs of the Spirit* (Geneva: WCC Publications, 1991), 37–47.

5 Judges, or Disasters of War

Alicia Ostriker*

This powerful modern midrash (interpretation) on war in the book of Judges touches on several important themes in feminist literature, most obviously the subject of violence against women. The scene is a crisis centre for abused women run by a descendant of the judge and warrior Deborah. As we shall see, however, some victims are less equal than others. Just as liberation theology has been criticized for its failure to address feminist concerns, so feminism here is warned against creating its own insiders and outsiders. To avoid anticipating the chilling denouement of this short story, I shall observe merely that Ostriker, a distinguished poet and author of works of feminist Bible criticism, brings psychological depth and complexity to a figure who, in the Hebrew Bible itself, is little more than a cartoon. We are reminded of Hagar, Abraham's Egyptian concubine, another female outsider who has only recently received the attention lavished on female insiders such as Sarah and Miriam. DL

> In those days there was no king in Israel: every man did that which was right in his own eyes.
>
> Judges 21: 25

> Turning and turning in the widening gyre,
>   The falcon cannot hear the falconer.
> Things fall apart; the center cannot hold;
>   Mere anarchy is loosed upon the world.
> The blood-dimmed tide is loosed, and everywhere
>   The ceremony of innocence is drowned.
>
> W. B. Yeats

The crisis center needs a paint job, which it will not receive for the foreseeable future since there is a war on and no available funds.

* Alicia Ostriker, 'Judges, or Disasters of War', from *The Nakedness of the Father: Biblical Visions and Revisions*. Copyright © 1994 by Alicia Suskin Ostriker. Reprinted by permission of Rutgers University Press.

When, we may ask, is there not a war on. What is human history but the history of that war, fought either against our neighbors or among ourselves. Therefore the plaster curls picturesquely on the ceiling. The phone bill is behind. A casement in the window was broken by a flying brick. The donated furniture is dented and wears a light coating of grease and dust. Down the street are a shoe repair shop, a butcher, a porno movie house, a diner, some warehouses. Outside the window, litter flies down the avenue like pieces of forgotten childhood learning. Inside there are flyspecked posters on the walls, a woman with a submachine gun, a woman nursing a child, an arm raised in defiance.

Several adolescent girls giggle in one corner. In another corner a pale woman in her mid-thirties with jet black hair, love beads, and bitten fingernails pours coffee into styrofoam cups, preparing for the afternoon group meeting in which some attempt is made at education. The leader tries to give the women who gather at the center a sense of personal identity and shared community. The afternoon discussions are always seething with tales, crackling with narratives. War stories, tales of horror.

Deborah tells her group the story of the Levite's concubine. Once there was a girl who fell in love with a travelling lawyer from the side of Mount Ephraim. He met her in the marketplace of Bethlehem-judah, gave her jewelry, and then bought her from her father. She travelled with him bringing her clothing and cooking things to his place. After some months, perhaps he beat her, perhaps she was merely lonely or bored, she went back to live with her father. She was sixteen. The lawyer came to fetch her home. The woman's father greeted the man as a son-in-law and feasted him for five days, with meat and wine, not permitting him to leave, hoping perhaps to keep both his daughter and the young man at his side. But finally they left. As it happened they lodged on the way in Gibeah, a Benjamite town. That night a hostile crowd of Benjamite men gathered outside the door, demanding to see the lawyer. Send him outside, they yelled drunkenly. We want to talk to him.[1]

Some of the women in the shelter already know what will happen. Surreptitiously they watch the new girls. They know this is the story to end all stories, a real shocker, and they like to see the new girls react.

Well, says Deborah, in this case there were no angels present. First the old man who was the host offered the mob his own daughter, a maiden, along with the lawyer's woman, saying do what you want with them, humble them, but leave my guest alone, don't commit your vileness with him. And then the lawyer pushed his woman out into the street.

Around the table they picture it, they know it, how the Levite's woman fell from the doorway and looked at the mob of men. The men were licking their chops. They were laughing, elbowing. She looked at their teeth and tongues in the chalky floodlight of a cool moon. They knocked her down, tore her dress off and began to bite at her face breasts belly. Someone poured the dregs of a bottle of wine over her. Use the bottle, use the bottle, the men yelled. Someone had the thigh-bone of a dog to thrust into her. She called and fought and fell silent. After some hours the moon set, the sky lightened. The woman crept to her host's doorsill. She put her hands on the threshold. After a while her man opened the door following his night's sleep and gazed out at the day. Time to go, he said, but nobody answered. I hope you are all paying attention because this is a true story, says Deborah. The lawyer lay the girl's corpse over his donkey and brought it home. Then with a knife he divided it into twelve pieces and sent one piece to each of the twelve tribes of Israel, demanding a judgment against the Benjamites who had insulted him. The Benjamites refused to surrender the culprits, and the upshot was war, a vast slaughter of men and destruction of cities. Well, let's have some comments.

The married women are shy, looking down at the table. This is not a good moment in history. Their husbands for the most part are drunkards, or crazies, with or without the excuse of combat experience. The women visit the center from time to time, mostly all they hope for is peace, they should raise their children in good health, their husbands should quit breaking dishes, cursing in front of the children, slapping them around in public. They try to be obedient wives, for everyone says if the husband is unhappy the wife is to blame, they truly try their best. The women who have been divorced by their husbands are perhaps worse off. They remember a room of men in black, saying holy words, refusing to look at them, refusing to touch them, men without pity. And then the agunot, women who have been abandoned by their husbands and can never remarry, who become like lifeless sticks. Red hands, evasive eyes, emaciation. The whiners and the beggars, the desperate marketers of their own bodies. Voices coarsened from screaming. Each with a tale to unfold that would wither your spirit. Drowning people gasping air, Deborah thinks, what is the use, mere straws I throw them. God help us regain our womanly strength, Deborah says to herself when she regards the flotsam thrown on her cement doorsill. God help us through this age of brother fighting brother, tribe murdering tribe. Turn us, Oh Lord, prays Deborah silently. A dull-normal girl, pregnant, who never speaks at meetings, has tears running down her cheeks. The rest look at her with some contempt.

A young runaway from a wealthy family raises her hand smirking, crossing her legs under the chipped table. The plot resembles that of the Iliad, and that of the Mahabarata and Ramayana, if you're looking at epics, she says. The men always fight wars over their wounded honor with some woman as pretext. Their inflated egos is more like it. And remember Jephthah's daughter, who got sacrificed because her father, that idiot, promised to sacrifice whoever first came out of his house if he was victorious in some battle? And Jacob's daughter Dinah, who got used as an excuse for our men to murder all the men of Schechem? Did anybody for one minute care how Dinah felt about being raped?[2] No news here, she yawns. The pigs are the same everywhere. Wait, says Deborah. We are speaking of Jews not gentiles. Remember that among Jews these stories are not heroic but scandalous. A symptom of social chaos, when men forget to obey God as their Lord and King, and therefore fall into abominations. For us it is tragic when women suffer. Doesn't that prove that Jews respect women? Don't you remember our saying that the price of a virtuous woman is far above rubies? Sure, right, says the runaway. Fools grow without rain. That's why the Levite is never punished, and Jephthah is never punished, and the rabbis never condemn them. No, the stories are to make us afraid. To terrify us into submission. She glares around the table but the other women are shrinking, disinclined to meet her eyes.

Deborah thinks it is time to tell something inspirational, a story of the old days, the days of faith. She squares her massive shoulders. Many years ago, says Deborah, my ancestress was a judge in Israel. A prophetess, a mother, and a judge. She was famous for defeating the Canaanites who oppressed us with their nine hundred iron chariots.[3] It was she under her palm tree in Mount Ephraim who mobilized our armies, she who promised our timid general Barak that she would go with him, and she who predicted that the enemy general Sisera would be killed by a woman. O my soul, thou hast trodden down strength. For the stars in their courses fought against Sisera, at the foot of Mount Tabor, and his people fell upon the edge of the sword, and not a man was left alive. Fleeing before us, Sisera stumbled into the tent of Jael, wife of Heber, thinking he would be safe there. Water, he croaked. And now hear what a heroine was this Jael. She gave him milk, she brought forth butter in a lordly dish, she covered him with a blanket and told him to sleep. Then while he slept she drove a tent stake through his head.

So perish all our enemies! Victory! Go for it, Jael! yell the women. Yes, continues Deborah, feeling herself at last a queen bee in her own hive. Yes, and think how that night the mother of Sisera looked through her lattice, wondering why Sisera was so long in arriving with his chariot. She expected him any moment to appear with his armies, having captured one or two of our Israelite women for each of his men. Boo, hiss, yell the women. They are picturing the general with the nail through his skull, they are elated with patriotism, and also something else.

For how good it is to kill, to kill in revenge. For the times they squeeze your breasts with their thick fingers. For the times they pretend you do not exist, while you beg them to listen to you. For the times they beat you and you creep away to wash your own blood, and make excuses for them to the children. For their indifference when you are sick and weak, although if a mosquito bites *them* they think the sky is falling. For the times they travel and forget to telephone. For the times they shit themselves, drunk, and you have to clean them. For their disgusting vomit. For their evil language, their laughter, their sarcasm, their warning index fingers. For the way they look at you with revulsion, pressing their lips together. For their joviality whenever any woman is humiliated. For their comradeship among themselves which excludes you. A nail, yes, a nail through the head, that would teach them. The women all sigh, they never have such wicked fantasies, they permit themselves a crude joke sometimes to communicate a shared fury. Why don't women have any brains? Because they don't have any pricks to put them in. They have their little litanies of grievances. He said, then I said, and then the sonofabitch had the nerve to say.

A new woman, a redhead in a black dress and gold necklaces has arrived, is standing by the door, they motion her to the table. She drinks the bad coffee with the rest and listens. Now the women are discussing personal problems, this week's bad news. They offer each other strategic advice and support. When her turn comes, the redheaded woman describes her relationship with her husband. As she speaks she becomes pale and pushes her rings up and down her fingers. The man was a bully, an animal, you can't tame somebody like that except by killing him. My love was infatuation, madness, she says. How his handsome arrogance dragged her like gravity. How her enthralled nervous system would start hanging up crepe paper, flinging tinsel, flicking the strobes, when he walked into a room, even when she felt most hatred for him. The other women nod, oh sister, they know all about it. The hyperventilation express, the jungle juice special, what woman doesn't.

Yet her heart resisted, she explains. He was a brute, the enemy, not even intelligent enough to argue with, his God and his country meant nothing to him, he was just a killing machine, a criminal. Imagine a man who called himself a servant of God in one breath, then in the next breath bragged about the fights he picked, his technique of feinting at a man's head with one hand and stabbing him in the gut like lightning with the other. The stories he told! Ripping a lion apart barehanded! Killing thousands of men with the jawbone of an ass— and the men are *her* countrymen, and he was telling her this as some kind of preface to lovemaking, he was *proud* of it, his eye whites and teeth gleaming like a wolf's, he was a complete wilful *infant*. She tried not to love him. You disgust me, she said. He would go back to his own people but then he would appear again in her doorway, rippling his pectorals. And in the city of her flesh, as this destructive child approached, swaggering, the shopkeepers of her body would be flinging open doors, rolling out awnings, ripping padlocks from windows, setting forth the tempting goods.

The redhead tells her story gaspingly. I have to get some counseling, she says. I was desperate, without a choice, I was like a goddamned leaf in the wind. I even thought he was asking for it. Please help me. Please try to understand. She beats her fist against her breast, where the golden chains dangle.

One by one the women understand who the redhead is. Whore, instrument of the devil. Philistine bitch. They look at her with horror and confusion. Get out of here, says Deborah. But I did less than Jael, says the redhead, I didn't kill him. I only weakened him. All I did was cut his goddamned hair. And you must have heard that Samson was a total psychopath, murdering my countrymen, my own relatives, for nothing, just to show off his strength.[4] Please, says Delilah, looking around the shabby room, can't I stay, I really need counseling. Get out, says Deborah. And I mean now.

Notes

1. Judges 19 is a replay of the scene at Sodom, obviously; but, as Mieke Bal points out, the replay is in the context of a shift from patrilocal to virilocal possession of women, which the Benjamite men are represented as resisting. The girl *is*

murdered in the story, and the Levite *is* attacked through the butchery of his property, which he then further butchers as if to re-establish control. I have followed Bal in seeing the Book of Judges as a book whose subtext is the war of the sexes, and in disregarding the supposed chronology of the book, which scholars assume to be its central theme but which is in fact very weakly rendered.

2. The episodes of Jephthah's daughter and the rape of Dinah are in Judges 11 and Genesis 34 respectively. Rabbinical commentary typically blames Dinah for her rape. In Deena Metzger's novel *What Dinah Thought*, Dinah and Schechem are secretly married, and Dinah curses the sons of Jacob after they massacre Schechem; violence between Israelites and Schechemites (i.e., Palestinians) will plague both nations throughout history.

3. The story of Deborah and the defeat of Sisera is in Judges 4–5.

4. The story is in Judges 13–16.

6   Beyond God the Father

Mary Daly*

Mary Daly is the feminist theologian most likely to be known to feminists outside the ranks of organized religion. *Beyond God the Father* remains a prophetic book, raising concerns that later become central in both English-speaking and French feminist theory. Daly accuses Christian theology of the heresy it most opposes—idolatry. Like liberation theology, feminist theology highlights the way that 'false gods' kill genuine hope for a better world. Daly is a sophisticated analyst of religious language and, drawing implicitly on Feuerbachian theories of projection, anticipates the French philosopher and psychoanalyst Luce Irigaray in saying that women need to name God (correctly) in order newly to name themselves.

JMS

WHY SPEAK ABOUT "GOD"?

It might seem that the women's revolution should just go about its business of generating a new consciousness, without worrying about God. I suggest that the fallacy involved in this would be an overlooking of a basic question that is implied in human existence and that the pitfall in such an oversight is cutting off the radical potential of the movement itself.

It is reasonable to take the position that sustained effort toward self-transcendence requires keeping alive in one's consciousness the question of ultimate transcendence, that is, of God. It implies recognition of the fact that we have no power *over* the ultimately real, and that whatever authentic power we have is derived from *participation in* ultimate reality. This awareness, always hard to sustain, makes it possible to be free of idolatry even in regard to one's own cause, since

---

* Mary Daly, excerpt from 'After the Death of God the Father', from *Beyond God the Father* (Women's Press, 1986).

it tells us that all presently envisaged goals, lifestyles, symbols, and societal structures may be transitory. This is the meaning that the question of God should have for liberation, sustaining a concern that is really open to the future, in other words, that is really ultimate. Such a concern will not become fixated upon limited objectives. Feminists in the past have in a way been idolatrous about such objectives as the right to vote. Indeed, this right is due to women in justice and it is entirely understandable that feminists' energies were drained by the efforts needed to achieve even such a modicum of justice. But from the experience of such struggles we are in a position now to distrust token victories within a societal and structural framework that renders them almost meaningless. The new wave of feminism desperately needs to be not only many-faceted but cosmic and ultimately religious in its vision. This means reaching outward and inward toward the God beyond and beneath the gods who have stolen our identity.

The idea that human beings are "to the image of God" is an intuition whose implications could hardly be worked through under patriarchal conditions. If it is true that human beings have projected "God" in their own image, it is also true that we can evolve beyond the projections of earlier stages of consciousness. It is the creative potential itself in human beings that is the image of God.[1] As the essential victims of the archaic God-projections, women can bring this process of creativity into a new phase. This involves iconoclasm—the breaking of idols. Even—and perhaps especially—through the activity of its most militantly atheistic and a-religious members, the movement is smashing images that obstruct the becoming of the image of God. The basic idol-breaking will be done on the level of internalized images of male superiority, on the plane of exorcising them from consciousness and from the cultural institutions that breed them.

One aspect of this expurgation is dethronement of false Gods— ideas and symbols of God that religion has foisted upon the human spirit (granted that the human spirit has created the religions that do this). . . . it might be well to focus specifically upon three false deities who still haunt the prayers, hymns, sermons, and religious education of Christianity. The three usurpers I have in mind have already been detected and made the targets of attack by liberal male theologians, but the point in mentioning them here is to indicate the specific relevance of feminism to their demise.

One of the false deities to be dethroned is the God of explanation, or "God as a stop-gap for the incompleteness of our knowledge," as

Bonhoeffer called him.[2] This serves sometimes as the legitimation of anomic occurrences such as the suffering of a child, a legitimation process which Peter Berger lucidly analyzes in discussing the problem of theodicy.[3] Such phenomena are "explained" as being God's will. So also are socially prevailing inequalities of power and privilege, by a justifying process which easily encourages masochistic attitudes. Clearly, this deity does not encourage commitment to the task of analyzing and eradicating the social, economic, and psychological roots of suffering. As marginal beings who are coming into awareness, women are in a situation to see that "God's plan" is often a front for men's plans and a cover for inadequacy, ignorance, and evil. Our vantage point offers opportunities for dislodging this deity from its revered position on the scale of human delusions.

Another idol is the God of otherworldliness. The most obvious face of this deity in the past has been that of the Judge whose chief activity consists in rewarding and punishing after death. As de Beauvoir indicated, women have been the major consumers of this religious product. Since there has been so little self-realization possible by the female sex "in this life," it was natural to focus attention on the next. As mass consumers of this image, women have the power to remove it from the market, mainly by living full lives here and now. I do not mean to advocate a mere re-utterance of the "secularization" theology that was so popular in the sixties. This obvious shape of the God of otherworldliness has after all been the target of male theologians for some time, and the result has often been a kind of translation of religion into humanism to such an extent that there is a kind of "self-liquidation of theology."[4] What I see beginning to happen with women coming into their own goes beyond this secularization. The rejection of the simplistic God of otherworldliness does not mean necessarily reduction to banal secularism. If women can sustain the courage essential to liberation this can give rise to a deeper "other-worldliness"—an awareness that the process of creating a counter-world to the counterfeit "this world" presented to consciousness by the societal structures that oppress us is participation in eternal life.

It should be noted that the God lurking behind some forms of Protestant piety has functioned similarly to the otherworldly God of popular Roman Catholic piety. In his analysis of the effects of Luther's doctrine of salvation by faith alone, Max Weber uncovers serious problems of ethical motivation, involving a complicated series of phenomena: "Every rational and planned procedure for achieving salvation, every reliance on good works, and above all every effort to surpass normal ethical behavior by ascetic achievement is regarded by religion based on faith as a wicked preoccupation with purely human powers."[5] Trans-worldly asceticism and monasticism tend to be rejected when salvation by faith is stressed, and as a result there may be an increased emphasis upon vocational activity within the world. However, as Weber explains, emphasis upon personal religious relationship to God tends to be accompanied by an attitude of individualism in pursuit of such worldly vocational activity. One consequence is an attitude of patient resignation regarding institutional structures, both worldly and churchly.[6] It is precisely this schizophrenic attitude that combines personal vocational ambition within the prevailing set of social arrangements and passive acceptance of the system that radical feminism recognizes as destructive.

A third idol, intimately related to those described above, is the God who is the Judge of "sin," who confirms the rightness of the rules and roles of the reigning system, maintaining false consciences and self-destructive guilt feelings. Women have suffered both mentally and physically from this deity, in whose name they have been informed that birth control and abortion are unequivocally wrong, that they should be subordinate to their husbands, that they must be present at rituals and services in which men have all the leadership roles and in which they are degraded not only by enforced passivity but also verbally and symbolically. Although this is most blatant in the arch-conservative religions, the God who imposes false guilt is hardly absent from liberal Protestantism and Judaism, where his presence is more subtle. Women's growth in self-respect will deal the death blow to this as well as to the other demons dressed as Gods.

WOMEN'S LIBERATION AS SPIRITUAL REVOLUTION

I have indicated that because the becoming of women involves a radical encounter with nothingness, it bears with it a new surge of ontological hope. This hope is essentially active. The passive hope that has been so prevalent in the history of religious attitudes corresponds to the objectified God from whom one may anticipate favors. Within that frame of reference human beings have tried to relate to ultimate reality as an object to be known, cajoled, manipulated. The tables are turned, however, for the objectified "God" has a way of reducing his producers to objects who lack capacity for autonomous action. In contrast to this, the God who is power of being acts as a moral power summoning women and men to act out of our deepest hope and to become who we can be. I am therefore in agreement with Johannes Metz that authentic hope will be active and creative.[7] The difference is that I see the specific experiential basis for this as an ontological experience. This experience in its first phase is one of nonbeing. In its second phase it is an intuition of being which, as Jacques Maritain described it, is a *dynamic* intuition.[8] Clearly, from what has preceded in this chapter, I see this ontological basis of hope to be particularly available to women at this point in history because of the marginal situation of females in an androcentric world.

This hope is communal rather than merely individualistic, because it is grounded in the two-edged courage to be. That is, it is hope coming from the experience of individuation *and* participation. It drives beyond the objectified God that is imagined as limited in benevolence, bestowing blessings upon "his" favorites. The power of being is that in which all finite beings participate, but not on a "one-to-one" basis, since this power is in all while transcending all. Communal hope involves in some manner a profound interrelationship with other finite beings, human and nonhuman. Ontological communal hope, then, is cosmic. Its essential dynamic is directed to the universal community.

Finally, ontological hope is revolutionary. Since the insight in which it is grounded is the double-edged intuition of nonbeing and of being, it extends beyond the superstitious fixations of technical reason. The latter, as Tillich has shown, when it is cut off from the intuitive knowledge of ontological reason, cannot get beyond superstition.[9] The rising consciousness that women are experiencing of our dehumanized situation has the power to turn attention around from the projections of our culture to the radically threatened human condition. Insofar as women are true to this consciousness, we have to be the most radical of revolutionaries, since the superstition revealed to us is omnipresent and plagues even the other major revolutionary movements of our time. Knowing that a Black or White, Marxist or Capitalist, countercultural or bourgeois male chauvinist deity (human or divine) will not differ essentially from his opposite, women will be forced in a dramatic way to confront the most haunting of human questions, the question of God. This confrontation may not find its major locus within the theological academy or the institutional churches and it may not always express itself in recognizable theological or philosophical language. However, there is a dynamism in the ontological

45

affirmation of self that reaches out toward the nameless God.[10] In hearing and naming ourselves out of the depths, women are naming *toward* God, which is what theology always should have been about. Unfortunately it tended to stop at fixing names *upon* God, which deafened us to our own potential for self-naming.

Notes

1. Unfortunately, in the Christian theological tradition this 'image' was recognized as existing unambiguously only in the male. While Augustine saw the male as being to the image of God, he conceded that woman is restored to the image only where there is no sex, that is, in the spirit (*De Trinitate*, XXI, 7). Aquinas was a little more generous, granting that the image of God is in both man and woman, but adding that in a special sense it is only in the male, who is 'the beginning and end of woman, as God is the beginning and end of every creature' (*Summa theologiae* 1, 93, 4 ad 1).

2. Dietrich Bonhoeffer, *Letters and Papers from Prison*, p. 190.

3. Peter Berger, *The Sacred Canopy: Elements of a Sociological Theory of Religion* (New York: Doubleday, 1967; London: Faber and Faber, 1969), 53–80. Berger, however, does not recognize implications of this from the standpoint of radical feminism.

4. Peter Berger, *A Rumor of Angels: Modern Society and the Rediscovery of the Supernatural* (New York: Doubleday–Anchor Books, 1970; Harmondsworth: Penguin, 1971), 12. Unfortunately, Berger goes rather far in 'liquidating' the work of theologians whose views are less orthodox than his own.

5. Max Weber. *The Sociology of Religion*, trans. Ephraim Fischoff (Boston: Beacon Press, 1963; London: Methuen 1965), 198.

6. Ibid. 198–9.

7. Johannes Metz, 'Creative Hope', in *New Theology No. 5*, ed. Martin E. Marty and Dean G. Peerman (New York: Macmillian, 1968), 130–41. See also Metz, *Theology of the World*, trans. William Glen-Doepel (New York: Herder & Herder, 1969).

8. Jacques Maritain, *Existence and the Existent*, trans. Lewis Galantiere and Gerald B. Phelan (New York: Doubleday–Image Books, 1956). Although he was hardly a feminist or social revolutionary, Maritain had an exceedingly fine sensitivity to the power of this intuition, which, if it were carried through to social consciousness, would challenge the world. See also *Distinguish to Unite: The Degrees of Knowledge*, trans. from the 4th French edn. under the supervision of G. B. Phelan (New York: Scribner's, 1959).

9. Paul Tillich, *Systematic Theology I* (Chicago: University of Chicago Press, 1951; London: Nisbet, 1953), 74: 'Whenever technical reason dominates, religion is superstition and is either foolishly supported by reason or rightly removed by it.'

10. Maritain, in *Existence and the Existent*, 76, remarks: 'When a man [*sic*] is awake to the intuition of being he is awake at the same time to the intuition of subjectivity. . . . The force of such a perception may be so great as to sweep him along to that heroic asceticism of the void and of annihilation in which he will achieve ecstasy in the substantial existence of the *self* and the "presence of immensity" of the divine Self at one and the same time.'

Part II. Identity: Who Do You Say I Am?

When women began to study academic theology in significant numbers they were often shocked by the sheer maleness of its texts. It was no surprise to them to learn that biblical texts were written by men in times and cultures different from their own, and that they had been commented upon for millennia almost entirely by men. No one expected the sacred writings to advocate votes for women, but women might have expected more feeling for their dignity before God. Not only was this hard to find in narratives that commented impassively on the rape, murder, and general dispensability of women (the Levite's concubine in Judges comes to mind), but even where women were central to the narrative they remained silent and, all too frequently, nameless. The women on the ark are known to us as 'the wives' of Noah and his sons (Genesis 7:13); the woman who went to her death so that her father could keep his vow to God is known simply as 'Jephthah's daughter' (Judges 11:34–40); and the woman to whom an angel promised a heroic son is known to us only as Samson's mother (Judges 13:2–24). Even the woman commended by Jesus as one who will be remembered forever (watched resentfully by the disciples, she anointed Jesus' head with precious ointment) is nameless (Mark 14:3–9).

As religious schools and seminaries gradually opened their doors to them, women approached the study of their religious traditions with optimism and joy, confident that their sacred texts were sources of truth and life. Disheartening then that the texts, at least as read by generations of male readers, seemed more attuned to the sources of life for men than for women. Even if the past is truly 'another country', why had later generations of religious leaders and scholars made so little, often nothing at all, of the absence of women in sacred texts? It became important to look at women in scriptures from a woman's point of view (examples can be found in the 'Sacred Texts' section of this volume). It also became important for scholars—mostly women—to examine the treatment of women as a theological topic in post-biblical religious writings, to look for the few and fragmentary texts written by women in the antique period (see Elisabeth

Castelli), and to examine the more extensive material from medieval and Renaissance women (see Kari Vogt and Jane Dempsey Douglass).

The requirement that women name themselves after centuries of silence is a feature of other branches of feminism. In feminist theology we find ourselves considering not just what tenth-, twelfth-, or twentieth-century men thought about women, but what they claimed to be the divinely ordained truth about woman, her relationship to man, and their relationship to God. Even in modern times, and where least expected, gender subordination vitiates major theological projects (see Rachel Muers' discussion of Karl Barth and Hans Urs von Balthasar).

We cannot assume that, because women must finally speak for themselves, they can speak synoptically for all women. This shortcoming in feminist rhetoric was soon exposed (especially in the United States) by critics who saw the so-called 'universal women's experience' as distinctly white and middle-class. In Christian thought, Womanist and *mujerista* theologies are just two examples of a movement that spans the globe, as women from Africa, south-east Asia, China, and Latin America, and indeed every state and circumstance, begin to do theology (see Ada María Isasi-Diaz and Elsa Tamez in this section, and Jacquelyn Grant and Sharon Bong in 'Incarnation and Embodiment').

The feminist battle against assumed homogeneity is by no means restricted to nationality, ethnic origin, or social class. Two women of the same religion with all these in common might yet respond very differently to questions about their identity as members of a faith community and as women. It is not only 'progressive' women who wrestle with their religious heritage, wondering if a woman's lot could have been otherwise in the past and asking whether it might be different in the future (see Haviva Ner-David on being an Orthodox Jewish feminist).

JMS

'Becoming Male': One Aspect of an Early Christian Anthropology

Kari Vogt*

'Virtue', from the Latin *vir*, 'male', had its origins in designating male perfections. Early Christian theologians, as well as some Hellenistic (Greek-speaking) Jews of the period, were familiar with a moral ascendancy in which 'womanish' or sensual elements were to be surpassed by masculine rationality. In this influential essay, Kari Vogt shows how a common Graeco-Roman phrase for moral growth, 'becoming male', took on new shading when used by Christian authors informed by New Testament writings. JMS

Like its variants on the theme 'becoming male', the metaphorical expression 'woman turned into man' is relatively frequent in early Christian literature. Similar metaphors occur in non-Christian texts also, and all the indications are that this usage comes from the *Koine* culture of the time: there is a common scale of values of which masculine and feminine contrast, and the term 'becoming male' refers without exception to development from a lower to a higher state of moral and spiritual perfection.[1] As a religio-literary metaphor common to Christians and non-Christians, the term 'becoming male' does not necessarily have to be interpreted any more specifically.

For our part, we consider that when the term (or one or other of its variants) is used by Christian authors it acquires a specifically Christian content, because it ties in with the main New Testament metaphors and therefore fits into a specific theological and anthropological system. This can lead one to perceive a connection between early Christian anthropology and the social reality of the age.

The first part of our article will establish the connections between use of the metaphor and anthropological ideas in two authors who are

* Kari Vogt, ' "Becoming Male": One Aspect of Early Christian Anthropology', translated by Ruth Murphy, from *Women: Invisible in Theology and Church*, edited by Elisabeth Schüssler Fiorenza and Mary Collins (*Concilium* 6, 1985).

typical of Christian antiquity, Clement of Alexandria and Origen. In the context of this article, it is interesting to note that both writers engaged actively in polemic against gnostic systems in which the metaphors 'woman turned into man' and 'becoming male' were in common use.[2] This is a very large subject which we can do no more than outline.[3]

ANTHROPOLOGICAL METAPHORS IN CLEMENT OF ALEXANDRIA

Clement of Alexandria calls the male Christian gnostic 'the perfect man', *teleios aner*, and describes in the same way the woman who, 'when she has freed herself of the cravings of the flesh', achieves perfection in this life as the man does, '. . . for souls are . . . neither masculine nor feminine, when they no longer marry nor are married. Perhaps *she is* thus *turned into a man*, the woman who is no more feminine than he, *the perfect, manly, woman*'.[4] This passage raises the question of a common human nature versus sexually determined nature; it also raises the question of the salvation of the believer and of his/her way to salvation. These are both central themes in Clement's anthropology. He is the earliest Christian writer to draw widely on Ephesians 4:13.[5] Obviously, then, 'perfect man' (*teleios aner*) is one of the crucial metaphors in Clement of Alexandria's work, and his use of other metaphors such as 'woman turned into man' or 'the perfect, manly, woman' should be viewed in relation to it.

Common Human Nature and Sexually Determined Nature

'The name of human being (*anthropos*) is common to men and women', says the *Paedagogus*.[6] This is the basis of Clement of Alexandria's whole anthropology: both sexes have the same chances of fulfilling virtue (*areté*), and thus of attaining perfection.[7] Common human nature contrasts with the singularity conferred by sex.[8] This singularity can be described as *skema* or *morphè*, and consists in external anatomical difference and different biological functions.[9] Biology and psychology are not unconnected and, with the backing of 1 Corinthians, the link between biology and the various tasks and social authority is stressed.[10] A man is superior to a woman in as much as he is a man.[11] However, individuals are not determined morally by belonging to one or the other sex; thus a man may be morally and physically weaker than a woman.[12] A married woman should obey her husband, true; but if he becomes morally degraded, she is under a duty to guide him and remonstrate with him.[13] In this sense, 'manliness' has to be striven for by both sexes: women may act in manly wise, that is, they may achieve virtue (*areté*), while men may become effeminate, that is, they may degenerate morally.[14]

Nature Determined by Sex and Desire (*epitymia*)

Differentiation into sexes is bound up with desire, *epitymia*, 'the root of evil'.[15] The differentiation is willed by God, because it serves procreation, but at the same time it is a passing state belonging to this life, which exists because of the desire (*epitymia*) that sustains it.[16] In heavenly life *epitymia* disappears, as also therefore does differentiation into sexes: 'human beings [are] freed of the desire that separates them into two distinct beings'.[17] In the *Stromateis*, *epitymia* is contrasted with *apatheia*,[18] and differentiation into sexes thereby acquires a negative connotation: plurality is contrasted with oneness.[19] Christ, who represents oneness and draws all the virtues together, is there described as *aepitymia*,[20] and whoever wants to be united with him must be freed of desire.[21]

The Doctrine of the Image and Spiritual Progress

Clement's doctrine of the image of God is christocentric: Christ is the image of God, human beings are in the image of Christ and therefore of God. The image of God in woman is accepted without further discussion, and as is so often the case with the Alexandrians, the image of God is linked with the asexual soul although Clement of Alexandria will in certain cases allow the human body (that is the male body) to represent the image of God;[22] as for the likeness of God, man has to achieve it by moral actions and a process of reassimilation.[23] Only Christ has both *eikon* and *homoiosis* from the start, and only the Christian gnostic 'who imitates God as much as possible' will reach the point of resembling Christ in that also.[24] The gnostic becomes 'the living image of the Lord',[25] and is the example offered to other Christians: '. . . we should thus make haste to become, like the gnostic, *manly and perfect*', we read in the passage of the *Stromateis* that quotes Ephesians 4:13 in full.[26] In Clement of Alexandria, the idea of a realisation of the image of God comes structurally to resemble the idea of transformation into *teleios aner*, with both ideas indicating spiritual progress.

The Christian Gnostic—Man or Woman—as *teleios aner*

Transformation into *teleios aner* is characterised by not being fully achieved before the next life, and by the possibility of reaching the celestial state during life on earth.[27] The perfect man, the gnostic, is like the angels during his earthly life;[28] he is described as 'son of God', 'friend of God',[29] or as 'divine'.[30] The sexually differentiated state can be nullified even in this life, and *teleios aner* includes both sexes. So to become 'perfect man' is something more than just the metaphor Clement uses in the *Stromateis*, where we read for example that women show manliness in action. The *teleios aner* metaphor and the expression 'the manly woman' mark a change to a new level in which the sexes are transcended, and so acquire symbolic meaning. 'To become perfect and male' emerges then as the final aim of both men and women. The metaphors 'woman turned into man' and 'the manly woman' relate therefore to woman as *anthropos* and are used as soteriological terms. In other words, a form of expression typical of the age and culture here converges with a scriptural base in which *teleios aner* happens to be the key metaphor. At the same time, this metaphor can be supported by or even replaced by other male metaphors such as becoming like Christ; it can also be combined with metaphors which refer directly to the asexual sphere, such as becoming like the angels. (The paradox of using a male metaphor to refer to a state in which sex is transcended will not pass unappreciated!)

ANTHROPOLOGICAL METAPHORS IN ORIGEN

In Origen, the categories 'male' and 'female' stand in contrast with each other and are sharply defined. The metaphor 'becoming male' occurs with relative frequency and in direct connection with spiritual progress. On several occasions, spiritual progress is described as transformation into *vir perfectus* or *teleios aner*, though Eph. 4:13 is less important than in Clement of Alexandria.[31]

Male and Female: Two Aspects of the Inner Man

To show the place of the categories male and female in Origen's anthropological thought, we shall refer to his *Homiliae in Genesim* I, 12–14.[32] This text is concerned with the creation of the celestial and immaterial man. As in Philo, the two creation narratives are interpreted as two different acts of creation. Origen distinguishes between Genesis 1:26–27a 'God created man in his image', and Genesis 1:27b 'He created them male and female', the latter being connected with fecundity and not directly with the *imago*. His interpretation of Genesis 1:26–27a stresses that for man (*homo*), the fact of being in the image of God is constitutive. It is the inner man (*homo interior*), and not the body, which is in the image of God. Only Christ is *imago*; a human being is 'an image of the image', and like Clement of Alexandria's, Origen's doctrine of the image is bound up with the idea of spiritual progress.[33] A human being's aim is to be changed 'ad similitudinem imaginis Dei'.[34] In the allegorical presentation of Genesis 1:27, we read that *homo interior* consists of spirit (*spiritus*) and soul (*anima*), the spirit being described as male (*masculus*) and the soul as female (*femina*).[35] The ideal and hierarchical relation between *spiritus* and *anima* is described as a marriage, lawful union being necessary if the offspring are to be legitimate. But if the feminine part of *homo interior* turns away from the spirit towards the senses, it commits adultery and its offspring are illegitimate. The metaphorical meaning that 'male' and 'female' acquire in Origen's ethical and anthropological thought has to be seen in the light of the fact that he links these categories with his notion of the soul; he describes the masculine part of *homo interior* as higher and qualitatively better than the feminine part.

'Male' and 'Female' as Moral Categories

'Male' and 'female' not only make up the inner human hierarchy, but may be used also as metaphors for moral qualities. Woman and the feminine then represent 'the flesh and carnal affections', and on occasions, weakness, laziness and dependence.[36] The feminine may also be directly linked with the sphere of sin: 'he is a true male who does not know sin, which is the lot of fragile woman'.[37] There are two types of action whose moral qualities are characterised as male or female: 'If our action is female, it is corporeal or carnal'.[38] In *Homiliae in Exodum* Origen interprets the pharaoh's order to kill all the male children and let the girls live as an attack by the devil on rational sense and the intelligent spirit (of boys). The girls represent the flesh and its passions.[39] The midwives, who in Origen stand for the Old and New Covenants, kill the girls and let the boys live, which shows the Church banishing sin and promoting virtue.[40] Whoever has a manly soul is advised to let the male child within him/her live.[41]

Sexual Appartenance as a Spiritual Category

When Origen calls good actions male and bad actions female, as he does in *Selecta in Exodum* 23, 17, he ends: '. . . what is seen by the Creator's gaze is male and not female. For God does not deign to look at what is feminine or material'. This statement, like other similar ones, has to be seen in the light of the fact that Origen gives a spiritualised meaning to the category 'sex'. Which sex an individual belongs to is a matter of moral quality and spiritual intelligence.[42] We read in *Homiliae in Josue*: 'Men and women are distinguished according to differences of heart. How many belong to the female sex who before God are strong men, and how many men must be counted weak and indolent women.'[43] This text is of especial interest because it expressly links the metaphor and the extra-metaphorical reality. A woman, by virtue of her moral and spiritual qualities, may be turned into a man, i.e. may be saved, while man may 'become a woman', i.e. degenerate and be lost. In Origen, then, sexual appartenance is defined soteriologically and determined by spiritual progress. The formulation of the fragment concerning Ephesians 5:28–29: '. . . so that their wives may become men . . .' should be read in this light.[44]

'Becoming Male' through Spiritual Progress

The words 'woman' and 'feminine' describe a negative state, that of 'the category of women who can do nothing manly'.[45] The same words can also describe the soul which, though weak and immature, nevertheless has the possibility of changing into a man and becoming a 'perfect man'.[46] The metaphor is used in a particularly instructive way in *Homiliae in Canticum Canticorum*: human beings who have not yet reached the state of perfection are the girls accompanying the Bride (the Church),[47] while the angels and those who have attained perfection are represented by the young men with the Bridegroom (Christ).[48] This text links Ephesians 4:13 to an initiatic theme and urges the believer to join the Bridegroom's companions. The aim is to become *vir perfectus*.[49] Those who find this demands too much of them can stay among the girls.[50] '... I fear many of us are girls', we read in the address to believers.[51]

Ephesians 4:13 and the Theme of Progress

Origen may also interpret Ephesians 4:13 eschatologically; he then refers to the final transformation of the soul into *vir perfectus*,[52] and states clearly that this transformation is the purpose of the soul on earth. In *Homiliae in Numeros* 24 there is a particularly detailed development of this theme, apropos of the way the passage on vows (Num. 30:3–16), where the different vows correspond to degrees of perfection, should be interpreted. It describes the evolution of the soul from the stage in which it is still female in sex up to its highest stage of masculine autonomy in which, 'freed of its vows', it is freed of all that is female and childish and can become perfect man.[53]

There are several very clear parallels in the way Clement of Alexandria and Origen use the metaphors 'woman turned into man', 'becoming male', 'perfect man', which are all ways of expressing spiritual progress from the vocabulary of soteriology.

In the following centuries the terms 'becoming male' and 'perfect man' continue to be used metaphorically in connection with proleptic eschatology and spiritual progress. 'Becoming male' has sometimes been linked with Galatians 3:28,[54] but is most often used as in Ephesians 4:13. Referring to this latter verse, Didymus the Blind presents a very clear picture of the soul becoming manly through spiritual progress,[55] and St Ambrose develops the notion of woman becoming *vir perfectus* when she comes to faith.[56] St Jerome also, referring like Didymus and Ambrose to Ephesians 4:13, uses the metaphor of woman becoming manly in several texts.[57]

A number of early fourth-century texts, such as St Jerome's letter 108, show that the question of 'woman turned into man' may also be tied in with the debate on the resurrection of the dead.[58] Should women rise again as men? In *De Civitate Dei* 22, 17 St Augustine points out that some people interpret Ephesians 4:13 in that sense, but he is careful to make clear that he disagrees.[59]

'BECOMING MALE' IN MONASTIC LITERATURE

Yet more aspects of the use of this metaphor were to be seen in other literary genres. St Perpetua's formulation *facta sum masculus*[60] is well known, and fourth- and fifth-century hagiographic literature stresses that (female) saints are 'manly women'.[61] A woman's holiness is often presented as the contrast of masculine and feminine; her holiness is a 'transcending of the measure of her sex' which in turn is a prerequisite for 'manly actions';[62] or, as a fifth-century text has it, 'all women who are pleasing to God rank as men'.[63] In St Jerome's letters there are a number of such expressive formulae; in letter 71, 3 for example Jerome addressing Lucinus and speaking of Theodora says: '... she has become your sister, has changed *from woman to man, from subject to equal*'. After Lucinus' death, he writes to Theodora: '... even on earth he saw you as a sister, or better, as a brother'.[64]

'De femina virum, de subjecta parem'

The fourth- and fifth-century women who chose the ascetic life could develop much more freely than their married sisters, and the metaphors that express transformation have recently been seen as proof that some women enjoyed the same life-style as men.[65] With sex thought of as neutralised, social relations, friendship and collaboration between Christian men and women could be given as foundation and justification: Christians were 'brothers' and 'sisters' or, to take the idea to its conclusion, a woman was no longer woman, and could be said to be man (*dicetur vir*).[66] In *Vita Melaniae*, the heroine goes visiting in the desert of Nitria where 'the holy fathers welcome her like a man'. Her biographer adds: 'It is true she had transcended the measure of her sex and acquired a manly or rather a celestial mentality'.[67] We see then that when this literature has recourse to metaphors that express transformation, it redefines interpersonal relations, and many writings that were widespread at the time, like the *Apophtegmata Patrum* or the *Historia Lausiaca*, make the sense of the metaphor even clearer.

Woman as Exemplary Man

The life of ascesis in the desert is presented as a restoration of life in paradise and an anticipation of life in heaven. Around a central motif on the theme of the restoration of man's relation to God, there grew up a rich symbolic language in which 'woman turned into man' has a role that may be described as important, that of representing heavenly life restored.

It is clear that besides this symbolic function, the metaphor has other more concrete ones. The texts have to stimulate *imitatio*,[68] and in several cases women can serve as a model for both sexes; the monk Piteroum says of a sister from the Tabennesi convent: 'she is both my *amma* and yours'.[69] *Amma* was the honorific title given to women who could be offered as models; the Greek collection of *Apophtegmata* gives us the names of three *amma* whose *dicta* it also reports: Amma Theodora, Amma Sarra and Amma Synclatica.[70] The question of their historicity is unimportant in our context. On the other hand it is interesting to note that when the *dicta* were set down, the charismatic authority of women was taken for granted. The purpose of the text was in effect to put forward an example and to emphasise what the readers or listeners should engrave in their hearts.[71]

Woman and Charismatic Authority

Apophtegmata Patrum presents the lives and deeds of the *amma*, and the stories are in no way different from those about men: the women fight against the same temptations, and show the same endurance; simple brothers and 'great anchorites' visit them, and all receive their *dicta*. It is related as naturally as can be that Amma Theodora addressed a question of exegesis to the patriarch of Alexandria, and in another context that she herself is asked a question with thorny dogmatic nuances.[72] Two *dicta* attributed to Amma Sarra will throw light on the *ammas'* activity. In the first, two great anchorites visit Sarra and attempt to humiliate her: 'Watch that you do not elevate your thought, saying: anchorites are coming to see me, a woman. Amma Sara replied: By nature [*physis*] I am a woman, but by my thought [*logismoi*], not.' Elsewhere we are told: 'She said to the brothers: I am a man, and you, you are women'.[73] This reveals a hidden hierarchy in which authority is accorded to whoever deserves it, i.e. to whoever has progressed furthest in the spiritual life. Both sexes equally could have this charismatic authority, and the texts we possess show that it was not limited to spiritual matters but extended also to matters affecting the material well-being of the community. In *Historia Lausiaca*, it is the visionary virgin Piamoun who has the village priests summoned in order to warn them of an imminent enemy attack, and they who beg her to intervene. The enemy is halted, 'thanks to God and the prayers of Piamoun'.[74] Although this story is not considered historical, we should stress that it met contemporary criteria for historical credibility.

CONCLUSION

The different early Christian literary genres use different metaphors on the same theme of 'becoming male'. These variants depend on the New Testament and seem to come from the anthropological thought of the authors we have been discussing. The expressions 'becoming male' or 'becoming perfect man' fit the well-known *Urzeit-Endzeit* model and are used to reinforce or to suggest the main ideas in Christian anthropology, in which man comes to be 'in the image of God' or 'like Christ'. In several cases, *teleios aner* or *vir perfectus* is used within a soteriological vocabulary. Ephesians 4:13, Galatians 3:28, and the many New Testament passages which emphasise *bios angelikos* as the aim of all human life are all concerned with spiritual progress and salvation.

'Becoming male' or 'becoming perfect man' involves both sexes and refers to an asexual sphere; 'man' and 'male' can therefore describe human nature (in what is common to the sexes) and relate to a state in which sex is transcended. 'Woman' and 'female' on the other hand always refer in such contexts to the inferior and temporary state of human beings in this world. All this literature redefines and spiritual-ises the category 'sex': belonging to one or the other sex is not some-thing given; it has to be achieved by the inner man. In this context, sex depends on spiritual progress, and it has a decisive role in the attainment of salvation.

The metaphor of man becoming woman expresses moral degener-ation or perdition, but is less often used than that of 'woman become man', which has a long history in female hagiography.[75] 'Woman turned into man' emerges, then, as that element in a symbolic language which represents paradise regained, and fifth-century monastic literature refers to the link that binds doctrine, symbolic language and social reality together: in certain conditions, and in given milieux, some women achieved 'the rank of man'. This implies, within the same context of course, that saints of both sexes were accorded the same charismatic authority.

Notes

1. Philo, *Quaest. in Exodum* I, 8. See R. A. Baer, *Philo's Use of the Categories Male and Female* (Leiden, 1970), 46 ff. Porphyrios, *Epistula ad Marcellam*, Monographien zur klassischen Altertumswissenschaft Heft 20, 87 ff. On the notion of women turning into men after death as a Pythagorean idea, see J. Carcòpino, *Aspects mystiques de la Rome païenne* (Paris, 1941), 276 ff., and by the same author *Le Mystère d'un symbole chrétien: l'ascia* (Paris, 1945), 45. For the many gnostic examples see C. Blanc in Sources Chrétiennes [SC] 157, pp. 27–31.

2. Clément d'Alexandrie, *Extraits de Théodote*, SC 23, pp. 99–101 and 203: *Ex. de Theodoto* 21, 3; 22, 3; 79. Origène, *Commentaire sur S. Jean* VI, 20, 111; SC 157, p. 213.

3. A theme not treated here is that of the role of the metaphor 'becoming male' in fifth-century theological thinking; on the masculine state of the Logos, in whom carnal generation of the Son of God is only fully accomplished by the masculine phase succeeding the feminine phase, see P. Hadot, pp. 855–7 in Marius Victorinus, *Traité théologique sur la Trinité* I, SC 68, *Adversus Arium* 51, 28–43.

4. *Stromates* IV, 100, 6, 'woman turned into man', *gunaika eis andra metatithesthai*. At this point it is interesting to note the linguistic coherence: Clement of Alexandria uses the verb *metaithemi* in *Strom.* VI, 100, 3 (PG (*Patrologia Graeca*) 9, 321) and *Ex. de Theo* 21, 3, and 79. Origen uses the same verb to give his opinion of Heracleon in *Com.s.S. Jean* VI, 20, 111; SC 157, p. 212.

5. According to *Biblia Patristica, Des origines à Clément d'Alexandrie et Tertullien* (Paris, 1975), Eph. 4:13 occurs 16 times in the works of Clement of Alexandria: 12 times in *Strom.* VI and VII, in *Strom.* IV, 132, 1 and VII, 40, 3. But its use in *Strom.* VII, 88, 3 is not recorded. and there are many allusions to Eph. 4:13 in *Strom.* IV, V, and VII.

6. *Le Pédagogue* I, 4, 11.

7. For the Stoic influence on Clement of Alexandria see M. Spanneut, *Le Stoïcisme des Pères de l'Eglise* (Paris, 1957), 166 and 254.

8. *Strom.* III, 93, 3.

9. *Strom.* IV, 59, 1–4.

10. Ibid. 60, 1.

11. *Le Péd.* III, 19, 1.

12. *Strom.* IV, 62, 4; *Le Péd.* II, 107, 2.

13. *Strom.* IV, 67, 1; 68, 2; 123, 2.

14. On woman's manly actions see ibid. 48, 1; 120, 2. On effeminate man, see n. 12 above.

15. *Le Péd.* II, 51, 2.

16. *Le Péd.* I, 4, 10; I, 31, 2.

17. Ibid. 4, 10.

18. *Strom.* VII, 40, 3.

19. *Strom.* III, 93, 3; 69, 3.

20. *Strom.* VII, 72, 1.

21. Ibid.

22. *Le Péd.* III, 20, 4 and 5; II, 64, 3.

23. *Strom.* II, 131, 6; III, 42, 4–6.

24. *Strom.* II, 97, 1.
25. *Strom.* VII, 52, 3.
26. *Strom.* IV, 132, 1.
27. *Strom.* VII, 46, 7.
28. *Strom.* VI, 105, 1; VII, 57, 5.
29. Ibid. 68, 1.
30. *Le Péd.* III, 5, 3; *Strom.* VII, 56, 6.
31. Eph. IV, 13 is used 29 times in the works of Origen: *Biblia Patristica* Origène (Paris, 1980).
32. For the text see PG 12, 146 ff.; SC 7, pp. 79–86.
33. For a fuller treatment of this theme, see H. Crouzel, *Théologie de l'image de Dieu chez Origène* (Paris, 1956). See also *Dictionnaire de spiritualité* VI, 'Image et ressemblance', 814.
34. PG 12, 157; SC 7, p. 83.
35. PG 12, 158; SC 7, p. 84.
36. *Homélies sur Josué* IX, 9; *De Principiis* IV, 3, 12; *Hom. sur le Lévitique* IV, 8; *Hom. sur les Nombres* I, 1. Numerous references will be found in H. Crouzel, *Virginité et mariage selon Origène* (Paris, 1963), 135–9.
37. *Hom. sur Lév.* I, 1; SC 286, p. 75.
38. *Sel. in Ex.* 23, 17; PG 12, 296D.
39. *Hom. sur Ex.*, SC 16, p. 93; PG 12, 305B.
40. *Hom. sur Ex.*, S.C. 16, p. 96; PG 12, 305C.
41. Ibid. 307D.
42. This theme is found also in Didymus the Blind, *Sur la Genèse* I, SC 233, pp. 158–63: 'In the sensible order, it is impossible to change nature, but in the spiritual order . . . whoever is . . . in the situation of a *woman* may one day by progress become *male* . . .' In Didymus the idea of a change of nature is connected with the idea of becoming 'perfect man', see SC 233, p. 162. On the idea of changing nature, 'being born as a male', see also Gregory of Nyssa, *La Vie de Moïse*, SC I, pp. 106–9.
43. *Hom. sur Jos.*, SC 71, p. 267.
44. PG 14, 1298; see also n. 57 below.
45. *Hom. sur Jos.* IX, 9, SC 71, p. 267.
46. Ibid. 8, SC 71, p. 265.
47. The femininity of the soul before God is a common metaphor which may also alternate with metaphors intended to express the soul becoming manly. We have not the space here to treat the question in depth, but can point out that when the metaphor that presents the soul as feminine is used, it is the soul's dependence and inferiority in relation to God which are stressed. Didymus the Blind expresses this with great precision; after describing the soul becoming male through spiritual progress he adds: 'But if we apply this to the Word of God, it is the whole rational nature which in relation to him has the female role.' *Sur la Genèse*, SC 233, pp. 160 ff. For Philo, see R. A. Baer, in the work cited in n. 1 above, p. 66.
48. *Hom. sur le Cantique des Cantiques* I, 1; SC 37, p. 69.
49. Ibid.
50. Ibid. 71.
51. *Hom. sur Cant. Cant.* II, 7, p. 127.
52. *Commentaire sur S. Matthieu*, SC 162, p. 152.

53. *Hom. sur les Nombres* XXIV, 2; SC 28, p. 471.

54. PG 28, 264A, 'Discours de Salut à une Vierge', trans. J. Bouvet in Saint Jérôme, *Lettres* V, ed. J. Labourt (Paris, 1954), 34; *Historia Lausiaca* 49, ed. Butler, p. 144.

55. *Sur la Genèse*, SC 233, pp. 160–3.

56. PL (Patrologia Latina) 15, 1843 ff.

57. PL 26, 567, and *Contre Rufin* I, 28 ff.; SC 303, pp. 77–81.

58. Saint Jérôme, *Lettres* V, ed. Labourt, 190–3.

59. Saint Augustin, *La Cité de Dieu*, Bibliothèque Augustinienne 37 (Paris, 1960), 620–3. See Marius Victorinus on resurrection from the dead as passing from femininity to masculinity, the work cited in n. 3 above, SC 68, p. 856.

60. *The Acts of the Christian Martyrs*, ed. H. Musurillo (Oxford, 1972), 118.

61. Palladius, *Hist. Laus.* 9 and 41, ed. Butler, pp. 29 and 128; by the same author, *Dialogus* chs. 16 and 17; Grégoire de Nysse, *Vie de Macrine*, SC 178, p. 140; *Vie de Sainte Mélanie*, SC 90, p. 90; *Vie de Sainte Synclétique*, trans. B. Begrolles, 1972, pp. 29, 102, 103; Paulin de Nole, Ep. 29, 2, *Vie d'Olympias*, SC 13, p. 413; Socrates Scolasticus, *Hist. Eccl.* IV, 23.

62. *Vie de Sainte Mélanie*, SC 90, pp. 127, 200, 202.

63. PG 28, 264A, 'Discours de Salut à une Vierge', in *Vie de Sainte Synclétique*, p. 124.

64. Ep. 71, 3; Ep. 75, 2; in Saint Jérôme, *Lettres* IV, ed. Labourt, 10, 34.

65. E. Clark, 'Ascetic Renunciation and Feminine Advancement', *Anglican Theological Review* 63 (1981), 245.

66. '. . . mulier esse cessabit et dicetur vir . . .' PL 23, 533.

67. *Vie de Sainte Mélanie*, SC 90, p. 200.

68. PG 65, 72 and 73A; *Hist. Laus.*, ed. Butler, Introductory Pieces, pp. 1–3.

69. Ibid. 98.

70. Amma Théodora, PG 65, 201–4; Amma Sarra, PG 65, 419; Amma Synclétique, PG 65, 422–8. J. C. Guy, *Les Apophtegmes des Pères du Désert* (Begrolles, 1972), 116–19, 298–306.

71. Later recorders of the tradition were not afraid to rebel against this and quote the sayings anonymously. 'In der späteren Überlieferungen tauchen die Logien der Frauen vielfach anonym auf . . . Es scheint eine Scheu bestanden zu haben, Frauen als Autoritäten zu zitieren': W. Bousset, *Apophtegmata: Studien zur Geschichte des ältesten Mönchtums* (Berlin, 1923), 39.

72. Théodora 1 and 10; Sarra 1 and 2; Sarra 4 and 8.

73. Sarra 4 and 9.

74. *Hist. Laus.* 31, ed. Butler, 86. On the social function of the exemplary man, see P. Brown, 'The Rise and Function of the Holy Man in Late Antiquity', in *Society and the Holy in Late Antiquity* (London, 1982).

75. E. Patlagean, 'L'Histoire de la femme déguisée en moine et l'évolution de la sainteté féminine à Byzance', *Studi Medievali* (1976), 597–623. M. Delcourt, 'Le Complexe de Diane dans l'hagiographie chrétienne', *Revue de l'Histoire des Religions* (1958), 1–33.

8   Female Martyrs

Elizabeth A. Castelli*

While enjoining women to 'become male' seems, at this historical distance, a supreme example of bad faith, Elizabeth Castelli in this excerpt directs us to its subversive possibilities, especially when deployed by early Christian women. The lives of early Christian women, she says, were shaped by 'paradoxical ideological conditions'. Christianity offered new freedoms, but women had access to holiness 'only through the manipulation of conventional gender categories'. Castelli analyses here an astonishing document, the martyr diary of Perpetua. This account of the imprisonment of a group of North African Christians, including a pregnant slave, Felicity, is 'the earliest Christian text indisputably attributed to a woman'. Perpetua, imprisoned with her baby still at the breast, was put to death in the arena.   JMS

Just such a manipulation of the constraints of gender and the social conventions linked to them can be found in the intriguing *Martyr-dom of Perpetua and Felicitas*, included in a well-circulated collection, *The Acts of the Christian Martyrs*.[1] A third-century text combining a narrative with Perpetua's own diary of her last days in prison, it represents the earliest Christian text undisputedly attributed to a woman. The story recounts the arrest, imprisonment, and eventual execution of a group of Christians in Carthage (North Africa)— including Vibia Perpetua, a young (apparently wellborn) woman who has recently given birth to a child, and a slave woman, Felicitas, whose pregnancy threatens to keep her from being executed with the rest of the group. In the course of the imprisonment, Perpetua experiences and records a number of visions which assure her that her fate is to die in the arena but which promise that her reward will be access to heaven. Her death itself is narrated as a profound act of will, as she is reported to have guided the gladiator's sword to her throat; the narrator speculates that "it was as though so great a

* Extract from Elizabeth A. Castelli, ' "I Will Make Mary Male": Pieties of the Body and Gender Transformation of Christian Women in Late Antiquity', from *Body Guards: The Cultural Politics of Gender Ambiguity*, edited by Julia Epstein and Kristina Straub (Routledge, 1991).

woman, feared as she was by the unclean spirit, could not be dispatched unless she herself were willing" (21.10). Most striking is the highly elaborated weaving together of Perpetua's female body with its social functionings, and how her series of visions lead her ultimately to cast off the female body ("I became a man") and the social roles and ties it has enacted in her life.

The Martyrdom of Perpetua and Felicitas is an unusual text because it includes two genres of writing, a fairly standard martyrological narrative written in the third person, and a first-person memoir generally accepted as the diary Perpetua wrote while in prison. The introduction to the narrative indicates that the writer understands this text to stand in a tradition of texts which prove God's favor and provide for the spiritual strengthening of human beings; these fairly recent events are being written down because the examples they articulate will one day be ancient and therefore take on an authority that at the moment only ancient examples hold. The closing paragraph of the martyrdom reiterates this assertion of the power of the narrative to transform and to possess significance "no less than the tales of old." The narrative comes to its unified and singular conclusion; the story is written to testify to the glory of God.

Within this teleological narrative is embedded Perpetua's own, complicating narrative which strains against so simple a reading. Part of the strain has to do with the contradiction of the genre of autobiography itself; by its nature, no autobiography can come to closure, no writing about oneself within the conventions of narrative autobiography can ever finish the story. As much as Perpetua's narrative attempts to bring closure to the conflicts in her own existence, ultimately she must give over the power of narrative to some other writer. Her diary closes after the fourth vision with the statement, "About what happened at the contest itself, let him write of it who will" (10.15). While by the end of the fourth vision, Perpetua is persuaded that she will "be victorious" (i.e., be killed), and so in that sense she has brought her story to a close, it remains that at the textual/generic level, the narrative remains unfinished, open-ended, resistant to closure. Just as her narrative remains open-ended and therefore ambiguous, it also narrates an ambiguity toward gendered imagery and gendered identity on the part of its main character; whereas Perpetua's own story calls narrative closure and fixed gender identity into question, the framing narrative finishes the story and puts Perpetua back into the conventions of gender, as a "woman [femina]."

Perpetua's account of her imprisonment and her dreams and visions is an extended narrative of conflicts and their resolutions, all pointing forward to the final conflict, the final battle, Perpetua in the arena with her executioner. These conflicts have to do with fundamental issues of social relation, with her understanding of her status as a woman in her social network, with the very category of femininity. Each event and vision narrated is part of a movement of resistance against the dominant cultural narratives of relationship, paternal authority, and femininity. As Perpetua moves closer to the arena, she strips off the cultural attributions of the female body—first figuratively in leaving behind her child and in the drying up of her breast milk, and then finally and "literally" in her last vision, in the transformation of her body into that of a man; here she has stripped off all the physical marks of femaleness. Perpetua's spiritual progress is marked by the social movement away from conventional female roles and by the physical movement from a female to a male body; these processes of transformation signify her increasingly holy status.

Perpetua's narrative begins with a description of her conflict with her father who wants her to recant her confession of Christian faith in order that she might be released from prison. She makes a kind of Socratic argument, pointing to a vase and asking whether it might be known by any other name than what it is; when he responds, "no," she argues, " 'Well, so too I cannot be called anything other than what I am, a Christian' " (3.2). The argument produces such anger in her father that he moves toward Perpetua "as though he would pluck my eyes out" (3.3). He departs, taking his diabolical arguments with him, and Perpetua spends several days comforted by her father's absence.

Part of the emerging pathos of Perpetua's story has to do with the ongoing renegotiation of conventional family relations. As the father disappears temporarily from the narrative, Perpetua's mother, brother, and baby appear on the scene. For the moment, Perpetua takes her child into her care in the prison. During this period, she experiences the first of her four visions, a vision she has requested from God to determine whether she will be condemned or freed.

This vision resonates with biblical allusions and other complex imagery, and begins Perpetua's journey toward the resolution of certain social conflicts. In the vision, she sees "a ladder of tremendous height made of bronze, reaching all the way to the heavens, but it was so narrow that only one person could climb up at a time" (4.3). The ladder is studded with swords, spears, hooks, daggers, and spikes, promising to mangle the flesh of the unwary climber. At the foot of the ladder a dragon of enormous size is positioned, ready to attack those who wish to climb the ladder. "Slowly," Perpetua recounts, "as though he were afraid of me, the dragon stuck his head out from underneath the ladder. Then, using it as my first step, I trod on his head and went up" (4.7). Arriving at the top of the ladder, Perpetua sees a pastoral scene of heaven, and is offered milk by an elderly shepherd who has been milking sheep. As she comes out of the vision, Perpetua still has the sweet taste of the milk in her mouth. The vision communicates to her that she "would no longer have any hope in this life" (4.10).

These images have some roots, certainly, in the biblical tradition; the ladder may well refer back to Jacob's ladder, the dragon a recurring demonic image, the woman's foot on the serpent's head, an echo of Genesis 3:15, "I will put enmity between you and the woman and between your seed and her seed; he shall bruise your head, and you shall bruise his heel." Perhaps, however, there are other resonances to be heard from these powerful images. In reading this text against another fascinating ancient text, the second-century handbook for the interpretation of dreams, Artemidorus' *Oneirocritica*,[2] one discovers some remarkable and suggestive clues for interpretation. Artemidorus documents the symbolism of a whole catalogue of objects and images, both everyday and fantastic; he is particularly interested in the imagery of the human body and its varied meanings, but he addresses other issues at length as well. The ladder, for example, is a well-known symbol for travel and its rungs signify both progress and danger (2.42). More interesting for our purposes is Artemidorus' analysis of the meanings of body imagery and of serpents. The *Oneirocritica* includes a lengthy and elaborate interpretation of different varieties of snakes, which signify a variety of ethical positions. "Venomous animals," writes Artemidorus, "that are formidable, mighty, and powerful as, for example, the dragon, the basilisk, and the hollow oak viper signify powerful men" (4.55). He argues elsewhere that the head signifies parents, in that both the head and parents are the cause of life (1.35); putting these two readings together, Perpetua's trampling on the head of the dragon may be read as one of her first gestures against paternal authority, the dragon signifying his power, the head signifying his personage.

This reading would be more capricious were it not for the repetition of imagery emphasizing the connection between power and Perpetua's feet later in the narrative. In a last desperate gesture of supplication to Perpetua, narrated just after the account of this vision, her father throws himself down at her feet, addressing her no longer as a daughter but as a woman. "Have pity on my grey head," he says (5.2). He also calls up the familial relationship Perpetua will be abandoning—those with him, her brothers, her mother, her child. She rejects his entreaties, and the father disappears once again, temporarily, from the narrative. In her last vision, Perpetua is victorious over against her Egyptian opponent, a victory signified by her placing her foot on his head. By this advanced point, her female body has been replaced by a male body, and her rejection of paternal authority and the concomitant abandonment of her subjectivity in the feminine are complete. But even the first vision of her foot on the head of the dragon begins Perpetua's movement beyond the confines of gendered conventions as they are articulated in family relationships, especially those with her father. This vision which combines imagery of paternal authority with the demonic imagery of the dragon reinforces here the suggestion that Perpetua's father's actions are in some fashion "diabolical," a suggestion first made explicit in their first set of interactions.

The scene that follows this first vision, in which her father begs her to pity his grey head, suggests a complexity of gendered meanings. Perpetua writes, "This was the way my father spoke out of love for me, kissing my hands and throwing himself down at my feet. With tears in his eyes, he no longer addressed me as his daughter but as a woman" (5.5). This scene is confounding of gendered meanings in at least two ways: first, the actions of the father in his desperation can be read as feminizing actions—crying and kissing the hands of his daughter, throwing himself down before her feet. At the same time, there is an additional ambiguity in the statement that he addresses her not as a daughter but as a woman. In a psychoanalytic reading of this story, classicist Mary Lefkowitz has cited the interpretation of Jungian analyst Marie-Louise von Franz who has read the scene as an articulation of "unconscious incest," the desperate attempt on the part of the father to keep the distintegrating family together.[3] Perpetua's husband—the father of her baby—is completely absent from the narrative, and Perpetua's mother appears on the scene only briefly and passively when Perpetua speaks to her out of anxiety for her own baby. One might be hesitant to read back into this ancient document modern categories of analysis in this way; this particular reading seems overly reductive, because it appropriates psychoanalytic categories ahistorically and unproblematically and because it ignores the complexity of the textuality of the story, reading the account provided in Perpetua's diary as though it were a simple rendering of the "truth" of Perpetua's actual, real-life experience rather than as, at some level, a fiction. Nevertheless, the scene at the very least suggests another layer of complexity in the family constellation, and may function to decenter certain conventional family relations in Perpetua's journey beyond these networks.

The next scene continues the conflict between paternal authority, family relationships, and Perpetua's own competing self-understanding apart from these relations. Having been brought, together with the other prisoners, to a hearing, Perpetua stands on the prisoner's dock. Her father appears in the crowd, carrying Perpetua's baby, and drags her from the step; the governor himself at this point begs Perpetua to "have pity on your father's grey head; have pity on your infant son" (6.3). Perpetua continues to confess her Christian identity, and when her father persists in trying to dissuade her, the governor Hilarianus orders him to be thrown to the ground and beaten with a rod. The continuing feminizing of the father matches the movement of Perpetua away from her identity within the family.

At her condemnation to death in this scene, Perpetua's ambivalent relationship to her child is both highlighted and then resolved by divine intervention. The baby had been accustomed to breast feeding, and so Perpetua sends to have the baby retrieved from her father. Her father refuses to turn over the infant—reinscribing his increasingly feminized role, now as mother. At the same time, Perpetua reports that "as God willed, the baby had no further desire for the breast, nor did I suffer any inflammation; and so I was relieved of any anxiety for my child and of any discomfort in my breasts" (6.8). Perpetua moves further away from the conventional positions she has occupied in the society—no longer dutiful daughter, she is also separated from her role as a mother, in a miracle of immediate and divinely inspired weaning of her child. The detail of this description is poignant, for Perpetua is still very much embodied in the specificity of female flesh—the emphasis on the absence of the physical pain she would have experienced under ordinary circumstances underscores her continuing life in a female body. At the same time, she complicates her identification with the social roles that accure to that female body—she gives her baby up, refusing thereby the maternal function.

Having detached herself from these two foundational relationships, with her father and with her son, Perpetua now experiences two visions concerning a third relationship with another important male relative, her brother Dinocrates who died of a facial cancer when he was seven years old. In the first dream/vision, Perpetua sees Dinocrates emerging from a dark hole, still bearing the wound on his cheek. In the dream the child cannot reach to the rim of a pool of water, and though parched, cannot get a drink. In the second vision of Dinocrates several days later, Perpetua sees that her brother has been refreshed, and no longer has an open wound, but a scar. The rim of the pool of water had been lowered, and he could drink easily from the golden bowl. These visions are interpreted by Perpetua to mean that Dinocrates was suffering, but has now been redeemed through her prayers offered in the days intervening between the two visions. Again, for Perpetua, the visions function to resolve conflict.

One might well read these visions at a somewhat different level, through the matrix of relationships in which Perpetua is both implicated and in the process of extricating herself, and through the symbolism again of the body in dreams. Mutilated cheeks, according to Artemidorus, signify mourning (1.28); wounds on any part of the body should be interpreted as having the same meaning as that part of the body when it is uninjured, while a scar indicates an end to all one's anxieties (3.40). If this story can be read as Perpetua's movement from more self-evident to more fluid understandings of gender, then the wound and the scar may be interpreted as standing for both the loss of this male family member, but also for the resolution of that loss. Further, given the pattern of disengagement that is being traced out here—disengagement from familial relations, from male relations, and by implication from conventional gender understandings—the resolution of Dinocrates' suffering in the vision may be read as a resolution of the relationship itself. The resolution is further reinscribed by the image of Dinocrates drinking from a gold drinking vessel which, Artemidorus argues, is "auspicious for everyone" and "symbolize[s] great safety" (1.66).

In one psychoanalytic reading of this text, the relationship of the details of the story to Perpetua's own journey across and beyond gender has been read in this way: First of all, Perpetua and Dinocrates are linked in both of them having come out of a dark hole—he, in her vision; she is being released from the dark hole of the prison. Dinocrates' wound is read as a symbolic marker of his pregendered position, as a possibility of femininity. In this interpretation, the sex and the smallness of the brother both contribute to Perpetua's journey, marking the path along a continuum away from femininity.[4]

This vision is followed by the final encounter with Perpetua's father, an encounter which is beyond dialogue. The old man is desperate, and appears for the final time in the narrative, tearing out his beard and throwing himself on the ground. The loss of the beard, even self-inflicted, marks the further feminization of the father.

The final vision by Perpetua marks her radical transformation in terms of gender. The vision is lengthy, but significant, and worth quoting at length:

Pomponius the deacon came to the prison gates and began to knock violently. I went out and opened the gate for him. He was dressed in an unbelted white tunic, wearing elaborate sandals. And he said to me: 'Perpetua, come; we are waiting for you.'

Then he took my hand and we began to walk through rough and broken country. At last we came to the amphitheatre out of breath, and he led me into the centre of the arena.

Then he told me: 'Do not be afraid. I am here, struggling with you.' Then he left.

I looked at the enormous crowd who watched in astonishment. I was surprised that no beasts were let loose on me; for I knew that I was condemned to die by the beasts. Then out came an Egyptian against me, of vicious appearance, together with his seconds, to fight with me. There also came up to me some handsome young men to be my seconds and assistants.

My clothes were stripped off, and suddenly I was a man. My seconds began to rub me down with oil (as they are wont to do before a contest). Then I saw the Egyptian on the other side rolling in the dust. Next there came forth a man of marvelous stature, such that he rose above the top of the amphitheatre. He was clad in a beltless purple tunic with two stripes (one on either side) running down the middle of his chest. He wore sandals that were wondrously made of gold and silver, and he carried a wand like an athletic trainer and a green branch on which there were golden apples.

And he asked for silence and said: 'If this Egyptian defeats her he will slay her with the sword. But if she defeats him, she will receive this branch.' Then he withdrew.

We drew close to one another and began to let our fists fly. My opponent tried to get hold of my feet, but I kept striking him in the face with the heels of my feet. Then I was raised up into the air and I began to pummel him without as it were touching the ground. Then when I noticed there was a lull, I put my two hands together linking the fingers of one hand with those of the other and thus I got hold of his head. He fell flat on his face and I stepped on his head.

The crowd began to shout and my assistants started to sing psalms. Then I walked up to the trainer and took the branch. He kissed me and said to me: 'Peace be with you, my daughter!' I began to walk in triumph towards the Gate of Life. Then I awoke. (10)

This fourth vision brings to its narrative height the journey of

69

Perpetua through the conventions of gender. As she is brought into the arena where she will play out the role of an athlete—a common enough trope in early Christian literature for spiritual struggle— Perpetua is stripped of her clothing and of her feminine identity, located in the physical body. She becomes a man. As in the case of the *Gospel of Thomas* texts, this scene produces a paradox: Perpetua has stretched the conventional bounds of gender identity, at the same time as her spiritual ascendancy is figured in gendered terms, or more precisely, in terms of maleness.

Commentators have frequently argued that this transformation occurs in the interests of feminine modesty, but I believe that something else is at stake here. The pinnacle of Perpetua's struggle is described in this scene, and she is victorious in the battle—*and* victory is described *as* and *by* the stripping off of feminine gender. It is not simply that Perpetua's victory is assured through becoming a man— rather it is marked by the emblem of her new male body, it is signified by the transformation itself. Now clearly, Perpetua is not the only early Christian woman to be narrated in this way; as the tradition develops, particularly in narratives about the lives of ascetic holy women, the mark of true holiness is that the women become men. The trope, by the time it is repeated in the ascetic materials, has become domesticated, even a cliché. The transformation itself is never narrated, as it is here in Perpetua's diary; it is *fait accompli*. Perpetua's account then becomes a kind of double narrative, I would argue— about victory in spiritual struggle, and about shifting gender identity as the major signifier for a woman's journey toward that victory. The battle is between Perpetua and the forces of evil *and* between competing understandings of gender.

The scene itself is worth reading briefly. It is remarkable for its sensual imagery and for its continuation of the already established themes of victory over the father/devil. The Egyptian stands for both father and devil, and the battle itself is ambiguously sexual. Once again, Perpetua's feet serve her well, and her ascendancy over her opponent is narrated through the image of her foot on his head. The irony and double meaning of martyrdom itself are called up in this scene, when the trainer announces that if the Egyptian is successful, he will slay Perpetua; if she is successful, she will receive the branch of victory. If her opponent succeeds, Perpetua will die—and just so, Perpetua knows that if her father "saves" her, she is doomed. If she succeeds, she gains life—but in the ideology of martyrdom, she can only do so by losing her life. Perpetua's victory, signified by her walk toward the Gate of Life, is a spiritual victory and a final victory over the father and over gender conventions.

Notes

1. Herbert Musurillo (ed. and trans.), *The Acts of the Christian Martyrs* (Oxford: Clarendon Press, 1972), 106–31. References to *The Martyrdom of Perpetua and Felicitas* will be included parenthetically in the text.
2. Artemidorus, *Oneirocritica/The Interpretation of Dreams*, trans. Robert J. White; Noyes Classical Studies; Park Ridge, NJ: Noyes Press, 1975). All references to this edition (Artemidorus' book and chapter numbers) will be included in the text.
3. Mary R. Lefkowitz, 'The Motivations for St. Perpetua's Martyrdom', *Journal of the American Academy of Religion* 44 (1976), 417–21.
4. Mieke Bal, 'Perpetual Contest', in *On Storytelling* (Sonoma, Calif.: Polebridge Press, 1991), 227–41.

Luther on the Image of God in Women

Jane Dempsey Douglass*

'So God created humankind in his image, in the image of God he created them; male and female he created them' (Genesis 1:25, New Revised Standard Version). Given the natural subordination of women (an overwhelming presumption until the twentieth century), Christian theologians had difficulty with the Genesis teaching that both male and female were made in the image of God. If both were in God's image, why then not equal? Was it the Fall that brought on Eve's subservience? In the reforming debates of the sixteenth century, traditional teachings on sex, women, and marriage were questioned. The Magisterial Reformers, Luther and Calvin, in grounding authority in Scripture, could appeal to Genesis to enhance female dignity. Yet they had equally to keep in mind St Paul, who implies in 1 Corinthians 11:7 that men were more truly in God's image than women. Jane Dempsey Douglass expands here on Luther's position with regard to women and the *imago dei*. Her original essay continues beyond this excerpt to discuss Calvin.

JMS

In view of the many significant shifts in theology which took place within the various Reformations of the sixteenth century, both Catholic and Protestant, it is important to ask whether the doctrine of the image of God, particularly as it relates to distinctions between men and women, was among those doctrines disputed or reformulated.[1]

As we examine the writings of Luther and Calvin, it appears that this doctrine was not singled out by them as one in need of such major reformulation as were, for example, the doctrines of justification and the sacraments. Both Reformers take up the traditional question of the nature of the image of God, with heavy dependence on the Fathers of

---

* Extracts from Jane Dempsey Douglass, 'The Image of God in Women as Seen by Luther and Calvin' (Solum Forlag, 1991).

the ancient church, especially Augustine, and desire to show their continuity with that tradition. On the other hand, questions had arisen in the Renaissance which shape the discussions of Luther and Calvin somewhat differently than had been the case in the ancient and medieval church. Calvin, more deeply steeped in the Renaissance tradition than Luther, shows this influence more clearly.

Physicians of the Renaissance had taken up again the issue of the physical nature of women, putting the writings of Galen (somewhat imperfectly understood) against the views of Aristotle which had dominated the Middle Ages. By the late sixteenth century the physicians generally had given up Aristotle's view that women were misbegotten males in favor of a view that the female sex is normal in itself, just as the male sex is. As important as this scientific shift may have been for the dignity of women, one must note that the physicians continued to believe, nonetheless, that women are weaker and more frail than men, needing to remain under the protection of the home.[2] Another biological question under discussion was whether women as well as men contributed "seed" in the procreative process. Increasingly the older view that women merely nurtured the male seed was being replaced by the opinion that women, too, contributed seed to the fetus.[3]

The question of the possibility and the propriety of women holding public office was alive in the sixteenth century. At stake were several questions closely related to the nature of the image of God: whether women have the inherent capacity to govern, whether God wills for them to hold public office, and more generally, what their relationship should be to men. Though a very few queens and other noblewomen in the fifteenth and sixteenth centuries did in fact exercise considerable political and social influence, many more women discovered the extent of their vulnerability in the hysteria of the witch trials, which extended even beyond the Reformation period.

Deeply contradictory assumptions about women are also evident in intellectual circles from the end of the fourteenth century into the sixteenth in the Renaissance *querelle des femmes*, the literary debate by both men and women about women's nature. During 1404–5 in France Christine de Pizan in her *Book of the City of Ladies* described her difficulty reconciling her own experience and that of other women with the vilifying portrait of women drawn by the male authors she read. Yet she so respected their authority above that of her own experience that she came to detest herself and the whole female sex as monstrosities in nature.[4] A visit from three ladies, Reason, Rectitude, and Justice, freed her from these false assumptions by teaching her about women's true nature and place in history. Reason countered male views of the shameful imperfection of the female body, among other arguments, retelling the Genesis story of Eve's creation in Paradise and asserting that the Supreme Craftsman was not ashamed to create a female body.

... she was created in the image of God. How can any mouth dare to slander the vessel which bears such a noble imprint? But some men are foolish enough to think, when they hear that God made man in his image, that this refers to the material body. This was not the case, for God had not yet taken a human body. The soul is meant, the intellectual spirit which lasts eternally just like the Deity. God created the soul and placed wholly similar souls, equally good and noble in the feminine and in the masculine bodies.[5]

As the debate continued, women were alternately viciously deprecated and extravagantly lauded. One common question discussed was whether women's weaknesses are the result of nature or nurture— poor education and limited experience outside the home.[6] Women's defenders often made the point that the Scriptures as a whole and especially the writings of Paul are read onesidedly emphasizing all negative statements about women and suppressing those that favor women's equality and freedom.[7] They often attacked the assumption of Paul that Adam's creation prior to Eve guarantees his natural superiority.[8] Finally in 1598 came a treatise entitled "A New Disputation against Women, in which it is proved that they are not human beings." Usually attributed to Valens Acidalius, and certainly satirical, it was seriously debated by theologians, doctors, and lawyers. The last academic trial on the question was held in Wittenberg in 1688; Lutheran theologians refuted the treatise. But the text and its refutations were republished into the late eighteenth century.[9]

Since the question of the nature of women was a lively question, particularly in Renaissance culture, at the end of the Middle Ages and through the Reformation period, one should be alert for evidence of Luther's and Calvin's awareness of it as they discuss the image of God. For twentieth-century readers to explore the issue of gender in relation to the image of God in the Reformation period is by no means anachronistic.

Reformation theologians like Luther and Calvin, committed to the authority of "Scripture alone," worked differently than most of the medieval theologians. Though they knew and valued the theological tradition, were more deeply shaped by it than they acknowledged, and often explicitly dialogued with it, they tried to start freshly with the biblical text, accepting the theological tradition only where they believed it was in accordance with Scripture. Since the Renaissance, biblical scholarship had been able to profit from the new knowledge of Hebrew and Greek and from textual criticism, was much more restrained in its use of the allegorical method than the medieval tradition had been, and was more interested in the historical context out of which the biblical passages arose. Because earlier theologians had depended heavily on allegory at many points in their discussions of men and women in the image of God,[10] the nature of that discussion changed. Emphasis on "Scripture alone" reinforced the warnings against rash speculation beyond revelation which the Reformers inherited from late medieval scholasticism.[11]

Since Luther did not leave us a systematic theological work with a discussion of the image of God, the most useful focus for study seems to be his extensive commentary on Genesis from 1535, a product of his mature thought.[12] Some comparisons will be made with commentaries on such key texts as I Timothy 2 from 1528 and Galatians 3:28 from 1535. Unfortunately no sermon or commentary from Luther is available for I Cor. 11, containing the much-discussed verses 7 and 8: "man is the image and glory of God; but woman is the glory of man. For man was not made from woman, but woman from man." We will see that this text is in his consciousness, and so we wonder about the significance of its omission.

In Luther's 1535 commentary on Genesis, he takes the first three chapters of Genesis as a single narrative of creation, imagining that both God's instruction about the forbidden fruit and the fall take place on the sabbath, though he acknowledges that he cannot be certain of the dating.[13] Critical of Hilary and Augustine, as propounded by Nicholas of Lyra, Luther believes that Moses' six days of creation should be taken literally rather than allegorically. Moses "wants to teach us, not about allegorical creatures and an allegorical world, but about real creatures and a visible world apprehended by the senses."[14]

[. . .]

An important function of the image of God in humanity, Luther believes, is to show that human beings, though sharing many similarities with animals in their physical lives, were created "by a special plan and providence of God" for a better, spiritual life in the future. Even if Adam had not sinned, when the determined number of saints had been reached, "Adam and his descendants would have been translated to an eternal and spiritual life" without eating, drinking, and procreating.[15] So special was the act of creation of humanity that Moses even uses a different phrase than he had used earlier: "Let us make," which expresses God's "obvious deliberation and plan."[16]

The image of God in Paradise was far more excellent than modern people can imagine, Luther explains. Adam's "inner and outer senses were all exceedingly pure. His intellect was the most faultless, his memory was the best, and his will was the most sincere—all in the most beautiful composure, without any fear of death and without any anxiety."[17] Added to this was a superb body, strong, with acute senses. Still another description of the image of God includes Adam's possessing it in his own being, not only his knowledge of God as good, but also his godly life, his fearlessness, and his contentment with God's favor, and also Eve's fearlessness in speaking to the serpent.[18] Or Luther will list Adam's enlightened reason, his true knowledge of God, his will to love God and his neighbor so that he immediately embraced Eve as his own flesh, and also his remarkable knowledge of other living things.[19]

The reason this image is so unknown to modern people, Luther thinks, is that God's declaration proved true: when Adam and Eve sinned, disobeyed God, they lost the image of God. The remaining powers of the image have become "leprous and unclean," impaired and weakened.[20] But in Luther's day the Gospel, he thought, was bringing about a restoration of the image of God in humanity, with the hope of eternal life. Though that image was still unfinished in the godly, when the kingdom comes all the powers of the image will be renewed, there will be freedom from fear, and all the creatures will be even more completely under human rule than in Paradise. Until then there can be no truly adequate knowledge of the lost image of God, except that it included eternal life, freedom from fear, and all that is good. Humankind hardly knows what it has lost.[21] But God takes pleasure in this work of restoration through Christ just as God rejoiced in the creation of humanity.[22]

Already Luther has alluded to the dominion of humanity over all creatures in his discussion of the image of God. When he reaches the section of Gen. 1:26 where God commands humanity to have dominion over all the animals, it seems evident that ruling, dominion, is part of the image of God. Luther seems not so much to identify ruling as a separate aspect of the image as to connect it with the intellect, knowledge: Adam and Eve had insight into all aspects of the natural world. Because they knew so deeply all the creatures and all the plants and herbs, they were able to obey God's explicit command to rule over all the animals even though they were naked, "without weapons or walls." Indeed Luther introduces his discussion of ruling with a description of Adam and Eve which mentions their knowledge of God, their enlightened reason, justice, and wisdom. They become models of an outstanding philosopher with their most perfect knowledge of God, whose similitude they feel within themselves. Luther thinks people in his own day retained as a mere vestige of the image of God the capacity to rule some creatures through industry and skill, but not through the intimate knowledge of nature which Adam and Eve had.[23] A little farther along, on Gen. 1:28, Luther will suggest that people in his own day can hardly even imagine what the nature of "dominion" was in Paradise, but creatures were surely used with less greed and more admiration of God and holy joy than among his contemporaries.[24]

So far Luther in discussing humanity in Paradise has sometimes spoken simply of "Adam," as though he were alone, or as though "Adam" means humankind of both sexes, sometimes of "Adam and Eve." Perhaps this is because Luther in dealing with the first three chapters of Genesis as a single narrative is faced with the problem of creation of humanity in both sexes in chapter one, then the creation of Eve in chapter two. Whatever the explanation for this language, Luther has not appeared to make distinctions between male and female with regard to the image of God or their non-reproductive capacities.

Here, however, after speaking of the remarkable knowledge of nature and capacity for dominion which Adam and Eve possessed, Luther feels it necessary to emphasize that "Eve had these abilities equally with Adam . . ." Luther is certainly aware of the practice of most patristic writers to identify dominion with the male, and he must be consciously refuting that tradition. Eve knew the purpose of her creation and the source of her knowledge of it. "Therefore she not only heard these things from Adam, but her own nature was pure and full of the knowledge of God, so that by herself she understood and reflected on the word of God."[25]

But already in the following verse, where the text declares that God created both male and female in the image of God, Luther introduces gender distinctions. On the one hand Luther understands that Moses includes mention of women in order to be clear that they, too, share the image and the likeness of God, as well as the rule over all things.

They will share eternal life and are joint heirs of the same grace, and they may not be excluded from any glory of human nature.[26] He rejects Talmudic tales of a bisexual creature split apart into male and female and also such pejorative and ridiculing terms for women as Aristotle's "damaged male" or "monster." Luther clearly rejects Aristotle's view of women as botched or imperfectly formed men. He insists that woman as well as man was expressly made by God's special counsel as a most excellent work in which God took delight.[27] Women seem here to share fully in all human dignity.

On the other hand, still commenting on this same biblical verse which makes no distinction between men and women, Luther observes that:

... woman seems to be a somewhat different sort of being from man, because she has both dissimilar members [of her body] and a nature [ingenium] which is far weaker. And although Eve was a most extraordinary creature, similar to Adam with respect to the image of God, that is in justice, wisdom, and soundness, still she was a woman. For just as the sun is more extraordinary than the moon (although the moon is also a most extraordinary body), so even though the woman is a most beautiful work of God, still she does not equal the glory and worthiness [dignitatem] of the male.[28]

Luther draws the parallel to a household where "the wife is a partner in managing the household affairs and has common possession of the children and property, yet still there is a great difference between the sexes."[29]

This ambivalence between Eve as fully equal to Adam in Paradise before sin and Eve as inherently inferior to Adam because she is female continues through the discussion of the first three chapters of Genesis. Since often there is nothing in the immediate biblical text to explain Luther's inconsistency, one must assume that he feels the tension between biblical texts like Gen. 1:27 where there seems clearly to be an equality in the creation of man and woman on the one hand, and on the other hand the weight of his cultural and theological tradition, which had usually read these texts through the perspective of other biblical texts which assume the subordination of woman.

Once again Eve is portrayed as the equal of Adam in what Luther believes to be the institution of marriage and the family, already in Paradise. Luther sees Gen. 2:18, where God determines to make a help for Adam, as Moses' way of emphasizing that woman as well as man was created according to a unique counsel of God, suitable for the life planned for Adam and useful for procreation. "Had the woman not

78

been deceived by the serpent and sinned, she would have been in all things the equal of Adam . . . [before sin] she was in no respect inferior to Adam, whether you count the qualities of the body or of the mind."[30] This point is repeated twice in the discussion of Gen. 3:16 about Eve's punishment after sin. Eve is placed "under the power of her husband, she who previously was very free and, as the sharer of all the gifts of God, was in no respect inferior to her husband . . . If Eve had persisted in the truth, she would not only not have been subjected to the rule of her husband, but she herself would also have been a partner in the rule which now entirely belongs to males."[31]

These themes come together in a somewhat different way in Luther's commentary on Gen. 2:23: "This one will be called woman, because she has been taken from the man." Though he thinks the Hebrew cannot be fully imitated in Latin, he proposes as an equivalent for the Hebrew "Ischa:" "virago" or "vira," "she-man," "a heroic woman who does manly deeds."[32] Luther sees this term for Eve as revealing marriage to be a partnership in which the wife possesses in entirety all that the husband has: money, children, home. "For whatever the man in the home has and is, that the woman has and is, differing only in sex. Then also there is what Paul notes in I Tim. 2: she is woman, "virago," by origin, because the woman descends from man, not man from woman."[33] Eve and—by extension in Christ's teaching in Mt. 19: 5—all wives can be said to be of one flesh with their husbands. This point that woman differs only in sex from man is repeated three times in two paragraphs: once the point is made very explicitly that, apart from her difference in sex, she is "clearly man" (vir).[34] Here again Luther argues that had sin not intervened, Eve would not have been subject to her husband but would have shared "equal governance" (gubernatio aequalis) with Adam.[35]

Luther's ambivalence about the nature of Eve in Paradise can be seen also in the discussion about her temptation by the serpent. He acknowledges that at first Eve resisted the serpent admirably, because she was still led by Spirit, having been created perfect in the likeness of God, but then she allowed herself to be persuaded.[36] In what did her sin consist? Although she was not aware at the time that she was sinning, she fell into doubting God's Word, unbelief, "inquisitive discussion" beyond God's Word," desire to eat the forbidden fruit, disobedient action, lying.[37] ". . . Eve, created a most wise woman, longs for another wisdom beyond the Word and on account of this wisdom thus sins in many ways with all her senses by seeing, thinking, desiring, and acting."[38] Why did the serpent approach Eve rather than Adam?

Because just as in all of nature, the male is stronger than the female, so even in Paradise, though Adam and Eve were created "equally righteous," still Adam surpassed Eve. Therefore the serpent approached "the weak part of human nature," Eve, "for he sees that she trusts so confidently in her husband that she does not believe that she is able to sin."[39] Luther believes that if the serpent had tempted Adam, Adam would have triumphed by stamping upon the serpent and ordering him to be quiet, for "the Lord commands otherwise."[40]

This assumption by Luther that the serpent chose the weaker person to tempt stands strangely in the context of an argument for the cleverness of the serpent; Luther has just argued for the serpent's cleverness because he assails precisely the greatest strength of the human being, the very likeness of God, the will properly disposed toward God.[41] One might assume such a clever tempter would challenge the strongest, not the weakest human being. So Luther must be drawing uncritically on the tradition of Eve's weakness. Yet in this commentary he is noticeably freer of the carping about women's frailties and vices which is so common in medieval and Renaissance popular literature than in his first commentary on Genesis.[42]

On the other hand, Luther criticizes the whole exegetical tradition for its unsatisfactory dealing with Gen. 3:1–6, especially because Augustine has influenced Gregory and even Nicholas of Lyra to see here an allegory where the woman refers to the "lower reason." Luther believes the story should rather be read according to the "historical and literal meaning" as dealing with a real man, woman, and a serpent dominated by Satan. But he also regards it as absurd to see Eve as the lower part of reason because "she was in no respect, either in body or in mind, inferior to her husband Adam."[43]

How does Luther share the blame between Adam and Eve for original sin? We have seen that he devotes considerable comment to Eve's encounter with the serpent and her yielding to his temptation. But Luther notes that in Gen. 3:9, it is specifically Adam who is at first called to trial by God. This seems appropriate to Luther because it was Adam alone on the sixth day to whom the command about the forbidden tree was addressed. But because Eve also sinned, she also hears God's judgment and shares the punishment.[44] Luther seems somewhat concerned about the fact that the Genesis text does not indicate that Eve was present when the command not to eat of the tree of knowledge was given. However the church was established even before Eve's creation, before the creation of the home, when God preached to Adam, commanding what he could lawfully eat.[45] So he explains that though Adam alone heard God's sermon, he later informed Eve of God's Word.[46] In fact he suggests that early on the sabbath day Adam preached to Eve about God's will, perhaps even taking her to see the forbidden tree.[47] At the trial which God conducts, both Adam and Eve try to pass along the blame: Adam to Eve, whom God created, Eve to the serpent, whom God created. Yet finally Eve admits her sinful deed, while Adam tries to hide it.[48]

When the question arises why God allowed Satan to tempt Eve, Luther cautions strongly against attempting to investigate such questions. Job teaches us that God cannot be called to account. Luther thinks only one answer ought to be given: "it pleased the Lord that Adam [!] should be put to the test and should exercise his powers."[49]

Luther reflects on Paul's statement in I Tim. 2:13–14: "For Adam was formed first, then Eve; and Adam was not deceived, but the woman was deceived and became a transgressor." Luther believes nearly everyone understands this to mean that Adam was not seduced by the Devil but sinned willingly. He wanted to please his wife and placed his love of his wife ahead of his love to God. This common view, he says, presumes the serpent was afraid to approach Adam, the master, but thought Eve, though holy, was weaker and could more easily be seduced. Either Adam was seduced by the woman, who gave him the apple, or he seduced himself by noticing that she did not immediately die, therefore thinking they might escape punishment. Luther "does not disapprove" of this interpretation.[50]

Indeed this material is traditional. Much of it can be found in Augustine, for example: the view that Adam's personal sin was in obeying his wife out of affection for her; that the serpent approached Eve as the weaker of the two; that Adam and Eve each pass the blame to another.[51] But there are differences from Augustine. Whereas Augustine stresses pride as the essence of original sin,[52] Luther begins with unbelief. There is no indication in this material that he agrees with Augustine's view that Eve fell into sin because she was weaker intellectually than Adam, since he was created first.[53]

A few years earlier, 1527–28, Luther had prepared a commentary on I Timothy, which treats the text in greater detail. Whereas Luther in his two references to this text in the Genesis commentary[54] has shown little interest in the point about the order of creation, in the earlier commentary on I Timothy Luther took this context very seriously. Here he argues that because Adam was first, man has greater authority than woman. This is God's intent, demonstrated also from the story of Adam and Eve. He understands verse 14 to function as evidence for

Paul's view that man is to be dominant over woman. God chose to create Adam first, making him superior to Eve because of "primogeniture." Furthermore Adam was wiser and more courageous than Eve. "Thus it has been proved by divine and human law that Adam is the master of the woman. That is, Adam did not err. Therefore there was greater wisdom in Adam than in the woman, and thus greater dominion."[55] Then Luther goes on to make some of the same arguments he had made in the Genesis commentary from "common interpretation:" Adam was not deceived quite simply because the serpent did not approach him but rather Eve, the weaker one. Adam sinned knowingly to please his wife. He states here, in contrast to the Genesis commentary, that we do not know whether Adam would have sinned had he listened to the serpent. He also clarifies that Adam received God's command directly from God, Eve indirectly through Adam. Adam was deceived by the woman, believing that disobedience was not a very important matter. The woman became the transgressor and therefore was punished by becoming subject to her husband and bearing children in pain.[56]

Though much of the content of the argument is similar to the discussion on Genesis, the later Genesis commentary lacks the self-conscious focus on the order of creation, the rights of primogeniture so conspicuous in the commentary on I Timothy, Adam's superiority just because God created him first. Even where Luther in the later Genesis commentary cites the I Tim. text on Eve's coming from Adam, it is to stress their solidarity as one flesh. The Genesis commentary also lacks the single-minded focus on Eve as the transgressor which Paul's letter to Timothy exhibits. It is not clear how much of the difference should be attributed simply to the different nature of the biblical text on which Luther is commenting and how much to change in Luther's thought over time.

One further point should be made concerning Luther's view of woman in Paradise: even there, though he usually portrays Eve as possessing equally all the gifts Adam had, he focuses on Eve's role in home and family. According to Moses God does not "form" or "create" her like other creatures but "builds" her; Luther claims that Scripture commonly refers to a wife as a household building because of her role in bearing and rearing children.[57] The vision of affectionate couples moving away from their parents to their own homes, raising their own families, but visiting their parents and praising God together is part of Luther's picture of Paradise. Fertility would have been even greater than now because of the absence of illness and other impediments. In the absence of lust, children would be conceived chastely and without shame.[58] Sexual union would be as honorable as eating or talking at the table with one's wife. Bearing and rearing children would be very easy, without any difficulty, and full of joy.[59] Luther realizes, however, that as he believes the fall took place on the first sabbath, the day after Eve was created, none of this idyllic family life which he envisions ever in fact took place in Paradise.

In Luther's discussions of the wonders of God's plan for pro-creation, it is interesting that although he has repudiated Aristotle's view of the formation of the female sex, he continues to assume that women are without "seed", merely nurturing the child which comes from a drop of the father's blood or semen.[60]

Since the fall of Adam and Eve, Luther believes, the whole human situation has changed. As we have seen, Luther thought people after the fall can scarcely imagine what original humanity was like, and they can only picture what humanity is intended to be through the Gospel of Jesus Christ. The powers of the intellect and of the body are ser-iously weakened, and human dominion over the creatures is only a vestige of its former effectiveness. Eve has lost her freedom and become subject to her husband, and she must bear children in pain. Luther regards this punishment as a very serious one. In fact, he claims that Eve has received a far more severe punishment than Adam.[61] Not only must she suffer many physical ills in conjunction with pregnancy and childbirth,[62] she must stay at home, caring for the household, "like a nail driven into the wall," deprived of any share in the govern-ance of public matters outside the home.[63] But Adam, too, has been punished, Luther believes. He must contend with raging lust. His duty to support and govern his family as well as to rule over the world beyond is a very great burden. The earth is cursed with decreased fertility, weeds and harmful plants, disease, natural disasters, and the air is less pure.[64] He must see his wife's misery in childbearing.[65]

In short, one cannot discover the true nature of humanity as God created it by looking at the present inhabitants of the world. The very existence of "damage" such as lust, ignorance, the difficulties of the "work of procreation," and the loss of the righteous will leads Luther to disagree with those scholastics who claimed that "natural endowments" remain unimpaired after the fall.[66]

Human relationships are disrupted still further because of sin, Luther observes. Women are impatient of the burden of subjection to their husbands' rule and seek to regain what they lost through sin. At least they grumble about their situation.[67] The papists force people into celibacy, ignoring the blessings and promises relating to God's gift of sexuality, pretending wrongly that they are neither male nor female, despising marriage.[68] The heathen who do not know God see the great sufferings of women in pregnancy and childbirth and discourage marriage.[69] Many people (apparently among Christians), especially the nobility, also refrain from marriage in order not to have children. Luther finds this aversion to parenthood a "more than barbaric savageness and inhumanity."[70] The lack of respect for procreation, aggravated by celibacy, leads to insult or abuse against the female sex. "However it is a great favor that God has preserved woman for us almost against our will for generation and also as a medicine against the sin of fornication . . . we are hardly able to speak of her without shame, and we are certainly not able to use her without shame."[71] Sexual union, such a noble delight in Paradise, created and blessed by God, is now, "alas, such a shameful and dreadful pleasure that it is compared by the doctors with epilepsy . . ."[72] ". . . we are begotten and also born in sin because our parents do not come together only for the sake of duty but also for the sake of remedy or avoiding sin."[73] Like the earlier theological tradition, Luther regards sexual union even within marriage as at least somewhat sinful if it is the result of sexual desire rather than simply the intent to have children.

Still marriage remains for Luther a very significant vestige of the life of original humanity. We have seen that Luther regards marriage as essential for most people to avoid sin and loneliness, and we have seen that there remains some vestige of partnership between the sexes in the management of the family. Procreation remains a blessing, though marred by sin.[74]

Especially for women, Luther sees marriage and childbearing, despite its suffering, as revealing something of God's intention for humanity and as a source of hope. He tries to help women to think positively about their situation, emphasizing the hope of immortality and eternal life, the virtue of suffering in teaching humility, and the remaining outstanding glory—even since the fall—of motherhood and the blessing of the womb. The marvels of mothers' care for infants before and after birth are other gifts which remain even in fallen humanity. Luther seems quite sincere in his eloquent admiration for women's skill, even as young girls, in caring for children. He contrasts women's deftness in handling a fussy baby with men's clumsiness, like a camel dancing! Since the fall "women cannot administer manly offices, like teaching and ruling. But they are mistresses [magistrae] of bearing, feeding, and nurturing children."[75] Luther's personal warmth here about motherly skills suggests that he is drawing on his own family experience of a decade with Katie. He believes Eve would have had a joyful heart even in her sorrow at God's punishment:

... Eve hears that she is not rejected by God ... that she is not being deprived in this punishment of the blessing of procreation promised and given before the fall. She sees that she retains her own sex and is a woman ... that she is not separated from Adam ... that the glory of motherhood is left to her ...[76]

When one adds to all this that she has the hope of eternal life and the promise of bearing the Seed who will crush the head of Satan, Luther believes that Eve must have been very greatly encouraged, even joyful.[77]

This same mingling of punishment and promise is present in the story of Adam's naming of Eve, Luther thinks. He emphasizes that Adam's right to name Eve is part of the power over her given as punishment for sin. He relates this story to the custom of his own day that a wife takes her husband's name when she marries, losing her own family name. It would be monstrous for a husband to wish to take his wife's name, Luther declares. Wives in Luther's day were also compelled to follow their husbands if they moved, another evidence for Luther of the husband's power over his wife.[78] But Adam gives Eve a delightful name, Eve, Mother of all living. Luther attributes this wisdom to Adam's having been enlightened by the Holy Spirit to understand the promise of the coming Seed who will crush the tempter, the promise of the forgiveness of sins. The name was a very beautiful witness to Adam's faith and his recreated spirit, and it comforted him and strengthened his faith.[79] Nothing at all is said by Luther here concerning Eve's feelings about her name.

We have seen several examples of Luther's forbidding women to hold public authority since the fall, to speak outside the home. Frequently he refers to I Tim. 2:11 as justification. In his commentary on this text from 1528, he does indeed emphasize that this text has to do with public affairs. In public assemblies, including the church, the woman must be a hearer, subject to men. She must not teach or pray in public gatherings—at least where men are present, because God's good order and the peacefulness of the assembly would be broken. Luther thinks Paul believes women are clever, but he is concerned that they would argue against men in public. Yet in an awkward insert into the argument, Luther raises the opposing point that women are spoken of in Scripture as having authority: Queen Candace, Huldah, Deborah, Jael, for example. Luther responds that these women, like Philip's daughters who prophesied, were unmarried; "women" in the text means "wife," and wives should not have authority over their husbands. Yet Luther nowhere in this discussion offers hope to unmarried women that they could hold public office. Indeed the basic concern seems to be the problem of uppity women like Miriam who upset the proper order of male dominance.[80] After the discussion we have detailed above on Adam and Eve from I Tim 2:14, Luther moves to verse 15 where women can be saved through childbearing, if they are faithful. He repeats his familiar theme that the penalties of sin: pain in childbearing and subjection to husbands, must be borne till judgment. The guilt of sin is taken away, but the penalty remains. But suddenly at the very end of the chapter Luther interjects: "And if the Lord should raise up a woman so that we should hear her, we would allow her to rule like Hulda."[81] One wonders how Luther would recognize that she had been raised up by God!

Finally we should see how Luther deals with Gal. 3:28: ". . . there is neither male nor female; for you are all one in Christ Jesus." Here Paul is dealing with the restoration of fallen human nature through the Gospel. Luther says in 1535 that one could add: "There is neither magistrate nor subject, neither professor nor listener, neither teacher nor pupil, neither lady nor servant, etc. Because in Christ Jesus all social stations, even those that were divinely ordained, are nothing."[82] In salvation, the Law which makes such distinctions has been abolished, and all are saved by putting on Christ. Still,

In the world and according to the flesh there is a very great difference and inequality among persons, and this must be observed very carefully. For if a woman wanted to be a man, if a son wanted to be a father, if a pupil wanted to be a teacher, if a servant wanted to be a master, if a subject wanted to be a magistrate—there would be a disturbance and confusion of all social stations and of everything. In Christ, on the other hand, where there is no Law, there is no distinction among persons at all.[83]

Luther makes no mention here of any consequences at all for the sixteenth-century hierarchical social structure—indeed in Luther's Germany still feudal—of this spiritual oneness in Christ.

What conclusions can we draw from an examination of these selections from Luther's commentaries written during his mature years? Perhaps that Luther is a theologian in transition between two worlds. Educated a scholastic, he has so deeply imbibed the older tradition of understanding the image of God and the different relation of men and women to it that he simply cannot consciously lay aside that tradition, though he tries very hard to do so. He has abandoned allegorical interpretation like that of Augustine as a way to deal with the image of God in woman,[84] along with the double-creation schemes of several of the Fathers.[85] The connection of "male and female" in Genesis 1:27 to the image of God is taken for granted by Luther, though it has not always been so. Luther's intent is to substitute a biblically-derived picture of humanity as created in God's image for the traditional one he regards as too much derived from Greek philosophy. In fact he regards the mixing of Aristotle with theology as a serious mistake. He perceives his own view from Genesis to be a much more positive picture of humankind and especially of woman's nature than the scholastic one, giving her greater dignity. He also believes he offers a much more positive picture of the home and childrearing, woman's special sphere, than that of the Fathers.

For the most part in the 1535 Genesis commentary Luther argues that before the fall Eve was equal in endowments to Adam, despite her different body, and shared equally in governance over the other creatures. Female subjection to men is punishment for the fall. But at times the older view of Eve's subjection to Adam from creation itself creeps back into the discussion, and what is different from the male becomes necessarily inferior. The theology of women's subordination in passages like I Cor. 11:7 and I Tim. 2:14, both of which he attributes to Paul, influences his reading of Genesis[86] and perhaps also of another key Pauline text, Gal. 3:28. There is no evidence that he sees any real tension between the Galatians text and those clearly teaching women's subordination to men.

Insofar as Luther places the beginning of women's subordination after the fall, as the result of sin, he contributes to genuine reform in theology, stressing a full equality between women and men as intended by God at creation. This teaching has come to dominate modern theology. But Luther does not see women's subordination as simply an unfortunate disordering of human relationships as a consequence of sin; rather he sees it as God's express punishment of women which must endure till the end of time.[87] By giving women's inferior place in society the full weight of God's command, Luther effectively eliminates any possible practical consequences flowing from the creational equality of women with men for the earthly lives of real women.

Notes

1. Early versions of this discussion were included in broader presentations given in 1989 as the Scott Lecturer at Brite Divinity School of Texas Christian University and the Schaff Lecturer at Pittsburgh Theological Seminary. Those opportunities for engagement with these issues are most appreciated.
2. See Ian Maclean, *The Renaissance Notion of Woman: A Study in the Fortunes of Scholasticism and Medical Science in European Intellectual Life* (Cambridge: Cambridge University Press, 1980), 28–46.
3. Ibid. 35–7.
4. Christine de Pizan, *The Book of the City of Ladies*, trans. Earl Jeffrey Richards (New York: Persea Books, 1982), 3–5.
5. Ibid. 23.
6. See Joan Kelly, 'Early Feminist Theory and the *Querelle des Femmes*, 1400–1789', *Signs* 8 (1982), 4–28. Cf. Jane Dempsey Douglass, *Women, Freedom, and Calvin* (Philadelphia: Westminster Press, 1985), 66–73.
7. For examples from Marguerite of Navarre, Henricus Cornelius Agrippa of Nettesheim, and Marie Dentière in Geneva, see ibid. 68–71, 103–4.
8. See ibid. 68.
9. Maclean, *Renaissance Notion of Woman*, 12–13; Manfred P. Fleisher, ' "Are Women Human?" The Debate of 1595 Between Valens Acidalius and Simon Gediccus', *Sixteenth Century Journal* 12 (1981), 107–20.
10. See e.g. Karl Elisabeth Børresen, *Subordination and Equivalence: The Nature and Role of Woman in Augustine and Thomas Aquinas*, trans. Charles H. Talbot (Washington, DC: University Press of America, 1981), 26–9.
11. Heiko A. Oberman, *The Harvest of Medieval Theology: Gabriel Biel and Late Medieval Nominalism* (Cambridge, Mass.: Harvard University Press, 1963), 50–5. Gerhard Ebeling, *Luther: An Introduction to his Thought* (Philadelphia: Fortress Press, 1964), chs. 5, 14. William J. Bouwsma, *John Calvin: A Sixteenth Century Portrait* (New York: Oxford University Press, 1988), 106–27, 157.
12. 'Vorlesungen über 1. Mose von 1535–45', ed. G. Koffmane and D. Reichert, *D. Martin Luthers Werke; Kritische Gesamtausgabe* (Weimar, 1911), vol. 42. Hereafter cited as WA 42. Though there has undoubtedly been more extensive editing of this Luther text than in the case of some other writings of Luther, it should serve our purpose adequately. For a discussion by Jaroslav Pelikan of the questions of authenticity raised by Peter Meinhold, see Pelikan, 'Introduction to Volume 1', in *Luther's Works 1: Lectures on Genesis Chapters 1–5* (St Louis, Mo.: Concordia, 1958), pp. ix–xii.
13. Gen. 2:3, WA 42, 61–2; cf. Gen. 2:16–17, WA 42, 80 where God's sermon is on the sixth day, before Eve's creation.
14. Gen. 1, preface, WA 42, 4.
15. Gen. 1:26, WA 42, 42.
16. Gen. 1:26, WA 42, 41–2.
17. Gen. 1:26, WA 42, 46.
18. Gen. 1:26, WA 42, 47.
19. Ibid.
20. Gen. 1:26, WA 42, 46–7.
21. Gen. 1:26, WA 42, 48–9.
22. Gen. 1:27, WA 42, 51.

23. Gen. 1:26, WA 42, 49–51.
24. Gen. 1:28, WA 42, 54.
25. Gen. 1:26, WA 42, 50.
26. Gen. 1:27, WA 42, 51–2.
27. Gen. 1:27, WA 42, 53.
28. Gen. 1:27, WA 42, 51–2. See parallel WA 42, 52 ll. 18–21.
29. Gen. 1:27, WA 42, 52.
30. Gen. 2:18, WA 42, 87.
31. Gen. 3:16, WA 42, 151.
32. Gen. 2:23, WA 42, 103.
33. Ibid.
34. Despite Luther's protestations about women's likeness to men, his use of the term *vir* suggests that at least to some degree he assumes the woman's humanity to be secondary to that of men.
35. Gen. 2:23, WA 42, 103.
36. Gen. 3:1, WA 42, 113.
37. Gen. 3:3–6, WA 42, 116–22.
38. Gen. 3:6, WA 42, 121.
39. Gen. 3:1, WA 42, 114.
40. Ibid.
41. Gen. 3:1, WA 42, 113.
42. Cf. e.g. Luther's sermons on Genesis from 1519–21: WA 9, 332–4.
43. Gen. 3:14, WA 42, 138.
44. Gen. 3:9, WA 42, 129.
45. Gen. 2:16–17, WA 42, 79.
46. Gen. 2:16–17, WA 42, 80.
47. Gen. 3:1, WA 42, 108.
48. Gen. 3:13, WA 42, 135.
49. Gen. 3:1, WA 42, 109.
50. Gen. 3:13, WA 42, 136.
51. See Børresen, *Subordination and Equivalence*, 53–6.
52. Ibid. 54–5.
53. Ibid. 53.
54. Gen. 2:23, WA 42, 103; Gen. 3:13, WA 42, 136.
55. I Tim. 2:14, WA 26, 47.
56. I Tim. 2:13–15, WA 26, 47–8.
57. Gen. 2:22, WA 42, 98–9.
58. Gen. 2:18, WA 42, 87–90; Gen. 2:22–3, WA 42, 98–103.
59. Gen. 3:16, WA 42, 151.
60. Gen. 2:7, WA 42, 64; Gen. 2:21, WA 42, 94–8; Gen. 3:15, WA 42, 145.
61. Gen. 3:16, WA 42, 150.
62. Gen. 3:16, WA 42, 149–50.
63. Gen. 3:16, WA 42, 151; cf. on Eccl. 7:28, WA 20, 148–9.
64. Gen. 3:17–19, WA 42, 152–63.
65. Gen. 3:16, WA 42, 150.
66. Gen. 3:1, WA 42, 106; Gen. 3:14, WA 42, 139–40.
67. Gen. 3:16, WA 42, 151.
68. Gen. 4:1, WA 42, 177.
69. Gen. 3:16, WA 42, 150.

70. Gen. 2:18, WA 42, 89.
71. Ibid.
72. Ibid.
73. Gen. 2:18, WA 42, 88.
74. Gen. 1:28, WA 42, 54.
75. Gen. 3:16, WA 42, 150–1.
76. Gen. 3:16, WA 42, 148.
77. Ibid.
78. Gen. 3:20, WA 42, 163–4.
79. Gen. 3:20, WA 42, 164–5.
80. I Tim. 2:11–12, WA 26, 46–7.
81. I Tim. 2:14–15, WA 26, 48–9.
82. Gal. 3:28, WA 40, 1, 542.
83. Gal. 3:28, WA 40, 1, 544–5.
84. Børresen, *Subordination and Equivalence*, 26–30.
85. Ibid. 16–21, 153–63.
86. See in Luther's sermons on Genesis from 1519–21 the *catena* of New Testament passages, including those mentioned here, which he adduces to explain Gen. 3:16. WA 9, 336, cf. 333.
87. In Luther's sermons on Genesis from 1519–21, he seems to suggest that whereas Adam's punishment is remedial, Eve's is merely punitive. WA 9, 334.

10 *Mujerista* Theology

Ada María Isasi-Diaz*

'To be called a name is one of the first forms of linguistic injury that one learns. But not all name-calling is injurious. Being called a name is also one of the conditions by which a subject is constituted in language' (Judith Butler, *Excitable Speech: A Politics of Performance* (New York: Routledge, 1997), 2).

In her explanation of the origins and aspirations of *mujerista* theology, Ada María Isasi-Diaz sees naming oneself as 'one of the most powerful human acts'. Her framework is liberation feminist theology. *Mujerismo* derives its particularity from the lives of Hispanic women, especially in the United States, and their struggle for survival. In this excerpt, Isasi-Diaz expands on the questions of identity she addresses here in the fourth chapter of her book *Mujerista Theology*. The conclusion of that chapter is worth quoting in full and is given here too.

All theology is subjective because one of its main elements is the historical circumstances of the theologian along with the community of faith to which she or he relates. The theology I have been involved in articulating is born out of my experience and that of other Hispanic women living in the United States. For the last fifteen years those of us who struggle against ethnic prejudice, sexism, and in many cases, classism, have been at a loss as to what to call ourselves. The majority of Hispanic women have simply called ourselves *cubanas, chicanas, puertorriqueñas*, and most probably will continue to do so. Some of us have called ourselves *feministas hispanas*. Though *feministas hispanas* has been an appellation riddled with difficulties, we have felt the need for a name that would indicate the struggle against sexism that is part of our daily bread while also helping us identify one another as we struggle for our survival within Hispanic communities and

* Ada María Isasi-Diaz, 'Roundtable Discussion: *Mujeristas*, Who We Are and What We Are About'. This article appeared first in the *Journal of Feminist Studies in Religion* 8(1) (spring 1992), and was reprinted, with the 'Conclusion' which appears here, in *Mujerista Theology* (Orbis Books, 1996). Reprinted by permission of the author.

US society as a whole. But using *feminista hispana* has required long explanations of what such a phrase does *not* mean.[1]

Feministas hispanas have been consistently marginalized in the Anglo feminist community because of our critique of its ethnic/racial prejudice and lack of class analysis. Though Anglo feminists have worked to correct these serious shortcomings in their discourse, in my experience their praxis continues to be flawed.[2] *Feministas hispanas* have also been rejected by many in the Hispanic community who consider feminism a concern of Anglo women. Yet Hispanic women widely agree with an analysis of sexism as an evil within our communities, an evil that plays into the hands of the dominant forces of society and helps to repress and exploit us in such a way that we constitute a large percentage of those in the lowest economic stratum. Likewise Hispanic women widely agree that, though we make up the vast majority of active church-goers, we do the work but do not participate in deciding what work is to be done; we do the praying but our understanding of the God to whom we pray is ignored.

Hispanic women understand how sexism works in our lives and we struggle against this oppression daily. In spite of our understanding and struggle, however, we have not had a way to name ourselves. To name oneself is one of the most powerful human acts. A name is not just a word by which one is identified. A name also provides the conceptual framework, the point of reference, the mental constructs that are used in thinking, understanding, and relating to a person, an idea, a movement. In our search for a name of our own, we have turned to our music, an intrinsic part of the soul of our culture. In our songs, love songs as well as protest songs, we are simply called *mujer*. And so, those of us who make a preferential option for *mujeres*, are *mujeristas*.[3]

CREATING A NAME OF OUR OWN—BEGINNINGS

The task at hand is to create the meaning of *mujerismo*. We want to start by recognizing that for *mujerismo* to become a term that refers to the struggles of Hispanic women against oppression, the meaning of the term has to remain open, in flux—alive! Those of us who have come up with the term and have been the first to use it wish to encourage Hispanic women to appropriate this term, fully aware of the fact that such a process also includes adaptation. We have no intention of ever claiming exclusive authority to decide that what others mean by *mujerismo* is not correct, that a given person should not be called a *mujerista*. But we do believe we have the responsibility of establishing certain flexible parameters of meaning for these terms and of insisting on organic development rather than artificial changes. This is why instead of using a definition, we have chosen to use descriptions; instead of establishing criteria, we have chosen to indicate context; instead of demanding correct usage we have chosen to explain our methodology. We do not ask others to conform to our understanding and use of the terms *mujerismo* and *mujerista*. But we do ask those who use these terms to participate in constructing, rather than rejecting, this world of meaning, and to engage in this task openly, fueled by the desire and need for our liberation as Hispanic women.

We come to the task of establishing parameters from a religious perspective—not only because we are theologians but also because of the centrality of religion in the Hispanic culture. It is particularly Christianity, and within Christianity, Roman Catholicism, that continues to be the faith tradition to which the majority of Hispanic women relate. We will attempt to deal with these terms in language that is accessible to our Hispanic community. Some may consider this language lacking in precision. But for us the most important thing is to contribute to the struggle of Hispanic women. Though we believe that we must impact the world of ideas and the academic world as part of this struggle, we choose clarity to our main community of accountability over academic correctness and linguistic precision.

This discussion has already provided much information about *mujerismo*. But, to be more explicit: a *mujerista* is a Hispanic woman who struggles to liberate herself not as an individual but as a member of a Hispanic community. She is one who builds bridges among Hispanics instead of falling into sectarianism and using divisive tactics. A *mujerista* understands that her task is to gather the hopes and expectations of her people about justice and peace. In the *mujerista*, God chooses to once again lay claims to and revindicate the divine image and likeness of women made visible from the very beginning in the person of Eve. The *mujerista* is called to gestate new women and new men—Hispanics who are willing to work for the common good, knowing that such work requires us to denounce destructive self-abnegation.[4]

MUJERISTA THEOLOGY

Because the term *mujerismo* was conceived by a group of us working from a religious perspective for the liberation of Hispanic Women, the first application of this term has been to our theological task. Such an application further illumines how we have used the term *mujerismo*.

Mujerista theology, which includes both ethics and theology, is a liberative praxis: reflective action that has as its goal liberation. As a liberative praxis *mujerista* theology is a process of enablement for Hispanic women insisting on the development of a strong sense of moral agency, and clarifying the importance and value of who we are, what we think, and what we do. Second, as a liberative praxis, *mujerista* theology seeks to impact mainline theologies that support what is normative in church and, to a large degree, in society.

How does *mujerista* theology accomplish this two-pronged liberative praxis? A first task of *mujerista* theology is to enable Hispanic women to understand the many oppressive structures that strongly influence our daily lives. It enables us to understand that the goal of our struggle is not to participate in and to benefit from these structures but to change them radically. In theological and religious language this means that *mujerista* theology helps us to discover and affirm the presence of God in the midst of our communities and the revelation of God in our daily lives. We must come to understand the reality of structural sin and find ways of combating it because it effectively hides God's ongoing revelation from us and from society at large.

The second task of *mujerista* theology is to help us define our preferred future: What will a radically different society look like? What will be its values and norms? In theological and religious language this means that *mujerista* theology enables Hispanic women to understand the centrality of eschatology in the life of every Christian. Our preferred future breaks into our present oppression in many different ways. We must recognize those eschatological glimpses and rejoice in them and struggle to make those glimpses become our whole horizon. Third, *mujerista* theology enables Hispanic women to understand how much we have already bought into the prevailing systems in society—including the religious systems—internalizing our own oppression. *Mujerista* theology helps us see that radical structural change cannot happen unless radical change takes place in each and every one of us. In theological and religious language this means that *mujerista* theology assists us in the process of conversion, helping Hispanic women to see the reality of sin in our lives. Further, it enables us to understand that to resign ourselves to what others tell us is our lot and to accept suffering and self-effacement is not necessarily virtuous.

To coin a new term is not complicated but to have it become common usage is another matter. What moved us to create the terms *mujerismo* and *mujerista* was our experience in the struggle for our liberation as Hispanic women. We felt a strong need to have a name of our own. And as community, allowing ourselves to be inspired by one of the best expressions of the soul of our culture, our music, we birthed these terms. Now we eagerly wait for all Hispanic women to add their understandings to the meaning of *mujerismo* so that we all, as Hispanic women struggling for liberation, will be able to call ourselves *mujeristas.*

CONCLUSION

In many ways what has guided *mujerista* theology from the beginning are those wonderful words of Miriam in the book of Numbers, "Has Yahweh indeed spoken only through Moses?" (Num. 12:2). Well aware of the fact that she suffered severe penalties for daring to scold Moses, for daring to claim that Yahweh also spoke to her and through her, our sister Miriam invites *mujerista* theologians to throw our lot with the people of God and to hope that, just as in her case, the authorities will catch up with us, that they will eventually also see that we have no leprosy, that we are clean. But their declaration of cleanliness is *not* what makes us clean; their saying is *not* what makes *mujerista* theology a worthwhile and important task for us. It is rather the fact that *mujerista* theology is part of the struggle for survival, the struggle for liberation—that is what makes it right and just for us to pursue it. Doing *mujerista* theology is an intrinsic element of our struggle, of our lives, because indeed, for Latinas in the USA to struggle is to live, *la vida es la lucha.*

Notes

1. Ada María Isasi-Diaz, 'Toward an Understanding of *Feminismo Hispano* in the U.S.A.', in *Women's Consciousness, Women's Conscience*, ed. Barbara H. Andolsen, Christine E. Gudorf, and Mary D. Pellauer (New York: Winston, 1985), 51–61.
2. Ada María Isasi-Diaz, 'A Hispanic Garden in a Foreign Land', in *Inheriting*

Our Mothers' Gardens, ed. Letty Russell, Kwok Pui Lan, Ada María Isasi-Diaz, and Katie Cannon (Philadelphia: Westminster Press, 1988), 91–106.

3. I am much indebted to the work of African–American feminists who have preceded us in this struggle to name ourselves. Their use of the term *womanist* has indeed influenced me. I am particularly grateful to Katie Cannon, Joan Martin, and Delores Williams, with whom I have had the privilege of sharing much. See especially Delores Wiliams, 'Womanist Theology: Black Women's Voices', in *Christianity and Crisis* (2 Mar. 1987), 66–70; and Cheryl J. Sanders, Katie Cannon, Emile M. Townes, M. Shawn Copeland, and Bell Hooks, 'Roundtable Discussion: Christian Ethics and Theology in Womanist Perspective', *Journal of Feminist Studies in Religion* 5 (2) (fall 1989), 83–112.

4. Rosa Marta Zarate Macias, '*Canto de Mujer*', in *Concierto a Mi Pueblo,* audio tape produced by Rosa Marta Zarate Macias, PO Box 7366, San Bernardino, Calif. 92411. Much of this description is based on this song, composed and interpreted by Rosa Marta. I have known her for many years. She composed this song in response to the insistence of several Hispanic women that we needed a song that would help us express who we are and would inspire us in the struggle. For the full text of her song in English and Spanish see Ada María Isasi-Diaz, '*Mujeristas:* A Name of Our Own', *The Christian Century* (24–31 May 1989), 560–2.

11 Interview with José Míguez Bonino

Elsa Tamez*

Liberation theology broke upon the world stage in the late twentieth century through the writings of a number of Latin American men. The liberationists, so powerful in speaking for the poor, were nonetheless not quick in the early days to recognize the presence of women as the poorest of the poor, excluded even by those church structures which aimed to assist them. In a groundbreaking little book, Elsa Tamez sought to speed the process of recognition. Her authorial strategy was part of the cure. Instead of writing a single-authored tract, she recorded and published interviews with twelve major liberation theologians. The exchange of views and the courtesy of the voices demonstrate that theology is often best done in dialogue. The extract here is from her interview with Methodist theologian José Míguez Bonino. JMS

Míguez: One of our problems is that we still don't know what a "women's perspective" is. What's the difference between the way men and women address different subjects? Are the differences due to real differences between men and women? Or are they due to the roles that they have played in society, which have created different ways of thinking, of conceiving things, of relating to the world, of qualitatively and quantitatively evaluating things? That is, the modality or the viewpoint of the feminine perspective will be apparent only to the degree that women have full access to the totality of human activity and so are able to recreate this feminine modality. I am very curious to know, for example, what is going to happen to the conception and exercise of pastoral ministry when half the pastors, or even a third, have been women over a period of twenty years. What formulation, what reconception of the ministry, will be produced by the presence of women over a period during which they can fashion their own way of doing things? This will be extremely significant.

* Elsa Tamez, excerpt from *Against Machismo: Interviews by Elsa Tamez* (Meyer Stone Books, 1987).

To get back to your question, let me answer in a somewhat tentative, imaginative way. For in the first place I'm not a woman, and in the second I'm not sure how much we can talk about a women's perspective. But I do think that one of the characteristics of a women's approach to theology is the overcoming of some of the dichotomies that have affected theology for centuries. Perhaps it is precisely because their approach is through the concrete, that is, through unity and not distinctions. Scholastic thought, which has dominated theology, proceeds by distinction. Distinction is no doubt necessary at a certain stage in thought, but when distinction becomes the principal concern, we unavoidably become involved in dichotomies. Perhaps a women's approach is more concrete and comprehensive.

I am thinking specifically about the question of justification, where we suffer under a basic dichotomy that is reflected in all our discussions. What is the dichotomy between God's initiative and human action? The question arises from the concern to attribute to each what corresponds to it, and to attribute exclusively, that is, what is attributed to one cannot be attributed to the other. And since in theology we must attribute everything to God we must then in some way or another take everything away from human beings. If we really think from a feminine perspective, if we think comprehensively, starting from unity and not separation, then love is more important than rational understanding, and we start from the basic fact of the relationship of God with human beings. Our starting point is not difference or distinction, but relationship. What is most important is to know what happens in this relationship, and not to whom the different elements of the relationship should be attributed.

I imagine that a theology of justification in a feminine perspective would have as its starting point the relationship of God with human beings, a relationship that generates a dynamic of love pervading all of reality, the whole universe. This relationship comes before the distinction between the justice of God and human justice, between initiative and response. It's possible that at a later point we need to get into the distinctions. But I'm more and more convinced that we have posed the problem backwards and so, perhaps, have not only distorted reality, but have also distorted the biblical perspective. In the Bible the starting point is an action of God in which the people are involved. Human beings are in a relationship with God, a covenant, if you will, where understanding—even carnal, physical knowledge—is assimilated into love.

Elsa: Míguez, can't we say that when you are making this effort to re-read justification by faith from a women's perspective, what you are doing is rather a more complete theology, not a feminist theology, but a theology that by including the feminine dimension complements a more masculine theology. Would you agree?

Míguez: Of course. I believe that in the last analysis we are not going to have a masculine theology and a feminine theology.

Elsa: But isn't our present theology incomplete?

Míguez: It is clear that our present theology is incomplete. It is incomplete because there are subjects who have been excluded from theology, not only women, but also the people, particular races, particular classes, whose experiences of faith and of reality have been excluded from reflection. Theological reflection has been not only a reflection of males, but of males situated in a particular place in society, namely, the clerical state, in a particular social class that has usually been linked with the ruling classes. And this has determined their concept of power, of love, of life, and the result has been a deficient theology, a defective theology. Perhaps we are for the first time approaching the possibility of a theology that is really the result of the participation of all the actors of faith and that can reflect this diversity.

Elsa: That's why I think it's important to promote the reading of the Bible from a women's perspective. Otherwise we miss certain things that we should see and that would help us to have a more complete reading of the Bible. The Bible in itself is problematic because it was written in a patriarchal context, but even so we can discover certain liberating elements for women. What is your opinion on the question of the Bible and women?

Míguez: I think that we must start from the fact that the Bible was written in certain historical circumstances, within a social structure where women had particular roles and men other roles; it was a patriarchal society. So I think it's unnecessary and a little annoying to be continuously looking in the Bible for places where women appear in subordinate positions. Because you're always going to find them. You're going to find them everywhere because this was the social structure and the ideology of the people who wrote the Bible and who lived that experience.

I think it's much more useful to find the points where in some way the liberating acts of God are reflected in events, in phrases, in texts, in

99

sudden flashes. Points that break apart in a small way the total pre-dominance of the structure of the oppression of women, and of others as well. That is, the places where we find atypical things happening. And I think these places exist and those who are sensitive to them will find them, namely, women. I already mentioned your reference to "brother and sister" in your reading of James.[1] I had never noticed this and I know of no one else who had either. Another example is the story of Hagar. I can recall only two presentations of Hagar that have impressed me as significant theological readings of the episode. One is yours and the other is that of the North American Phyllis Trible, who has a slightly different interpretation.

I think that in the case of the poor the need for such a rereading is much more obvious than in the case of women. But even so I think the task is worthwhile. On the other hand I think that the distinction, which is sometimes made so sharply, between finding in the text what we are looking for and accepting the text as it is, is a distinction that can be deceptive. Nobody finds in the text what they are not looking for, whether they know what they are looking for or not. And I think it's preferable that women, or blacks, or the poor know with what questions they approach the text and are aware of what they are look-ing for. Otherwise we are controlled by the questions that the prevail-ing ideology would have us ask. So we have every right to a controlled exegesis, not simply self-serving, but controlled, with questions that flow from our experience.

To speak in a slightly heretical way—and I feel more and more heretical on this point—I do not think that we can consider revelation as closed. If by closure to revelation we mean that in the mystery of Jesus Christ all is contained, very well. But that is not closure. The mystery of Jesus Christ is a mystery of openness of the love of God, and revelation is not closed as long as we continue to experience the redeeming presence of Jesus Christ. And when this presence enters into a new sphere of human existence and opens it up from within, as in the case of women's experience, or the experience of a particular race that begins to ponder its faith, then revelation is made manifest. No mere literal or conceptual harmonization of perspectives is enough; we have to go to a much deeper level of relationships. I think there is a place for a reading of Scripture from this perspective. In this case it is from the perspective of a sex, but it could also be from the perspective, for example, of a region, or a social group, or the like.

Elsa: Thank you very much, Míguez.

Note

1. Míguez is referring to my study of James, *Santiago: una lectura de la epístola* (San José, Costa Rica: DEI, 1986), 42, English translation *Faith Without Works Is Dead: The Scandalous Message of James* (New York: Crossroad, 1990).

12 Life on the Fringes

Haviva Ner-David*

Sally Priesand, the first female rabbi in the USA, was ordained in 1972 at Hebrew Union College; Jackie Tabick soon followed at Leo Baeck College in the UK. Yet both were years behind the first woman to be ordained in modern times. Regina Jonas, a graduate of Berlin's Hochschule für die Wissenschaft des Judentums, was ordained privately in 1935. Tragically, she died in Theresienstadt in 1942, and the memory of her extraordinary achievement almost died with her. In some respects, Haviva Ner-David, who is pursuing ordination as an Orthodox rabbi in Israel, has more in common with Jonas than with Priesand and Tabick. The latter two women belonged to movements by then pledged to equality of the sexes, and both were ordained by their movements' official seminaries. Since no Orthodox Jewish movement yet sanctions the ordination of women, Ner-David, like Jonas, will be ordained (once she has successfully completed her studies) by a rabbi acting without the approval of movement or peers. Her book's title, *Life on the Fringes*, alludes both to her relationship to her own community—not beyond the pale, but hardly mainstream—and to the fringed garment worn by non-Orthodox Jews at prayer and by Orthodox male Jews at all times. Ner-David describes here her decision to take upon herself the mitzvah (obligation) of wearing tefillin (phylacteries) and tzitit (fringes).

DL

I first put on tefillin ten years after my bat mitzvah. I was married and living in Washington, DC, worlds away from the close-knit Orthodox community in which I had grown up.

One evening on the phone, I told my mother that I planned to have a second bat mitzvah at Fabrangen, an informal and completely egalitarian prayer community, the *havurah* in which I had become active. It would be on Shabbat, and I would read from the Torah. I had not yet confessed to my mother that I had been regularly participating in egalitarian services. The geographic distance between us made me brave.

* Haviva Ner-David, excerpt from *Life on the Fringes: A Feminist Journey Toward Traditional Rabbinic Ordination* (JFL Books, 2000).

My mother's disappointment was evident in her silence, and then in the tension in her voice. "Joining an egalitarian havurah isn't a good answer to your religious questions," she said. "You're settling for quick and easy solutions, and that will get you nowhere. You'll be sorry later. The people in this havurah of yours aren't committed to halakhah. They'll never provide a solid Jewish community for you."

I told her that I agreed with much of what she was claiming. In fact, I would later leave this havurah for the very reason that she mentioned. "It's true that most of them don't observe Shabbat or *kashrut* strictly," I explained, "but the *tefillah* is more sincere and uplifting than any I have experienced before. It's real prayer, not just words they're mumbling out of habit."

"You're trying to tell me that you can't find any Orthodox shul with nice *tefillot*? There are plenty of Hasidic shuls with beautiful *tefillot*. You aren't being fair."

She was right. I hadn't looked for a Hasidic shul, although I doubt that there were any in Washington, DC, but that wasn't the point. My mother was trying to tell me that she knew that my choice of prayer community was not just about finding spiritual *tefillah*. It was also about egalitarianism, and she was correct.

I tried to explain to my mother: I wanted to be part of a Judaism that was both egalitarian and committed to halakhah, tradition, and mitzvot, or at least in a serious dialogue with the tradition. In other words, ideally I wanted to be part of a community struggling with the integration of modernity into a living Judaism, without casting off all laws that seemed inconvenient, irrelevant, distasteful, or difficult— and one that also viewed greater women's participation in ritual as increasing the community's capacity for holiness, not watering it down.

"If and when I have daughters," I told my mother, "I want them to do all the mitzvot, including the ones they aren't obligated to perform."

"Like what?" my mother asked.

"Like tefillin," I immediately answered, as though it were obvious. *Of course my daughters would pray with tefillin*, I thought. Yet in that moment I realized: How could I expect a daughter of mine to put on tefillin if I didn't do so myself? I would have to be a role model for her. I would have to commit to putting on tefillin every morning, and I would have to start before my children were born.

The next morning, Jacob presented me with my first pair of tefillin. They had belonged to his great-uncle. They were old and worn; the black paint was chipping from the leather, and they were significantly larger than the ones that contain the scrolls of the size that most *sofrim*, religious scribes, write today.

Jacob showed me how to put on my new tefillin. Standing behind me, he demonstrated how to wrap the straps that attach to one of the boxes around my arm and put the other box on my head, letting the straps from that box hang down over my chest. He told me at which point in putting on the tefillin I should say the various *b'rachot*. My hands trembled as I wrapped the straps; my voice shook as I recited the words.

Wearing tefillin for the first time felt so strange. I had seen only men do it, and even though I knew intellectually that I was permitted according to halakhah to wear these ritual objects, I still felt as if I were breaking a taboo. Some rabbis maintain that a woman should not perform this mitzvah because she does not have a *guf naki*, a clean body. That idea resonated in my head, along with the strong visual image of men and boys praying in tefillin. I had never seen a woman in tefillin, yet I felt reborn as a religious Jewish feminist. The two worlds of my childhood, the modern and the Orthodox, actually met fully within me. For the first time in a long time, I did not feel torn apart.

As I recited the biblical verse that refers to tefillin while wearing them, I felt a strong connection to generations past. Our Torah, our most ancient religious Jewish document, tells us to wear tefillin. Although we do not know exactly when the verse was first interpreted to describe the ritual objects we use today, I knew that Jews have been wearing tefillin similar to mine for thousands of years!

Wearing the tefillin was distracting at first, as I imagine it is at the beginning for any person who starts performing this mitzvah, including bar mitzvah boys. I was so aware of their presence on my arm and head that I had trouble meditating on the prayers themselves; I was too busy thinking about the tefillin and why I was wearing them. It was also difficult to get used to the actual physical sensation. I have come to see this heightened awareness of the tefillin as one of the reasons for wearing them. When the novelty of wearing the tefillin wore off, they helped me focus on my prayers and the words I was saying. Prayer has become a more physical act that requires my whole self, my entire being, body and spirit.

Other aspects of Jewish prayer have a similar effect—synchronized bowing, standing, sitting, swaying, covering our eyes, stepping forward and backward—but none of these movements is as regular or tangible as tefillin. They are "signs," as they are called in the Shema, physical reminders of our love for God and the mitzvot.

Wearing tefillin has also helped me to take *tefillah* more seriously. Prayer now includes the concrete physical act of wrapping the tefillin and the commitment to perform this act every day. Prayer can feel so amorphous and subjective. It would be easier to tell myself on busy mornings, "Well, I'll just pray on the bus or as I walk the kids to school." My prayer has had to become more serious and deliberate. My commitment to wearing tefillin when I pray has forced me to set aside much-needed time and space each morning to spend with God—no excuses accepted.

When I finished my morning prayers that first day of wearing tefillin, Jacob showed me how to rewrap the straps around the boxes and put them away in their bag. Reversing precisely the steps of putting them on, we unwind the straps from around the fingers, take off the head tefillin and put them away, unwind the straps from around the arm and put the arm tefillin away. Everything about these objects is ritualized; they are to be treated with such care and attention to detail that one cannot help but be aware of their holiness.

It was obvious to me, as I put the tefillin back in their bag, that discouraging women from wearing tefillin is only one of the ways the Rabbis surrounded these ritual objects with rules and regulations. There is a specific time to wear them, a prescribed way to put them on and take them off, and a particular group who should wear them. Guarding their holiness also means restricting and structuring their use.

Yet I believe that I bring a new holiness to the mitzvah of tefillin when I don them to pray. By wearing tefillin I am, perhaps, chipping away at some of the restrictions intended to intensify their holiness. However, my adoption of this mitzvah works toward the same goal the Rabbis had in mind. My decision to lay tefillin every morning, and to take this as a serious religious obligation, is a testament to the beauty and spiritual power of this mitzvah, so charged with spiritual and historical meaning. Now that, thank God, most contemporary Jews (even within Orthodoxy) would agree that a woman's body is no more physically unclean than a man's, a woman taking on this mitzvah no longer desecrates the tefillin; instead, she affirms their sanctity.

This is a male tradition; male scholars interpreted this biblical verse with only men in mind. Why choose to make this mitzvah my own?

Why not create a new ritual, a female reinterpretation of this commandment?

This is the mitzvah we were given in the Torah. It is our tradition, practiced by Jews through the Crusades, the Inquisition, pogroms, and the Holocaust. It is a profound practice, beautiful and powerful. Because I saw my father pray this way each morning, this image is ingrained in my mind: a person absorbed in prayer, swaying meditatively in deep concentration, wearing a tallit and tefillin. It is possible to draw the image anew for our children and ourselves, making the body of a woman in that mental picture interchangeable with that of a man. I have to step into that picture in order for it to become flexible for my children.

The tradition about who should wear tefillin can evolve in a changing world without detracting from the spiritual power of the tefillin themselves. The adoption of this mitzvah by more serious observant Jews enhances their significance. Since I began wearing tefillin, I feel as if my prayers are lifted to a higher plane, coming from a deeper place. I feel bound to God as I bind God's words to my arm and head with these holy straps, wind them around my finger like a wedding ring, and recite the verses from Hosea: *I will betroth you to Me forever; I will betroth you to Me with righteousness, justice, kindness, and mercy. I will betroth you to Me with fidelity, and you will know God.*

As a child, putting on tefillin would have felt almost as transgressive as eating pork. I did not know the intricacies of the laws relating to women wearing tefillin; I just knew that women did not wear them. No one *told* me that my body was unclean; the words were not necessary. I was a girl and would someday become a woman. Somehow my skin and my entire body were different from that of my brothers.

The first time that I pressed the holy leather of Jacob's great-uncle's tefillin next to my skin, I knew I had taken back a mitzvah that had been stolen from me, that was rightfully mine. Smiling to myself, I imagined the man whose tefillin I was inheriting somewhere in another realm, shaking his head and sighing, "Oy! What is this world coming to? Women putting on tefillin! Next thing you know, men will be changing diapers!"

Once I began laying tefillin, Jacob kept encouraging me to take on the mitzvah of tzitzit, which would mean wearing a tallit while praying in the mornings, and a *tallit katan* underneath my shirt while it is light outside. It is one of his own favorite mitzvot. He could not understand why I would take on laying tefillin every day yet not wear tzitzit.

"Tzitzit are so much easier," he would tell me over and over again. "You just put them on, and then you're done."

It made sense rationally, but it felt like a bigger emotional step for me. The tzitzit would be with me, on me, all day long. Unlike tefillin, the tallit is worn even on Shabbat. If I took on the obligation to perform this mitzvah, I would have to wear my tallit in shul on Shabbat, even in Orthodox synagogues (where I often pray) and even at my parents' and my in-laws' synagogues when I was visiting. It would mean coming out of the closet as a "radical" religious Jewish feminist. I would be making a statement every time I prayed in any Orthodox shul. If I was going to have to defend myself at every turn, I needed to first feel absolutely certain that I was on the right path.

One morning, that feeling of certainty came over me as I was praying the morning service, reciting the Shema. The third paragraph in that prayer (a passage from the biblical book of Numbers), which Jews (or, according to Orthodox halakhah, Jewish men) are obligated to recite three times each day, contains God's commandment to wear fringes, tzitzit, on the corners of our garments. Once a day during the daylight hours, when we recite this prayer and say the word "tzitzit" (which appears three times in the prayer), the traditional practice is to kiss the fringes on the *tallit katan* or *gadol*.

Although a woman is not halakhically required to recite the Shema, traditionally boys and girls, men and women, are expected to recite this paragraph as part of our daily morning prayers. Somehow, as a child, it never seemed strange to me to recite God's commandment to us to wear tzitzit even though it was clear that my female peers and I were not considered obligated to wear them—and even more, that we *shouldn't* wear them.

On that particular morning, as I recited the Shema, the words jumped out at me. The contradiction aroused me from years of empty recitation. For twenty-two years I had been reciting this prayer without truly meaning what I was saying, and I knew that I would never again recite that paragraph during morning prayers without wearing tzitzit and kissing the fringes while I said the word "tzitzit," just as I had seen the men and boys around me doing since my childhood.

I believe that I am commanded by God to wear tzitzit. The traditional rationale behind a woman's exemption from this mitzvah is that it is a time-bound commandment. The commandment to wear tzitzit only applies during daylight hours, when they can be seen by natural light (although there is no prohibition against wearing them at night), and women are exempt from most positive commandments connected with a particular time of day or year. However, I cannot find a reason that women as a class today should be exempt from performing this mitzvah, which sanctifies our bodies and the clothing with which we cover our nakedness. It is a constant reminder of what is expected of us as Jewish people bound by the mitzvot. As the verse in Numbers 15:39 tells us, the mitzvah of tzitzit is to remind us of all of God's mitzvot so that we will perform them, not sway after our hearts and eyes, and therefore be holy. The essence of the mitzvah has no relation to time. It seems as though women are missing out on the power of performing this mitzvah because of a technicality. I imagine that God is, as it were, waiting for Jewish women to reclaim this mitzvah, to say, "It is ours, too! How dare you take it away from us!"

For a woman to perform this mitzvah, as well as the others from which she is exempt, the drive must flow from within her. There are many women who feel comfortable in the ritual role that halakhah has thus far carved out for them. I do hope that masses of women will eventually see the beauty in these mitzvot and set aside their exemption, as they have historically done with other positive timebound mitzvot, such as *shofar* (hearing the blowing of the ram's horn on Rosh Hashanah) and sukkah (sitting in a temporary hut on Sukkot). Until then, the smaller number of us who feel a deep connection to the mitzvot of tefillin and tzitzit should be able to grow in our religious practice, free of discouragement from others.

13   The Mute Cannot Keep Silent

Rachel Muers*

If human beings are created in the divine image, then what might be the theological significance of sexual difference itself? Insofar as sexual difference was discussed by pre-feminist theology, there was a tendency to a theological and ontological complementarity in which woman was invariably man's other. Here, Rachel Muers discusses Karl Barth's infamous 'woman as the answer' account. Her essay goes on to address the same topic in the writings of the Catholic theologian Hans Urs von Balthasar.   JMS

Feminist theology is one of the few theological areas in which silence is ever talked about; but readings of silence within feminist theology tend to be negative—they are critiques of the silencing of women.[1] My current work is an attempt to incorporate the insights of feminist theology into a more positive, or at least a more nuanced, reading of silence. That is the larger context out of which this paper arises.[2]

SILENCE AND MUTENESS

I should, first, explain my title: The mute cannot keep silent. The act of keeping silent, as philosophers and literary theorists alike have noted, can have a multiplicity of meanings. A silence in conversation can be the avoidance of speech on a particular subject, a recognition that no words can be an adequate response to the situation, an affirmation of an intimacy that includes but is not exhausted by verbal exchange. Responding to a question with silence can indicate agreement, indifference, ignorance, deep thought, refusal to acknowledge the questioner. The keeping of silence is not equivalent to an utterance, but is equally a part of human communicative behaviour.[3]

* Rachel Muers, 'The Mute Cannot Keep Silent: Barth, von Balthasar, and Irigaray on the Construction of Women's Silence', from *Challenging Women's Orthodoxies in the Context of Faith*, edited by Susan Frank Parsons (Ashgate Publishing Ltd, 2000).

In the Gospels and in Christian theological texts, appearing amid the polyphony of significant sayings, we find significant silences. Mary falls silent in the second chapter of Luke's Gospel, "treasuring" all the words of the birth narrative. Jesus' opponents are reduced to silence; the disciples at the transfiguration can find no words. The Gospel of Mark ends with a paradoxical silence. Jesus stands silent before Pilate.[4]

All of these acts of significant silence must be distinguished from the silence of Zechariah at the beginning of Luke's Gospel, when he disbelieves the angel's message and is deprived of speech. Zechariah is rendered mute.[5] Speech is impossible for the mute person, but so is keeping silent. As Heidegger puts it in Sein und Zeit: "If a man is dumb, he still has the tendency to speak. Such a person has not proved that he can keep silence; in fact he entirely lacks the possibility of proving anything of the sort".[6] The mute person's silence, in and of itself, communicates nothing.

In commentaries on Luke's Gospel, theologians from the patristic period onwards have linked the muteness of Zechariah with the "silence of the prophets" before John the Baptist. Speech was impossible before, but now through the coming of the incarnate Word and through the Holy Spirit which gives the power of speech, creation has been given back its voice.[7] Muteness is a possibility that the coming of Christ negates. The dumb are among those healed by Christ; if the disciples become mute, the stones themselves will lose their muteness and cry out.[8]

Christian feminist theology, from its earliest years, has belatedly claimed this promise of the Gospel for women. Attention has been drawn repeatedly to the muting of women within the churches and within academic theology. Women have been summoned to speech, exhorted to "find a voice". Criticism has been directed, not only at the institutional and cultural muting of women in the doing of theology, but also at the construction of women *as silent* within theological texts. Luce Irigaray's words concerning psychoanalysis could equally have been said of theology: "[Women's life] is assigned within a discourse that excludes, and by its very 'essence', the possibility that it might speak for itself".[9]

This paper will look at aspects of the construction and function of women's silence in the work of Karl Barth and Hans Urs von Balthasar. In the case of Barth I shall consider a specific text—the discussion of the creation of Eve. In the case of von Balthasar I shall make use of *Word and Silence* by Raymond Gawronski, a recent work that brings together various texts on women's silence in von Balthasar.[10] Both of these theologians develop readings of gender difference in which the silence of women, or woman, is both extremely important and a major point of weakness. After discussing their work I shall introduce, for contrast, a brief discussion of Luce Irigaray's treatment of woman's silence in her 'Epistle to the Last Christians'.

The central point to be made about the silence of woman in Barth and von Balthasar is that, to fulfil its role in their theological scheme, it needs to be an act of keeping silent. It needs to be a significant silence, not the result of muteness. However, in the process of constructing "woman" as the bearer or embodiment of that silence, the theologians in question render it a meaningless silence, an imposed muteness; the mute cannot keep silence.

I hope to bring out three interconnected features of the construction of woman's silence, which relate to this central point. Firstly, there is a tension between woman as object-to-be-talked-about, by definition excluded from speech, and woman as fully human subject—the latter point being essential to the anthropologies of both Barth and von Balthasar. Secondly, there is a tension between inexplicability and explanation. Both Barth and von Balthasar want to state that woman and her silence are in some way inexplicable, irreducibly "other"; at the same time, both find it necessary for their theological systems to give a full explanation of woman's silence and its significance. Thirdly, in this explanation of silence, there is the tension between silence as a free act and silence as muteness.

Much of the first section of the paper might sound like purely negative criticism, fired off at what we all know are easy targets. I hope the later parts will bring out some more positive suggestions—but to some extent the paper is intended to open up discussion, rather than to provide complete answers to its own questions.

BARTH'S SILENT WOMAN

In the first division of the third volume of Barth's *Church Dogmatics*, he develops a theological account of creation by following the Genesis narrative, introduces woman as the "answer" to man. Man, the male, is said to constitute a "question" to which woman provides, or crucially, *is*, the answer. Man is incomplete without woman, as the question is incomplete without its answer. In the words of Genesis 2:18, "It is not good for the man to be alone".[11]

"Question" and "answer" is a model based on speech. But note that the woman is characterized as "answer" rather than as the "one who answers"; it is this feature of the presentation that allows Barth to portray woman's existence as essentially silent from the moment of her creation. Barth follows what he takes to be the logic of the Genesis text: the man acknowledges the woman ("This at last is bone of my bone . . .") and the woman makes no response. Her silence is for Barth a sign that "She does not choose: she is chosen"; her acknowledgement of man is implied in his acknowledgement of her. As Barth develops from this a full account of the created interrelation between the sexes, "silence" and "quiet" are described as the "distinctive features of woman" revealed by the New Testament, features which, Barth assures us, are in no way to be regarded as "lack".[12]

The characterization of woman as "answer" brings out the first tension to which I alluded earlier, and raises the question: How human is woman? It is essential for Barth's purposes that she should be fully human, because he uses the man–woman relation as the paradigm of human community and an "image" of the Trinitarian God—that is his reading of Genesis 1:27: "In the image of God he created them, male and female he created them".[13] Gender difference is for him fundamental to human existence. In the discussion of Genesis 2, however, a male standpoint is tacitly assumed. It is the existence of *woman* that is a matter for theological reflection, not the existence of man, nor simply of sexual difference. Although the original Adam is in some sense sexless (Barth explicitly states, on the basis of biblical exegesis, that Adam is not "male" before the creation of the "female") it nonetheless becomes male in the discussion of sexual difference. The "woman" is from the first a problem, an object of the text's enquiry, and it is the nature of an object of enquiry to be silent. On the one hand, then, woman is fully human. So if she is silent, her silence cannot simply be assumed; it must, to some extent, be explained as an action. On the other hand, woman is an object, and her silence is an inevitable consequence of her positioning within the text.

Barth describes woman as a "mystery" to man, and therefore able to meet him as an inalienable Other. He refers, for example, to "the reality and multi-dimensional depth of the unmistakable mystery of the existence of woman and the sex relationship".[14] Her mystery is, however, not allowed to remain multi-dimensional; her silences must be explained, until in the discussion of the New Testament passages her silent existence is fully transparent: "She cannot be mistaken, but can be recognized without any effort on her part".[15] The logic of rendering women mute requires from them not only silence, but unambiguous silence.

Michel de Certeau's comments on the logic of torture are instructive here.[16] The torture victim, for de Certeau, is required to speak a word of surrender and then fall silent, but, paradoxically, the speech must not be heard, for it simultaneously reveals the violence that produces the victim's silence. The woman in Barth's text is made to give an unheard consent to her own silencing. Of course, we hear from Barth, she accepted man's choice of her and the place she was thus allocated in the order of creation. Of course the women who keep silent in the churches do not perceive their own silence as lack.

What function is this silence of women made to serve within the text? In its context in Genesis, it provides the basis for a crucial comparison between sexual difference and the ontological difference. Woman's silence, which accepts man's election, is held in a precarious analogical relation to human acceptance of God's election. Barth writes: "Woman is as little asked about her attitude to man as was solitary man about his attitude to God when God animated him by His breath".[17] The silence of woman is the silence of one who hears and accepts the word of electing love.

What can we say of this specification of women's silence? If we ignore its association with "woman", we can see its theological importance. It signals the perfect adequacy of the word of election to the one who hears it, so that nothing more needs to be said. It is the intimate silence of the disciples with Jesus at the end of John's Gospel: "No one dared to ask, 'Who are you?'; they knew it was the Lord".[18] It is the silence of the disciples who, in the words of Whittier, in response to "the gracious calling", "without a word/Rise up and follow".[19]

The crucial point about this silence, however, is that it relies for its significance on its status as a free act. Muteness cannot keep silent. It cannot, therefore, keep silent as a sign of complete and joyful acceptance of God's call. Barth's interpretation of the silence of the woman in Genesis relies on her being paradoxically both free and unfree. She must be free, because she must signal by her silence her acceptance of her election. She must be unfree, because her silence is decreed from the beginning and by her nature; her creation out of man means she has no choice. Man, in the story as Barth tells it, has a choice: to speak or keep silent; woman is required to be silent in order to symbolize, for man, what his silence might mean.

VON BALTHASAR'S *JAWORT*

A similar problem appears in von Balthasar's development of a theology of sexual difference. Like Barth, he uses the image of woman as "answer" to man. In von Balthasar's discussion, however, the "woman's answer" is from the start a "double answer". There is the personal answer which constitutes the completion of the I–Thou relationship, in terms already familiar from Barth; man "requires the existence of the other . . . in order to make his own perfection possible".[20] Beside this, and inseparable from it, however, is the answer which transcends that relationship, the answer expressed in terms of *Fruchtbarkeit*, fruitfulness or fertility. The female or the feminine principle does not carry and bring forth a form determined by the male, but "something new, in which his gift is indeed integrated, but which encounters him in an unexpected, renewed form".[21] In von Balthasar's Mariology and Ecclesiology this double answer is developed in terms of the "bridal" and "maternal" roles of Mary and the Church. Again, woman *is* the answer and does not *give* it; so again, despite the use of a "conversational" image to depict sexual difference, woman is constructed as silent. In a later section of the *Theo-Drama*, Mary's relation to the life of Christ is portrayed as a silent one; she conceives and bears the child in silence and shares the silence of the crucifixion.[22]

Here, again, the characterization of woman as answer, rather than as the one who answers, points to a tension between the need to render her a fully human subject and the tendency to objectify her. The immense significance of Mary in von Balthasar's *Theo-Drama* heightens this and the other tensions to which I have referred.

An utterance by Mary—the *Jawort*, the word that accepts what is promised in the annunciation—is central to von Balthasar's *Theo-Drama*. The whole possibility of that drama rests on the establishment of a position from which she can give that response. In terms of the "theo-drama" of the male–female encounter, von Balthasar's insistence on the "double answer" and the requirement that woman's answer should be "something new" makes it even more important that she should be given an independent subject-position from which to respond. The inexplicability of woman, the irreducibility of her otherness, is the precondition of her "double answer". Yet Mary is characterized as pure "answer"—and as pure "femininity". She gives her consent, her *Jawort*, silently, and falls silent.[23]

Gawronski's discussion of "Word and silence" in von Balthasar's theology is illuminating partly for its portrayal of sexual difference in relation to silence and speech. Mary's silence before God, her listening obedience, is characterized as "feminine", and at the same time presented as the primary stance of the whole Church, indeed of the whole of redeemed creation. "Masculine" approaches to prayer—the use of prayer techniques, the attempt to take possession of God—are condemned as the spiritual equivalent of the "sin of Sodom".[24] Men within the Church, it seems, are enjoined to learn to keep silent; to discover, spiritually, their "feminine side", or to play a "feminine" role. We saw in Barth, also, that man by virtue of his positioning within the text has the ability both to speak and to keep silent.

But gender difference, Gawronski insists with von Balthasar, must be preserved; so women are not to play a "masculine" role, not to participate themselves in the interweaving of speech and significant silence which forms the Church's activity.[25] They are not to keep silent but to *be* silent, in a silence whose significance is known primarily to the male theologian who observes and speaks of it. They are to remain mute, speaking only to reaffirm their muteness. If this line of thought is taken much further, the inevitable conclusion is that women, in these theologies, are not and cannot be fully human or fully part of the redeemed relationship of humanity to God. If silence is their nature, it cannot be their act. It cannot be a vocation they accept or a role they play. Like Mary in the *Theo-Drama*, all women, in von Balthasar's vision of the Church, are defined by and confined to their "feminine" silence.

THE EXPLANATION OF THE INEXPLICABLE

In both Barth's and von Balthasar's treatments of the silence of women, we see both a determination of woman as inherently silent and a determination of woman's silence as significant in a particular way for the observers—supposedly the whole Church, but often implicitly limited to men. Women are not just mute persons who might at some future time retain the possibility of speech; they become less than persons. They are symbols, images, "answers". An answer is spoken, read, or interpreted; it does not speak, read, or interpret itself. The construction of women's silence constructs necessary silences. It is necessary, within the theological systems of Barth and von Balthasar, that there should be silence in creation so that the Word of God can be heard and creation can respond obediently. It is necessary that there should be silence, in order for dialogue to take place. It is necessary to preserve the possibility of silence being kept within the Church. Woman is used to mark the place of this necessary silence.

It is also important to note, however—this is the second tension to which I referred—that von Balthasar, and Barth to a lesser extent, make a double demand of woman's silence. On the one hand, they require woman's silence to have a clear significance—the obedient hearing of God's Word. On the other hand, insofar as sexual *difference* is itself important to them, they require woman's silence to be in some way inexplicable. Woman's silence denotes her difference, her mysteriousness, the impossibility of assimilating her to the monologue of male discourse. For von Balthasar, this difference is what permits the "double answer" of woman to man (and, within the *Theo-Drama*, of creation to God), the "fruitful" answer, which brings about something "new" and unexpected. For Barth, this difference is what makes human existence inescapably relational, constituted by "I" and "Thou". Woman's silence marks this indispensable difference. But, at the same time, woman's silence is constructed, interpreted and controlled, assimilated to the monologue.

IRIGARAY'S SILENT WOMAN

It is worth noting that both Barth and von Balthasar derive woman's silence from biblical narratives, particular narrated silences of women, which are taken to reveal some essential aspect of the feminine nature, and are developed into explorations of aspects of the relation of God and humanity. The interpretation of narrated silences is rarely straightforward, as the diversity of opinion among biblical commentators regarding the silence of Christ before Pilate, for example, clearly shows. Is it possible to re-read the narrated silences of women, not as imposed muteness but as significant silence?

Luce Irigaray's 'Epistle to the Last Christians' concludes with a tentative question: "Grace that speaks silently through and beyond the word?"[26] A recurring theme throughout the piece is the silence of Mary. The proclamation of Christianity makes her, as Irigaray describes it, the "dumb virgin, with her lips closed", not permitted to speak herself, but only to hear and reproduce the "Word of the Father". Irigaray identifies the paradoxical demand made by the theological tradition of Mary; that she should utter a "silent yes" to the divine will and, in doing so, establish her own silence. Christianity can be "saved" from the erasure of difference—and of embodiment—by ending Mary's muteness. She must be "unsealed" from her "silent yes" and "given the Word".[27] Irigaray's central question is: "Who listens to the annunciation Mary makes?"

What Irigaray offers, however, is not straightforwardly a critique but rather a reinterpretation of Mary's silence. The "annunciation Mary makes" is intimately connected with her keeping of silence. Irigaray re-describes Mary's silence as that of "the only one left who still has some understanding of the divine . . . who still listens silently".[28] Her silence both learns and expresses the "grace that speaks silently through and beyond the word"; it signals the revelation of God in what cannot be completely assimilated to one word, one discourse, or one philosophical system. It signals the unrecognized implications of incarnation—the "Word's faithfulness to the flesh" above and beyond the "redemptory submission of flesh to the Word".[29]

Asking "Who listens to the annunciation Mary makes?" points to a dramatic revaluation of Mary's silence. It becomes a communicative silence deliberately chosen. Like all communicative silences, it is not replaceable by speech, but makes sense only in the context of the possibility of speech.

In the introduction to this paper, I referred to the muteness of Zechariah. Luke's birth narrative contains a contrasting instance of silence in Luke's Gospel: "But Mary treasured all these words, and pondered them in her heart".[30] The verbs used, συντηρέω and συμβάλλω, both have the component συν . . . "with", together with. What seems to be indicated here is a "gathering" of the words. Mary "takes in" all that is said, in order to "draw it together". Commentaries often suggest that this verse is intended to identify Mary as a witness; she recounted the story faithfully to the evangelist or the disciples. If we accept that explanation, Mary becomes again a silent "receptacle" for the words of others, for the Word of the Father. She can contribute nothing of her own, she can say nothing of her own. Her silence is fully transparent to the interpreter, its meaning and use fully within his control; and she herself means nothing by it.

We can, however, re-read this narrated silence. Mary's "treasuring" of the words is open-ended; she never speaks again in the Gospel narrative, except briefly to question the young Jesus in the Temple.[31] If her listening is described in order to identify her as a witness, it remains the case that her "witness" itself is never mentioned within the confines of the text. The possibilities created by this listening are never stated. Is she acting only as a "receptacle" for the words? Or is she gathering them actively, drawing them together in her thoughts, to allow new words or thoughts to emerge? Her silence contains the whole Gospel narrative, because it gathers together the words of prophecy spoken at the birth of Christ and carries them forward to their fulfilment; but it also points to the incompleteness, the openness to new speech, of this or any theological narrative. It points to and reveals the limitless, unassimilable and endlessly generative grace of God. Unless, of course, Mary never speaks again because she is forced to be silent, because nobody hears her, or because she has handed over her silence and its interpretation to the Gospel's author. The silence can only be revelatory if there is the possibility of Mary speaking and being heard.

Von Balthasar affirms the "second answer" given by woman to man; he wants to make Mary other than a silent and passive receptacle of the Word; he wants to affirm the centrality of difference to his theological scheme; he wants, it seems, to "listen to the annunciation Mary makes". Barth likewise wants to retain irreducible difference within his system as the basis for human community. They try to develop the "silence of woman" in order to do precisely this, but by defining women as inherently silent, and by presenting their silence as something that can be fully explained and controlled, they lose its capacity to signify difference. The silence they are left with is a meaningless emptiness in which the monologue of their theological discourse resounds. Developing a theology that gives genuine value to sexual difference will involve analysing and critiquing women's muteness. But it may also involve attending to the possibilities signalled by the keeping of silence.

Notes

1. For a summary of these critiques see M. Dumais, *Le Sacre et l'autre parole selon une voix féministe*, in E. D. Blodgett and H. G. Coward (eds.), *Silence, the Word and the Sacred* (Waterloo: Wilfred Laurier University Press, 1989).
2. See also R. Muers, *A Question of Two Answers: Difference and Determination in Barth and von Balthasar*, in *Heythrop Journal* 40(3) (1999).
3. See, for a lengthy consideration of this, B. Dauenhauer, *Silence: the Phenomenon and its Ontological Significance* (Bloomington: Indiana University Press, 1980).
4. Luke 2:19; Mark 3:4; Mark 9:6; Mark 16:8; Mark 15:5.
5. Luke 1:20.
6. 'Der Summe hat umgekehrt die Tendenz zum "Sprechen". Ein Stummer hat nicht nur nicht bewiesen, daß er schweigen kann, es fehlt ihm sogar jede Möglichkeit, dergleichen zu beweisen.' M. Heidegger, *Sein und Zeit* (Tübingen: Niemeyer, 1993 (1927)), 164 f. Trans. as *Being and Time* by J. Macquarrie and E. Robinson (Oxford: Blackwell, 1962), 208.
7. See on this R. Mortley, *From Word to Silence*, vol. ii: *The Way of Negation* (Bonn: Hanstein, 1986), 37, 63 ff.
8. Mark 9:17 ff:, Luke 19:40.
9. L. Irigaray, *This Sex Which is Not One*, trans. C. Porter and C. Burke (Ithaca, NY: Cornell University Press, 1985), 91. For a discussion of this theme in Irigaray, see M. Walker, 'Silence and Reason: Women's Voice in Philosophy', *Australian Journal of Philosophy* 71(4) (1993).
10. R. Gawronski, *Word and Silence* (Edinburgh: T. & T. Clark, 1995).
11. K. Barth, *Church Dogmatics*, trans. G. W. Bromiley (Edinburgh: T. & T. Clark, 1948), vol. iii(1), 290.
12. Ibid. 303, 327.
13. Ibid. 186 ff.
14. Ibid. 297.
15. Ibid. 327.
16. M. de Certeau, *Heterologies*, trans. B. Massumi (Manchester: Manchester University Press, 1986), 40 f.
17. Barth, *Church Dogmatics*, vol. iii(1), 303.
18. John 21:12.
19. J. G. Whittier, 'Dear Lord and Father of Mankind', in *Quaker Faith and Practice* (London: Religious Society of Friends (Quakers), 1995), extract 20: 03.
20. H. U. von Balthasar, *Man in History*, trans. W. Glen-Doepel (London: SCM, 1968), 306.
21. H. U. von Balthasar, *Theo-Drama*, trans. G. Harrison (San Francisco: Ignatius Press, 1988), vol iii, 286.
22. Ibid. 358 ff.
23. See on this L. Gardner and M. Moss, 'Something Like Time: Something Like the Sexes', in L. Ayres *et al.* (eds.), *Balthasar at the End of Modernity* (Edinburgh: T. & T. Clark, 1998).
24. H. U. von Balthasar, *Sponsa Verbi* (Einsiedeln: Johannes Verlag, 1961), 198. Published in English as *Spouse of the Word*, trans. A. V. Littledale with A. Dru (San Francisco: Ignatius Press, 1991), quoted passage p. 188.
25. See H. U. von Balthasar, *New Elucidations*, trans. M. Skerry (San Francisco: Ignatius Press, 1986), 189 ff.

26. L. Irigaray, 'Epistle to the Last Christians', in *Marine Lover of Friedrich Nietzsche*, trans. G. C. Gill (New York: Columbia University Press, 1991).
27. Ibid. 171.
28. Ibid. 175.
29. Ibid. 169.
30. ἡ δὲ Μαριὰμ πάντα συνετήρει τὰ ῥήματα ταῦτα συμβάλλουσα ἐν τῇ καρδίᾳ αὐτῆς. Luke 2:19.
31. Luke 2:48.

Part III. Sacred Texts: Your Word is a Lamp to My Feet

Feminist philosophy of science (to take an arbitrary example) may affect many women indirectly, but its primary readers are professional philosophers and scientists, and its direct impact limited in the main to the women who read it. Feminist theological writing, on the other hand, is read by many women who are not professionals, and it affects directly the lives of millions of women in faith communities. Most Jewish or Christian women need to negotiate between their identities as women and as members of faith communities, and wherever these negotiations occur, sacred texts are bound to loom large. Women who wish to remain within a faith community must seek points of contact between their lives and their sacred texts. The nature of their search varies in detail, but can be divided into four broad areas of concern: the maleness of the biblical God; the use (usually by men) of the Bible to determine practical aspects of women's lives, from ritual to romance; the relationship of female readers to texts written by men, for men, primarily about men; and membership of a perceived guild of 'qualified' readers, living and long dead. Women who belong to avowedly egalitarian denominations may encounter fewer problems than others in the third and fourth of these areas, but egalitarianism by no means signals an end to all tensions.

If women from all walks of life seek significance and relevance in their sacred texts, with many turning to feminist theological writing for illumination if not answers, it is worth asking how directly and effectively feminist Bible scholars treat the challenges confronting female readers of the Bible. Not all feminist approaches mesh well with the needs of women in faith communities. Exposing the misogyny inherent in the history of interpretation or revealing that the Bible is biased against women is one thing. Working to show that the Bible as a whole is irredeemably misogynistic is something else again, and women who reach this conclusion may feel obliged to sever the thread binding them to their sacred text and to organized religion as a whole. Yet although responding to the needs of women is not necessarily an objective of feminist Bible scholarship, professional feminists seem to be remarkably successful in addressing the grassroots

121

requirements of women outside the academy. Let us briefly count some ways in which they engage with the four areas of difficulty mentioned above.

First, God's maleness is an important theme for feminists who study the Hebrew Bible in its ancient Near Eastern context (see Athalya Brenner). Some women may find it helpful to consider God's maleness in its original historical and sociological context, bearing in mind the imagery available at the time and the need to counteract polytheism and the influence of fertility cults. (Other women may, of course, be further alienated by posited links between the scarcity of feminine imagery in relation to God and sociopolitical conditions in ancient Israel.) Second, while attempts to demonstrate female authorship of the Bible are few and far between, much feminist scholarship is devoted to the twin tasks of showing that sacred texts yield new fruits when read from a woman's perspective and foregrounding female characters (see Phyllis Trible). The latter shares much in common with the midrashic interest in imaginative expansion of biblical characters. Anita Diamant's fictional treatment of Dinah in *The Red Tent* might be described as modern midrash, as might the first-person narratives in which feminist Bible scholars and others develop marginal characters through the genre of pseudo-autobiography. Third, feminist re-readings of biblical texts support women who seek greater or enhanced participation in organized religions. The creation of woman in Genesis 2 is an important proof text in many religious debates about the rights and roles of women, and feminist Bible scholars have contributed here by showing that the text does not necessarily envisage woman as second to be created, let alone secondary or second-rate. At the same time, they have drawn attention to prominent roles for women in some biblical (especially New Testament) texts that seem at odds with their low profile in post-biblical Judaism and Christianity (see Pheme Perkins). Fourth, feminist Bible scholars have addressed in at least three different ways the feeling shared by many women of being excluded from a perceived guild of authorized interpreters: women can, if they wish, join the guild, reading successfully according to traditional methods of exegesis; they can operate effectively outside the guild by inventing or adapting their own rules for textual interpretation; and they can call into question the validity of the guild and its rules. Examples of these approaches can be found in what follows and in other sections of this book.

It will be clear by now that we are concerned here with the sacred texts of Judaism and Christianity, but women from other religious traditions are beginning to reread their own sacred texts through a feminist lens. Though by no means extensive, a literature is emerging (see for example *Daughters of Abraham: Feminist Thought in Judaism, Christianity, and Islam*, edited by Yvonne Y. Haddad and John L. Esposito (Gainesville: University of Florida Press, 2001)). It will be fascinating to follow the development of this new enterprise.

DL

14 The Hand that Rocks the Cradle

J. Cheryl Exum*

A useful feature of Cheryl Exum's chapter on the female characters in the early Exodus narrative is that it contains a brief history of interpretation of the author's own views on her chosen text, the story of the midwives in Exodus 1 and 2. Here is a woman who is not afraid to say that she has changed her mind. As well as providing a personal case study of the development of feminist Bible scholarship, the article offers insights into such issues as the unintended side effects of certain methodologies. She points out that the popular practice of 'reading against the grain'—identifying the writer's ideology and reading the text for the opposite message—risks giving the impression of being out of step with the plausible majority that reads with the grain. Exum is equally concerned about the 'logocentric constraints' on the kinds of literary analysis that have proved so popular with feminist critics, recommending instead an approach that combines textual exegesis with sociological questions about the condition of women in ancient Israel. While there is a sense in which the biblical text serves here as a focus for Exum's thoughts on feminist hermeneutics, it also generates some excellent exegesis. Of particular interest in relation to Alicia Ostriker's modern midrash on Judges is Exum's observation that Miriam's objection to Moses' Cushite wife may serve as an unhappy corrective to the dangerous cooperation across ethnic boundaries between the women of Exodus 1 and 2.   DL

> Why did Moses have a sister?
>
> Edmund Leach

> . . . each reading of a book, each rereading, each
> memory of that rereading, reinvents the text.
>
> Jorge Luis Borges, *Seven Nights*

* J. Cheryl Exum, 'The Hand that Rocks the Cradle', from *Plotted, Shot and Painted: Cultural Representations of Biblical Women*. Copyright © Sheffield Academic Press, 1996. Reprinted by permission of The Continuum International Publishing Group.

This chapter is a story, somewhat autobiographical, about reading—a story about reading and rereading the account of Moses' birth, a biblical narrative in which women play a central role. The story is autobiographical because it documents one reader's changing responses to the text in the light of feminism and of the critical responses feminists have developed for dealing with androcentrism in the fundamental texts of the Western literary canon (and with the androcentric history of their interpretation). The story begins in the modulated tones of the male-defined academic discourse in which I was trained and ends (for now) also within an academic discourse, within which I of necessity operate, but one whose terms I insist on having a role in defining.

In 1983 my article, ' "You Shall Let Every Daughter Live": A Study of Exodus 1.8–2.10', appeared in an issue of *Semeia* devoted to *The Bible and Feminist Hermeneutics.*[1] I never liked the article. It would be more accurate, and more honest, to say that I never liked the text. A story of five women and a baby. Women, it is true, are very important in these opening chapters of Exodus, but the subject of their activity is a male infant, Moses, who soon takes over the story and dominates it, while women fade into the background. His mother, his sister, and the pharaoh's daughter (accompanied by women servants) are directly involved in preserving the infant Moses' life; and although the midwives do not interact with him directly, by implication they save his life when they do not obey the pharaoh's command to kill male babies. We never hear of Shiphrah, Puah, and the pharaoh's daughter again after Exodus 2, and Moses' mother appears again only in his genealogy (Exod. 6.20; Num. 26.59). Of the many active female characters in Exod. 1.8–2.10, only Moses' sister has a role in the subsequent narrative, one that, apparently, the biblical writers felt the need to suppress (cf. Exod. 15.21 with 15.1–18)[2] or discredit (Num. 12).

Exod. 1.8–2.10 was not a text that I would have chosen for analysis of my own accord. My article was a revision of a position paper that Letty Russell invited me to present in a joint symposium of the Women and Religion Section and the Liberation Theology Group of the American Academy of Religion, which took place at the 1981 Annual Meeting of the American Academy of Religion and Society of Biblical Literature. Exod. 1.8–2.10 seemed an obvious choice as one of the topics for a panel discussion of the intersecting interests of feminist and liberation theology. The existence of a special joint session called 'The Feminist Hermeneutic Project' was an indication of the attention feminist interpretation was beginning to receive in the field of Religious Studies. At that time, one of the goals of the emerging feminist biblical criticism was to uncover positive portrayals of women in the Bible—as if one could simply pluck positive images out of an admittedly androcentric text, separating literary characterizations from the androcentric interests they were created to serve.[3]

A few years later, in a short essay that discussed a number of biblical 'mothers', I turned again to Exod. 1.8–2.10, this time using the opportunity to express my dissatisfaction with my earlier work. My conclusion bears citing here as much for what it does not say as for what it does say.

I have dealt at length in another study with the women in the prologue to the exodus ... I must confess that I was never satisfied with the results. The reason, I believe, has to do with disappointment that the narrative quickly and thoroughly moves from a woman's story to a man's story. While a feminist critique might want to seize onto the affirmative dimension of our paradox [without Moses there would be no exodus, but without these women there would be no Moses], accenting the important consequences of women's actions for the divine plan, it must also acknowledge that being mothers of heroes—albeit daring, enterprising, and tenacious mothers—is not enough; acting behind the scenes is not enough.[4]

Whereas I recognized the limitations of the portrayal of women in Exodus 1–2, I had nothing to offer by way of response beyond this kind of feeble objection, and thus was left with disappointment. It took me years to see that what was needed to move beyond this impasse was a reading strategy that could expose and critique the ideology that motivates the biblical presentation of women. I adopted such a strategy in my 1993 book, *Fragmented Women* (published ten years after the Exodus article), but I did not take up the Exodus story again in that work. I had no intention of writing about this text again until Athalya Brenner approached me about reprinting ' "You Shall Let Every Daughter Live" ' in *A Feminist Companion to Exodus to Deuteronomy*. I felt I could not let that article stand without some comment about how my thinking had changed, and so I wrote a companion piece entitled, 'Secondary Thoughts about Secondary Characters', indicating what I would do differently if I were writing about Exodus 1–2 in 1994 instead of 1983.[5] Even now, I have no desire to offer another detailed study of Exod. 1.8–2.10 and other texts related to it. I propose rather to build on my most recent contribution to the debate by indicating some of the questions I believe a feminist critique attentive to gender politics should ask and by looking more closely at the reader's role in producing meaning in the light of postmodern literary theory. In doing so, I will address two major problems with my 1983 article. Although I address them with specific reference to my own article, they are problems that, in my opinion, still characterize some of the work that goes under the rubric of feminist interpretation today.[6] The first problem is that because I used a literary method that remained within the ideology of the text, I was able only to describe the view of women expressed in the text and not to critique it. The second is that although I mentioned the problem of the absence of women in the narrative after one moves beyond the first few chapters of Exodus—an absence as striking as the presence of so many women in the first four chapters—I did not investigate the relationship of this absence to the noticeable presence of women in the opening chapters in terms of gender politics.

LITERARY ANALYSIS AND THE IDEOLOGY OF THE TEXT

The approach I used to analyze the text in ' "You Shall Let Every Daughter Live" ' was essentially a form of New Criticism as biblical scholars were practicing it in the 1960s and 1970s under the names of 'close reading' and 'rhetorical criticism', an approach that 'investigates the narrative in its present form on the premise that an understanding of its literary contours will aid us in perceiving its meaning'.[7] The method led me to focus on such stylistic features as narrative arrangement, key words and phrases, the paralleling of characters, as well as tropes, such as irony, and unusual details, such as the fact that the names of the two midwives are reported. All of these devices, I argued, work together to foreground the important role of women in the story. In terms of narrative arrangement, I divided the account of Exod. 1.8–2.10 into two parts with three movements. In the first part (1.8–22), which deals with the threat to the Hebrews as a people, my analysis sought to show how the pharaoh, though he initiates the action by proposing rather absurd solutions to the problem of Hebrew overpopulation, yields his narrative centrality to women, as the midwives change the course of events by defying his command to kill the Hebrew male babies. In the second part (2.1–10), which deals with the threat to one particular Hebrew, the baby Moses, many women appear but men are strikingly absent (Moses' father disappears from the story after v. 1) or passive (Moses cries, v. 6, and grows up, v. 10, but otherwise is the object of the women's actions). Thus, I argued, not only do women take over the story in Part 1, but also 'the speech and action of women shape the contours of [Part 2 of] the story'.

Moses' mother acts but, interestingly, does not speak. In contrast, his sister and pharaoh's daughter both act and speak. The story begins with a detailed account of the action of one woman, a daughter of Levi (vv. 2–3). A small but significant role is assigned to Moses' sister (v. 4). Next we hear of considerable activity on the part of yet another woman, the daughter of pharaoh (vv. 5–6), followed by the vital speech of the sister (v. 7). Though she has little action and only one speech, the sister is crucial to the development of the story. She has the critical linking role between the two daughters (vv. 4, 7). Once all three women are involved, narrative attention moves quickly back and forth between them (vv. 7–10), until finally an unnamed daughter gives our hero his identity: 'she called his name Moses'.[8]

The three movements of the story (1.8–14; 1.15–21; 1.22–2.10)[9] are concerned with the pharaoh's three attempts to curb the growth of the Hebrew population. In the first of these, his people carry out his command to afflict the Hebrews with hard service, but this solution is unsuccessful and the Hebrews only increase all the more. The next two movements are both stories of defiance in which the pharaoh's plan to kill the Hebrew male babies, among whom the baby Moses should be numbered, is thwarted by women. The subtle defiance of the mid-wives, who act by choosing not to act in accordance with the pharaoh's death edict, is followed by the open defiance of Moses' mother and of the pharaoh's daughter, who, in direct opposition to her father's command, saves the infant Moses from death by exposure on the Nile.[10] The narrative progression, then, is from action determined by the pharaoh in the first movement (but not successfully), to the pharaoh sharing the stage with the midwives in the second—where the midwives, in fact, have the last word with their clever explanation of their failure to obey the pharaoh's decree ('before the midwife comes to [the Hebrew women] they are delivered', 1.19)—to the third movement, where the pharaoh drops out of the story immediately after issuing the directive to kill male babies, and the stage is shared by a mother, a sister, and a daughter (his daughter), whose initiatives determine the course of events. 'This increasing concentration on women', I concluded, 'invites us to consider the significance of the fact that ancient Israelite storytellers gave women a crucial role in the initial stages of the major event in the nation's history'.[11]

I looked not only to narrative arrangement but also to key words for clues to the narrative emphasis on the women's important roles; for example, the key terms 'son' (*ben*) and 'daughter' (*bat*) are strategically placed at key points in the narrative. The semantic range of *ben* becomes increasingly narrow as the focus shifts from the '*sons of Israel*' as a people to one particular *son*, Moses, while the occurrences of *bat* alert us to the vital roles played by daughters in a story about a famous son. The pharaoh's last words, 'every son that is born you shall expose on the Nile, but every daughter you shall let live' (1.22), are followed immediately by the introduction of a *daughter* of Levi (2.1) and soon thereafter (2.5) by the *daughter* of the pharaoh himself, both of whom defy his edict, with his own daughter adopting the boy and raising him as her own. Thus the story of Moses' birth begins with the birth of a son (*ben*) to the daughter (*bat*) of Levi (2.2) and ends with his becoming a son (*ben*) to the daughter (*bat*) of the pharaoh (2.10). Aesthetically this is really nice, I thought, and, rhetorically speaking, it maintains emphasis equally on sons and daughters. Key phrases function similarly; for example, the pharaoh is identified as the source of death by means of his repeated command to kill boy babies but let the girls live (1.16, 22), while the midwives are identified as the source of life through the repetition of '[they] let the male infants live' (1.17, 18). The implication is that Moses owes his life to the midwives.

The paralleling of characters was yet another device in which I found evidence of narrative interest in the women's roles. A significant series of actions, for example, is attributed both to Moses' mother and to the pharaoh's daughter, and I interpreted these as the narrator's way not only of indicating the importance of both women but also of showing his positive assessment of the pharaoh's daughter.[12]

At two points the narrative pace slows to describe in detail the actions of women, the daughter of Levi and the daughter of pharaoh. The attention they give to the child is comparable, and in fact some of the same terms are used (ראה [see], לקח [take]). By the end of the story, the two daughters have something more in common—a son.[13]

The daughter of the pharaoh who has compassion on the Hebrew baby and saves him by drawing him out of the Nile is also, of course, a counterfoil to her father who seeks the deaths of boy babies by means of the Nile.

These are just some of the features on the surface structure of the text that function to highlight the role of women in this account. I also might mention irony (as in the pharaoh's proposal to kill newborn sons when the logical way to control overpopulation would be to kill daughters; the serious blunder the pharaoh makes in neglecting to exclude Egyptian male babies from the command to expose 'every son' on the Nile in v. 21 of the Hebrew text;[14] the fact that daughters are the real threat in this story), and literary flourishes that put female characters in a positive light, such as the demonstration of rhetorical skill by Moses' sister (her proposal to 'call *for you* a nurse from the Hebrew women to nurse *for you* the child' both provides the idea that the princess keep the baby and creates the impression that she makes the proposal for the princess's sake), or the pun that carries with it the suggestion that the pharaoh's daughter charts Moses' destiny when she gives him a(n Egyptian) name that in Hebrew means 'the drawer out'.

I hope this brief summary of my main points in ' "You Shall Let Every Daughter Live" ' is sufficient to indicate that such a literary approach was, and still is, useful. I still would not question its conclusions that the women in Exodus 1 and 2 are portrayed positively, that they are active and enterprising, and that their actions are important for the future of the Israelite people. The sustained focus on women, the subtle comparisons created by paralleling characters, the ironic twists, the artistic use of the *bat/ben* contrast to make a point—all these things contribute to a striking affirmation of the role of women in the opening chapters of Exodus. Jopie Siebert-Hommes, in articles published in 1988 and 1992,[15] describes further artistic details that highlight the women's roles. When, for example, her stylistic analysis reveals that the twelve tribes owe their deliverance to *twelve daughters*, she shows that the potential of this method is far from exhausted and that it can profitably be used to gain new insights from textual details.

Siebert-Hommes's essays and mine demonstrate, quite persuasively I believe, how positively women are portrayed in Exod. 1.8–2.10. I might note, however, that even in ' "You Shall Let Every Daughter Live" ', I recognized the limits of the portrayal I was describing:

Discussion of women in Exod. 1.8–2.10 requires consideration of their place within the total configuration of the narrative—a narrative which does not become a woman's story until 1.15, and, even then, has as its goal the birth of a *son* who will become the leader of his people.[16]

It is a woman's story in so far as their action determines its direction. But while narrative attention focuses on the activity of women, their attention centers on Moses. Referred to as a בֵן [son], a יֶלֶד [boy], and a נַעַר [lad], at the end of the story *he* is given a name. Thereafter he becomes the central character of the exodus.[17]

Such statements are in tension with my central thesis about the portrayal of women in this text, and considering them now, I would want to seize upon their potential for disrupting my rather sanguine evaluations of the important roles women play in the events preceding the exodus.

This brings me to the problem with this kind of literary analysis: it places logocentric constraints on feminist criticism. By focusing solely on the surface structure of the text, on the ways literary devices and structures serve as guides to meaning, it limits us to describing, and thus to reinscribing, the text's gender ideology. I now see this method as confining, and as representing, or at least serving, the phallocentric drive to control and organize reading (and reality) into clearly defined categories. If we read according to the ideology of the text available to us in the surface structure, and stop there, we are left with the ancient (male) authors' views of women, which, in the case of Exodus 1–2, happen to be affirmative. But to see how the positive portrayal of women in Exod. 1.8–2.10 nevertheless serves male interests, we need to interrogate the ideology that motivates it. Granted that women are given important roles here—and, indeed, precisely because women are given such important roles here—we need to ask, What androcentric interests does this positive presentation promote? Key questions for a feminist critique of these chapters are, What is it about the women in Exod. 1.8–2.10 that makes them characters with whom women in ancient Israel might have wished to identify?[18] And what is it about these female characters that makes those responsible for maintaining the social and symbolic order want to manipulate them?[19] I can only begin to address these questions here.

STEPPING OUTSIDE THE IDEOLOGY OF THE TEXT

As feminist critics have pointed out, even though men and women share in the making of history, symbolic production has been controlled by men.[20] Even if the Bible's authors were not all males, the dominant male world-view is the world-view that finds expression in the biblical literature. I begin, therefore, with the assumption that the biblical literature was produced by and for an androcentric community. I understand women in the biblical literature as male constructs. They are the creations of androcentric (probably male) narrators, they reflect androcentric ideas about women, and they serve androcentric interests. What Esther Fuchs observes about biblical mothers applies to other female characters as well: they 'reveal more about the wishful thinking, fears, aspirations, and prejudices of their male creators than about women's authentic lives'.[21] Since as long as we remain within the androcentric ideology of the text, we can do no more than describe ancient men's views of women, a feminist critique must, of necessity, read against the grain. It must step outside the text's ideology and consider what androcentric agenda these narratives promote.

The concepts of stepping outside the ideology of the text and reading against the grain are crucial to me as a feminist reader, but require perhaps some explanation in the light of two important methodological objections. One is that texts do not have ideologies.[22] I agree with this critical position in principle. Authors have ideologies and readers have ideologies; texts do not. But speaking of a text's ideology is nonetheless a convenient shorthand way for expressing the idea that texts arise in concrete social situations and reflect the social locations and world-views—in other words, the ideologies—of the writers who produced them. That the Bible may have a long history of transmission and redaction does not change this fact, though it may make analysis more complicated. To say that texts have ideologies is to personalize the text by projecting a reader's response—that is, a reader's perception of the ideology of its writers—onto it. I acknowledge a certain circularity in my argument about the ideology of the text: the androcentric ideology that is the subject of my critique is the one that I as a reader have identified as motivating the text. Similarly, reading against the grain involves first determining what I perceive the grain to be. For my purposes, the grain is another way of speaking about the ideology of the text.

The other objection to the concept of reading against the grain is that to describe one's reading as 'against the grain' gives the impression that it is an idiosyncratic or individualistic reading as over against the majority of readings that read with the grain. This could suggest to some that (androcentric) readings with the grain are somehow more 'accurate' interpretations of the 'meaning' of the text, what the text is 'really about', or that they are less subjective or less influenced by gender interests than feminist readings.[23] It seems to me that, in the present intellectual climate, any commentator who openly identifies her or his interests risks the charge of subjectivity from readers and critics who still believe that there is such a thing as a neutral or objective interpretation. The role gender and other interests play in the interpretive process should not be minimized. To think that interpretation can be neutral or objective would be to assume that meaning resides in the text. My position, and one borne out by the story of reading this chapter tells, is that meaning resides in the interaction between reader and text.

In response to these two objections to the concepts of stepping outside the ideology of the text and of reading against the grain, I appeal to certain properties of texts highlighted by recent critical practices that go under the name of deconstruction.[24] Deconstruction draws attention to the slipperiness of language and the instabilities of texts, with their infinite deferral of meaning. Because the logic of every text is non-unitary, a text inevitably undermines its main thesis. A text typically promotes or takes for granted some set of oppositions, privileging one term as prior to or positively valued over its partner; for example, good/evil, purity/pollution, rational/emotional, objective/ subjective, culture/nature, or what some feminists have identified as the primary opposition, male/female.[25] Deconstruction reveals the text's inability to sustain these oppositions by exposing chinks in the text's logical premises. It does not reverse the oppositions but rather challenges the conceptual system that makes opposition possible in the first place.

Deconstruction focuses primarily on how texts work, and not on the reading process, which is what concerns me most as a feminist critic. The ideology outside of which I stand and the grain against which I speak of reading is what, in a deconstructionist mode, I would call the main thesis of the text (here I refer especially to the privileging of male over female and related oppositions).[26] I want to expose the difficulty a patriarchal text like the Bible has in maintaining patriarchal authority, and to see how a focus on a (suppressed, displaced) female version of the story can subvert the privileged male version. Reading against the grain is not replacing one side of the hierarchy with the other any more than deconstruction is. Its aim is not to offer a reading in which women are privileged in place of a reading that privileges men—for every hierarchy is vulnerable to deconstruction. It seeks rather to subvert the shaky premises upon which the text's androcentric main thesis rests and to offer an alternative (not opposite) reading that gives women characters power by making them the subjects of their own discourse.

As the terms 'suppressed' and 'displaced' above indicate, my own reader-response approach is informed not only by deconstructive strategies but also by insights from psychoanalytic literary criticism.[27] Thus my critique in this chapter centers on investigating the ideology that motivates particular portrayals of women and on looking for the buried or encoded messages that these texts give to women. All of us, women and men, internalize a vast number of messages about gender roles and expectations as part of our socialization into a society built on gender distinctions.[28] And what we learn from reading plays a large role in this socialization process. And so, when I read Exod. 1.8–2.10, I ask, What does this text tell women about how to view themselves and how to behave? And, What does this particular message imply about the people who produced this text? As I indicated above, texts like this tell us as much about the beliefs and prejudices, fears and desires of the writers who created them as they tell us about women in biblical times.

In 1983 I said, 'The question is not *why* does a story of daughters form the prelude to the exodus, but rather: what effect do these stories about women have on the way we read the exodus story as a whole?'[29] That I now want to ask the very question I avoided then shows how my position as a reader of the text has shifted. Why are women allowed to play such an important role in the early chapters of Exodus? A traditional way of understanding the focus on women in Exodus 1–2 is to connect it to a familiar biblical theme: God (behind the scenes, in this case) uses the weak and lowly to overcome the strong and powerful. The inferior, but clever, women successfully defy the powerful Egyptian pharaoh. If there is a positive side to this characterization, there is also a negative one. This particular pharaoh, as I argued in my 1983 article, is exceedingly foolish, so foolish that even women can outwit him![30] Another way of looking at the important role women play in these chapters is to consider it a consequence of the focus on infants: it is only natural that women should appear in an account where babies are concerned. Both these explanations appeal to women's subordinate position and traditional domestic role to account for the emphasis on women in the opening chapters of Exodus, but neither interrogates the text's androcentric motivation.

In order to maintain and perpetuate itself, patriarchy depends on women's complicity.[31] Force, threat, and fear are often relied upon to keep women in their place. But rewarding women for their complicity is one of patriarchy's most useful strategies, because it can often achieve a level of cooperation that force or threat cannot guarantee. The honor of playing a decisive role in the future deliverance of the Israelite people is the reward the women of Exodus 1–2 receive for acting in the service of male power (the real contest in Exodus is, after all, between 'males'—between the Egyptian pharaoh and the male-identified Israelite god, or between the pharaoh and Moses). Women, Exodus 1–2 tells us, are important; without the courage and ingenuity of women, Israel might not have survived as a people. In Exod. 1.8–2.10, the women are accorded recognition as national heroes; their bravery, cleverness, and initiative are instrumental in the founding of a nation. The risks they take to preserve the lives of male babies, especially Moses,[32] guarantees that these women will be honored for generations to come; thus the names of the two midwives, Shiphrah and Puah, are recorded, and the story later supplies the names of Moses' mother Jochebed and sister Miriam.[33]

The text tells women how important mothers are and proposes that the domestic sphere can be a place of valor, where a woman's mettle is tested. Honor and status (the two are related) are rewards patriarchy grants women for assent to their subordination and cooperation in it. One of the few roles in which women can achieve status in patriarchal society is that of mother. Motherhood is not only patriarchy's highest reward for women, it is also presented as something women themselves most desire (witness the many biblical accounts of barren women who desperately desire and finally give birth to a long-awaited son). As Fuchs points out, this is a powerful ideological strategy.[34] The women in Exod. 1.8–2.10 perform traditional female, and especially motherly, activities, activities focused on children—though, of course, they give new meaning to their nurturing and protective roles. The midwives not only assist in birth, they save lives. As a reward for their defiance of the pharaoh's command to kill male babies, God builds them 'houses'; that is, he gives them families.[35] Figuratively speaking, the midwives, Moses' mother, Moses' sister, and the pharaoh's daughter are all mothers of the exodus.[36]

What is it about the women in Exod. 1.8–2.10 that makes them characters with whom women might wish to identify? They exhibit admirable qualities, such as heroism, fear of God (1.17), compassion (2.6), determination (2.2–4), and cleverness (2.7), and they show that women can contribute significantly to the life of their people. The story praises women in the spirit of the old adage that the hand that rocks the cradle rules the world. In essence, its message to women is: stay in your place in the domestic sphere; you can achieve important things there. The public arena belongs to men; you do not need to look beyond motherhood for fulfillment. In Exodus 1–2, Hebrew women do not need to kill Egyptians (fighting is men's work or the work of their male-identified god (Exod. 12.29; 15.24–31)) but only to keep Hebrew males alive.

Sayings like 'the hand that rocks the cradle rules the world' and 'behind every great man is a woman' are meant to make women feel important, while in reality they serve an androcentric agenda by suggesting that women should be satisfied with their power behind the scenes.[37] Exod. 1.8–2.10, where women actively determine Israel's future, serves a similar agenda. It compensates women on the domestic front for the role denied them in the larger story of the exodus and journey to the promised land. But like its modern counterparts in the sayings above about women's indirect power, it has something to hide: the fear of women's power that makes it important to domesticate and confine it.

THE SUBVERSIVE FEMALE PRESENCE AND ITS SUPPRESSION

The women in Exodus 1 and 2 are literary creations, male constructs—and they are powerful. They outwit and overcome men. Precisely because women have power that they can use to subvert authority, they present a threat to patriarchal society. Having acknowledged this threat, the text must somehow circumscribe and control this female power. It is therefore in the interest of those who maintain the social and symbolic order to represent women characters as using their power in the service of patriarchy.

Historically patriarchy has relied on class divisions and ethnic divisions among women to prevent women from forming alliances that might further the cause of their sex. Michal's introduction in 2 Samuel 6:20 of a class distinction between herself and David's 'male servants' women servants' allowed the narrator to isolate her from other women at the very moment he was isolating her so effectively from David, thus making it easier for the narrator, and David, to do away with her. Women do not often interact or speak to one another in the Bible, yet here in Exodus 2 we find Moses' mother, his sister, an Egyptian princess, and the princess's women servants all engaged in protecting the infant Moses from the pharaoh's death edict. Whereas the text offers a glimpse of the formidable threat posed to male authority when women cooperate across class and ethnic lines, it co-opts women's power for its own ends: it uses an alliance between women to defy the foreign authority that oppresses the Hebrew people. Moreover, the text describes a fairly unlikely alliance. That an Egyptian princess would openly defy her father's command to expose male babies on the Nile by taking the infant out of the Nile, and that she would adopt a Hebrew baby, could be considered 'providential'. Indeed, by having the sister appear suddenly to put the idea of adopting Moses in the princess's mind, the narrator suggests that the deity, rather than any decision by women to work together, is responsible for the propitious outcome.

One way of dealing with women's power is to diffuse it. In Exodus 1–2 this is accomplished by having three (or five) 'mothers' rescue Moses, rather than one. Imagine the power one woman would have had if she alone had saved Moses.[38] Diffusing the influence of women, I believe, is also the reason Moses' mother and sister are anonymous in this account; by withholding their names until later in the narrative, the narrator accords them less recognition and renders them less imposing.

The role the women play in the birth of the nation is comparable to the role usually played by mothers in the Bible: they yield their power, and their stories, to their husbands and sons.[39] Like a child dissociating itself from its mother, Moses must separate from his 'mothers' and exchange his passive role for an active one. Thus, almost immediately after he is rescued by *daughters* (recall the meaningful use of *bat* in Exod. 1.8–2.10), Moses rescues *daughters*. In Exod. 2.16–22, Moses—who in the space of five verses has grown up, killed an Egyptian, and fled the country—delivers seven daughters from shepherds who threaten them when they come to water the flock of their father Reuel (Jethro), the Midianite priest. He marries one of these daughters and has a son of his own (the contrast between *ben*, 'son', and *bat*, 'daughter', continues throughout the chapter). But the reversal of roles is not complete. In Exod. 4.24–26, a foreign woman again saves Moses' life: Zipporah, Moses' wife, prevents the divine Father from killing her husband, through a rite of circumcision that makes him her 'bridegroom of blood'.[40] Typically, she drops out of the picture, and is not mentioned again until Exod. 18.2–5, where we learn that Moses had sent her away.[41] Perhaps we might view the reappearance of a woman to deliver Moses violently as an instance of women refusing to be written out of the text without a struggle; in other words, as a symptom of a guilty narrative conscience. In any event, Moses, unhampered by the woman's presence, moves on to deliver not just women again, but rather a whole people.

After Exodus 4, women are conspicuously absent in much of the narrative of the exodus and journey to the promised land in Exodus, Leviticus, Numbers, and Deuteronomy.[42] The feminine, however, resurfaces in another form. Patriarchy seeks to diffuse, or suppress, or appropriate female power, as the Bible's classic illustration of womb envy dramatically demonstrates: in Genesis 2, the creative power of women is assumed by the prototypical Man who, like Zeus who gave birth to Athena from his head, symbolically gives birth to woman with the help of the creator god (and in the absence of a creator goddess). Perhaps 'womb envy' prompts the application of female metaphors to God and Moses later in the exodus story. In Numbers 11, when the people complain to Moses about not having meat to eat, Moses complains to God about his responsibilities.

Did I conceive all this people? Did I bring them forth, that you should say to me, 'Carry them in your bosom, as a nurse carries the sucking child, to the land which you swore to give their fathers?' . . . I am not able to carry all this people alone, the burden is too heavy for me. (Num. 11.12–14)

Moses, cast in a nurturing, maternal role, finds it too hard, and his rhetorical questions imply that it is God who conceived the people of Israel and who is not doing an adequate job of mothering them. God and Moses are imaged as mother and midwife—roles played by *real women* in Exodus 1–2—not so much because they are better at women's roles (here they seem to have problems, but their difficulties will be resolved), but because male figures in these roles do not threaten the status quo. Applying maternal imagery to the deity and the human hero of the story is a way of appropriating maternal power. Patriarchy does not have to worry that God and Moses, acting as mother and midwife, will subvert androcentric interests and undermine the social order because they are the guarantors of the patriarchal social order.

I suggested above that Exod. 1.8–2.10 serves as a kind of compensation for the fact that women are not given a larger role in the bulk of the account of the exodus and wanderings. When the one woman from Exodus 2 to reappear in an important role does speak out for herself, claiming a position of leadership, she is put in her place. In Num. 12.1–2, we learn that Miriam (and Aaron)[43] speaks out against Moses 'because of the Cushite woman he married'. It is noteworthy that here Miriam is set over against a foreign woman, whereas Exodus 1–2 showed the cooperation between women across ethnic boundaries. Perhaps it is because such a level of cooperation cannot be tolerated that Miriam is used to speak out against a foreign woman in Numbers 12. Once gender solidarity across ethnic lines has been shattered, the complaint shifts abruptly from an objection to the woman to the issue of leadership: 'Has the Lord indeed spoken only through

Moses? Has he not spoken through us also?' (v. 2). The strange account has baffled commentators, not least because only Miriam is punished for challenging Moses' authority. She becomes leprous and must be 'shut up outside the camp seven days', after which she is brought in again.

It is not without significance that this story appears just after the account in which female imagery is used for Moses and God. In Num. 11.16–30 the problem of nurturing the people is resolved by allowing seventy *men*, elders of the community, to share the task. There Moses had proclaimed, 'Would that all the Lord's people were prophets'; here he denies that role to Miriam and undermines her status as prophet (Exod. 15.20). Miriam's punishment of being quarantined outside the boundary of the camp is suggestive of the position that feminist critics have argued is occupied by women in the phallocentric symbolic order.[44] Women are at the boundary of the symbolic order, the border between men and chaos. As borderline figures, women partake of the properties of a border: they are neither inside nor outside. When women are viewed as inside the border, they are seen to have protective qualities (as in Exod. 1 and 2); when viewed as outside, they are dangerous (as here in Num. 12). Miriam's claim to a position of authority comparable to Moses'—and the rhetorical questions imply that God has spoken through her also—threatens to blur the distinction between Moses' role and hers. It challenges male hegemony. Punishment is swift and devastating. For threatening to disrupt the social order, Miriam is put outside the boundary of patriarchal order, symbolized by the camp, where she becomes, literally, the outsider, the other—until she is allowed to come back *inside* the camp/symbolic order in her proper, submissive role. Some commentators have argued that Aaron does not share in Miriam's punishment because he is a priest, and that the Priestly writers of the Pentateuch would not have wanted to dishonor him by portraying him as leprous and having him put outside the camp. Gender politics are also at work, I suggest: as a man, Aaron poses no threat to the symbolic order. On the contrary, his proper place is inside it, and so he remains within the camp. While leaving Aaron unblemished and unpunished, Numbers 12 effectively humiliates and eliminates the woman.

The case of Miriam in Numbers 12 offers but one example of the way women's experience, in the biblical as in other patriarchal texts, is expressed but has been displaced and distorted. But in Miriam's challenge to Moses and in her insistence on speaking out against male hegemony, traces of the woman's point of view remain to unsettle patriarchal authority.

More remains to be done to provide an effective feminist critique of the exodus and wandering traditions. Attempting, as I have done here, to account for the distortion or absence or suppression of female presence after the opening stories in Exodus 1 and 2 in terms of biblical gender politics, rather than treating it as if it were unmotivated, is, I think, a step in the right direction. It is not the last word on this text, and perhaps not even my last word on it.

Notes

1. ' "You Shall Let Every Daughter Live": A Study of Exodus 1:8–2:10', in *The Bible and Feminist Hermeneutics*, ed. Mary Ann Tolbert; Semeia 28 (Decatur, Ga.: Scholars Press, 1983), 63–82; repr. in *A Feminist Companion to Exodus to Deuteronomy*, ed. Athalya Brenner; The Feminist Companion to the Bible 6 (Sheffield: Sheffield Academic Press, 1994), 37–61.

2. For discussion of the relation of Miriam to the song in Exod. 15, see the essays by Trible, Janzen, van Dijk-Hemmes, Meyers, and Bach in Brenner, *A Feminist Companion to Exodus to Deuteronomy*.

3. Phyllis Trible's groundbreaking *God and the Rhetoric of Sexuality* (Philadelphia: Fortress Press) appeared in 1978.

4. J. Cheryl Exum, ' "Mother in Israel": A Familiar Figure Reconsidered', in *Feminist Interpretation of the Bible*, ed. Letty M. Russell (Philadelphia: Westminster Press, 1985), 82.

5. J. Cheryl Exum, 'Second Thoughts about Secondary Characters', in Brenner, *A Feminist Companion to Exodus to Deuteronomy*, 75–87. The reprinted version of ' "You Shall Let Every Daughter Live" ' in *A Feminist Companion to Exodus to Deuteronomy* (pp. 37–61) is incorrectly cited on p. 37 as first appearing in 1993 instead of 1983.

6. Phyllis Trible, for example, practices essentially the same close-reading approach in 'Bringing Miriam out of the Shadows' that she used in *God and the Rhetoric of Sexuality* (1978). Though appeals to the reader and comments about the suppression of a woman's story give the impression of a more postmodern stance, for Trible the task remains one of 'unearthing the fragments [of an earlier tradition in which Miriam figured importantly] and assembling them' (p. 183). The ideology that motivates the portrayal of Miriam is never questioned; it is simply assumed that later androcentric redactors have sought to discredit Miriam.

7. ' "You Shall Let Every Daughter Live" ', 63. See, especially, James Muilenburg's now classic call for the practice of rhetorical criticism in his 1968 address to the Society of Biblical Literature, 'Form Criticism and Beyond', *Journal of Biblical Literature* 88 (1969), 1–18.

8. ' "You Shall Let Every Daughter Live" ', 75–6.

9. Exod. 1.22 functions as the end of what I called the first part and the beginning of the third movement, producing an overlapping structure. I used

Tzvetan Todorov's concept of narrative embedding to clarify its function. Exod. 1.22 supplies 'something excessive' to the story of the midwives, 'a supplement which remains outside the closed form produced by the development of the plot. At the same time, and for this very reason, this something-more, proper to the narrative, is also something-less. The supplement is also a lack; in order to supply this lack created by the supplement, another narrative is necessary' (T. Todorov, *The Poetics of Prose*, trans. Richard Howard (Ithaca, NY: Cornell University Press, 1977), 76).

10. There is a nice irony here. Pharaoh commands that every newborn male baby be exposed on the Nile; following M. Cogan ('A Technical Term for Exposure', *Journal for Near Eastern Studies* 27 (1968), 133–5) in rendering *hashlik* as 'abandon, expose', Moses' mother seems to be obeying the command when she places Moses in the Nile, but her *placing* (*wattasem*) stands in stark contrast to the pharaoh's 'abandon, expose' (NRSV, 'throw'). Pharaoh wanted the babies exposed on or thrown *into the Nile*; his daughter takes the baby *out of the Nile*.

11. ' "You Shall Let Every Daughter Live" ', 68.

12. Here I was taking issue with James S. Ackerman's negative assessment of the Egyptian princess in 'The Literary Context of the Moses Birth Story (Exodus 1–2)', in *Literary Interpretations of Biblical Narratives*, ed. K. R. R. Gros Louis, with J. S. Ackerman and T. S. Warshaw (Nashville: Abingdon Press, 1974), 86–96.

13. ' "You Shall Let Every Daughter Live" ', 80.

14. The versions (Syriac Peshitta, Septuagint, Targum, Targum Jonathan) 'correct' the Masoretic text by supplying the qualifier 'every son born to the Hebrews'. The omission of 'born to the Hebrews' in the MT produces the comical result that in his zealousness to be 'all' inclusive ('*all* his people', '*every* son', '*every* daughter'), the pharaoh forgets to exempt Egyptian boy babies from his death edict! This is entirely in keeping with his humorous characterization as a blundering fool.

15. Jopie Siebert-Hommes, 'Twelve Women in Exodus 1 and 2: The Role of Daughters and Sons in the Stories Concerning Moses', *Amsterdamse Cahiers voor Exegese en Bijbelse Theologie* 12 (1988), 47–58; Siebert-Hommes, 'Die Geburtsgeschichte des Mose innerhalb des Erzählungzusammenhangs von Exodus i and ii', *Vetus Testamentum* 42 (1992), 398–403. Detailed discussion of stylistic features can be found in Gordon F. Davies, *Israel in Egypt: Reading Exodus 1–2* (Journal for the Study of the Old Testament Supplement Series, 135; Sheffield: JSOT Press, 1992), who, curiously, provides a one-half page 'Excursus' on 'Women in Exodus 1–2' in a 181-page analysis of Exod. 1 and 2 (p. 63).

16. ' "You Shall Let Every Daughter Live" ', 64.

17. Ibid. 75.

18. I speak here of women in ancient times, for whom texts like this served as a means of social control. To the extent that modern women might wish to identify with these biblical models, the Bible still serves as a means of social control. As Renita J. Weems ('The Hebrew Women Are Not Like the Egyptian Women: The Ideology of Race, Gender and Sexual Reproduction in Exodus 1', *Semeia* 59 (1992), 25–34) points out, the text does not question but only reinscribes the ideology of difference.

19. Julia Kristeva, 'Stabat Mater', in *The Female Body in Western Culture: Contemporary Perspectives*, ed. S. R. Suleiman (Cambridge, Mass.: Harvard University Press, 1986), 113–14.

20. See e.g. Gerda Lerner, *The Creation of Patriarchy* (New York: Oxford University Press, 1986), 5–6, 199–211, 231–3 and *passim*.

21. Esther Fuchs, 'The Literary Characterization of Mothers and Sexual Politics in the Hebrew Bible', in *Feminist Perspectives on Biblical Scholarship*, ed. Adela Yarbro Collins (Chico, Calif.: Scholars Press, 1985), 118.

22. Stephen Fowl, 'Texts Don't Have Ideologies', *Biblical Interpretation* 3 (1995), 15–34.

23. This is Yvonne Sherwood's point in suggesting caution in the use of this concept: *The Prostitute and the Prophet: Hosea's Marriage in Literary-Theoretical Perspective* (Journal for the Study of the Old Testament Supplement Series, 212; Gender, Culture, Theory, 2; Sheffield: Sheffield Academic Press, 1996), 256.

24. Particularly the work of its 'founder', Jacques Derrida; see, *inter alia*, *Of Grammatology*, trans. Gayatri Chakravorty Spivak (Baltimore: Johns Hopkins University Press, 1976); *Writing and Difference*, trans., with introd. and notes, by Alan Bass (Chicago: University of Chicago Press, 1978); *Dissemination*, trans., with introd. and notes, by Barbara Johnson (Chicago: University of Chicago Press, 1981); and for a helpful introduction, see Christopher Norris, *Deconstruction: Theory and Practice* (London: Methuen, 1982).

25. Hélène Cixous and Catherine Clément, *The Newly Born Woman*, trans. Betsy Wing (Minneapolis: University of Minnesota Press), 63–132.

26. Although I acknowledge the importance of looking beyond gender to broader issues of race, ethnicity, class, etc., my focus here is on gender. At this particular point in time I am not ready to see criticism of a specifically feminist persuasion subsumed into a larger project before it has had an opportunity to make its full impact felt. Fortunately this kind of broader analysis is being done by others; see Weems, 'The Hebrew Women Are Not like the Egyptian Women'; Ilse Müllner, 'Tödliche Differenzen: Sexuelle Gewalt als Gewalt gegen Andere in Ri 19', in *Von der Wurzel Getragen: Christlich-feministische Exegese in Auseinandersetzung mit Antijudaismus*, ed. Luise Schottroff and Marie-Theres Wacker (Leiden: Brill, 1996), 81–100.

27. See Peter Brooks, 'The Idea of a Psychoanalytic Literary Criticism', in *Discourse in Psychoanalysis and Literature*, ed. Shlomith Rimmon-Kenan (London: Methuen, 1987), 1–18.

28. To give an example from 'real life': I recently attended a picnic where there were three small children, two girls and a boy. Many comments were made to the little girls about their cute outfits, matching shoes, and adorable little hats. Almost nothing was made of the boy's attire, though he was as smartly dressed as his sister. I am sure this was not nor will be the only time these children receive this kind of well-meaning attention from adults, through which the girls but not the boy are getting a message about the importance of physical appearance (and nice clothes) that will have some effect on their self-perception as they grow older. I am not saying that this effect of this message is inescapable, but it places an extra burden upon the girls: they will have to unlearn a message about clothes and appearance whereas the boy will not.

29. ' "You Shall Let Every Daughter Live" ', 82.
30. For example, his problem is overpopulation, but he fears the Israelites will leave; putting the Hebrews to hard work and killing male infants are absurd 'solutions' to the present problem; he is gullible enough to accept without question the midwives' explanation for their failure to execute his command; he orders all male babies, not just Hebrews, exposed on the Nile; and the very things he seeks to prevent come to pass—male babies, including Moses, are spared, and the Hebrews do, eventually, leave the land.
31. See Lerner, *The Creation of Patriarchy*, 5–6, 233–5.
32. As I pointed out in ' "You Shall Let Every Daughter Live" ', the pharaoh's question to the midwives, 'Why have you done this?', takes the form of an accusation found in juridical contexts. It suggests therefore that the midwives face a serious charge, and the fact that they get away with the incredible explanation they provide shows just how foolish this pharaoh is. Moses' mother and the pharaoh's daughter take a risk by openly defying the pharaoh's command, which was publicly issued to all his people.
33. This means that only the woman who is clearly non-Israelite, Pharaoh's daughter, is not given a name. It is not entirely clear whether the midwives are Hebrew or Egyptian; the Masoretes construed the word 'Hebrew' as an adjective, but the consonantal text is ambiguous and the Septuagint and Vulgate read, 'the midwives of the Hebrews'. On the names Shiphrah and Puah, see ' "You Shall Let Every Daughter Live" ', 70, 72. Miriam is not identified as Moses' sister in Exodus, but only as Aaron's sister; she is identified as Moses' sister in Num. 26.59 and 1 Chron. 6.3. On the unexpected appearance of a sister in Exod. 2, and different approaches available to exegetes in dealing with logical contradictions in the narrative, see Jürgen Ebach, 'Die Schwester des Mose: Anmerkungen zu einem "Widerspruch" in Exodus 2, 1–10', in '*Mit unsrer Macht ist nichts getan . . .*': *Festschrift für Dieter Schellong zum 65. Geburtstag*, ed. Jörg Mertin, Dietrich Neuhaus, and Michael Weinrich (Herchen, 1996), 101–15.
34. Fuchs, 'The Literary Characterization of Mothers', 130.
35. See the discussion of the difficulty of v. 21 in ' "You Shall Let Every Daughter Live" ', 74.
36. Exum, ' "Mother in Israel" ', 80.
37. The sayings have something else in common with Exod. 1.8–2.10; both popular adages and text assume that women have power but they do not have authority. Power is the ability to achieve one's goals and to get others to comply with one's will; women have always had power through a variety of means. Authority, power that is recognized and legitimated by society, has traditionally been a male prerogative; see Louise Lamphere, 'Strategies, Cooperation, and Conflict among Women in Domestic Groups', in *Woman, Culture, and Society*, ed. Michelle Zimbalist Rosaldo and Louise Lamphere (Stanford, Calif.: Stanford University Press, 1974), 99; Michelle Zimbalist Rosaldo, 'Woman, Culture, and Society: A Theoretical Overview', also in *Woman, Culture, and Society*, 21–2; Carol Meyers, *Discovering Eve: Ancient Israelite Women in Context* (New York: Oxford University Press, 1988), 40–4, 181–7.
38. See Athalya Brenner, *The Israelite Woman: Social Role and Literary Type in Biblical Narrative* (Sheffield: JSOT Press, 1985), 99–100.

39. See Exum, *Fragmented Women*, ch. 4, 'The (M)other's Place', 94–147.
40. This strange text has posed numerous problems for interpretation. It is interesting that a woman here performs the rite of circumcision. For suggestive comments on this passage, see Ilana Pardes, *Countertraditions in the Bible: A Feminist Approach* (Cambridge, Mass.: Harvard University Press, 1992), 84–93.
41. Jethro brings her and her two sons with him to meet Moses after the exodus from Egypt, but Zipporah is not mentioned in the reconciliation scene.
42. Exodus 19 indicates that the covenant at Sinai is made with men; the people are addressed with the command, 'Do not go near a woman' (v. 15). That the ten commandments, for example, are addressed to men is clear from the second person masculine singular pronouns and a command such as, 'You shall not covet . . . your neighbor's wife' (v. 17); on the difficulties, see Athalya Brenner, 'An Afterword: The Decalogue—Am I an Addressee?' in Brenner, *A Feminist Companion to Exodus to Deuteronomy*, 255–8; David J. A. Clines, 'The Ten Commandments, Reading from Left to Right', ch. 2 in his *Interested Parties: The Ideology of Writers and Readers of the Hebrew Bible* (Journal for the Study of the Old Testament Supplement Series, 205; Gender, Culture, Theory, 1; Sheffield: Sheffield Academic Press, 1995), 26–45. On women's general invisibility in the laws, see Phyllis Bird, 'Images of Women in the Old Testament', in *Religion and Sexism*, ed. R. R. Ruether (New York: Simon & Schuster, 1974), 48–57.
43. The verb is third person feminine singular, suggesting either that Aaron is a later addition to the story (if one takes a historical-critical approach) or that the story is primarily concerned with making only Miriam look bad.
44. For this discussion, see Toril Moi, *Sexual/Textual Politics: Feminist Literary Theory* (London: Methuen, 1985), 167.

15 # Genesis 22: The Sacrifice of Sarah

Phyllis Trible*

Phyllis Trible's *God and the Rhetoric of Sexuality* is a strong contender for the book most often described in citations as 'groundbreaking'. Reproduced below is the second half of an article in which Trible managed to break ground with one of the most extensively analysed texts in the Hebrew Bible: the sacrifice, or binding, of Isaac in Genesis 22. The first half of the article, in common with the vast majority of exegesis that came before it, focuses on Abraham (the tested) and Isaac (the bound or sacrificed). Trible conducts a close reading that develops the themes of attachment (Abraham and his beloved son Isaac go together up Mount Moriah), detachment (Abraham is willing to raise the knife), and non-attachment (though Abraham had expected to return to his two servants with Isaac, he returns alone). The second half of her article approaches the same text from the perspective of the conspicuously absent Sarah. She, not Abraham, Trible argues, needed to learn the lesson of non-attachment (considered by Trible to be a liberating ideal), but her name is not mentioned and she is removed from the scene as soon as the narrative is over. What happens if Sarah becomes the parent who is tested? DL

Our rhetorical-critical reading demonstrates the ways structure, vocabulary, and content embody meanings. What a piece of work is Genesis 22! And yet, hardly do I complete the first two verses before a great uneasiness descends. So attached to patriarchy is this magnificent story that I wonder if it can ever be what it purports to be, namely a narrative of nonattachment.[1]

With all-consuming power, the patriarchal bonding of father and son threatens to destroy not only Abraham and Isaac but also another—Sarah. Why is she not in this story? Where is she? What does it all mean for her? Over centuries, many commentators have

---

* Phyllis Trible, extract from 'Genesis 22: The Sacrifice of Sarah', from *'Not in Heaven': Coherence and Complexity in Biblical Narrative*, edited by J. Rosenblatt and J. Sitterson (Indiana University Press, 1991).

answered such questions by composing stories outside the text to fill gaps within it.[2] Another approach wrestles from within, using scripture to interpret scripture. Adopting this procedure, I should like to show how the biblical depiction of Sarah works to expose the patriarchy of Genesis 22, how that exposure alters the meaning of the story, and how the resultant interpretation challenges faith. A feminist hermeneutic takes over the rhetorical analysis to yield a different reading.

In the genealogical preface to the so-called Abrahamic narratives, Sarai receives special attention. A recital of descendants originating with Shem lists, in each case, a single male heir followed by reference to "other sons and daughters" (11:10–25). The pattern ceases with the introduction of Terah, "father of Abram, Nahor, and Haran" (11:26). Of the three sons named, only Haran, who dies early, is identified by a male descendant, his son Lot. All three, however, are associated with women:

> And Abram and Nahor took wives.
>> The name of Abram's wife was Sarai,
>> and the name of Nahor's wife, Milcah,
>>> the daughter of Haran the father of
>>>> Milcah and Iscah.
>> Now Sarai was barren; she had no child. (11:29–30)

Here male genealogy relinquishes structure and content to herald a story that names characters.

Contrast emerges between Sarai and Milcah, whose names appear in alternating sequence. The contrast moves between the silence and voice of the text. Nothing is said of Sarai's lineage, but Milcah is "the daughter of Haran"; she also has a sister. On the other hand, nothing is said about Milcah's fertility (cf. 22:20–23), but "Sarai was barren; she had no child." These ominous words haunt the narrative to come. They bring Sarai to center stage while Milcah recedes, as does her husband Nahor. The three remaining men, Terah, Abram, and Lot, go forth with the lone woman Sarai, the one who has neither pedigree nor fertility, neither past nor future.

> Terah took Abram his son and Lot the son of Haran, his grandson,
>> and Sarai his daughter-in-law, his son Abram's wife,
> and they went forth together from the Chaldeans ... to Haran. ...
> (11:31)

Unique and barren, Sarai threatens the demise of genealogy. The death of her father-in-law Terah in Haran reduces the generations to two.

The generational preface stops (11:32), and the call of Abram begins (12:1–3).

In his journey from Haran to the promised land, Abram takes Sarai his wife as well as Lot his brother's son (12:5). Upon their arrival, Yhwh assures Abram descendants but does not take account of Sarai's condition. When famine sends the group to Egypt, the tension builds. Speaking for the first time, Abram addresses Sarai (12:11–13). With flattery he manipulates her to justify deception and protect himself. He disowns the beautiful Sarai as wife, calls her his sister, and allows Pharaoh to use her, thereby ensuring his own survival, even his prosperity. For her sake Pharaoh dealt well with Abram (12:16) but also for her sake Yhwh afflicted (*ngʿ*) Pharaoh (12:17). Sarai remains the pivot in the story. At the end, Pharaoh reprimands Abram and holds him accountable for the use of his wife (12:18–20). Pharaoh respects another man's property. Throughout it all, Sarai has neither voice nor choice. Though she is central in the episode, patriarchy marginalizes this manhandled woman.

Object of special attention, Sarai eventually speaks, seeking to fulfill herself within cultural strictures. Her words concern fertility and status; they also reveal her as a voice of realism, decisiveness, and command:

> And Sarai said to Abram,
> "Because Yhwh has prevented me
>   from bearing children,
>   go to my maid.
>   Perhaps I shall be built up from her." (16:2a)

Thus this barren woman proposes a plan whereby she may obtain children through her Egyptian maid Hagar (15:1–6). As property of Sarai, Hagar is female enslaved, used, and demeaned. Abram once gave Sarai to Pharaoh; Sarai now gives Hagar to Abram. This time, however, no deity intervenes; the arrangement is legal and proper.

But no happy solution results (16:4–6). Inevitably the women clash. The pregnant maid sees the lowering of hierarchical barriers, and the barren mistress resents loss of status. Reasserting power, Sarai afflicts (*ʿnh*) Hagar, who then flees to the wilderness. The blessed and exalted woman has become malicious and tyrannical. Her authority reaches into the wilderness. Finding Hagar by a spring of water, the messenger of Yhwh orders her not only to return to her mistress but also to "suffer affliction (*ʿnh*) under her hand." The cruelty of Sarai continues, this time with heavenly sanction. Who will deliver Sarai from such disease? Who will make possible healing reconciliation? Not Abraham, not her son, not the narrator, and not even God. To the contrary, the story countenances the division between the women.

As the narrative proceeds, God makes clear that only Sarai, no other woman, can bear the child of promise. She is destined for great things:

> And God said to Abraham:
> "As for Sarai your wife,
>   Call not her name Sarai[a][b]
>   for Sarah (is) her name.[b'][a']
> I will bless her
>   and also will give from her to you a son.
> I will bless her
>   and she will become nations;
>   royal people from her will be." (17:15–16)

Sarah's apotheosis is complete. If Hagar is woman in the gutter, Sarah is woman on the pedestal. Their positions illustrate well the strictures of patriarchy.

The exaltation of Sarah continues as Abraham responds to the divine words. Falling on his face and laughing,[3] he utters two speeches. The first, inward dialogue, poses through rhetorical questions an impossible situation:

> Abraham . . . said in his heart
> "Shall a son be borne to one
>   who is a hundred years old?
> Shall Sarah, the daughter of ninety years old,
>   bear?" (17:17)

These words of Abraham specifically name Sarah. His second response, outward dialogue, pleads for the legitimacy of Ishmael, but it does not name Hagar:

> And Abraham said to the God,
> "If only Ishmael might live in your presence!" (17:18)

Abraham's responses bring yet again divine sanction for Sarah as the sole designated mother of the chosen heir. A single speech makes three declarations (A, B, C, below). It begins by citing Sarah and Isaac (A). Conversely, it closes with Isaac and Sarah (C). Hers, then, is the first and last proper name. Between the two declarations occurs a promise of blessing for Ishmael, without reference to Hagar (B). Although central in the structure, the promise becomes peripheral to the story line. In other words, the beginning stress upon Sarah and

Isaac and the ending stress upon Isaac and Sarah confine Ishmael. The extremities of the divine speech show in particular the special, exalted role of Sarah as mother.

God said,

(A)   "No, but Sarah your wife will bear for you a son,
     and you will call his name Isaac.
I will establish my covenant with him
  as an everlasting covenant
  for his descendants after him.

(B)   As for Ishmael, I have heard you.
Surely I will bless him
  and I will make him fruitful
  and I will increase him more and more.
Twelve princes he will bear
  and I will make him a great nation.

(C)   But my covenant I will establish with Isaac
  whom Sarah will bear to you by this time next year."

(17:19–21)

Yet another story ensures the status and destiny of Sarah (18:1–16). Disguised as three men, Yhwh visits Abraham by the oaks of Mamre. After receiving the hospitality of rest and food, the guests inquire about Sarah (18:9). Told that she is in the tent, the visitor (now singular) promises to return in the spring "when surely a son will be to Sarah your wife" (18:10). At this point the narrator intervenes to focus on Sarah. Four times her name appears in a report about her location and activity, her old age and infertility, and her immediate response to the promise.

Now-Sarah was listening at the entrance of the tent
  behind him.

Abraham and-Sarah (were) old, advanced in the days;
it was past to be to-Sarah (in the) manner of women.

So-laughed Sarah within herself. . . . (18:10b–12a)

Only after this narrated intervention does Sarah's direct response to the divine promise come:

After being worn out, (is there) to me pleasure—
  and my lord, (who) is old? (18:12b)

Yhwh replies, however, not to Sarah but to Abraham. Questions of reprimand precede a reiteration of the promise, with the name Sarah occurring at the beginning and end.

> Why (is) this, <u>Sarah</u> laughed saying
> "Now shall I indeed bear when I am old?"
> Is anything too difficult for Yhwh?
> At the appointed time I will return to you in the spring
> and to <u>Sarah</u> (will be) a son. (18:13–14)

Sarah's laughter "within herself" (18:12) has been heard,[4] but out of fear she denies (*khs*) that it ever happened. "Not I-laughed." This time the divine reply comes directly to her. "No, for you-did-laugh." For the first and only time the deity speaks to Sarah. Yet not even this curt rebuke diminishes her exalted and unique status.

Elect among women, only Sarah can bear the legitimate male heir. And so, at long last, it comes to pass. "Yhwh visited Sarah . . . and did to Sarah as Yhwh had promised" (21:1). She bears a son to Abraham in his old age. Abraham names him Laughter (*Yishaq*) but Sarah interprets its meaning:

> Laughter God has made <u>for-me</u> (*lî*).
> All who hear will laugh <u>for-me</u> (*lî*). (21:6)

If Laughter (Isaac) is special to Abraham, how much more to Sarah! She claims the child for herself, "for-me." After all, he is her, not Abraham's, one and only son.

Ishmael, the other male child in the family, is thus a threat. So jealousy continues to breed rivalry between the two women: Sarah, wife of Abraham, and Hagar, wife of Abraham; Sarah, woman on the pedestal, and Hagar, woman in the gutter; Sarah, mother of Isaac, and Hagar, mother of Ishmael. Potential equality between sons counters actual inequality between their mothers. Power belongs to Sarah; powerlessness to Hagar. Sarah asserts authority against the other woman, as she did once before, and now against her child. Speaking to Abraham, she orders:

> Cast out this slave woman and her son,
> for the son of this slave woman
> will not inherit with my son,
> with Isaac. (21:10)

Language of contrast achieves several effects. First, the single phrase "her son" and the double phrase "with my son, with Isaac" show the lack of equality between the sons. Second, the name Isaac accords him dignity and power in contrast to the namelessness, and hence powerlessness, of both the slave woman and her son. Third, the combination "my son Isaac" bespeaks possessiveness, indeed attachment.

It foreshadows language that in Genesis 22 applies to Abraham, rather than to Sarah. Yet in chapter 21 Abraham has no exclusive relationship with Isaac. He uses no speech of intimacy for either son. But the narrator and the deity attach him to Ishmael and to Hagar:

> The matter was very distressing
>> in the eyes of Abraham
>> on account of his son.
> But God said to Abraham,
>> "Do not be distressed in your eyes
>>> on account of the lad
>>> and on account of your slave woman." (21:11–12a)

Possessive language, "his son," links Abraham and Ishmael, a paternal–filial connection that endures until Abraham's death (25:9).

Through direct and narrated discourse Genesis 21:1–11 delineates a decisive parental difference between Sarah and Abraham. Sarah speaks directly, using the vocabulary "my son Isaac." Her exclusive speech owns her one and only son. On the other hand, Abraham speaks not at all; he claims no father–son relationships. They appear only in the distancing of narration. The storyteller makes the claim for Abraham regarding both sons, "his son Isaac" (21:4, 5) and "his son" Ishmael (21:11). Accordingly, unlike the bond between Sarah and Isaac, no unique tie exists here between Abraham and Isaac. Other texts support the observation. Before Genesis 22:7 Abraham never utters or implies the possessive "my son" for Isaac, though he does imply the epithet for Ishmael (17:18). Such witnesses, most especially chapter 21, dispute the father–son pairing of Genesis 22 to compel a closer look at Sarah's relationship to Isaac.

With single, unqualified attachment to "my son," Sarah prevails once more over against Abraham because God supports her.

> Everything that Sarah says to you, heed her voice;
> for in Isaac will be named to you descendants. (21:12)

Sarah, the chosen vessel of the legitimate heir, remains secure on the pedestal that patriarchy has built for her. To keep her there protects her from a test, but in doing so it exacerbates her tyranny, deprives her of freedom, and renders impossible reconciliation with Hagar.

If the phrase "my son Isaac" in 21:10 foreshadows the language of chapter 22, while reversing the parental figures, other associations similarly challenge the content.[5] In the wilderness with his mother Hagar, Ishmael comes close to death; a messenger of God intervenes to save him. On the mountain with his father Abraham, Isaac comes close to death; a messenger of God intervenes to save him. Thus are joined the two sons and the divine representatives. The presence of Hagar the mother and Abraham the father, however, skews the pairing. Chapter 21 shows that the proper match in parents are the mothers, Hagar and Sarah. This pairing argues correspondingly for the appearance of Sarah, not Abraham, in Genesis 22. As Hagar faced the imminent death of Ishmael, so Sarah ought to have faced the imminent death of Isaac. Explicit parallels between chapters 21 and 22 sustain the logic of the argument, and yet a bias for father–son bonding has defied the connection.

Another observation demonstrates the inappropriateness of Abraham as the parental figure for Genesis 22. Nowhere else in the entire narrative sequence does he appear as a man of attachment.[6] To the contrary. When Yhwh calls him, Abram obediently leaves his country, his clan, and his father's house to journey to an unknown land (12:1–4). Immediately after that commendable relinquishment comes an unflattering one: Abram passes his wife Sarai off as his sister (12:10–20). Later he even repeats this act of extraordinary detachment (20:1–18). In reference to the land, Abraham shows no possessiveness but instead allows Lot to choose (13:2–12). After warring with kings from the East and recovering all the goods and people captured, Abraham gives the king of Salem a tenth of everything, besides refusing to take anything not his own (14:1–24). Similar behavior appears in his less generous treatment of Hagar. On two occasions he gives power over her to Sarai and God (16:1–6 and 21:1–14). Hints of his involvement with Ishmael (17:18; 21:11) are negated when he sends the child away, along with Hagar. In another episode he gives gifts to Abimelech as they settle a dispute over wells (21:22–34). Be the incident an occasion for weal or woe, nowhere prior to Genesis 22 does Abraham emerge as a man of attachment. That is not his problem. How ill-fitted he is, then, for a narrative of testing and sacrifice.

Attachment is Sarah's problem. Nevertheless, Genesis 22 drops Sarah to insert Abraham. The switch defies the internal logic of the larger story. In view of the unique status of Sarah and her exclusive relationship to Isaac, she, not Abraham, ought to have been tested. The dynamic of the entire saga, from its genealogical preface on, requires that Sarah be featured in the climactic scene, that she learn the meaning of obedience to God, that she find liberation from possessiveness, that she free Isaac from maternal ties,[7] and that she emerge a solitary individual, nonattached, the model of faithfulness. In making Abraham the object of the divine test, the story violates its own rhythm and movement. Moreover, it fails to offer Sarah redemption and thereby perpetuates the conflict between her and Hagar. As long as Sarah is attached to Isaac (both child and symbol), so long Sarah afflicts Hagar.[8]

The text, however, permits the banished Hagar to forge for herself a future that God and Sarah have diminished. She chooses an Egyptian wife for her son and so guarantees the identity of her descendants (21: 21; cf. 25:12–18). If it yield but small mercy, her act is nonetheless a sign of healing for this abused woman. By contrast, the biblical story allows no opportunity, however small, for Sarah to be healed. It attributes to her no action or word that might temper her affliction. Instead, it leaves her a jealous and selfish woman.

Patriarchy has denied Sarah her story, the opportunity for freedom and blessing. It has excluded her and glorified Abraham. And it has not stopped with these things. After securing the safety of Isaac, it has no more need for Sarah; so it moves to eliminate her. The process begins obliquely, yet with the telling phrase, "and it came to pass after these events" (22:20). As this phrase introduced the story of testing and sacrifice (22:1), so it returns to make a transition that continues the larger narrative.

Once again, continuation holds surprise. The narrative begets a genealogy (22:20–24). Its subject reverts to the family of Nahor, thereby recalling the genealogical preface to the entire saga (11:27– 32). An unidentified speaker addresses only Abraham, who has just returned from the mount of sacrifice. Unlike the preface, this passage says nothing explicit about Sarah. Silence begins her removal. The words commence, "Behold Milcah also (*gam*) has borne children to your brother Nahor" (RSV). The particle "also" contrasts the two wives.[9] Though Sarah has borne only the singular child Isaac, Milcah has birthed eight sons. Bethuel, the last of them, holds special meaning because "Bethuel became the father of Rebekah" (22:23). Reference to this daughter forecasts a future for Isaac. The concluding item in the genealogy likewise implies contrast between women: "Moreover, his concubine, whose name was Reumah, bore Tebah, Gaham, Tahash, and Maacah" (22:24, RSV). Though Hagar, second wife of Abraham, bore the one son Ishmael, Nahor's concubine Reumah bore four sons. Yet the small family of Abraham and Sarah, excluding Hagar, and not the large family of Nahor and Milcah, including Reumah, carry the promise. The two families join later when the one and only child Isaac finds a wife in the daughter Rebekah (24:1–67).

If at the beginning of this entire saga barren Sarai threatened the demise of genealogy (11:30), at the end genealogy portends the demise of Sarah. Immediately after the report of 22:20–24, patriarchy dismisses Sarah. It has no further need of her, and so it writes a lean obituary (cf. 25:7–8).

> Sarah lived a hundred and twenty-seven years;
>   these were the years of the life of Sarah.
> And Sarah died at Kiriath-arba (that is, Hebron)
>   in the land of Canaan. . . . (23:1–2a, RSV)

The place of Sarah's death suggests another facet of her story. After the test, Abraham returns to dwell in Beersheba. But Sarah dies in Hebron. Thus the text reads as though husband and wife were never reunited in life. Indeed, "Abraham *went* to mourn for Sarah and to weep for her" (23:2b).

Sarah died alone. Then Abraham went to her. But immediately the story turns from Sarah to a long section in which Abraham bargains with the Hittites for burial ground (23:3–18). Only after some sixteen verses does Sarah re-enter the narrative. "After this, Abraham buried Sarah his wife in the cave of the field of Mach-pelah east of Mamre (that is, Hebron) in the land of Canaan" (23:19). Where she died, there was she buried. If early on patriarchy casts out the woman in the gutter (Hagar), the time comes when it also dismisses the woman on the pedestal (Sarah). Moreover, it allots Sarah no dying words. It leaves the reader to remember as her last words only the harsh imperative, "Cast out this slave woman with her son; for the son of this slave woman shall not be heir with my son Isaac" (21:10). This utterance haunts Sarah's portrait, crying out for release from possessiveness and attachment. And though the story for healing is at hand, it remains captive to a patriarchal agenda.

From exclusion to elimination, denial to death, the attachment of Genesis 22 to patriarchy has given us not the sacrifice of Isaac (for that we are grateful) but the sacrifice of Sarah (for that we mourn). By her absence from the narrative and her subsequent death, Sarah has been sacrificed by patriarchy to patriarchy. Thus this magnificent story of nonattachment stands in mortal danger of betraying itself. It fears not God but holds fast to an idol. If the story is to be redeemed, then the reader must restore Sarah to her rightful place. Such a hermeneutical move, wed to rhetorical analysis, would explode the entrenched bias to fulfill the internal logic of the story. And it would do even more: it would free divine revelation from patriarchy. Yet even there the matter does not end.

Notes

1. Despite the salutary warning by Carol Meyers about problems inherent in the word 'patriarchy', the term appears likely to remain. As shorthand, it designates male-centered and male-dominated cultures and texts with an implied critique of them. It names a pervasive social system. Meyers rightly pleads for an understanding of historical specificities in descriptions and evaluations of patriarchy. See *Discovering Eve: Ancient Israelite Women in Context* (New York: Oxford University Press, 1988), 24–46.

2. See e.g. Louis Ginzberg, *Legends of the Bible* (Philadelphia: Jewish Publication Society of America, 1968), 128–38; also Shalom Spiegel, *The Last Trial* (New York: Pantheon Books, 1967). Cf. Yaakov Elbaum, 'From Sermon to Story: The Transformation of the Akedah', *Prooftexts* 6 (1986), 97–116. On ancient interpretations, Jewish and Christian, see *inter alia* P. R. Davies and B. D. Chilton, 'The Aqedah: A Revised Tradition History', *Catholic Biblical Quarterly* 40 (1978), 514–46; Sebastian Brock, 'Genesis 22: Where Was Sarah?', *Expository Times* 96 (1984), 14–17; C. T. R. Hayward, 'The Sacrifice of Isaac and Jewish Polemic Against Christianity,' *Catholic Biblical Quarterly* 52 (1990), 293–306.

3. Note that the verb 'laugh' (*shq*) forecasts the name of the son, 'Isaac' (*yshq*).

4. Note the parallel to Abraham's laugh in 17:17 and the corresponding play on the name 'Isaac'. Note also other similarities and contrasts between Abraham and Sarah: 'Abraham said in his heart' (17:17a); 'Sarah laughed within herself' (18:12a). Two rhetorical questions by Abraham, asked inwardly (17:17), are matched in part by Sarah's one question, perhaps also asked inwardly (18:12b); cf. S. Bar-Efrat, *Narrative Art in the Bible* (Sheffield: Sheffield Academic Press, 1989), 63 f.

5. For comments on these two stories, chs. 21 and 22, from the perspective of the abandonment of children, see John Boswell, *The Kindness of Strangers* (New York: Pantheon Books, 1988), esp. 141, 144–5, 155.

6. The thesis of this paragraph emerged in a discussion with Professor Tikva Frymer-Kensky of the Reconstructionist Rabbinical College, Wyncote, Pennsylvania.

7. Genesis 24:67 suggests that the problem of mother–son bonding continued even beyond Sarah's death.

8. For a womanist perspective on the Hagar and Sarah stories, see Renita J. Weems, 'A Mistress, a Maid, and No Mercy', in *Just a Sister Away* (San Diego, Calif.: LuraMedia, 1988), 1–19.

9. C. Westermann, *Genesis 12–36: A Commentary*, trans. J. Scullion (London: SPCK, 1986) 366–7.

16 The Hebrew God and His Female Complements

Athalya Brenner*

What do feminist Bible exegetes and archaeologists have in common? Both uncover remains and reconstruct whole worlds from fragments. Jewish and Christian commentators have spent two thousand years burying biblical women. Through her own scholarship and the widely read Feminist Bible commentaries she edits, Athalya Brenner has been a pioneer in the tasks of recovery and reconstruction. Here she takes on the challenging subject of God's gender. Noting that the Hebrew Bible contains competing voices and that feminist Bible scholars also disagree, Brenner argues that God is most often identified as a father with female elements incorporated in the form of a consort or stereo-typically female attributes such as compassion. Far from being incidental or a historical accident, she sees God's male identity as performing a crucial function in the Hebrew Bible; it provides the model of 'just father' with 'errant sons' that exonerates God from seeming abandonment of his children. Brenner's personal postscript, though not unique to feminist Bible scholarship, is certainly a hallmark.   DL

....

THE HEBREW GOD'S GENDER

....

Was God a woman at the dawn of Religion (Stone 1977: 17)? The Hebrew god, as described in the Hebrew Bible (Old Testament), was not. The Hebrew god's gender, from the very beginning as documented in the Bible, was almost invariably referred to as M (male/masculine).

It would be an error to attribute this gender definition of the Hebrew divine being to the restrictive usage of the Hebrew language alone. Indeed, Hebrew has no N (grammatical neuter) class, no

* Athalya Brenner, 'The Hebrew God and His Female Complements', from *Reading Bibles, Writing Bodies: Identity and The Book*, edited by T. Beal and D. Gunn (Routledge, 1997).

equivalent of the English "it." Thus every animate as well as inanimate entity, abstract concept or concrete phenomenon, has to be grammatically gendered in the language as either M or F (female/feminine). The linguistic practice of relating to the divine through M terminology seems like a matter of deliberate choice and world view. YHWH is, of course, not simply a male. How can "he" be, given "his" lack of physical characteristics beyond metaphor, a lack reinforced by the severe—albeit also transgressed—command not to supply "him" with plastic representation?[1] He is male nevertheless, and a specific kind of male at that. He is rational and intellectual. Hence, he creates the cosmos and its contents by speech acts, that is, through language (Genesis 1:1–2:4a). At least according to the mainstreams of the biblical canon, that male god is omniscient, omnipotent, immanent. The question of his morality and justice, the so-called "theodicy," is not easily settled (Crenshaw 1983). Sometimes, as in the book of Job or in Ecclesiastes (Qohelet), his moral constitution seems questionable. He undoubtedly has a dark side, as well as a graceful and loving side (Exodus 20:5–6; 34:6–7; Jonah 4:2).[2] But, first and foremost, he is a paternal figure.

God is primarily depicted as a single M parent, cast and stereotyped from the outset as the Great Father. In the Garden of Eden narrative (Genesis 2:4b–3:24) he is a father who exiles Adam and Eve, his rebellious children, from the original homestead after they have eaten from the forbidden tree of knowledge. He makes explicit his fear that, if not expelled, the humans might act to resemble him in divinity (3:22), that is, knowledge and unlimited life. Throughout the Eden story he maintains an authoritative if benevolent stance. His commands are inexplicable and unexplained but to be obeyed. All humanity, but particularly the Hebrews (Amos 9:7; Hosea 11:2), and especially King David and his dynasty, are depicted as his "sons."

Humankind, M and F together in that order, is created in god's image (Genesis 1:26–8).[3] Does that actually mean that the Hebrew god embodies both M and F principles and that he is genderless, beyond gender or bi-gender? We shall see that this is perhaps so in places, but infrequently.[4] At any rate, humankind's destiny is set immediately at the time of its inception: to control the world, much the same as males are to control females (Genesis 3:16) and fathers their inferiors— women, minors, slaves, foreigners, everyone. The model for this societal image is obvious. Biblical law[5] and narratives imply that a patriarch of the premonarchical period was like a god: his was the right to judge and even condemn to death; see the Tamar and Judah story, where Judah condemns Tamar to death by burning for alleged "fornication" and her pregnancy, of which he is the unwitting agent (Genesis 38). In short, thus man creates his god in his father's image through the statement that god created man in his own divine image.

From a psychological perspective, god-as-father corresponds to Freud's analysis of the beginning of religion in the eventual deification of ancestral (mainly M) spirits, and to Rudolf Otto's attribution of religious sentiments primarily to horror/fear of the holy. The identification of the father idea with intellect, rational behavior, justice and control—considered self-evident by orthodox religious and theological systems, and by twentieth-century M psychology and psychotherapy—seems to inform the biblical texts.

A sociological perspective should also be considered. Literature is often reflexive of social attitudes, mores and norms. It is not too far-fetched to expect the social realities of the patriarchal order to be reflected in the design of the biblical construction known as the Hebrew god. *Contra* the revisionist feminists, Christian and Jewish alike (e.g., Trible 1973; 1978), who attempt to salvage the Hebrew god for their faith, it can be said emphatically that this god was never a "woman," was never even fully or largely metaphorized as a woman (but see below). Nor was he ever, on the whole, a womanly male. Therefore, it is difficult to relate to him—a common feminist practice—as "s/he," or as anything more than incorporating some features of femaleness or female symbols or deities.

To what extent does the assigning of an M gender to a communal god illustrate the social and legal inferiority of women in that same community? This is a separate issue which, strictly speaking, lies outside the scope of the present inquiry. We shall, however, briefly return to it later. Let us also note in passing that, even in cultures that partly admit goddess influence, women's status is not automatically superior.

YHWH IS THE SUPREME FATHER: HOW A LACK IS CONCEALED

One way of evaluating the M parent–child relationship between YHWH and his children (his sons, really) is to pronounce this relationship a continuous failure and increased disillusion in biblical myth (Clines 1990: 49–66, 85–105). In the origin myth (Genesis 1–11), the relationship deteriorates rapidly and steadily. The newly created woman initiates the eating of the fruit from the forbidden tree, and the human couple is driven out of the Garden. The first murder, a fratricide (4:1–16), soon follows the birth of Cain and Hebel, or Abel (Pardes 1992: 39–59). A brief erotic encounter between the sons of god (who are they anyhow?) and the daughters of man (6:1–4) threatens to bring together heaven and earth, reported earlier (chap. 1) to have been drawn asunder by god himself (cf. Davies 1993: 194–201). Humanity's morals have become so corrupt that god decides to destroy his children by a flood (chaps. 6–8). And what happens to the family chosen to survive? No sooner is Noah saved than he starts a vine culture and gets drunk; then two of his sons either show disrespect by looking at his nakedness or, as some Jewish sages interpret the passage in their commentaries, castrate him or have homosexual intercourse with him (chap. 9). Humanity now attempts to consolidate by building a city and a tower so as to stay together and speak one language. This, once more, is a threat to the divine plan. God frustrates it and scatters his children further afield (11:1–9).

God now concentrates on Abraham's family (chap. 12 onwards), calling to Abraham to leave his homestead and go to a new, divinely appointed land: this is of course a replay in reverse of the expulsion from the primeval Garden. But does the new beginning, so promising since Abraham obeys god without hesitation, signify an end to the chain of disappointments? Not so. Soon after the entry to the land, Abraham has to leave it because of a famine. His wife is in danger of being violated by a foreign king (12:10–13:2; and cf. the two other versions of the same story, chaps. 20 and 26). He has no son to inherit the extravagant divine promises liberally bestowed upon him. When he has two sons, Yitzhak and Yishmael, Sarah makes him send the firstborn away (chap. 21). Two generations later, Jacob steals the inheritance rights from his older brother Esau, and has to leave the country for many years (chap. 25 onwards). Then his son Joseph is sold to Egypt by his brothers, who eventually follow him there (chap. 37 onwards). Through strife, trickery, and dishonesty, the promised land is evacuated by its presumed inheritors for many years.

After a prolonged sojourn in Egypt, Yhwh sends Moses to deliver the Hebrews back to their land. He saves them from bondage by inflicting plagues upon the Egyptians and by parting the Sea of Reeds for them (Exodus 1–15). He reveals himself at Sinai and gives them the Ten Commandments and the Law, formalized as a political treaty binding both sides to one another (chaps. 19–24). He protects, feeds, and guides his children, the Children of Israel. What does YHWH get in return? Crises. Complaints. A golden calf (chap. 32). Rebellions. Incidents of fear, skepticism, distrust, and disobedience recur throughout Numbers and Deuteronomy too. The corrective measure required yet again is, as in the case of the Primeval flood, extinction. The people are sentenced to roam the desert for a formulaic period of forty years. The desert generation—including Moses—has to die before a new beginning, the re-entry to the land, is embarked upon.

The remaining biblical books, which narrate the "history" of Israel and Judah until the destruction of the first temple and Jerusalem and the first exile in 586 B.C.E. (Joshua, Judges, Samuel, Kings: the so-called first biblical historiography), are informed by the same vision of failure and disappointment. It is claimed again and again that the Israelites keep turning away from their god, to whom they are supposedly bound orthogenetically as well as by legal covenant. He tries to save them from the consequences of their own follies by sending intermediaries—judges, leaders, prophets (see the prophetic books), kings—but to no avail. Finally, and against his will, he has to punish them by taking away both political organization and territory. They have to go into exile.

The second "historiographical" cycle—Chronicles, Ezra, and Nehemiah—takes us again to the very beginning of the world through to the restoration of Jerusalem and the temple into the fifth century B.C.E. In it, as well as in prophetic works which relate to the same period (Isaiah 40–66, for instance), the exile is understood as a period of re-education for the erring children. Here the general tone is more optimistic. Nonetheless, is the rehabilitation program considered wholly successful? Only partially so, as the various transgressions of the Law reported in Ezra and Nehemiah show. The Book of Daniel, the last and latest chapters of which refer to the very last years before the Hashmonaean revolt against Hellenized Syria (towards the middle of the second century B.C.E.), ends with a message similar to its predecessors. Only a few, the chosen ones, will survive the forthcoming political and religious tribulations. Thus the biblical story concludes with a message of hope but, once more, the hope is underlined by human anxiety over divine disappointment.

I have here summarized the story of Israelite/Judahite history, as narrated in the Hebrew Bible. Many details, especially of the earlier "history," cannot be verified by external (archaeological and other) evidence, thus their historicality—in the modern sense of the term—must remain questionable. However, the cultural/ideological thrust of the biblical macro-story is quite clear. It seems that the father-and-child model which informs the origin myth continues to operate in "history." This, by and large, is the societal model operative in the Bible as a literary configuration. While individual passages or story-lines may advance a different message, it seems that the overall framing ideology is conditioned by the pressing need to exonerate YHWH of his apparent periodic abandonments of his children. Rather than destroy the father image (as sons do, either metaphorically and symbolically or figuratively, in many non-monotheistic myths), biblical authors and editors opted for an ethos of *human* responsibility. The sons are blamed for their own bad fortunes, whereas the fatherhead's theodicy remains intact.

In Lacan's terms, the psychological and cultural construct "Father" is perceived by his children as the supreme phallic symbol. It is easier, perhaps, to plead recurrent instances of collective non-integrity than to demolish an ideal. However, three observations seem to be in order at this point.

First, it is difficult if not impossible, within the process of education and socialization, to draw a clear demarcation line between the failure of a child and that of a parent or to distinguish their respective burdens of responsibility. The process is one of mutuality, as is the outcome.

Second, one cannot help but wonder whether the singularity of the divine parent, and the insistence on his M attributes (justice and morality as prerequisites for gaining love, in so many instances) in his dealings with his children, is not at least one of the reasons for the continuous mutual failure of both partners throughout myth and "history."

Third, other solutions in the Hebrew Bible present the Hebrew god in images other than the ultimately fair Father with errant sons. Broadly speaking, these images fall into two main categories. The first supplies YHWH with various types of F consorts; the second supplies him with F attributes. It remains to be seen to what extent each of these categories is successful in removing the blame from YHWH. Both categories, though, illustrate an admission of the problematics involved in the divine lack of an overt F element and, also, the need to fill this lack.

HUMAN SEXUALITY AND DIVINE SEXUALITY: MATTERS OF FERTILITY AND F PRINCIPLES

The Bible establishes that the Israelites, whatever exactly their origins and history, were familiar with various cults practiced in the land that they eventually came to regard as theirs. Moreover and dialectically, in spite of zealous disparagement of those cults, they assimilated elements of them into their own cult. Deuteronomy and the related editorial framework of the books of Kings make it abundantly clear, through their heated and frequent polemics, that the fertility aspects of the so-called "Canaanite" rites were too attractive for the Israelites and Judahites to ignore. In the reigns of Jezebel and Athaliah, the Bible tells us (1 Kings 17 to 2 Kings 11), the cult of Baal and his female consort Asherah became official state cult in the northern kingdom ("Israel") as well as in the southern kingdom ("Judah"), alongside the cult of YHWH. A passage in Jeremiah (7:17–18) reports of such cults in Jerusalem itself, just before its destruction.

Do you not see what they are doing in the cities of Judah and in the streets of Jerusalem? The children gather wood, the fathers kindle fire, and the women knead dough, to make cakes for the queen of heaven;[6] and they pour drink offerings to other gods, to make me angry.

In other words Jeremiah the prophet (if he is a historical person), or whoever wrote under that name, is able to narrate the worship of the "queen of heaven" as an eyewitness. He disapproves of what he knows: the cult is a widely practiced family cult, in which the women are dominant, and this is considered one of the reasons for YHWH's wrath (cf. Jeremiah 44:15–30). As Carroll writes (1986: 212–13; see also 734–43),

An idyllic picture of egalitarian religion with a strong emphasis on the family worshipping together! The cakes have impressed on them the image of the queen of heaven, the mother goddess of the ancient world . . . or they may be cakes in the shape of a star . . .

Who is this "queen of heaven"? Carroll rightly maintains that her precise name—the Babylonian Ishtar, the Canaanite Anat or Astarte, the Egyptian Isis—is less than important. All the names point to the same cultural manifestation of great mother goddess. Significantly, the people claim that her worship brings peace and economic prosperity (44:16–19). Jeremiah, of course, is indignant: YHWH's anger is provoked by this cult. In his view, that of YHWH's messenger, the goddess

161

cult ultimately helped bring about the destruction of temple, city, and land.

A few points are worth noting here. It appears that as late as the sixth century B.C.E. cults of a/the mother goddess were popular even in Jerusalem, the supposed stronghold of YHWH's exclusive worship. Therefore, although it constituted an unwanted subculture for the author of the relevant biblical passages, the modern reader is under no obligation to label it as such. Furthermore, it seems that the goddess cult or cults flourished—and, significantly, as family cult—in times of political and economic stress. In such times people, especially women, seem to have turned back from the cult of the disappointing Hebrew Father to a divine Mother in a quest for maternal love and assistance. It follows that the accusations expressed by the literary "Jeremiah" have a sound basis in the reality of "his" day. The Father's disappointment in his children appears to be mirrored by his daughters' disappointment in him! Ironically, the information concerning this muted (minority?) view of the "daughters" is preserved by the atavistic patriarchal opposition to it.

Most narrators of the Hebrew Bible were probably males narrating for M consumption. They often accuse women of turning to non-monotheistic religious practices. And when the women are of foreign descent, the accusation becomes stereotypic. Such an approach is a useful ideological device, since it makes women the chief culprits in the drama of divine disappointment. For example, the religious influence of Solomon's many foreign wives is cited as a factor justifying the division of his kingdom into two kinglets immediately upon his death (1 Kings 11:1–13). In the age of Ezra and Nehemiah (mid-fifth century B.C.E.), foreign wives and mothers are divorced for their cultural and religious influence on the newly organized Jewish community. In other words, the usual societal, political, and economic rationale for exogamy and endogamy (Lévi-Strauss 1966; 1985) becomes secondary to the ideology of the Father. This ideology must be safeguarded against F religiosity and devotion to alternative cults.

Goddess cults were celebrated all over the ancient Near East, including the southern Levant or ancient "Israel." These cults had hallmarks. In them, the F divine element was dominant and often symbolized by the earth. The female deity stood for both fertility and sexuality: she was a lover and mother combined, but almost never enacted the socially inferior role of a daughter. She often had an M consort. He started his career by being her son, lover, and husband rolled into one. He died, sometimes because of her wrath, while she reigned eternal.

She would in places rescue him from death back into divine life, only for the script to be repeated periodically. Later on, who knows when, the tables were turned: the M consort became the chief symbol for fertility/sexuality—perhaps through his recurrent resurrection, perhaps as an imitation of the seasonal fertility cycle. The goddess then became *his* demoted consort (Neumann 1955).

It is important to realize that, whatever the internal gender dominance might be, so-called pagan pantheons from the third millennium B.C.E. onwards were organized mostly in F/M couples. Imitative fertility rites of the *hieros gamos* (sacred marriage) type—a dramatically enacted "marriage" of a priestess and a priest, a king and the goddess's priestess, an F commoner and an M priest—were an integral part of Mediterranean culture and known as such to the "Hebrews," who finally defined themselves as Israelites and Judahites. Sexual intercourse indulged in under the auspices of a religious sanctuary or custom, which looks like—at least in part—"white" magic for encouraging fertility in the biological and human cosmos, could not fail to be attractive. The prophetic books, as well as Numbers and Deuteronomy, acknowledge this attraction indignantly. They demote the practice to no more than fornication, adultery, and prostitution. However, surprisingly, they put the non-monotheistic reality which surrounded them and which, by their own testimony, was practiced by their compatriots to a fresh literary use. They incorporated it into their own metaphorical/symbolical world, thus providing YHWH with his lack: the missing F consort. To use Jungian terminology, YHWH's animus is provided with its complementary anima.

....

GOD THE HUSBAND: LOVE, MARRIAGE, AND COVENANT IN THE PROPHETIC BOOKS

....

The beginning of the book of Hosea (chaps. 1–3), which refers to political events of the end of the eighth century B.C.E., might be the earliest passages to contain the new metaphor. The relationship between YHWH and his people, formalized in the Torah (Pentateuch) in terms of a binding covenant, is metaphorized in terms of a marriage situation. God is depicted as a steadfast, supportive, responsible, and loving husband. The Israelites are his adulterous, promiscuous, immature wife. There is no doubt that the scenario is a takeoff of sexuality/fertility rites. The metaphorical woman's illicit "lovers"—in the plural!—are named *ba'alim* after Baal, the Canaanite male god of storm and rain and hence the fertilizer of the earth. In Hosea, the speaker himself (the prophet?) reports an illustration of this marriage principle: "he" takes a "woman of harlotry" for a wife (chap. 1), and accuses women of participating in that cult freely, with the knowledge of their male kin (4:13).

In chapters 2 and 3 of Hosea we learn how a change can be effected. The woman-nation is clearly in need of re-education. First, a divorce by the divine husband; a period of isolation and training will follow.[7] Then, and only then, will the woman-nation be worthy again of the divine husband's honorable intentions, and he will remarry her.

The same metaphor is employed in the Book of Jeremiah, which refers to a later period (beginning of the sixth century). The roles have not changed. On the contrary, they have become further polarized through the exaggerated imaging of the "wife." The woman-nation (Judah, in fact, since the northern kingdom was destroyed by the Assyrians in 722 B.C.E.), once more in danger of being divorced (Jeremiah 3), is even likened to a she-ass in heat (Brenner 1993a: chap. 2). In the book of Ezekiel, referring roughly to the same period or a little later, YHWH is both foster father and husband to the woman-Jerusalem; once grown, she becomes a common whore who commits religious and political adultery (chap. 16). This description, as well as that of the twin sisters Jerusalem and Samaria in chapter 23, is extremely pornographic (Setel 1985; van Dijk-Hemmes 1993).

Only in prophetic literature relating to the period after the destruction of Jerusalem and the exile do we get different versions of the same metaphor. Now, after the punishment (the exile) has been carried out, YHWH promises to reinstate his "wife" as mother and spouse in his/her land (Isaiah 49:14–23; 50:17–23, 54; 62:4–5; 66:7–13). Within the context of Isaiah 49–66, the image of god-as-husband is as frequent as that of god-as-father.

What can be gleaned from the continuing literary life of the divine husband/human spouse convention? The attribution of (metaphorical) matrimony to YHWH was probably facilitated not only by his exclusivity but also by his pronounced maleness. In stereotypic thinking, this maleness implies both a lack of and need for an F complement. The tendency to preserve YHWH's reputation of justice and fairness operates here as in the metaphor of the divine father. And last but not least, this religious-literary convention reflects societies in which the androcentric ethos, world view and vision are the norms. The negative F imagery consistently applied to the "erring" people becomes progressively more extravagant until, with Ezekiel, it achieves vulgar misogynistic proportions. It is designed to humble and intimidate the recipients. It must reflect, to a high degree, a reality of gender relations in an M world in which F sexuality is the Other, fatally attractive to males and because of that degraded and deemed in need of M control. To come back to Jungian terminology, YHWH is provided with an animal rather than an anima to complement his maleness.

THE THEOLOGICAL QUEST FOR A DIVINE FEMALE CONSORT: THE SONG OF SONGS

Within the Hebrew Bible, the Song of Songs is unique. It is an anthology of secular, non-matrimonial love lyrics, erotic and outspoken. Although the poetic material incorporated in it varies and has no clear plot line (in spite of many readers' attempts to find one), it has a well-organized structure (Exum 1973) which is probably due—like other features of the book—to the editor's or editors' efforts. One of the outstanding other features of the collection is the predominance of F voice(s) in it. Most of the lyrics assume the form of monologues and dialogues, and most of these are spoken by an F "I." Furthermore, those F voices compare favorably with their M counterparts. They are direct, articulate, loving, loyal, steadfast, imaginative, enterprising. The M lovers are weaker by comparison. No jealousy, no treachery, no accusations are admitted into the lovers' garden. There is no mention of a "father's house" or a father figure, as against references to a "mother's house" and mothers. The imagery employed by the M voices in regard to the F love object is strong, positive, beautiful. In short, egalitarian mutuality and gender equality—with a bias in favor of the F partner(s)—underlie the literary picture.

There may be many reasons for this unusual picture of gender roles in love and sexuality. One feasible explanation is the attribution of the Song of Songs, as a literary collection, to F authorship or editorship (Brenner 1989). This is probably less far-fetched than it seems at first, since love poetry is culturally tolerated for women even in patriarchal societies. What is most relevant to our agenda here, though, is not the biblical Song of Songs *per se* but, rather, the theological-allegorical exegesis attached to it by the orthodox Jewish and then Christian establishments from ancient times on.

Post-biblical Jewish interpretation coped with the uniquely secular nature of the Song of Songs and its apparent incompatibility with the rest of the Hebrew canon by promoting its allegorical interpretation as the only legitimate one. In the allegory, first hinted at in a text of the first century C.E., the M lover is once more the Hebrew god and the F lover is his nation. In contradistinction to the previous love stories and disappointments, this allegorized "story" is a happy affair in which mood, traditional role, and outcome are inverted. The nation-woman now actively and loyally seeks her master; other partners are out of the question. This allegory was taken over by the Christian church as well: here the partners are Jesus and the soul/church/community (the Christological approach) or Mary and the soul/community (the Mariological approach). Such traditional interpretations of the Song of Songs, which persist until our times, claim to decipher its original meaning through the negation of its profane erotic meaning, and by attributing the active role to the male (divine) partner rather than to the female (human) one.

The religious and theological advantages of such an allegorical interpretation are evident. To begin with, it chastises an unusual text and truly canonizes it. It also supplies god, finally, with a worthy loving partner. The allegory's therapeutic value almost cancels out the harsh harangues of the earlier prophetic books.

In passing, I would like to note that modern feminist critics share this ancient notion of the therapeutic import of the Song of Songs. Thus, for instance, Trible reads it as a counterfoil to the Garden of Eden story, a rectification of the gender relations and F social inferiority condoned there (Trible 1978).

YHWH AND HIS CONSORT: CONTEMPORANEOUS EXTRA-BIBLICAL EVIDENCE

At the beginning of the twentieth century, documents written on papyrus in Aramaic were found at Elephantine, a settlement on the small island in the Nile opposite Aswan. The documents discovered— legal, literary, religious—disclosed the existence of an organized colony of Jewish soldiers who populated the site from the beginning of the Persian rule in Egypt (525 B.C.E.) to the beginning of the common era. The Jewish settlers had a local temple and were conscious of their religious identity: their priests even attempted to correspond with the

Jerusalem priests on religious and cultic matters (Cowley 1923; Kraeling 1953).

Whom did the Jews of Elephantine worship? The Hebrew god, of course, whom they called Yhw (a shorter form of YHWH?). And alongside him, in the same temple, two goddesses: Asham (probably the Ashmat of Samaria named in Amos 8:14) of Beit El (a chief city in the northern, Israelite kingdom according to biblical historiography) and Anat of Beit El.

Scholars have found it relatively easy to affirm that Yhw of Elephantine is YHWH of the Hebrew Bible, even though Yhw has two (!) female consorts. They regarded the religious practice of Elephantine as Jewish, albeit not normative, and excused it on various grounds. The first excuse cites populist culture:

The Elephantine Jews brought with them to Egypt the popular religion combatted by the early prophets and by Jeremiah shortly before the destruction of the First Temple. It is true that this religion placed the God of Judah, Yahu . . . in the centre of the faith and worship. (Schalit 1971: 608)

Other scholars cite geographical distance and lack of communication with the prescriptive, normative Judaism of Second Temple Jerusalem, and/or assimilation to the foreign (non-monotheistic) environment. However, more recent archeological finds, earlier in date and closer to the Jerusalem centre, invalidate such apologies.

A Hebrew inscription in the old Hebrew script on a broken pythos, found in Kuntillet 'Ajrud in north-eastern Sinai (on the road from Gaza to the Red Sea) and dated to the beginning of the eighth century B.C.E., has three primitive figures drawn on it (fig. 1).

While the interpretation of these figures is still hotly debated by scholars (Dever 1984; Margalit 1989), I side with those who read it thus. The bigger figure in the foreground, on the left, is a crowned male figure; a smaller female figure, with breasts and a smaller crown, stands just behind him to the right.[8] Their arms are locked, spouselike. A third figure, probably a female (note the breasts again!) is seated to the far right, holding a musical instrument. The Hebrew inscription above the drawing reads: "I bless you by YHWH of Samariah and his Asherah" (Dever 1984; King 1989). Furthermore, a tomb inscription from el-Qom in Judea, dated approximately to the same period, also concludes with the words, "to YHWH and his Asherah" (Margalit 1990).

Asherah, like Anat, is a well-documented goddess of the north-west Semitic pantheon. We remember that, according to the Bible itself, at

Fig. I (Pirhiya Beck, Tel Aviv University)

times Asherah was officially worshipped in Israel; her cult was matron-ized by Jezebel who, supposedly, imported it from her native Phoeni-cian homeland. Other traces in the Bible either angrily acknowledge her worship as goddess—2 Kings 14:13, for instance, where another royal lady is involved—or else demote her from goddess to a sacred tree or pole set next to an altar (2 Kings 13:6; 17:16; Deuteronomy 16:21; and many more). The apparent need for the hostile and widely distributed polemics against Asherah worship constitutes evidence for its continued popularity. Margalit (1989) claims that, linguistically, "Asherah" signifies "[she who] walks behind," displaying a stereotypic if divine attitude that befits a wife (and is reflected in the Kuntillet 'Ajrud drawing). Thus both the partially suppressed and distorted biblical evidence and the archeological evidence combine to suggest one conclusion. The cult of a goddess, who was considered YHWH's spouse, was celebrated in more than one place during the First Temple era; and, beyond this period and the land, also by the Jewish settlement in Elephantine.

Readers and critics of the Hebrew Bible tend to balk at the idea that YHWH, the traces of canonical testimony notwithstanding, in fact had a divine consort in biblical times and well into the Persian period. They explain away the husband-wife imagery as "mere metaphor," as if metaphors are unproblematic figures of poetic expression.[9] But this is not so. The polemics of prophetic books appears to have been based on first-hand knowledge of the religious practice prevalent at the time. As hard as some elements fought to promote pure (M) monotheism, popular F cults continued to flourish. And in those cults, the unnatural deficiency of the Father god was supplemented by coupling him with a borrowed goddess figure. The archeological finds bear the most valuable witness to this phenomenon since, unlike the biblical texts, they are not overtly tendentious.

Finally, scholarly attempts to dismiss a consort status for Asherah in the Kuntillet 'Ajrud and el-Qom inscriptions, attempts motivated by the same purist ideologies found in the Bible itself, have been repudiated by many scholars. The need for an F complement was felt, the gap filled. Traditionalist protestations can no more obliterate YHWH's divine consort from the history of biblical religion, even if the Bible itself promotes her rejection with tell-tale vehemence. Patai's much criticized book, *The Hebrew Goddess* (1967), should therefore be revalued in the light of recent discoveries.

There are perhaps other and more traces in the Hebrew Bible for a divine F consort.[10] At this point, however, we shall turn to ancient Bible exegesis of another kind.

BEYOND THE HEBREW BIBLE: THE FEMALE PRINCIPLES OF THE SHEKINAH AND THE SHABBAT

Jewish mysticism does, of course, relate to the Hebrew Bible as to a canon and prooftext. Since Jewish mystical texts date from the first century C.E. on, they constitute another type of testimony for ancient Bible interpretation. And lest we think that mysticism is esoteric only, let us remember that esoteric it may be but it is theosophical too. At any rate, it has pervaded Jewish life and customs more and more over the ages.

The language of Jewish mysticism is erotic. The mystic's attempts to come closer to divine phenomena through the *Sefirot* ("stages") are depicted in sexual terminology (as well as in terms of light/darkness, letters and number combinations). It is therefore not too startling to find among the imaginative literature of the Qabbalah (mysticism) some fresh variations on YHWH's F complements. These hark back to biblical notions which are further developed, but with a twist. We shall name two such cases by way of illustrating this point.

According to the Bible, god's immanence (Hebrew *kabod*) "dwells" (Hebrew *shakan*) in certain parts of the world and among his people. Post-biblical Judaism developed the concept of immanence, and alongside it, that of god's *Shekinah*, "dwelling." In the Qabbalah, the *Shekinah* is the F element of the *Sefirot*, the first of the ten "stages." The mystic's ultimate purpose is to recover god's oneness through the reunification of his F and M elements—the oneness damaged by Israel's sins and other factors.

Another divine spouse is the Shabbat. In sixteenth-century Safed, a great Qabbalic centre, the Shabbat was hailed as the "queen": let us remember that one of the biblical god's appellations would translate as "the king of the royal kings." That the divine king is paired with the royal Shabbat becomes more explicit with the spreading of the custom to recite the Song of Songs for the Shabbat. Another poem recited for it was the biblical passage praising the woman or wife of valor (Proverbs 31:10–31). In time, the view of the Shabbat's divine matrimonial status spread beyond mystical circles.

YHWH AS MOTHER

God the father (as distinct from mother) is the norm in the Hebrew Bible. An additional partial list of passages referring to his paternal attributes includes the following: Deuteronomy 32:6; 2 Samuel 7:14; Isaiah 63:16; 64:7; Jeremiah 3:4, 19; 31:8; Malachi 1:6; Psalms 103:13; and three occurrences in Chronicles. Nevertheless, in some instances he is likened to a woman and, specifically, to woman-as-mother. The F images attributed to YHWH are infrequent but distributed throughout the Hebrew Bible. They occur in the Torah (Numbers 11:12), the Psalms (123:2), and Hosea 11, but mainly in Isaiah 40–66.[11] These chapters in Isaiah are, by scholarly consent, poems written and delivered not earlier than the middle of the sixth century B.C.E., from the time of the return from the Babylonian exile. In some passages (e.g., 42:13–14; 45:9–10; 49:14–15; and 66:13), YHWH is compared to a mother and a woman in labor. Gruber rightly states that, within these same poetic collections, the image of god-as-father features too (in 42:13; 63:16; 64:7). Gruber explains the sudden proliferation of positive F imagery applied to god, in addition to the more traditional M imagery, as perhaps a deliberate response on the part of the exilic author to other earlier prophetic traditions which had intimated "that in the religion of Israel maleness is a positive value with which divinity chooses to identify itself. Perhaps, as a result of this realization our prophet deliberately made use of both masculine and feminine similes for God" (Gruber 1983: 358). Perhaps. But, on the whole, the literary situation remains unambiguous. References to the motherhood of god, even if they are more frequent in Isaiah 40–66 than elsewhere in the Hebrew Bible, are still rare. Although their existence cannot be denied, it should be neither overstated nor magnified out of proportion. Accrediting YHWH with motherhood is but another stratagem for filling his F lack.

A more traditional formulation of the problematics involved in a one-gender representation of the divine is offered by Gruber in his conclusion: ". . . a religion that seeks to convey the Teaching of God who is above and beyond both sexes cannot succeed to do so in a manner which implies that a positive-divine value is attached to one of the two sexes" (Gruber 1983: 359).

Indeed. The biblical god is not a bi-gender god. His predominant image is that of a male single parent. His lack of F components is filled by various means. In some passages he is provided with F consorts, human or divine, a line attested by external drawings and inscriptions[12] and continued in Jewish mysticism; in yet others he displays stereotypic F attributes. (Is not being a mother a biblical ideal for women?) The former solution has damaging consequences for YHWH's credibility as an exclusive god. The latter solution is too infrequent to be influential. The implications of this state of affairs for the women and men of the biblical communities, and for our Jewish and Christian cultures today, are the subject of intense debates among feminist critics of the Bible, and between them and non-feminists.

A PERSONAL POSTSCRIPT

I readily admit that my reading of the Hebrew Bible is motivated by what I am: Jewish, Israeli by birth and choice, middle class, an academic, a female, a feminist, a mother, divorced, non-religious, politically minded—in that or any other order. My emotional and intellectual sensibilities are the prisms through which I perceive and critique. My readerly location motivates me to ask the biblical text certain questions. The questions I ask condition, to a very large extent, the answers I attempt to glean.

From my perspective, gender issues in the Hebrew Bible can hardly be redeemed for many feminists. Small consolations can indeed be gleaned from one specific text or another; but, on the whole, the so-called Good Book is a predominantly M document which reflects a deeply rooted conviction in regard to woman's otherness and social inferiority. Its M god is made to pretend, most of the time and against all odds, that he does not really need F company or F properties. Paradoxically, the fight itself is testimony to its futility. In spite of this small victory, the post-reading sensation I experience focuses on the bitter taste in my mouth.

This is my heritage. I am stuck with it. I cannot and will not shake it off. And it hurts.

Notes

1. Cf. e.g. the command opening the Decalogue, Exodus 20:2–4, and the parallel passage in Deuteronomy 5:8–9.
2. Numerous feminists believe that Y<small>HWH</small>'s loving and caring traits should be equated with the female/feminine maternal principle, somehow incorporated/ taken over/motivating this obviously male deity. The equation of F and emotion/caring, as against M and discipline, constitutes in itself compliance with stereotypic gender norms. More on this below.
3. I use a lower-case 'g' for 'god' instead of the customary upper case, since the god we are discussing here is a literary figure like others in the biblical story. As such, I do not want to give him the privileged status of a privileged spelling.
4. For a sample of feminist discussions of and additional bibliography for the two creation stories—the creation of both humans together (Genesis 1) and the creation of each separately in the Garden story (Genesis 2)—cf. articles by various scholars in Brenner (1993b: 24–172).
5. See Pressler (1993: 113–14), who writes in her conclusion, 'Several recent scholars have argued that the Deuteronomic laws exhibit a "peculiarly humanistic" view of women or a non-hierarchical view of gender relationships within the family. An examination of the presuppositions and purposes of the Deuteronomic family legislation calls into question this assessment. . . . [The laws] do aim at protecting dependent family members, including women. . . . Nonetheless, none of these protective laws challenges that hierarchical, male-defined structure of the family in any fundamental way. Moreover, they presuppose the authority of the male head of the household even as they set limits on that authority.'

6. The vowel signs for the word translated 'queen' here actually obscure the word. However, ancient Bible translations are reliable witnesses that 'queen of heaven'—that is, the goddess of heaven—is the original sense of the (initially vowel-less) text.

7. In the Hebrew Bible the option of terminating a marriage is not given to the wife. Only the husband can initiate a divorce or legally accuse a wife of adultery.

8. In this interpretation, the overhang between both figures' legs is *not* defined as a penis (it is situated too much to the back which, even in the lack of perspective, can be seen clearly). Rather, that overhang is a tail, probably an Egyptian influence, signifying the divine status of both figures.

9. For the relations of metaphor, desire, and subconscious, and much more, see Lakoff and Turner (1989).

10. In the first collection of the Book of Proverbs, chaps. 1–9, a personified figure of Woman Wisdom appears again and again. She is often described, in erotic terms, as the right 'consort' for a human male. In chap. 8 she is depicted as YHWH's daughter; in chap. 9, a woman with her own household. Many scholars have noted that, in both cases, the Woman Wisdom cuts a goddess figure. Hence, they ask whether these descriptions of her do not point to her status as YHWH's divine consort. I think that the main source for this goddess description (Proverbs 9) is too isolated to provide any firm basis for conclusion. The imagery appears to be derived from a human rather than divine context. See Camp (1985: 23–147).

11. On Numbers 11, see Trible (1978: 32), and against her interpretation see Gruber (1985: 77); on Hosea, see Schüngel-Straumann (1986: 119–34); on Isaiah 40–66, see Gruber (1983; 1985) and Darr (1994).

12. For interpretations of the archaeological materials, see, recently, Hadley (2000, esp. 84–155).

References

Brenner, Athalya (1993a). 'On "Jeremiah" and the Poetics of (Prophetic?) Pornography', in A. Brenner and F. van Dijk-Hemmens (eds.), *On Gendering Texts: Female and Male Voices in the Hebrew Bible*. Leiden: Brill.

—— (ed.) (1993b). *A Feminist Companon to Genesis*. Sheffield: JSOT Press.

Camp, Claudia V. (1985). *Wisdom and the Feminine in the Book of Proverbs*. Decatur: Almond.

Carroll, Robert P. (1986). *Jeremiah: A Commentary*. London: SCM Press.

Cowley, A. E. (1923). *Aramaic Papyri of the Fifth Century BC*. Oxford: Oxford University Press.

Crenshaw, James L. (1983). 'Sapiential Rhetoric and its Warrants', *Vetus Testamentum Supplement* 32.

Darr, Katheryn Pfisterer (1994). *Isaiah's Vision and the Family of God*. Louisville: Westminster/John Knox.

Davies, Philip R. (1993). 'Women, Men, God, Sex and Power: The Birth of a Biblical Myth', in Brenner (1993b).

Dever, William G. (1984). 'Asherah, Consort of Yhweh? New Evidence from Kuntillet 'Arjud', *Bulletin of the American Schools of Oriental Research* 255.

Exum, J. Cheryl (1973). 'A Literary and Structural Analysis of the Song of Songs', *Zeitschrift für Altentestamentliche Wissenschaft* 85.

Gruber, Mayer I. (1983). 'The Motherhood of God in Second Isaiah', *Revue Biblique* 90.

—— (1985). 'Female Imagery Relating to God in Second Isaiah' (in Hebrew), *Beer Sheva* 2.

Hadley, Judith M. (2000). *The Cult of Asherah in Ancient Israel and Judah: Evidence for a Hebrew Goddess.* Cambridge: Cambridge University Press.

King, Philip J. (1989). 'The Great Eighth Century', *Bible Review* 5(4).

Kraeling, E. G. (1953). *The Brooklyn Museum Aramaic Papyri: New Documents of the Fifth Century from the Jewish Colony at Elephantine.* New Haven: Yale University Press.

Lakoff, George, and Turner, Mark (1989). *More than Cool Reason.* Chicago: University of Chicago Press.

Lévi-Strauss, Claude (1966). *The Savage Mind.* Chicago: University of Chicago Press.

Margalit, B. (1989). 'The Meaning and Significance of Asherah', *Vetus Testamentum* 39.

—— (1990). 'Some Observations on the Inscription and Drawing from Khirbet el-Qom', *Vetus Testamentum* 40.

Neumann, Erich (1955). *The Great Mother.* New York: Pantheon.

Pardes, Ilana (1992). *Countertraditions in the Bible: A Feminist Approach.* Cambridge, Mass.: Harvard University Press.

Patai, Raphael (1967). *The Hebrew Goddess.* New York: Ktav.

Pressler, Carolyn J. (1993). *The View of Women Found in the Deuteronomic Family Law.* Berlin: Walter de Gruyter.

Schalit, A. (1971). 'Elephantine', in *Encyclopaedia Judaica.*

Schüngel-Straumann, H. (1986). 'Gott als Mutter in Hosea 11', *Tübinger Theologische Quartalschrift* 166.

Setel, T. Drorah (1985). 'Prophets and Pornography: Female Sexual Imagery in Hosea', in L. M. Russell (ed.), *Feminist Interpretations of the Bible.* Oxford: Blackwell.

Trible, Phyllis (1973). 'Depatriarchalizing in Biblical Interpretation', *Journal of the American Academy of Religion* 41.

—— (1978). *God and the Rhetoric of Sexuality.* Philadelphia: Fortress.

van Dijk-Hemmes, Fokkelien (1993). 'The Metaphorization of Woman in Poetic Speech: An Analysis of Ezekiel 23', in A. Brenner and F. van Dijk-Hemmens (eds.), *On Gendering Texts: Female and Male Voices in the Hebrew Bible.* Leiden: Brill.

17 The Secret of Redemption

Avivah Gottlieb Zornberg*

An announcement for a lecture by Avivah Zornberg (standing room only, as all her talks are) billed her as possibly the greatest living female Torah scholar. I felt mildly irritated: which male Torah scholar is greater? And what is distinctively female about Zornberg's creative way with biblical and rabbinic texts? With regard to the second point, though not the first, I have reconsidered. On the one hand, Zornberg's appeal to rabbinic commentaries to elucidate biblical texts is highly traditional which, in her Orthodox Jewish circles, usually means male. On the other, her seamless transitions from midrash through Milton to existentialist philosophy, literary criticism, and child psychology are anything but traditional. But are they distinctively female? Zornberg might disagree, but one might specu- late that her semi-outsider status, acquired simply by virtue of being a woman in the predominantly male world of Orthodox Torah scholarship, made her more willing to blur boundaries between areas of learning and life experience that might otherwise have remained distinct. There is nothing linear about Zornberg's approach to her sources; to hear her teach is to witness the construction of a marvellous garment made from interlocking circles. Less speculatively, a sign of her gender is her tendency to highlight images and analogies, sometimes her own and sometimes elaborated from rabbinic interpretations, that are distinctively female; the crossing of the Red Sea is seen as a birthing. How fortunate that Zornberg's father, an Orthodox rabbi, was enough of a feminist himself to consider it worthwhile to teach his daughters Torah.   DL

THE SECRET OF REDEMPTION

The "secret of redemption," in its technical, coded form, consisted of the words *pakod pakad*—"He has taken notice." The one who knows the words will be the accredited redeemer. For Serach, the wise

---

* Avivah Gottlieb Zornberg, from 'The Secret of Redemption: a Tale of Mirrors', from *The Particulars of Rapture: Reflections on Exodus.* Copyright © 2001 by Avivah Gottlieb Zornberg. Used by permission of Doubleday, a division of Random House, Inc.

matriarch, this secret is reducible to "letters": in these letters, she hears the reconstituted words that represent redemption. The letters are *peh peh*, labials, panting, rudimentary sounds. They evoke the panting cries of the laboring woman. Rashi puts us in mind of these cries, when he treats the name Puah (one of the midwives) as a professional reference: identified in the midrash with Miriam, she is named for the panting breaths of the laboring woman, or the coaxing talk of the midwife (1:15). The name is an onomatopoeia, conjuring the sound-world of birth.

The letter *peh* is the same as the word for mouth, the site of language; that is, the place where redemption is constructed or suffocated. One who comes uttering these letters will, in the future, redeem, says Serach. And in saying so, in recognizing the letters, in decoding the secret signs, she makes redemption real in the world. The midrash subtly registers her sensibility, by using the two expressions, *othoth* and *othioth*. Of the signs, the miracles, the *othoth*, she declares dismissively, *ein bahem mamash*—"There is nothing solid in them." Only letters, *othioth*, the fluid shapings of language, only they have substance. Paradoxically, she declasses the miracle, and gives prestige to the letter, to the lips, the mouth.

The key to redemption is hers, but she is absent from the surface of the biblical narrative. The midrash detects her, extracts her from the "inner sphere," has her construct redemption. In this role she becomes not merely a custodian, but an agent of redemption.

A TALE OF WOMEN

However, a classic statement in the Talmud singles out that human group, quite visible in the biblical narrative, to which she belongs: "In reward for the righteous women of that generation, Israel was redeemed from Egypt."[1] Redemption, says the Talmud, came only because of "righteous women." In the narrative, we can think of the righteousness of Jochebed (Moses' mother) and Miriam, of Pharaoh's daughter, of the dissident midwives. But the Talmud seems to speak of something else, something that many women shared, without which the people would not have been redeemed. This "secret sharing," connoted by Serach, whose words create redemption, characterizes, I would suggest, all the righteous women of the time. What is it that, working in the semidarkness of Havel's "inner sphere," emerges with such explosive force as to shock the system of Egypt?

The Talmudic answer is the narrative that follows the statement. This is a narrative about women who feed and comfort their husbands in the field, have relations with them there, and bear children. That is, they defy the *gezera* of Pharaoh in the most literal sense, by being fruitful. Their answer to the decree is the answer of the body— sexuality, pregnancy, birth, nursing—assisted by God Himself. They act as God had done at the beginning of time, they create and nurture life: that is, in the simplest sense, the meaning of redemption. They live within the truth.

Another version of this midrash, however, gives us, I suggest, an answer of greater imaginative power:

"These are the records (pikudei) *of the Tabernacle"*: You find that when Israel were in harsh labor in Egypt, Pharaoh decreed (*gazar*) against them that they should not sleep at home nor have relations with their wives. Said Rabbi Shimeon bar Chalafta, What did the daughters of Israel do? They would go down to draw water from the river and God would prepare for them little fish in their buckets, and they would sell some of them, and cook some of them, and buy wine with the proceeds, and go to the field and feed their husbands, as it is said, "In all the labor in the field." (1:14) And when they had eaten and drunk, the women would take the mirrors and look into them with their husbands, and she would say, "I am more comely than you," and he would say, "I am more comely than you." And as a result, they would accustom them- selves to desire, and they were fruitful and multiplied, and God took note of them (*pakad*) immediately. Some of our sages said, They bore two children at a time, others said, They bore six at a time, yet others said, They bore twelve at a time, and still others said, Six hundred thousand . . . *And all these numbers from the mirrors . . .* In the merit of those mirrors which they showed their husbands to accustom them to desire, from the midst of the harsh labor, they raised up all the hosts, as it is said, "All the hosts of God went out of the land of Egypt" (12:41) and it is said, "God brought the children of Israel out of the land of Egypt in their hosts." (12:51)

When God told Moses to make the Tabernacle, the whole people stood up and offered whatever they had—silver, gold, copper, etc.; everyone eagerly offered their treasures. The women said, "What have we to offer as a gift for the Tabernacle?" So they brought the mirrors to Moses. When Moses saw those mirrors, he was furious with them. He said to the Israelites, "Take sticks and break their thighs! What do they need mirrors for?" Then God said to Moses, "Moses, these you despise! *These mirrors raised up all those hosts in Egypt!* Take them, and make of them a copper ewer with a copper stand for the priests to sanctify themselves—as it is said, 'And he made the ewer of copper and its stand of copper, of the mirrors of those who created hosts . . .' " (38:8) [This is a free, midrashic translation of the verse.]²

The midrash gains its momentum from the opening *gezera*: Pharaoh issues a decree, a cut-and-dried (the root of *gezera* means "to cut") formula that will separate men from women. In the context of the biblical narrative, the purpose is clear: ". . . so that they may not increase . . ." (1:10). Pharaoh has cut off the possibility of natural increase among the Israelites. But the midrash does not emphasize the effective purpose of the edict: merely that couples are sexually separated, since the husbands may not sleep at home.

The women enter the narrative as a question: "What did the daughters of Israel do?" The assumption is that the women, who are not most directly affected by the edict (since it is the men who are the laborers and who are prevented from going home at night), will adopt some measure against it. Since the edict is one of separation, of effective sterilization, the women's efforts naturally tend towards reunion. The little fish, archetypal symbols of fertility, become clear sexual signs, as they providentially swim up in the women's buckets. They are transformed, in the most pragmatic way—through cooking and the cash nexus—into a nourishing and stimulating meal for the exhausted husbands in the field.

It is striking that God appears twice in this narrative: first, He provides the little fish, the most "natural" of events. Thereafter, the women's planning takes over, the conscious use and reconstruction of the natural into the shape of desire. Having fed their husbands, the women contemplate themselves with their husbands as a couple in "the mirrors," which are described with the definite article, though we have not read of them till now. What follows is an intimate scene of erotic "boasting," shockingly unconventional in sentimental terms. Instead of praising each other, each praises her/his own beauty, by comparison with the other. This "mirror work" produces desire and procreation; through processes that are complex and willful, they are "fruitful and multiply," fulfilling the original blessing/command to humankind (Gen 1:28; 9:7).

And God acts a second time: He "takes notice"—*pakad*—of them. This one word, here most clearly signifying the mysterious gift of pregnancy, gathers multiple resonances. Its first use in the Torah was to narrate Sarah's pregnancy, after years of barrenness (Gen 21:1). God's promise of redemption—*pakod yifkod*—is fulfilled here, in the most "natural" mode imaginable. For what could be more "natural" than the women's conceiving, after they are reunited with their husbands? It is as natural as the shoals of fish that swarm up in the women's buckets. And yet in these two moments, particularly, in the fishing and in the conceiving of many children (and the midrash reminds us that the same word is used for both—*vayishretzu*—they "swarmed"), God enters the narrative, and gives a surrealistic turn to the natural events: fish-becomes-wine-becomes-desire, and babies are born in multiples of (perhaps) six hundred thousand. Why does the midrash require God here? Why does it bring into play the epic reson-ance of *pakod yifkod*, of the "secret of redemption"? And why the mirrored narcissism of the couple at the visual heart of the midrash? On the "plot" level, it would have been sufficient to have the women feed their husbands well, in order to achieve reunion and fertility.

The end of the midrash emphasizes the enigmatic character of events. The extraordinary fertility of the women leads to the Zen-like statement: "All these numbers were from the mirrors." The midrash deflects our attention from the "natural" level of reading, from the normal strategies of arousal of desire, the aphrodisiac function of wine and fish, although the calculated preparation of these delicacies was the opening subject of the narrative. Essentially, claims the midrash, it was all done with mirrors. And finishes with a bizarre dialogue, in which Moses violently deplores the women's gift of these same mirrors to the Tabernacle, while God overrides his objections: "these mirrors raised up all the Israelite hosts in Egypt."

Subtly, the midrash yields its meanings. The mirrors are not simply the means by which women adorn themselves, set in motion the pro-cesses of desire, procreation, the creation of a nation. A much larger claim is being made: through these mirrors, each woman conceived *six hundred thousand* babies at a time. These mirrors, when God asks for gifts to the Tabernacle, to create sacred space, are *all the women have*. In Rashi's version, God concludes: "These mirrors are more precious to Me than any other gift."[3]

Moses' anger at the apparent frivolity, the inappropriate sexual associations of the gift, makes it clear that the gift is not a "giving up" of vanity.[4] It becomes an installation at the liminal point of entry into the sacred space: the mirrors are used to plate the priestly ewer, where hands and feet are washed. Giving their mirrors for this purpose, the women are making no ascetic immolation of the accoutrements of desire: Moses' outraged rejection indicates this quite unmistakably. "Break their thighs," expresses an anger at sexuality that transgresses boundaries. It is God who speaks for the women and their mirrors:

"the mirrors *raised up* the hosts of Israel." The verb *he'emidu* is often used to mean "beget," so that God actually says: "These mirrors *begat* the hosts of Israel." It was all done with mirrors!

MIRROR WORK

The most direct effect of the mirrors, in the words of the midrash, is desire ("And they accustomed themselves to desire . . ."). The drama, the action of husband and wife in front of the mirror, the four faces speaking, challenging, affirming beauty, creates a culture of desire. For one of the most arresting phenomena in the narrative is its fusion of intimacy and the most public perspective. The subject is the relation between husband and wife, in its most delicate moment; but in watching the couple in front of their mirror, we see multiple mirror reflections of the scene. Every woman in Israel is enacting the same drama. Our subject is not one particular woman, one extraordinary heroic figure, but "the daughters of Israel," a title that gives honor and propriety to their acts. Strangely, there is a chaste, impersonal quality to the narrative: it tells, essentially, the story of redemption: "In reward for the righteous women of that generation, Israel were redeemed from Egypt" (B. Sotah 11b). In this way a nation of six hundred thousand men was formed: this is the demographic, public product of the story. But, at the same time, each individual woman is described as having given birth to six hundred thousand. The very thought concentrates the mind wonderfully!

The enigmas of the story clearly center on the mirror. What is its role here, in creating desire, fruitfulness, and the *pekida*, the transfiguring presence of God? Each woman says, "I am more beautiful than you." She initiates the boasting game. The midrash may well be evoking the verse from The Song of Songs: "I am black but beautiful—*na'avah*" (1:5). The word for beauty is the same as the one used in the midrash—*na'eh*—comely, harmonious. Literally, the verse reads, "I am black *and* beautiful," but since there is no alternative mode of indicating the disjunctive "but," a teasing ambiguity destabilizes the text. Clearly, in context, blackness is a reason for shame:[5] here, the beloved proudly claims a paradoxical beauty despite/within her swarthiness. This is no primary narcissism; but the difficult project of seeing beauty in the blackened self.

Classic midrashim tell of the beauty that God sees in His people, in their very blackness. In Rashi's commentary, for instance, although the lover has abandoned her because of her blackness, she asserts her *structural* beauty: the blackness is mere sunburn, but her limbs are well made. By analogy, even if her deeds are ugly, she affirms a true self, a genetic identity, in which beauty is always potential. To assert this, she must draw, not on the assurances of a lover, but on her own awareness of beauty-within-blackness.

She says: "I am more beautiful than you," not "You are more beautiful than I." Her boast, delivered as they gaze together at their reflection in the mirror, is a challenge to her husband, grimy with clay and mud, to see beauty within that blackness. What she initiates is a dynamic, loving game. What she says is not a statement of fact, but a performance of transformation. Against the *gezerah* of Pharaoh she sets up the mirror of desire. The hosts of Israel, the secret of redemption: it is all done with mirrors.

The peculiar nature of this gift of the women to the Tabernacle is discussed by Ramban.[6] Why was Moses so angry at this particular donation? After all, the women gave other female items associated with narcissism and sexuality—jewelry of all kinds. Ramban answers that the other gifts were melted down, gold, silver, copper, to make the accessories of the Tabernacle. Only the mirrors were preserved as mirrors and used for one specific object—the ewer. The burnished copper, "very beautiful," Ramban notes, was assigned to this one purpose, and so remains as an unmitigated reminder of the mirrors and their original uses, with all the erotic associations that Moses deplores. The ewer, at which priests consecrate themselves to the service of God,[7] retains the reflective surfaces, the form and function of the original gift.

There are even fascinating speculations in the midrashic literature that the ewer served as a kind of mirror-system, like a periscope or a telescope, giving people a view of the interior of the Tabernacle, for example.[8] Mirrors thus function to allow vision at oblique angles, round corners, at a distance. With all the distortion of mirrors of that period (polished copper, we remember[9]), we may say that they function as revealers of the inaccessible: one's own face, the banned interior of the Tabernacle. They offer, in a sense, a counterworld to the world of the *gezera*, of the "way it has to be." The natural limitations of vision are challenged and deflected by this instrument that distorts reality (even modern mirrors retain the right-left reversal) in order to extend perception.

A similar point is made by Rashi, in a comment on Isaiah 3:23.

Here, mirrors are referred to as *gilyonim*—"revealers." Since this expression never recurs, Rashi explains: "These are mirrors, called so because they reveal the forms of the face." The plural perspectives of the mirror—each movement of the head produces a different form in the mirror—yield a shifting, multiple revelation of the self.

In *The Unbearable Lightness of Being*, Milan Kundera uses the mirror as the means by which lovers explore unexpected possibilities. Sabina "looked into the mirror with the same long questioning stare, training it first on herself, then on him."[10] A bowler hat reveals the abyss between them, since it was a motif in her previous love relationship with Tomas, and its multiple meanings are meaningless to her present lover. Originally, it had evoked laughter and a strange excitement: "Is excitement really a mere step away from laughter?"[11] The mirror, opening up possibilities, raises questions about the *gezera*, about the restricted, cramped experience of what has to be. It also painfully reveals the loneliness of unshared idioms of love.

Mirrors, as Rashi comments on the women's gift to the Tabernacle, are used by women to adorn themselves. It is this possibility of self-adornment, of costuming, that is the gift of the mirror. The effect can be jocular, it can signify violence, or humiliation, as in the Kundera scene. The basic assumption is that this activity belongs to the realm of the *yetzer hara*, the evil inclination, as Rashi points out; that is, self-costuming, cosmetics, self-decoration are a masking of the true face, they are used to deceive, to seduce. And yet, in our midrash, God vindicates the mirror and its costuming function against Moses' predictable indignation. For the mirror is used against the *gezera*; when a couple gazes into it, it generates redemption.

Many things can function as mirrors, can reveal the human face, in all its possible forms, to itself. To this end the work of art has traditionally been described as a mirror. In the English Renaissance, indeed, this became something of a cliché: the literary device of the *Mirror for Magistrates*, for instance, became a popular moral genre. More famously, Hamlet exhorts the players, as they rehearse their play, to "hold as 'twere the mirror up to nature."[12] The play is to present a version of reality—but only "as 'twere"; it is to be a stylized rendering of the murderous act in which Claudius is to recognize himself. Similarly, when he attempts to touch his mother's moral imagination, he shows her a diptych, twin portraits of his father and his uncle, her past and her present husband. They are "a glass Where you may see the inmost part of you."[13] Looking outwards at this "glass" is in some deflected, undefended way to see one's own face; for Gertrude, it is to be shocked out of the lie she has been living.

Lionel Trilling notices that the manufacture of mirrors in the eighteenth century coincides with that point in history when "men became individuals." This he defines as the ability to imagine oneself in more than one role:

The individual looks into mirrors, larger and much brighter than those that were formerly held up to magistrates. The French psychoanalyst Jacques Lacan believes the development of the "*Je*" was advanced by the manufacture of mirrors: again it cannot be decided whether man's belief that he is a "*Je*" is the result of the Venetian craftsmen's having learned how to make plate-glass or whether the demand for looking-glasses stimulated this technological success. If he is an artist the individual is likely to paint self-portraits; if he is Rembrandt, he paints some threescore of them. And he begins to use the word "self" not as a mere reflexive or intensive, but as an autonomous noun referring, the O.E.D. tells us, to "that . . . in a person [which] is really and intrinsically *he* (in contradistinction to what is adventitious)", as that which he must cherish for its own sake and show to the world for the sake of good faith. The subject of an autobiography is just such a self . . .[14]

THE MIRROR STAGE

Trilling's reference to Lacan evokes the French psychoanalyst's important theory of the mirror. Lacan writes of the formation of the "Je," as experienced in psychoanalysis, which "leads us to oppose any philosophy directly issuing from the *Cogito.*" It is not pure thought that defines Being ("I think, therefore I am"—(Descartes)), but the ability of the human infant to recognize his own image in the mirror (the *aha*—realization), to play with his reflection: "a startling spectacle," writes Lacan:

Unable as yet to walk, or even to stand up, and held tightly as he is by some support, human or artificial . . ., he nevertheless overcomes, in a flutter of jubilant activity, the obstructions of his support and, fixing his attitude in a slightly leaning-forward position, in order to hold it in his gaze, brings back an instantaneous aspect of the image.[15]

This "mirror stage" constitutes the transformation that takes place in the subject when he assumes an image, an "Ideal-I": "the subject anticipates in a mirage the maturation of his power." "Still sunk in his motor incapacity and nursling dependence," he experiences a "jubilant assumption of his specular image," a gestalt, an imago, that is "capable of formative effects in the organism." Lacan cites a biological experiment, which shows that "it is a necessary condition for the maturation of the gonad of the female pigeon that it should see another member of its species, of either sex; so sufficient in itself is this condition that the desired effect may be obtained merely by placing the individual within reach of the field of reflection of a mirror."

The *mirror stage* is a drama whose internal thrust is precipitated from insufficiency to anticipation—and which manufactures for the subject, caught up in the lure of spatial identification, the succession of phantasies that extends from a fragmented body-image to a form of its totality that I shall call orthopaedic—and, lastly, to the assumption of the armor of an alienating identity, which will mark with its rigid structure the subject's entire mental development.[16]

The movement from fragmented body (*corps morcelé*) to "orthopaedic totality" is traced by Jane Gallop in her study, *Reading Lacan*.[17] In her reading, the mirror stage is crucial since it is not only the individual's *future* that is created in anticipation, but his *past*, the body in bits and pieces, that is also retroactively imagined, perceived for the first time in the illusory mirror moment, when the body seems to become coherent. Anticipation creates an awareness of the *corps morcelé* that must come *after* the mirror stage.

Since the entire past and present is dependent upon an already anticipated maturity—that is, a projected ideal one—any "natural maturation (however closely it might resemble the anticipated ideal one) must be defended against, for it threatens to expose the fact that the self is an illusion done with mirrors."

Gallop quotes a later article of Lacan, to focus the paradox of the mirror stage:

This illusion of unity, in which a human being is always looking forward to self-mastery, entails a constant danger of sliding back again into the chaos from which he started; it hangs over the abyss of a dizzy Ascent in which one can perhaps see the very essence of Anxiety.[18]

Self-mastery is, in some unavoidable sense, the realization of the falsity of the self. And yet, there is the infant's *jubilation*. In spite of the anxiety of the "dizzy Ascent," in spite of the risk of "sliding back again into . . . chaos," there is that "fleeting moment of jubilation" (Gallop) on the threshold of selfhood. This moment, then, is a "brief moment of doomed glory," like that of Adam and Eve, expelled from paradise into history: anticipating mastery, they actually gain a "horrified recognition of their nakedness."

THE PARADOX OF REDEMPTION

Like Adam and Eve, and the mirror-stage infant, we have the Exodus midrashic couple in the mirror. In a moment of illumination, they laugh at the anticipated beauty of their being. Inspired by the truth of her "inner sphere," the woman challenges her husband to recognize the mirror image of his own beauty. In this way the couple are "precipitated from insufficiency to anticipation." This is the secret of redemption: they are "thrown forward into history."

The tragic dimension of the experience, however, as Gallop points out, is that, like the infant, the couple have "assumed by anticipation a totalized mastered body." They must therefore retroactively perceive their own inadequacy. A vision of wholeness will give birth to the infinite variations of the whole Jewish people (the mythic six hundred thousand births); each woman senses the intimate immensity of the resources of self and other. But the new awareness that is redemption inevitably brings with it an awareness of the body "in bits and pieces." For it is, in essence, a moment of self-delusion, of captivation by an illusory image. Both future and past are thus rooted in an illusion.

Inevitably, we are confronting radical questions about whether the people are fit for redemption. Are they *re'uyim*, literally, are they "seeable" as redeemed? The power of the midrash lies in its affirmation of a transformative vision that anticipates a future beauty and thus reconstructs the past. This is the "secret" of the women, as they place the "inner sphere," the intimate arena of their love-relations with their husbands in the mirror of their desire. In doing this, they defy the *gezera*: instead of that which must be, there are multiple possibilities, jubilant, polymorphous, anticipatory:

Sublimated forms of love—political, social, religious, cultural—reclaim a totality on a historical as well as a personal scale. But in every form of love a past and a future are grasped as if present . . . What is *ahistorical* is the need to hope. And the act of hoping is inseparable from the energy of love, from that which "holds," from that which is art's constant example.[19]

At the same time, there is a recognition of the illusory image, the "horrified recognition of . . . nakedness," with the anxiety at "sliding back again into . . . chaos," of which Lacan writes. The self is not yet mastered, the body is still—and especially now, retroactively—"in bits and pieces."

The paradox of redemption, therefore, is a tragic one. When Moses, with perhaps unparalleled savagery, cries out, "Break their thighs," he does so out of this anxiety of the *gezera* mind. Things are what they are; to pretend otherwise, to anticipate, to create counter-realities is to assume a posture of mastery that is not justified. In the house of mourning, according to Jewish tradition, the bereaved cover the mirrors. Without illusion, without anticipation, we accept the *gezera*, the reality of the human condition, as God has imposed it upon us.

And yet God defends the women's mirror-practice; with all the anxiety that will ensue, the women, each in her intimate sphere of mirror work, have modeled redemption. Perhaps for this reason, the language of the midrash associated God's name with the most natural gestures in the narrative: the surge of the little fish into the women's buckets, the multiple births. Excessive, surrealistic, they offer access to the "secret," inexplicable knowledge that is called *peh peh: pakod pakad*.

Notes

1. B. Sotah 11b.
2. Tanchuma Pikudei 9.
3. Rashi 38:8.
4. Compare the commentary of Ibn Ezra (38:8), which makes just this ascetic suggestion.
5. See, e.g., 1:6: 'Don't stare at me because I am swarthy, because the sun has gazed upon me.' The aesthetics of blackness—and of tanned skin—here clearly appeal to convention, to the imagery of a laboring and sun-exposed slave class, and to a submerged association with moral taint.
6. Ramban 38:8.
7. The use of the ewer for the Sotah (the wife suspected of adultery who is put through a ritual involving water: see Num 5:11–31) ordeal is of central importance; it does not, however, enter my main area of discourse in this chapter. Thematically, of course, there are clear connections between the subject of this chapter and the problem of misarticulated sexuality, suggested by the Sotah.
8. See Torah Shelemah, Vayakhel-Pekudei, appendix 6.
9. The polished copper mirrors of Masada come to mind.
10. Milan Kundera, *The Unbearable Lightness of Being* (London: Faber and Faber, 1985), 84.
11. Ibid. 86.

12. *Hamlet* III.ii.21.
13. Ibid. iv.19–20.
14. Lionel Trilling, *Sincerity and Authenticity* (Cambridge, Mass.: Harvard University Press, 1973), 25.
15. Jacques Lacan, 'The Mirror Stage', in *Écrits* (New York: Norton, 1977), 1–2.
16. Ibid. 4.
17. Jane Gallop, *Reading Lacan* (Ithaca, NY: Cornell University Press, 1985).
18. Lacan, 'Some Reflections on the Ego', quoted in Gallop, *Reading Lacan*, 84.
19. John Berger, *Keeping a Rendezvous* (New York: Vintage International, 1992), 33–4.

Galatians

Carolyn Osiek*

Carolyn Osiek examines here one of the most contested passages in Christianity's rapprochement with feminism: 'for in Christ Jesus you are all children of God through faith. As many of you were baptized into Christ have clothed yourselves with Christ. There is no longer Jew or Greek, there is no longer slave or free, there is no longer male and female; for all of you are one in Christ Jesus' (Galatians 3.26–8, New Revised Standard Version). JMS

....

INTRODUCTION
....

No scholars seriously doubt that Paul wrote the letter to the Galatians. It contains some of the ideas considered most central to Paul's theology, namely, salvation through faith in Christ and the Gentile Christian's freedom from the Mosaic law. Galatians differs from the other authentic Pauline letters, though, in being addressed not to the cluster of house-churches in one urban area but to a group of churches in a larger geographical region as a circular letter. Those churches were located either in the Roman province of Galatia (the south Galatian theory) or in the larger, more northerly region that traditionally bore the name (the north Galatian theory). Though there are good arguments on both sides, the south Galatian destination is more likely the correct one because Paul usually uses Roman political names for places. Furthermore, Acts depicts Paul as having been active in the province of Galatia (at Pisidian Antioch, Iconium, Lystra, and Derbe).

The occasion of the letter, probably written in the mid-50s, seems to have been that, after Paul's evangelization of the area, other Christian

---

* Carolyn Osiek, 'Galatians', from *The Women's Bible Commentary*, edited by Carol A. Newsom and Sharon H. Ringe (SPCK, 1992).

missionaries threatened to replace Paul's gospel with their own. Their version of the gospel assumed that people's access to Christ required that they obey the Mosaic law, or at least some of its major requirements, including circumcision. Paul wrote in a state of agitation (his usual thanksgiving after the greeting is missing), to reaffirm his own way of preaching the gospel.

Chapters 1 and 2 rehearse events that establish Paul's authority as an apostle and some of the difficulties he encountered. Chapters 3 and 4 set forth the biblical and theological underpinning of the gospel as he preaches it. In chaps. 5 and 6 he develops the ethical and communitarian implications of the life in the Spirit that flows from his gospel of freedom in Christ.

....

COMMENT
....

Male-centered Language and Worldview (1:1–3)

The address of the letter provides a good illustration of the male-centered worldview of the New Testament writers, which is often compounded by noninclusive translations. For example, in 1:1, Paul identifies himself as an apostle called by God first and foremost and not by human authorities. The RSV translates the source of Paul's call as "not from men nor through man." In the NRSV the wording has been improved and clarified to "neither by human commission nor from human authorities." The same point is made again in 1:10–12. In this case, it is a question of translation. The problem is different when Paul includes with himself as senders of the letter "all the brothers with me" (1:2). This terminology is pervasive in the Pauline letters and in Acts (e.g., Gal. 1:11; 4:12, 31; 5:11, 13; 6:1, where it refers to the addressees of the letter). It could be assumed that the masculine language is meant to be generic, as the translators of the NRSV do in using "friends" to translate the plural of the word for "brother." The more astute interpretation, however, is that women are simply marginal to social communication and interaction and therefore need not be specifically addressed. Masculine language can apply to women as well as to men only when women belong to the social group solely as extensions of their male protective figures (fathers or husbands, for example). Including women on such terms was generally the practice in the New Testament world and continues to be so in more traditional societies. Although in other settings Paul demonstrates awareness and even appreciation of individual women (e.g., Phil. 4:2–3; Rom. 16:1–7, 12, 15), this does not change his habitual language, or his habitual social perceptions.

The Rite of Initiation (2:3–9)

Paul's terms for Jews and Gentiles, generally translated "the circumcised" and "the uncircumcised," are literally "the circumcision" and "the uncircumcision." These categories, which symbolize people's relationship to the whole law of God, express from the Jewish point of view the essential difference between people. In Judaism, however, circumcision is a wholly male ritual, which incorporates the male child (or adult in the case of "proselytes" or converts) into the community of the law. At about the time this letter was written, another rite was also coming into favor for initiation of proselytes—ritual immersion, or baptism—for both sexes. This practice probably grew out of the Jewish custom of purification by periodic ritual washing by immersion in a *miqveh*, or pool. As far as we know, baptism was always a ritual for both women and men.

Probably when it began, baptism symbolized cleansing from the total impurity of being a Gentile. As baptism came to be interpreted in Gentile Christian communities, more attention could be given to the idea of cleansing from the impurity of sin (see Rom. 6:1–8). This was especially true as Paul's version of the gospel, which did not require Gentile Christians to keep the law of Moses, came to represent the dominant theology of the church.

The Social Meaning of Sonship (3:23–26; 4:4–7)

In chap. 3, Paul has ingeniously used examples from scripture and from life to illustrate his argument that observance of the law of Moses is no longer necessary for Gentile converts to Jesus. He maintains that his argument is valid in spite of the fact that other Christian missionaries have made a good case to the contrary and have presented the practice of Jewish custom in an appealing way (3:1–2; 4:10). In one of those examples, Paul speaks of the law as a "custodian" (RSV) or "disciplinarian" (NRSV). The reference is to a slave assigned as tutor and guardian of the son of a well-to-do Greco-Roman family (3:23–25; 4:1–3). Paul says that we are like that son, heir to the estate but, as a minor, subjected to a mere slave of the household until we attain maturity. The coming of Christ marks that change in status which frees us from the authority of our guardian (the law) in order to enjoy our inheritance as adults.

In this context, Paul proclaims that we are "all sons of God through faith" (3:26, author's translation). Again the question of inclusive language versus social interpretation is important. The easy interpretation would be that the intention of the text is that all are sons and daughters—children—of God. But in the culture in which Paul wrote, a daughter did not have the same status as a son, especially the oldest son and heir referred to here. While daughters could also inherit property, their property was at least nominally always under the control of a male relative or patron who administered it. Even an oldest daughter could never be heir to the authority of the *paterfamilias*, the male head of the household. Though we know of households headed by women (e.g., Lydia in Acts 16:15; Mary in Acts 12:12), such women were probably widows and still operating under the legal fiction of a male authority. Therefore, the best interpretation of 3:26 is most likely that all, both male and female, have the equivalent of the legal status of son before God—that is, all stand with Christ as heirs of eternal life.

Continuing the analogy of our coming to maturity with the coming of Christ, in 4:4–7 Paul speaks of Christ's divine and human origins: God sent the son, who was also "born of woman." The semidivine, semihuman son of a god and a human mother is a familiar motif in Greco-Roman religion: Dionysus, for instance, the god of vegetation, ecstatic sylvan worship, and sometimes of drama, was said to have been born of the human woman Semele, whom the high god Zeus courted and seduced behind his wife Hera's back. The phrase "born of woman" does not, however, witness to the virginal conception of Jesus! The same expression is used in the Gospels of Matthew and Luke to refer to John the Baptist as one among many who are "born of woman" (Matt. 11:11 // Luke 7:28). In fact, it simply emphasizes Jesus' human origins and parallels the following statement about his religious origins, that he was "born under the law." He is fully human and fully Jewish. Christ redeems or ransoms those who, like himself, are under the law (the Jews) and bestows on all believers the status not just of children of the household, in status no better than slaves, but of "sons" and heirs.

"No Male and Female" (3:28)

Galatians 3:28 has long been a center of controversy, more so in recent years with the rise of feminist readings of the Bible. Two of the three pairs, Jew–Greek and slave–free, occur also in similar statements in 1 Cor. 12:13 and Col. 3:11. The third, male–female, occurs only here, and it will be the focus of comment. Whereas the other two pairs are connected by correlative conjunctions ("There is no . . . or . . ."), the male–female pair is connected by the coordinating conjunction ("there is no male and female"). This difference is seldom noted in translations, though it is in the NRSV. There are at least five possible interpretations of this difficult passage.

1. *Emancipation proclamation ahead of its time.* Some interpreters suggest that the statement endorses an end to sexism and discrimination of every kind. At face value, this may be a bit naïve, since it would seem that elsewhere in Paul's writing (1 Cor. 11:2–16; 14:34–35), he certainly did not understand it that way. Yet, if we believe that biblical texts can be prophetic beyond the vision of author, time, and place, there is some validity to this approach.

2. *A formula used in the baptism of new Christians.* According to this recent interpretation, in the background of Paul's words lies a baptismal ritual of the early church. The language of this ritual echoes the statement from the first creation narrative in Gen. 1:27–28. There God is said to have fashioned humankind after God's own image and likeness, "male and female" God created them. The words in quotation marks are exactly the same in the Greek translation (the Septuagint) of Gen. 1:28 and in Gal. 3:28, where they break the parallel structure, as noted above. In some Hellenistic Jewish exegesis of Genesis, notably that done by the great theologian Philo of Alexandria, a contemporary of Paul, the creation narrative is a metaphor for the makeup of the person. In that metaphor, the division of the original human being into two genders was the beginning of the internal division of the person into rationality (symbolized by the male principle) and sensation (symbolized by the female principle). Conflict is soon to follow and indeed does in the story. Against the background of such an understanding of the human condition, the baptismal proclamation quoted by Paul implies that the division and conflict in human nature, the source of sin, can be overcome in the saving grace of baptism.

3. *Reference to the order of creation but not to the order of the Fall.* In this view, the text refers to a fundamental equality of male and female as created by God, alluded to in Gen. 1:27–28. However, with the Fall,

that equality was broken, as evidenced in Gen. 3:16: "Your [the woman's] desire will be for your husband, and he will rule over you." Galatians 3:28 therefore has nothing to say about contemporary relationship, but looks back nostalgically to the good old days before equality was lost by sin.

4. *The time of salvation anticipated in the present.* Related to the first interpretation but with a different view of human nature, this view suggests that in God's future the tension between human opposites— Jew and Gentile, slave and free, male and female—will disappear. Because life in the grace of Christ anticipates in part what the future can be like, it is possible to live without these unhealthy tensions even now.

5. *A glimpse of the still-distant future.* Contrary to the previous two interpretations, this reading suggests that Gal. 3:28 speaks of the heavenly realm of relationships in Christ, possible only in a new and transformed creation, like that envisioned in Rev. 21:1–4; 22:1–5. Like the third interpretation, this one would assert that the text has nothing to say to the present time—Paul's or ours.

God as "Father" (4:4–7)

In addition to bringing about people's transformation from the status of minor children under guardianship of the law to that of mature heirs able to enjoy their inheritance (see above on 3:23–26), the coming of Christ had other consequences as well. One of those consequences is that the Spirit of God, the sign for Paul of the presence of God's action, is sent into our hearts and enables believers to address God as *Abba*, Father (see also Rom. 8:14–17). Surely this characteristically Christian way of calling on and speaking about God goes back to Jesus himself, since it is so well attested of him. Whether or not he was the first or only one to use it in such a personal way is a debated point and is really irrelevant. In memory of Christ, Christians felt entitled to use this word for God. In its day, this was a groundbreaking move in Jewish and Christian spirituality. Addressing God as Mother today is a contemporary cultural analogy; that is, the feelings it evokes, both positive and negative, are probably quite similar to those evoked by the use of "Abba" for God in the first century.

Paul as Mother to the Galatian Christians (4:19)

In a very unusual way, Paul here draws upon the metaphor of giving birth to speak of his own relationship to the Galatian communities.

Elsewhere he freely uses paternal expressions (1 Cor. 4:14–15; 1 Thess. 2:11; Philemon 10). In 1 Thess. 2:7, he compares his ministry style to the tenderness of a nurse with her children, but here Paul speaks of his own birth pangs in the process of giving birth to Christ in them—a somewhat complicated metaphor. The language of birth pain is a common way to speak about the approaching end time (e.g., Mark 13:8; Matt. 24:8; John 16:21–22; 1 Thess. 5:3; Rom. 8:22; Rev. 12:2). Such language may also imply the mystery of rebirth as spoken of in Hellenistic mysticism and mystery religions. However, the difference here is that it is not the apostle alone who suffers the pain of giving birth, nor the believer alone who is to be reborn through the initiation process, but Christ who is being born and formed within believers. Paul's vivid sense of living in a time when the end of history was near means that this birth process of which he speaks is not limited to the individual apostle and community but is part of the grand scale of suffering and tribulation (see Rom. 8:22). But what does the use of maternal imagery imply about Paul himself? Perhaps a man willing to use such an image is not as alienated from women's experience as Paul is often made out to be.

The Allegory of Sarah and Hagar (1:21–31)

The great allegory of the two Jerusalems is grounded in Jewish imagery in use at the time, but not with such a negative shadow cast on the earthly city. The heavenly Jerusalem and the heavenly Temple were used by other New Testament writers as well (e.g., Rev. 21:2; Hebrews 9) to symbolize eternal transformation. Paul begins his allegory with the story of Abraham's two wives, the first wife, Sarah (never named but clearly intended), and the slave, Hagar, who becomes Abraham's second wife (Genesis 16:21).

The use of the two women illustrates the importance of the matriarchs in what we call the patriarchal narratives. They are bearers of the lines descending from Abraham, the common ancestor in faith for Jews, Christians, and Muslims. Jews claim both ethnic and spiritual descent through Sarah; Christians, Paul suggests, can trace their spiritual roots back to her; Muslims, in an interpretation attributed to Muhammad himself, claim Hagar and her son, Ishmael, as their spiritual ancestors. There is no denying that for both Genesis and Paul, Hagar is rejected. But precisely because of this interpretation, she becomes the symbol and heroine for all those women who feel rejected or less desired because of personal, economic, ethnic, or racist practices. While Paul's allegory, for his own purposes, ends with Hagar still rejected, the reader of the Bible cannot forget Jesus' outreach to just such oppressed and forgotten ones.

Freedom in Christ (5:1, 13)

In the last part of the letter, after giving his theological exposition, Paul appeals to the Galatians to live in the true freedom for which they have been freed by Christ. Apparently Paul did not mean by this that they were also to consider themselves free from the restrictions imposed on them by social customs. In this letter, written to people who, Paul thinks, need to be liberated, Paul speaks forcefully about freedom. In 1 Corinthians, on the other hand, where the problem seems to be just the opposite, he does not mention it! It has been suggested that perhaps Paul began preaching freedom in Christ among the Corinthians as well (or that they obtained a copy of the Galatian letter) but that they then went on to take him more literally than he intended. Read in that light, Paul's restrictive measures in 1 Corinthians fall into place. In questions of dress, hairstyles, and public conduct socially appropriate to each gender, for instance (1 Cor. 11:2–16, 14:34–35), Paul sounds quite conservative. Where has his open-mindedness about freedom gone?

Galatians 5:13 gives us a clue: Paul understands freedom not as the opportunity to pursue one's own interests but to be even more at the service of others. That this is costly service can be seen in the fact that in this charter of Christian freedom he also refers frequently to the cross (2:19–20; 3:1; 5:11, 24; 6:12, 14, and perhaps 17). This ideal of service and even self-sacrifice poses definite problems for women of all generations and nearly all cultures, who are socially educated to expect that their true happiness lies in service to others, while men are brought up to pursue their own goals.

But Paul may be doing something quite radical here: he is holding up traditionally feminine values as ideals for everyone, male and female, and perhaps especially for the Christian men who are his principal addressees (see above on 1:1–3). Women too need to appropriate these values, but they need also to balance this ideal carefully against their legitimate psychological needs. Bearing the cross in freedom does not mean enduring abuse and victimhood, but living genuinely for others out of one's own inner freedom by claiming the inheritance of the "sons of God."

Bibliography

Betz, Hans Dieter. *Galatians*. Hermeneia. Philadelphia: Fortress Press, 1979.

Boucher, Madeleine. 'Some Unexplored Parallels to 1 Cor. 11:11–12 and Gal. 3:28: The New Testament on the Role of Women', *Catholic Biblical Quarterly* 31 (1969), 50–8.

Bruce, F. F. *The Epistle to the Galatians*. Grand Rapids, Mich.: Eerdmans, 1982.

Gaventa, Beverly R. 'The Maternity of Paul: An Exegetical Study of Galatians 4:19', in *The Conversation Continues: Studies in Paul and John in Honor of J. Louis Martyn*, ed. Robert Fortna and Beverly Gaventa. Nashville: Abingdon Press, 1990, 189–201.

Osiek, Carolyn. *Galatians*. New Testament Message 12. Wilmington, Del.: Michael Glazier, 1980.

19 Philippians

Pheme Perkins*

Paul's Letter to the Philippians shows women playing an active part in the early Christian movement and speaks of a female deacon, Phoebe. Pheme Perkins alerts us to the danger of assuming women are fully included amongst the 'brothers' addressed by Paul.   JMS

INTRODUCTION

Philippians was written to Christians in Philippi while Paul was in prison. The location of that prison is the first problem that must be addressed. References to the "praetorium" (1:13) and "Caesar's household" (4:22) suggest a locale where imperial officials were stationed. Since information has been exchanged easily between Paul and the community (1:26; 2:19; 2:23–30; 4:18), it was probably not Rome. Ephesus, which is referred to in 1 Cor. 15:32 and 2 Cor. 1:8–10, could have been the location.

In this letter Paul focuses on three issues: conflicts among those preaching the gospel that have resulted from his imprisonment (1:14–18; 4:2–4); thanks for assistance sent to him by the Philippians (4:10–20) and for the recovery of Epaphroditus, the bearer of the assistance (2:25–30); and warnings against those who seek to adopt Jewish customs and insist on circumcising male converts (3:2–4:1). Originally, the thank you note and the warnings may have been separate letters. In combining them, the Philippian community has preserved a legacy of Paul's teaching to guide the church in the persecutions it will face (1:27–30).

The letter stresses the necessity for unity. Christians are engaged in

* Pheme Perkins, 'Philippians', from *The Women's Bible Commentary*, edited by Carol A. Newsom and Sharon H. Ringe (SPCK, 1992).

197

an athletic contest (1:27; 3:13–14) and a military struggle (2:25) on behalf of the gospel. The famous hymn in 2:6–11, which proclaims that Christ surrendered divinity to accept slave status and death followed by glorious exaltation to divine dignity as Lord over all things, is employed to emphasize the need to subordinate one's own interests to those of the group (2:1, 5, 12).

Philippians (4:2–3) and Acts (16:14–15) indicate that women played important roles in founding the community and in its preaching mission. The letter, however, is ambiguous in the way it portrays their involvement. For example, the dominant images of athletic contest and military service do not reflect their experience. Neither does the exchange of authorized, male representatives: Epaphroditus, for the Philippians, and Timothy, for Paul (1:1; 2:19–24). Women's flesh cannot be marked by circumcision (3:2, 5). Lydia, who hosted the community in her household, might be called a servant (= deacon, like Phoebe in Rom. 16:1) and so be included among the leaders referred to in the greeting, but much of the imagery in Philippians speaks only of male experience. One must ask, therefore, in what sense women might be considered "brothers" called to imitate the example of the apostle (3:17). The role of Lydia and the fact that a generic translation like "brothers and sisters" (NRSV) might be possible here suggest that women might be included, but such a conclusion or translation disguises the masculine imagery that permeates this letter.

COMMENT

Partnership in the Gospel (1:1–30)

Paul's letters usually open with a thanksgiving for the faith of the recipients, assurances of his concern for them, and reference to the judgment (1:3–11). Each thanksgiving also mentions concerns addressed in the letter. Here Paul notes that the Philippians have entered into a partnership with him to spread the gospel (1:5). No other church has done so (4:15). In the commercial world, partnerships were established by groups for a specific purpose. Though individuals might contribute differently to the enterprise, all would share any profits. A partnership could be dissolved because the members no longer agreed about its goals; that is, they had ceased to be "of one mind" (see Phil. 1:27; 2:2). The death of a member also brought the arrangement to an end. Paul assures the Philippians that they will share the fruits of his imprisonment (1:7) and even of his death (2:17). Some Philippians were engaged in preaching (1:15); others provided financial support for Paul (4:16–18). Women involved in business or in running their own households, like Lydia, were a source of material support in the Pauline mission. They were also among those who preached the gospel. Paul refers to Euodia and Syntyche as part of a group of fellow workers who have labored with him in the gospel (4:2–3). Therefore, it seems reasonable to conclude that women were members of this partnership.

Since Paul fears that he may be executed rather than released, the rivalry that has broken out among those who preach the gospel (1:14–17) could reflect the expectation of some that the partnership is about to end. Paul is careful to temper any reference to his death with a reassurance that he will remain among the Philippians (1:24–26; 2:24). If he were to die, the Philippians could continue the original partnership on their own. They might also break up into a number of rival groups. Paul's reminders that all their activities are oriented toward the day of judgment (1:10–11; 2:16) provide a framework for his instruction that regardless of what happens to him, the Philippians should remain united in the effort they have already undertaken.

Just as members have shared financial resources and missionary activity with Paul, they also will experience sufferings like his (1:29–30). Could women members be imprisoned as the apostle was? In the second century C.E., women like Perpetua and Felicitas would be commemorated as martyrs. Romans 16:7 refers to a certain Andronicus and Junia, possibly a husband and wife, as "relatives who were in prison with me; they are prominent among the apostles." There a woman is numbered among those imprisoned for the gospel.

Having the Mind of Christ (2:1–18)

Though it was customary that persons in a partnership demonstrate dedication to the common effort, Paul's case for unity does not rest on merely human concerns. Love requires that they always put other persons ahead of themselves. In order to make this point, Paul cites an early Christian hymn (Phil. 2:6–11). The first section (2:6–8) describes Christ's self-emptying. Whether as preexistent divine wisdom or as the obedient "spiritual Adam," he deserves equality with God. Instead, Christ adopts the existence of a slave. Paul emphasizes Christ's

199

degradation by reminding readers that Christ suffered the death reserved for the worst criminals and slaves, crucifixion. The second section (2:9–11) describes the exaltation of the risen Christ. Christ has been given the divine name "Lord" and is the ruler of all the powers. Of course, this victory is invisible to all except believers, who are "lights" in an evil and distorted generation (2:15–16).

How does Paul apply this hymn to Christian experience? He refers to himself and Timothy as "slaves of Christ" (1:1). His own imprisonment honors Christ. He anticipates a future with Christ (1:20–23). He also considers his pre-Christian life as one in which he could claim a position of honor in the Jewish community (3:4–6). In order to "know Christ," Paul had to give up those standards of value. He suffered the "loss of all things," and considered them "rubbish" (3:8). As a Christian, suffering like Christ now, he anticipates a glorious resurrection (3:10–11).

The exhortation to suffer like Christ in expectation of future salvation was frequently used to admonish Christian women and slaves to submit to abusive husbands or masters (e.g., 1 Peter 2:18–3:6). Christians who believe that the present world will soon end often find the idea of a reward for suffering like Christ to be an excuse for failing to struggle against injustice in this world. They forget that the hymn starts not with the suffering Christ but with the Christ who is equal to God. The poor in Latin America who are told to suffer like Christ rather than struggle for freedom, or abused women whose ministers tell them to submit to husbands, are not in the position to copy the Christ of this hymn. Its challenge is addressed to persons of some status and power, just as Christ had the status of God. In order to preach a gospel that centers on a crucified person and that brings persecution in its wake, such people must empty themselves.

Epaphroditus and Timothy (2:19–30)

Although some women participated in the Philippian partnership, its imagery is taken from the masculine world. The rivalry between preachers of the gospel is a male form of rhetorical contest (1:15). Paul and Epaphroditus are referred to as soldiers (2:25). Paul's imprisonment is an opportunity to make Christ known in the world of Roman soldiers and imperial officials. Paul also describes himself as an athlete seeking a prize (3:14). In addition, those primary representatives of both the community and the apostle are male. Since Paul cannot come to Philippi, he will send Timothy, whose proven devotion to the gospel makes him Paul's "son" (2:21–22). We learn of two women associates only because Paul finds it necessary to ask someone to intervene in a dispute between them (4:2–3). Even there they are absorbed into a larger group of male fellow workers.

True Circumcision (3:1–21)

The polemical tone of 3:2 and the sudden shift in topic suggest that this section was taken from another letter. The problem (see Galatians) is caused by missionaries who insist that non-Jewish converts ought to adopt Jewish practices. The debate focuses on the mark of male Jewish identity, circumcision. Paul rejects this attempt to establish one's religious identity in the flesh. He had abandoned all the special privileges of a faithful Jew when he recognized that salvation comes to all people in Jesus. Paul accuses this opposition of being concerned with material things, which can lead only to destruction. In this context, Paul refers to Christians as persons whose commonwealth is in heaven. The word "commonwealth" refers to the political organization of a minority community within the larger city-state. The Jewish community in a city was often organized as a "commonwealth."

Paul directs Christians to look to a commonwealth in heaven, when they will be transformed into the bodily likeness of the risen Christ. They should not attempt to establish themselves through the fleshly sign of Jewish identity, circumcision, or to institute a separate, minority community as though Christians were a particular race among the peoples of the earth. Paul makes circumcision appear unthinkable by invoking the male anxieties that link it with castration. He makes an earthly "commonwealth" appear impossible because the risen Christ, its founder, is in heaven. As in the Christ hymn, this advice might suggest that Christians divorce themselves from political struggles. However, it was just such a gospel of salvation for all peoples, without regard to ethnic identity or gender, that had led to Paul's imprisonment. The social challenge of the gospel was felt in Paul's world.

Paul's Thanks (4:1–23)

The final section of the letter includes a note, apparently written before Epaphroditus became ill (4:10–20), thanking the Philippians for their assistance. Paul introduces a peculiar distance into this acknowledgment by claiming a philosophic detachment from his own material circumstances. He attributes this indifference to God's power. After acknowledging the extensive aid that the Philippians have given to his mission, Paul again denies seeking such gifts (4:17). This reserve might reflect a concern to distinguish himself from those popular preachers who sought to enrich themselves by their activities. Yet the special relationship between Paul and the Philippians would make it appropriate for others in the partnership to contribute material resources to his effort. Their "gain" is the spiritual reward that comes from bringing people to salvation. Some interpreters suggest that Paul's reserve stems from a desire to avoid the normal forms of patron and client obligation. Normally, Paul would become dependent on those who gave him assistance. Here he will not owe the Philippians anything for their generosity: God is the one who repays such gifts (4:19).

How can this strategy be applied to women's experience? Women are commonly the subordinate members of relationships that permit others to make extensive demands as return for assistance or benefits, as is the case in the traditionally structured roles of wife and mother. Paul's example suggests that Christian forms of mutual aid need not carry the weight of subjection and obligation that can constitute a steep hidden price for the recipient.

Bibliography

Craddock, Fred B. *Philippians.* Interpretation. Atlanta: John Knox Press, 1987.
Sampley, J. Paul. *Pauline Partnership in Christ: Christian Community and Commitment in Light of Roman Law.* Philadelphia: Fortress Press, 1980.

20 Women in the Pauline Churches

Elisabeth Schüssler Fiorenza*

A theologian dealing with biblical texts is often working at the same time
with established traditions of reading them. This is as true for the scholar
who wishes to contest a reading as for those who would confirm it. Elisabeth
Schüssler Fiorenza engages here in an applied study of Jesus' choosing of 'the
twelve'.   JMS

In his letter to the Corinthian church, Paul explicitly refers twice to the
behavior of women in the worship service of the community. However
both references, 1 Cor 11:2–16 and 14:33–36, present for the exegete
and historian great difficulties of interpretation. It is very doubtful
whether we will be able to reconstruct the correct meaning of these
passages at all. Not only is the logic of the argument in 1 Cor 11:2–16
difficult to trace, but it is also debated whether Paul demands the
veiling of women or pleads for a special form of hairstyle. Since both
passages seem to contradict Gal 3:28 and Paul's own theology of freedom from the Law, some scholars attribute 1 Cor 11:2–16[1] and most
scholars 14:33b–36[2] to the early catholic theology of the post-Pauline
school.

The exegesis of these texts is even more hampered by the apologetic,
theological controversy surrounding them. From the outset of the
women's movement these Pauline passages were used against women's
demand for equality.[3] Antifeminist preachers and theologians maintained and still maintain that the submission of women and their
subordinate role in family, society, and church was ordained and
revealed through Paul. Whenever women protest against societal
degradation and ecclesial discrimination Paul's arguments are
invoked: Woman was created after man, she is not the image of God,
she brought sin into the world and therefore she has to be submissive

* Elisabeth Schüssler Fiorenza, 'Women in the Pre-Pauline and Pauline Churches', *Union
Seminary Quarterly Review* 33 (3 and 4) (1978).

and is not allowed to speak in church or to teach men. And those theologians rejecting patriarchal submission but upholding an "equal but different" or "two-human-nature"[4] theology point out that Paul maintains the creational difference between women and men without denying their equality.

Feminist thinkers on the other hand argue that Paul's statements give evidence that Christianity was at a very early stage sexist and that therefore a revisionist feminist appropriation of Christian theology is doomed to failure. They criticize the Pauline texts for their patriarchal theology which legitimizes our contemporary patriarchal structures in society and church.[5]

Christian apologists respond to this feminist challenge by defending Paul as a "liberationist."[6] Paul's writings, they argue, correctly understood and interpreted, support women's equality and dignity.[7] Not the Pauline message but the patriarchal or feminist misunderstanding of this message preaches the subjugation of women. The gist of the controversy is summed up in a book title: "Paul: Male Chauvinist or Feminist."[8]

Because of the apologetic interest to defend Paul against his feminist critics this revisionist approach does not sufficiently take into account the methodological issues and hermeneutical decisions involved on both sides of the debate. The hermeneutical discussion[9] and the sociology of knowledge[10] have underlined how important it is for exegetes and theologians to reflect on their presuppositions and on the theoretical models which they employ to assemble historical "data." This is of special consequence for the reconstruction of early Christian history because our sources do not have an immediate historical interest but rather are written for pastoral and theological purposes. Our understanding of the significance of the Pauline injunctions therefore does not only depend on a perceptive historical-critical interpretation of the texts but much more on the theoretical model of early Christian history in the context of which we formulate our questions and organize our exegetical results.

Since not only Biblical exegesis but historiography in general is a selective view of the past, its scope is not only limited by extant sources and materials but also shaped by the interests and perspectives of the present. As contemporary societal-cultural perspectives shift, the historian's perception and selection of what was important in the past and is worthwhile studying today also shifts.[11] Historians are not able to abstract from their presuppositions, ideologies and the interests of the powerstructures determining the questions and models with which they assemble the accessible information. The reconstruction and understanding of the past is never determined solely by so-called historical facts but always also by the presuppositions and interests of historians whose methodological approaches are decisively influenced by personal experiences and social mythologies.

Feminist scholars have therefore rightly pointed out that historians study historical sources in general and Biblical texts in particular from a patriarchal[12] perspective. Our Western conceptual framework and historical paradigm is determined by the understanding that "humanity is male and man defines woman not in herself but as relative to him; she is not regarded as an autonomous being. He is the subject, the absolute. She is the other."[13] This conceptual framework functions as a social mythology that determines women's and men's socialization and self-perceptions.[14] It marginalizes women and justifies the present structures of power that make women to be the weaker, "second" sex.

The problem with revisionist apologetics therefore is not so much that it has Christian or feminist presuppositions and criteria but rather that it fails to question the androcentric or patriarchal model underlying the scholarly reconstructions of early Christian history. Insofar as scholars single out the "role of women" as a special problem they reflect our own cultural, androcentric perspective according to which male existence is the standard expression of human existence and Christian history. In such an androcentric paradigm only the role of women becomes a special historical problem while the androcentric presuppositions of such an historiography remain unexamined. In order to understand and theologically evaluate the Pauline injunctions for women it is therefore necessary to critically analyze how scholars reconstruct early Christian history and how they define the role of women in the early Christian communities.

THE ANDROCENTRIC RECONSTRUCTION OF EARLY CHRISTIAN HISTORY

Since the academic writing of early Christian history shares in the androcentric paradigm of Western culture, it reconstructs the history of the early church according to the model of male dominance that marginalizes women. This becomes evident when we analyze the presuppositions underlying the study of women in early Christianity.[15]

First: Such studies generally presuppose that men have initiated the early Christian missionary movement and that only they had leadership in it. The discussions of discipleship, apostleship,[16] church order, worship or missionary activity tacitly assume that these leadership functions were exercised by males only. In analyzing 1 Cor 11:2–16 and 14:33–36 exegetes neglect to place these texts into their historical situation and their immediate context. Instead scholars presume that only these texts speak about women, whereas the rest of chapters 11–14 deals with male prophets and enthusiasts. In a similar fashion the information which the "people of Chloe" gave to Paul is characterized as gossip.[17] The "people of Chloe" are not considered as her followers or associates but as her slaves,[18] although we find a similar genitive construction in the immediate context, where Paul speaks of the different parties that claim different apostles as their spiritual leaders (1 Cor 1:11 ff.). Another example of such an androcentric interpretation is the understanding that Rm 16:7 refers to two male apostles, although Junia or Julia was a common female name of the time and patristic exegesis acknowledged that the passage refers to a woman apostle.[19] Because of the unquestioned presupposition that the early church was a "man's church" such androcentric studies understand the women mentioned in the Pauline letters as helpers of the apostles who supported especially Paul in his missionary work. This androcentric model has no room for the alternative possibility that women were missionaries and leaders of churches *before* Paul and on the same level with Paul. It could well be that Paul had no other choice than to work with women whose leadership was already well established in the pre-Pauline and Pauline churches.

Second: In such an androcentric model masculine terminology[20] is understood in a twofold way: as generic and as gender specific. On the one hand most exegetes would agree that standard masculine terms as elect, saints, brothers or sons do not designate males over against females but apply to all members of the Christian community. Masculine language in these instances is not used in a gender specific but in a generic inclusive way. On the other hand, when discussing leadership titles as e.g. apostles, prophets, or teachers, exegetes assume that these titles apply to men only although we have one instance in the Pauline literature where such a masculine title is applied to a woman. In Rm 16:1 f. Phoebe is characterized by the masculine form of the title *diakonos*. Therefore, we can assume that NT androcentric language on the whole is inclusive of women until proven otherwise.

Third: Androcentric interpretations still propose that the available information on women in early Christianity reflects the actual situation and roles women had in the nascent church, although NT scholarship generally recognizes that the NT authors do not give us accurate historical information about the life of Jesus or about the earliest communities. Source- and redaction-critical studies have demonstrated that the NT writers did not incorporate all available information into their works, but that they selected the materials according to their own theological purposes. A few examples for such an androcentric traditioning process should suffice. Paul's letters refer to women as co-missionaries in the early Christian movement, whereas Acts only mentions the contributions of wealthy women as patronesses but does not picture women as missionaries. Or: While all four gospels know of Mary Magdalene as the first witness to the resurrection, Paul does not list any woman among the resurrection witnesses.[21] Or: The Fourth Gospel claims that a woman had an important role in the beginnings of the Samaritan mission (Jn 4:4–42), whereas Acts mentions Philip as the first missionary in Samaria (Acts 8:4–13). Since the NT authors write from an androcentric point of view and select their information accordingly we can conjecture that they transmit only a small fraction of the information on women available to them. Therefore, the sparse NT references to women do not at all adequately reflect women's actual role and contributions to the history of early Christianity. They allow us, however, a glimpse of the possibly rich traditions which we have lost.

Fourth: One could argue that such an androcentric model of interpretation is methodologically appropriate because early Christianity mirrored its patriarchal culture and religion. However, the studies of the socio-cultural attitudes of the Jesus movement in Palestine point out that this movement was a socially and religiously deviant group.[22] Jesus and his first followers were not well adjusted members of their society but were in opposition to many cultural and religious values of their time. Jesus did not call into his fellowship the righteous, pious, and powerful, but all those who "did not belong": tax collectors, sinners, prostitutes, poor people, and women. This inclusive egalitarian movement of itinerant disciples understood itself in kinship terms and thereby replaced traditional family roles and bonds. Women, like men, are no longer defined by patriarchal marriage and procreative family roles but by their allegiance to the community of disciples.

However, G. Theissen, whose work is influential in the social study of early Christianity, has argued that the early Christian missionary movement outside Palestine did not stand in conflict to its society but was well integrated into it. The radicalism of the Jesus movement in

Palestine was assimilated by the urban Hellenistic communities into a family-style love-patriarchalism which perpetuated the social, hierarchal relationships of the patriarchal family in a softened milder form.[23] The classic expression of this love-patriarchalism is found in the household codes of the Deutero- and post-Pauline literature (Col 3:18 f.; Eph 5:21–33; Tit 2:4 f.; 1 Petr 3:1–7). In my opinion, however, it must be questioned whether these can be used to establish such a love-patriarchalism for the pre-Pauline and Pauline communities. The allusions of the genuine Pauline letters to the leadership of women suggest that the subordination demands of the household codes were not yet operative in the earliest congregations of the urban Hellenistic centers. Not the patriarchal family but the egalitarian community structures of collegia or cultic associations which accorded women and slaves equal standing within the community, appear to have provided the model for the early Christian missionary movement in the Greco-Roman world.[24]

WOMEN IN THE PRE-PAULINE AND PAULINE CHURCHES

Only when we reconstruct the history of the early Christian movement according to an egalitarian, non-androcentric model are we able to adequately integrate the available information on women's leadership that is found in the letters of Paul. Although this information is very fragmentary it nevertheless permits us to trace women's role in the churches before Paul and associated with Paul.

First: The Pauline letters mention women as Paul's co-workers but they do not give any indication that these women were dependent on Paul or subordinate to him. Only five of Paul's co-workers (Erastus, Mark, Timothy, Titus, and Tychicus) "stand in explicit subordination to Paul, serving him or being subject to his instructions."[25] The genuine Pauline letters apply missionary titles and characterizations as e.g. co-worker (Prisca), brother/sister (Apphia), *diakonos* (Phoebe), and apostle (Junia) also to women. They usually equate co-workers and "those who toil." In 1 Cor 16:16 ff. Paul admonishes the Corinthians to be "subject to every co-worker and laborer" and to give recognition to such persons. 1 Thess 5:12 exhorts the Thessalonians to "respect those who labor among you, and are over you in the Lord, and admonish you." It is therefore significant that Paul uses the same Greek verb "to labor" or "to toil" not only to characterize his own missionary evangelizing and teaching but also with reference to women. In Rm 16:6, 12 he commends Mary, Tryphana, Tryphosa and Persis for having "labored hard" in the Lord.

Paul also affirms that women have worked with him on an equal basis. Phil 4:2 f. explicitly states that Euodia and Syntyche have "contended" side by side with him. As in an athletic race these women have competed alongside with Paul, Clemens, and the rest of Paul's co-missionaries in the cause of the Gospel. Paul considers the authority of both women in the community at Philippi so great that he fears that their dissensions could do serious damage to the Christian community.[26] These women missionaries commanded the same esteem and respect as Paul's male co-workers in the community at Philippi.

Second: The house-churches were a decisive factor in the missionary movement insofar as they provided space, support, and actual leadership for the community.[27] The house-churches were the place where the early Christians celebrated the Lord's supper and preached the good news. Theologically the community is called the "house of God," the "new temple" in which the Spirit dwells.[28] Since women were among the wealthy and prominent converts (cf. Acts 17:4.12), they played an important role in the founding, sustaining and promoting of such house-churches. The following texts which speak of women as leaders of house-churches demonstrate this: Paul greets Apphia "our sister" who together with Philemon and Archippus was a leader of the house-church in Colossae to which the letter to Philemon is written (Phm 2).[29] Paul also mentions twice the missionary couple Prisca and Aquila and "the church in their house" (1 Cor 16:19; Rm 16:5). In a similar fashion the author of the letter to the Colossians refers to Nympha of Laodicea and the "church in her house" (Col 4:15). According to Acts the church at Philippi began with the conversion of the business woman Lydia from Thyatira who offered her house to the Christian mission (Acts 16:14). We also know from Acts that a prayer meeting was held in the house of Mary, the mother of John Mark.

We have therefore no reason to assume that women were excluded from the leadership of such house-churches and from presiding at their worship. The love-patriarchalism of the household-code tradition could therefore be a later patriarchal reaction to the leadership of women within the house-churches, but cannot express the original order of the pre-Pauline churches. This hypothesis is supported by 1 Tim 2 where the injunctions that women should be submissive are given in the context of regulations for prayer meetings and teaching as well as in the context of patriarchal requirements for church leadership.

Third: One of the most prominent heads of a house-church and outstanding co-worker of Paul is Prisca or Priscilla who together with her husband Aquila worked with Paul. Yet like Barnabas or Apollos she too was independent from the Apostle and did not stand under his authority.[30] Paul is grateful to the couple because they have risked their lives for him. Yet not only he but all the Gentile churches have reasons to give thanks to these outstanding missionaries (Rm 16:4). Their house-church in Corinth, Ephesus, and Rome (if Rm 16 is addressed to that community) was a missionary center at each place. 1 Cor 16:19 has greetings from the couple. Even though Prisca is mentioned here after her husband, it is remarkable that she is referred to by name at all, since normally the husband alone is named in such greetings. However, it is significant that whenever Paul sends greetings to them (Rm 16:3f.) he addresses Prisca first, thus underlining that she is the most important of the two (cf. also 2 Tm 4:19).

Acts also mentions Prisca before her husband, which corresponds to the information of the Pauline letters (cf. Acts 18:2 ff.; 18.26).[31] Since Luke concentrates in the second part of the Acts on the greatness of Paul, he refers to the couple only in passing. Even these brief remarks, however, indicate the great influence of the couple. We therefore can assume that Luke had much more information about them than he transmits to us. Like Paul, Priscilla and Aquila were by trade tent-makers and supported their missionary activity through their own work. Like Paul they were Jewish Christians and financially independent from the churches they served. Like Paul they travelled to spread the gospel and suffered for their missionary activity. When Claudius banished the Jews from Rome, they were expelled from there and moved to Corinth. In Ephesus they converted Apollos, one of the greatest apostles and missionaries alongside Paul (18:26), and taught him "the way of God more accurately." The text clearly assumes that Prisca was the catechist and teacher of Apollos.[32]

While Prisca and Aquila are not explicitly called apostles, another couple receives this title in Rm 16:7. Like Aquila and Prisca, Andronicus and Junia (Julia) were a missionary couple who were apostles before Paul. Since apostles had to have had a missionary task and a vision of the resurrected Lord[33] we can conjecture that the couple was among the more than 500 "brethren" to whom the Lord appeared and of whom most were alive when Paul wrote 1 Corinthians (1 Cor 15:6). Andronicus and Junia are at the writing of Rm 16 fellow prisoners with Paul and they are praised as "outstanding" among the apostles. We can conclude from 1 Cor 9:5 that the couples Priscilla and Aquila and Andronicus and Junia were not exceptions among the early Christian missionaries since the other apostles on their missionary journeys had "sisters" with them as "wives" (lit. women). If the term "brother" can characterize a particular group of missionary co-workers (cf. Phil 4:21 ff.),[34] then we can surmise that "sister" refers likewise to the women as missionary co-workers. The double accusative obj. (sister, woman) is best explained in this way. We therefore can assume that many early Christian missionaries were couples. When Paul stresses celibacy as the best precondition for missionary work (1 Cor 7:23 ff.) he is expressing his own opinion but does not concur with the practice of the early missionary church. Moreover we have no indication that the work of such missionary women, who labored in tandem with their husbands, was restricted to women.[35]

Fourth: Phoebe appears to have been one of the most prominent women in the early church. In Rm 16:1 f. she is characterized by three titles: Paul calls her "our sister," a *diakonos* of the church at Cenchreae, and a *prostatis* "of many and myself as well." Exegetes take pains to downplay the significance of these titles because they are given to a woman. Whenever Paul uses the title *diakonos* to refer to himself or another male leader, scholars translate it with minister, missionary, or servant, whereas in the case of Phoebe they usually render it with deaconess. After characterizing Phoebe as an "obviously well-to-do and philanthropic lady" Lietzmann goes on to say: "Even at that time there had long been women deacons in the Christian church who, when *their sex made them especially suitable*, came forward and gave signal help in caring for the poor and sick, and at the baptism of women"[36] (emphasis mine). Unconsciously Lietzmann projects here back into the first century the duties of the deaconesses of a later period whose service was restricted to the ministry to women. Yet the text does not indicate any limitations of the office of Phoebe by prescribed gender roles. She is not a deaconess of the women in the church at Cenchreae but a minister of the whole church.

Paul uses the term *diakonos* in tandem with *synergos* (co-worker) in 1 Cor 3:5, 9 and 2 Cor 6:1, 4. According to 1 Cor 16:15 the co-workers and laborers are those who "have devoted themselves to the *diakonia* of the saints." However, in distinction to the co-workers the *diakonoi* appear to be not only travelling missionaries but leaders of local congregations. The term is used in the NT and in secular sources to refer to preaching and teaching.[37] Thus the *diakonoi* served in the recognized and designated, "official" capacity of teachers and preachers. We therefore can presume that Phoebe was an "official" minister and teacher in the church at Cenchreae.

The importance of Phoebe's position as minister in the church at Cenchreae is underlined by the title *prostatis* which is usually translated with "helper" or "patroness," although in the literature of the time the term has the connotation of leading officer, president, governor, or superintendent.[38] Since Paul claims that Phoebe was a *prostatis* "of many and also of himself," scholars reject here such a meaning. However, in 1 Thess 5:12 the verb characterizes persons with authority in the community and in 1 Tim 3:4f. and 5:17 it designates the functions of the bishop, deacon, or elder. We therefore can assume that Phoebe had a position of great authority within the community of Cenchreae and that her authority was not limited to this congregation but was widely respected, even by Paul himself. Phoebe receives a recommendation similar to that of Timothy in 1 Cor 16:10f.[39]

In conclusion: Paul's letters indicate that women were among the most prominent missionaries and leaders of the early Christian communities. They were co-workers with Paul but did not stand under his authority. They were teachers, preachers, and prophets. As leaders of house-churches they had great influence and probably presided also at the worship celebrations. If we compare their leadership with the ministry of the later deaconesses it is striking that their authority was *not* restricted to the ministry for women nor to specific feminine functions.

Such a leadership of women in pre-Pauline and Pauline Christianity was legitimized by the theology expressed in Gal 3:28. In the Christian community all distinctions of race, religion, class, and gender are abolished. All members are equal and one in Christ. Gal 3:28 probably is a traditional baptismal formula[40] which was quoted by Paul in this letter in order to support his view that there is no longer any distinction between Jew and Gentile in the Christian community. This pre-Pauline baptismal formula expresses the self-understanding of the newly initiated Christians over against the societal-religious differences accepted in the Greco-Roman culture of the time. It was a rhetorical commonplace that the Hellenistic man was grateful that he was born a human being and not a beast, a Greek and not a Barbarian, a man and not a woman. This pattern seems to have been adopted by Judaism and found its way into the synagogue liturgy. Three times daily the Jew thanked God that he did not create him a Gentile, a slave, or a woman. In distinction to this cultural-religious pattern shared by Hellenists and Jews alike[41] the Christians affirmed at their baptism that all cultural-religious differences are abolished among them.

It is important to note, however, that this baptismal formula does not yet reflect the same notion of unification and androcentric perspective found in later gnostic writings.[42] Whereas according to various gnostic texts to become a disciple means for a woman to become "male" and "like man" because the male principle stands for the heavenly, divine realm while the female principle is secondary, Gal 3:28 does not extoll maleness as the standard and form of the new life[43] but Jesus Christ, in whose body—the church—male and female gender roles are transcended. Since the pairs "Jews and Greek" as well as "free and slave" indicate the abolition of cultural-religious differences within the Christian community (cf. 1 Cor 12:12 ff.), we safely can assume that the same applies to the third pair "male and female." The legal-societal and cultural-religious distinctions between Jews and Greeks and slaves and free are transcended in the Christian community insofar as, on the one hand, Jews and Greeks and slaves and free remain legally and socially what they are, but on the other hand have equal standing in the church. In a similar fashion the biological-sexual-legal differences between men and women remain but gender roles and their cultural-religious significance[44] are no longer valid for the Christian community.[45] This new egalitarian Christian self-understanding did away with all distinctions and privileges of religion, class, and caste and thereby allowed not only Gentiles and slaves but also women to exercise leadership functions within the community. Since even wealthy women were marginal people in antiquity, they must have been very attracted to such an egalitarian movement, which granted them authority and leadership within the church. Therefore not the love-patriarchalism of the post-Pauline school but the egalitarian ethos of pre-Pauline and Pauline Christianity provides in my opinion the context for Paul's injunctions concerning the behavior of women in the Corinthian community.

WOMEN'S BEHAVIOR IN THE WORSHIP SERVICE OF THE COMMUNITY

Although we have only scanty information on women in early Christianity, we have seen that the community of Corinth had at least three outstanding women leaders in their midst. The followers of Chloe approached Paul with questions to which he responds in the letter and Prisca lived and worked at Corinth. Most renowned is of course Phoebe who was a minister of the church at Cenchreae, the nearby seaport of Corinth.

However, it is also significant that the Corinthian Christians understood their faith in terms of Hellenistic–Jewish Sophia theology.[46] "The Spirit" was believed to be "the 'Wisdom of God' and the Spirit-Wisdom bestows the gifts of wisdom upon those who cultivate her gifts, and who live upon her supramundane level."[47] The Corinthians understand the significance of Jesus Christ in terms of Jewish–Hellenistic Sophia-speculation which also has determined the pre-Pauline christological NT hymns[48] and which was developed in connection with the Isis-religion.[49] They are convinced that they are able to receive divine Wisdom because God has given them a pneumatic-spiritual nature (cf. Gn 2:7). This Sophia-theology is found not only here but also in the Synoptic tradition and we must be careful not to label it too quickly as "gnostic"[50] and therefore heretical.

Since in this theology Wisdom was conceived as a semi-hypostatic female figure we can surmise that women were especially attracted to become her devotees. In the worship service of the community where the divine Wisdom-Spirit was present and all received her "spiritual" gifts women as well as men were pneumatics and therefore had equal leadership within the community. The immediate context of Paul's injunctions concerning women's behavior in the worship service of the community gives evidence that women as well as men do share in the pneumatic gifts of Wisdom-Spirit and pray and prophesy publicly under the influence of the divine Spirit. Paul explicitly affirms that in doing so the Corinthians have followed his teachings and example (11:2) and he does not disqualify this "spiritual" self-understanding and practice of the Corinthian pneumatics. The contrast between 1 Cor 11:2 and 11:17 underlines that Paul does not refer here to any particular abuse but introduces regulations and customs which were observed in other Christian communities (11:16, 14:33).

The injunctions concerning women's behavior, however, are not peripheral to Paul's argument but of great concern to him as their place in the structure of the letter indicates. The whole section of chapters 11–14[51] speaks of the pneumatic worship service of the community and is composed in the form of a thematic inclusion insofar as the section begins and ends with the problem of women's correct behavior in the worship assembly. The concluding verses 14:37–40 indicate how serious the issues are for Paul and how much he expects resistance to his viewpoint. Paul appeals to the prophets and pneumatics to accept his arguments as a revelatory word of the Lord himself (v. 37).[52] He assures the Corinthians that he does not want to hinder prophetic and ecstatic speaking but that he is concerned that everything "should happen decently and in the right order" (v. 40). Thus it seems to be Paul and not the Corinthians who attempts to qualify or to change the pneumatic behavior of the community. His major line of argument is decency and the right order, values which are not specific Christian.[53] At the same time Paul is in a difficult position since he had originally spoken to them about the new life in the Spirit and the Christian freedom evolving from it.[54] In order to understand Paul's position more fully we have to analyze the injunctions of 1 Cor 11:2–16 and 14:33–36 more in detail.

1 Cor 11:2–16: We no longer are able to decide with certainty which behavior Paul criticizes and which custom he means to introduce in 1 Cor 11:2–16. Traditionally, exegetes have conjectured that Paul insists that the pneumatic women leaders should wear the veil according to Jewish custom.[55] Yet v. 15 maintains that women have their hair instead of a head-covering and thus militates against such an interpretation. It is therefore more likely that Paul speaks here about the manner in which women should wear their hair[56] when praying and prophesying (v. 13). It seems that the women prophets and pneumatics have let down their hair during the worship celebration as the worshippers of Isis appear to have done. For instance a woman friend of the poet Tibullus is said to have had to let her hair down twice daily in the worship of Isis to "say lauds."[57] Archeological evidence also shows that the female devotees of Isis usually wore long hair "with a band around the forehead and curls falling on the shoulder"[58] while the male initiates had their head shaven. Hence Paul's sarcastic statement in vv. 5f. that the women who loosen their hair might as well have it cut short or shaven. It is as disgraceful to loosen one's hair as it is to shave it.

The Corinthian pneumatics presumably took over such a hair fashion because they understood their equality in the community and their devotion to Sophia-Spirit in analogy to the Isis cult since Isis was also said to have made the power of women equal to men[59] and her associations admitted, like the Christian communities, women and slaves to equal membership and active participation.[60] Paul, on the other hand, insists on a different hairstyle probably because loose hair had a completely different meaning in a Jewish–Christian context.

According to Jewish sources loosed hair continued to be a sign of

215

uncleanness even to Paul's day.[61] Nm 4:18 (*LXX*) prescribes that the woman accused of adultery be marked publicly by loosening her hair. Similarly in Lev 13:45 (*LXX*) one of the signs for the uncleanness of a leper is loosed hair. The Jewish woman very artfully braided her hair and pinned it up so that it formed a kind of tiara on her head (cf. Judith 10:3; 16:8), an effect highlighted by adorning it with gold, jewelry, ribbons, or a silvery gauze.[62] In view of this hairstyle the exegetically difficult statement in v. 10 becomes more understandable. Paul argues: Since the angels[63] are present in the pneumatic worship service of a community that speaks the "tongues of angels", women should not worship as cultically unclean persons by letting their hair down, but they should pin it up in the form of a tiara or crown as a sign of their spiritual power.

However Paul not only insists on a different hairstyle but also on the differences between women and men. He adduces the following Scriptural and theological arguments for his position: *Firstly*, Paul sets forth a descending hierarchy: God-Christ-man-woman,[64] in which each preceding member as "head" stands above the other "in the sense that he establishes the other's being."[65] *Secondly*, Paul declares that man is created to be the image and manifestation of God, while woman is only the glory or reflection of man, because man was created prior to woman and woman was created because of him (vv. 7–9).[66] Of course, this interpretation of Gn 2 flies directly in the face of the Corinthian Jewish–Hellenistic interpretation of Gn 2:7 which insisted on the pneumatic-spiritual nature of all persons. "A rabbinic reason for denying women the image-of-God status was precisely that they did not have the same religious duties as men."[67] Another rabbinic tradition thinks that the image-of-God status consists in circumcision and therefore a woman is *ipso facto* not the image of God. *Thirdly*, In vv. 11–12 Paul maintains that his insistence on the creational difference and hierarchy between men and women does not deny the interdependence of men and women within the Christian community.[68] However, that Paul does not want to speak here of the equality of men and women is evident by the fact that he refers shortly afterward in 1 Cor 12:13 to the baptismal formula of Gal 3:28 but omits the pair "male and female." This is significant because it is exactly at this point that Paul stresses that all are equal members of the body of Christ although they have different pneumatic gifts and functions. *Fourthly*, Paul employs the Stoic argument from nature[69] which was widely used against emancipatory tendencies in the Greco-Roman world to insist on the difference between men and women. *Finally*, Paul has to resort to an authoritarian appeal, probably because he himself senses that his arguments are not very convincing theologically. Therefore he declares that it is party spirit and contentiousness if the Corinthians do not accept his injunctions and he insists that he and the other churches do not acknowledge another practice. Nevertheless, Paul's argument does not deny that women are pneumatics and pray and prophesy in the worship service of the community. He argues, however, that they should retain the traditional hairstyle and respect the differences between women and men.[70]

1 Cor 14:33–36: It is debated whether 14:33b–35(36) is an authentic Pauline injunction or whether the passage was added by a later editor of the Pauline school. However, since the verses cannot be excluded on textual-critical grounds but are usually declared to be inauthentic on theological grounds, it is exegetically more sound to accept them as an original Pauline statement and to explain them within their present context. As in chapter 11 so in chapters 12–14 Paul seeks to persuade the Corinthians that decency and order should be more highly esteemed than the spiritual status and exercise of the individual. While the Corinthians seem to have valued glossolalia most, Paul favors the gift of prophecy and interprets it in terms of reason, order, and mission (14:4, 5, 19).[71] The Corinthian pneumatics should not be concerned with the exhibition of their spiritual greatness but with the building up of the community (14:4 f.) and with the impression they make on interested outsiders (14; 16, 17, 23 ff.).

14:26–36 are best understood to be a church order[72] with rules for glossolalists (vv. 27 ff.), for prophets (vv. 29–32), and for wives (vv. 33b–36). These three rules are formulated in a structurally similar fashion. A general sentence of regulation (vv. 27, 29, 34) is complemented by a sentence that concretizes it (vv. 28, 30, 35). The second and third rules are expanded with reasons for the regulation (vv. 31–32, 34a, 35b). However, the rule for wives is different insofar as it has an introduction (v. 33a) and ends with a double rhetorical question (v. 36). These stylistic additions seem to underline the importance of the last regulation.

1 Cor 14:33–36 is often understood to speak about women in general and therefore to contradict 11:2–16 which presupposes that women are pneumatics and as such pray and prophesy within the worship of the community. However, the difficulty is resolved if we recognize that the injunction does not pertain to all women but solely to wives, since chapter 7 documents that not all women in the community were married and could ask their husbands at home. 1 Cor

7:32–35 confirms the interpretation that the prohibition in 14:33–36 applies just to wives. Although in 1 Cor 7 Paul acknowledges the equality and reciprocity of husband and wife,[73] his ascetic preference for the unmarried state is plain.[74] In 7:32–35 he interprets the apocalyptic "as if not" tradition of 7:29–31 in a christological missionary perspective. The married person, Paul argues, is divided and concerned with the issues of marriage and family while the unmarried person is completely dedicated to the affairs of the Lord. It is apparent that Paul, here, is "taking over bourgeois moral concepts which denote not absolute but conventional values."[75] Paul's argument is surprising, especially since we know of leading missionary couples who spent their life in the service of the Lord.

However, only the singleminded dedication of the unmarried woman and virgin and not that of the unmarried man is further qualified with the subordinate clause "that she may be holy in body and spirit" (7:34). Paul ascribes here a special holiness to the unmarried woman and virgin apparently because she is not touched by men (cf. 7:1).[76] We therefore can surmise that Paul is able to accept the pneumatic participation of such "holy" women in the worship service of the community but argues in 14:34f. against such an active participation of wives.

Paul derives his theological argument from the Jewish–Hellenistic propaganda tradition that places the demand for the subordination of wives in the context of the Law.[77] This tradition has also influenced the household codes of the post-Pauline literature. However one could argue that the *hypotassein* of v. 34 does not demand submission to husbands but to the regulations of the community. As in 7:35, so here Paul concludes his injunction by pointing to propriety (v. 35b).

The subsequent rhetorical questions in v. 36 indicate the counter-argument which Paul expects. It is often suggested that these questions refer to the whole community because the wives could not have argued that the word of God originated with them or that they were the only ones whom it has reached. However, when we consider that leading early Christian missionaries such as Prisca, Junia, and perhaps Apphia were married and that in general the other leading women mentioned in the Pauline letters are not characterized as virgins, widows, or unmarried, such a counter-argument becomes plausible. Since we have seen that wives were called to missionary preaching and were founders of house churches, Paul's claim that these women should be silent and ask their husbands at home sounds preposterous. Paul realizes that this regulation goes against the accepted practice of the missionary churches in the Hellenistic urban centers. He therefore claims for his regulations the authority of the Lord (v. 37). In the final analysis, however, not theological reasons but the concern for decency and order determines Paul's regulation concerning the behavior of pneumatic women and men in the worship service of the community (v. 40).

In conclusion: In the preceding analysis I have attempted to argue that the Pauline injunctions for women in 1 Cor should be understood in the context of women's leadership in early Christianity. 11:2–16 on the one hand does not deny women's prophecy and prayer in the worship assembly but insists that in the Christian community women and men are interdependent. However they should not deny in their behavior the creational differences and hierarchal relationships. The community rule of 14:33–36 on the other hand has a specific situation in mind, namely the speaking and questioning of wives in the public worship assembly. Here as in 7:34 and 9:5 Paul appears to limit the active participation of wives in the "affairs of the Lord." His conclud-ing rhetorical questions indicate that he does not expect his regulation will be accepted without protest by the Corinthian community which knows wives as leading Christian apostles and missionaries. Yet Paul is more concerned that order and propriety be preserved so that an outsider cannot accuse the Christians of religious madness. In both passages, then, Paul places a limit and qualification on the pneumatic participation of women in the worship service of the community. We do not know whether the Corinthian women and men accepted his limitations and qualifications. However, the love-patriarchalism of the Deutero-Pauline household codes and the injunctions of the Pastoral Epistles[78] are a further development of Paul's argument that will lead in the future to the exclusion of all women from ecclesial office and to a gradual patriarchalization of the church.[79]

In response to R. Scrogg's attempt to rescue Paul from the uninformed attacks of his feminist critics, Elaine Pagels has main-tained as a hermeneutical principle: "It is really not my intent to put Paul on trial before a panel of NT scholars or debate whether he is 30%, 75%, or 100% a feminist. After all, these are criteria that have emerged from our own present situation. To attempt simply to judge Paul by such standards seems to me anachronistic and a waste of time."[80] I have attempted to show, to the contrary, that firstly, the feminist quest for the equality of women was alive in pre-Pauline and Pauline Christianity, and that Paul for the sake of "order" and for the sake of attracting outsiders appears to react to it. Secondly, the hermeneutical discussion has driven home that a value-free historical inquiry unencumbered by present-day concerns is intellectually not possible. Feminist scholarship is not the exception of the rule but openly demonstrates that all scholarship is determined by contemporary issues. Finally, in my opinion, scholars cannot refrain from passing judgment on biblical texts because the NT is not just a historical work of the first century but functions as Holy Scripture for Christian communities today. Insofar as the Bible is not only a document of past history but inspired Scripture for today exegetical-Biblical studies cannot avoid the question of the *meaning* of NT texts for today.

A hermeneutic-theological approach that is concerned with the contemporary meaning and authority of the Pauline injunctions in a post-patriarchal society and church, however, has to insist that solely non-sexist and non-oppressive traditions of the NT and non-androcentric models of historical reconstruction and biblical interpretation do justice to divine revelation, if the word of God is not to become a tool for the patriarchal oppression of women and a theological justification of sexist societal and ecclesial structures. The theological significance of Paul's injunctions for today has to be judged accordingly. After all, Paul himself has insisted: "For freedom Christ has set us free; stand fast therefore, and do not submit again to a yoke of slavery" (Gal 5:1 RSV).

Notes

1. W. Munro, 'Patriarchy and Charismatic Community in "Paul"', in J. Plaskow and J. A. Romero (eds.), *Women and Religion*, 2nd edn. (Missoula: Scholars Press, 1974), 189–98; Wm. O. Walker, '1 Cor 11:2–16 and Paul's View Regarding Women', *JBL* 94 (1975), 94–110; and the critical review of this proposal by J. Murphy-O'Connor, 'The Non-Pauline Character of 1 Cor 11:2–16?', *JBL* 95 (1976), 615–21.

2. Cf. G. Fitzer, *Das Weib schweige in der Gemeinde* (ThE 110; Munich: Kaiser, 1963), and H. Conzelmann, *1 Corinthians* (Hermeneia; Philadelphia: Fortress, 1975), 246, for the arguments against the authenticity of the passage.

3. Cf. E. Cady Stanton, *The Original Feminist Attack on the Bible (The Woman's Bible)* (New York: Arno Press, 1974), esp. the introduction by B. Welter; cf. also the 'Pastoral Letter of the Massachusetts Congregationalist Clergy (1837)', in A. S. Kraditor (ed.), *Up From the Pedestal* (Chicago: Quadrangle, 1968), 50 ff.

4. Cf. 'Vatican Declaration: Women in the Priesthood', *Origins* 6 (1977), 518–24, and the supporting comment by D. Burrell, 'The Vatican Declaration: Another View', *America* (2 Apr. 1977), 289–92, 291: 'for I cannot but suspect that Lawrence would find the Vatican Declaration profoundly accurate in the way it links sexuality with the symbolic dynamics of human salvation.' For a

feminist analysis of the political implications of this 'two-human-nature' concept, cf. B. W. Harrison, 'The New Consciousness of Women: A Socio-Political Resource', *Cross-Currents* 24 (1975), 445–62; id., 'Sexism in the Contemporary Church: When Evasion Becomes Complicity', in A. L. Hagemann (ed.), *Sexist Religion and Women in the Church* (New York: Association Press, 1974), 195–216.

5. Cf. M. Daly, *Beyond God the Father* (Boston: Beacon Press, 1973), and the review article by C. Christ, 'The New Feminist Theology: A Review of the Literature', *Religious Studies Review* 3 (1977), 203–12.

6. Cf. e.g. R. Scroggs, 'Paul Chauvinist or Liberationist?', *Christian Century* 89 (1972), 307–9; id., 'Paul and the Eschatological Woman', *JAAR* 40 (1972), 283–303, and 42 (1974), 532–49.

7. e.g. A. Feuillet, 'La dignité et le rôle de la femme d'après quelques textes pauliniens: Comparaison avec *L'Ancien Testament*', *NTS* 21 (1975), 157–91; J. Massyngberde Ford, 'Biblical Material Relevant to the Ordination of Women', *JES 19* (1973), 669–94.

8. R. and J. Boldrey, *Chauvinist or Feminist? Paul's View of Women* (Michigan: Baker Book House, 1976); cf. also P. J. Ford, 'Paul the Apostle: Male Chauvinist?', *Biblical Theology Bulletin* 4 (1975), 302–11.

9. For a general discussion cf. K. Frör, *Biblische Hermeneutik* (Munich: Kaiser, 1961); R. Funk, *Language, Hermeneutic and Word of God* (New York: Harper & Row, 1966); E. Schillebeeckx, *The Understanding of Faith* (New York: Seabury, 1974); J. A. Sanders, 'Hermeneutics', *Suppl. Vol. IDB* (Nashville: Abingdon, 1976), 402–7, and my attempt to apply the hermeneutical principles of the Constitution on Divine Revelation of Vatican II to the problem of how to evaluate the teachings of the NT on women: 'Understanding God's Revealed Word', *Catholic Charismatic* 1 (1977), 7–10.

10. For the heuristic value of 'models' cf. I. G. Barbour, *Myth, Models and Paradigms* (New York: Harper & Row, 1974).

11. Cf. K. Mannheim, *Ideology and Utopia* (London: Routledge, 1954), 243: 'Every epoch has its fundamentally new approach and its characteristic point of view and consequently sees the "same" objects from a new perspective.' For a feminist analysis cf. H. Smith, 'Feminism and the Methodology of Women's History', in B. A. Carrol (ed.), *Liberating Women's History* (Urbana: University of Illinois Press, 1976), 368–84.

12. I use 'patriarchal' in the sense of a societal system of male dominance and female submission and marginality.

13. S. de Beauvoir, *The Second Sex* (New York: Knopf, 1953), pp. xv f.

14. E. Janeway, *Man's World, Woman's Place* (New York: Dell, 1971), 307, points to the emotional component of social mythology. Therefore not logic but only 'an answer *in reality* to those needs which the myth answers in phantasy' will bring about change in such a social mythology (emphasis mine).

15. Cf. my article 'The Study of Women in Early Christianity', in Thomas J. Ryan (ed.), *Critical History and Biblical Faith* (Villanova: Villanova University Press, 1979).

16. Cf. my articles 'The Twelve' and 'The Apostleship of Women in Early Christianity', in L. and A. Swidler (eds.), *Women Priests: A Catholic Commentary on the Vatican Declaration* (New York: Paulist Press, 1977), 114–23 and 135–40. In my writings I have consistently pointed to the apostleship of Mary

Magdalene; cf. E. Schüssler, *Der vergessene Partner* (Düsseldorf: Patmos, 1964), 57 ff.; 'Mary Magdalene: Apostle to Apostles', *UTS Journal* (Apr. 1975), 22 f.; 'Die Rolle der Frau in der urchristlichen Bewegung', *Concilium* 12 (1976), 3–9.

17. Cf. e.g. W. A. Meeks, *The Writings of St. Paul* (New York: Norton, 1972), 23: 1 Corinthians 'is a response to reports which have come to Paul by two means: (1) a letter, brought by an official delegation, Stephanus, Fortunatus, and Achaicus (16:17, cf. 7:1) and (2) *gossip* from ' "Chloe's people" (1:11), otherwise unknown' (emphasis mine).

18. Cf. the discussion by G. Theissen, 'Soziale Schichtung in der korinthischen Gemeinde. Ein Beitrag zur Soziologie des hellenistischen Urchristentums', *ZNW* 65 (1974), 255. However Paul writes *ek* with genitive when speaking about slaves of a household (cf. Rm 16: 10 f.; Phil 4:22).

19. Cf. Bernadette Brooten, 'Junia . . . Outstanding among the Apostles (Romans 16:7)', in Swidler and Swidler, *Women Priests*, 141–4, and J. M. Lagrange, *Saint Paul: Epître aux Romains* (Paris, 1916), 366.

20. For the problem of masculine language cf. R. Lakoff, *Language and Woman's Place* (New York: Harper, 1975); Miller and Swift, *Words and Women* (Garden City, NY: Anchor Press, 1976); L. Russel, 'Changing Language and the Church', in *The Liberating Word* (Philadelphia: Westminster, 1976), 82–98; and the extensive bibliographical review by M. R. Key, *Male/Female Language* (Metuchen: Scarecrow Press, 1975).

21. Cf. 1 Cor 15:3–10. The conclusion drawn by R. E. Brown is therefore questionable: 'The priority given to Peter in Paul and in Luke is a priority among those who became official witnesses to the Resurrection. The secondary place given to the tradition of an appearance to a woman or women probably reflects the fact that women did not serve at first as official preachers of the Church'; cf. R. E. Brown, 'Roles of Women in the Fourth Gospel', in W. Burkhardt (ed.), *Woman: New Dimensions* (New York: Paulist Press, 1977), 116 n. 12.

22. Cf. J. G. Gager, *Kingdom and Community: The Social World of Early Christianity* (Englewood Cliffs, NJ: Prentice-Hall, 1975), 22–37; R. Scroggs, 'The Earliest Christian Communities as Sectarian Movement', in J. Neusner (ed.), *Christianity, Judaism and Other Greco-Roman Cults* ii (Leiden: Brill, 1975), 1–23; G. Theissen, 'Itinerant Radicalism: The Tradition of Jesus Sayings from the Perspective of the Sociology of Literature', in *Radical Religion: The Bible and Liberation* (Community for Religious Research and Education, 1976), 84–93; id., *Sociology of Early Palestinian Christianity* (Philadelphia: Fortress, 1978).

23. Cf. Theissen, 'Soziale Schichtung', 268–72; id., 'Itinerant Radicalism', 91 f.; id., 'Die Starken und die Schwachen in Korinth', *EvTh* 35 (1975), 171 ff. Theissen owes the expression 'love-patriarchalism' to E. Troeltsch, *The Social Teachings of the Christian Churches* i (New York: Harper, 1960), 78: 'This is the type of Christian patriarchalism founded upon the religious recognition of and the religious overcoming of an earthly inequality.'

24. For the participation of women in cult associations and philosophical schools, cf. L. Swidler, 'Greco-Roman Feminism and the Reception of the Gospel', in B. Jaspert and R. Mohr (eds.), *Traditio-Krisis-Renovatio aus theologischer Sicht* (Marburg: Elwert, 1976), 49–52; W. A. Meeks, 'The Image of the Androgyne: Some Uses of a Symbol in Earliest Christianity', *History of Religion* 13 (1974), 169–74.

25. Cf. E. E. Ellis, 'Paul and his Co-Workers', *NTS* 17 (1970/71), 439; cf. also the essay of M. A. Getty on *synergos* in Swidler and Swidler, *Women Priests*, 176–82.

26. Cf. W. D. Thomas, 'The Place of Women in the Church at Philippi', *Expository Times* 83 (1972), 117–20; R. W. Graham, 'Women in the Pauline Churches: A Review Article', *Lexington Theological Quarterly* 11 (1976), 29 f.

27. Cf. F. F. Filson, 'The Significance of the Early House Churches', *JBL* 58 (1939), 105–12; E. A. Judge, *The Social Patterns of Christian Groups in the First Century* (London: Tyndale Press, 1960), 36: 'Not only was the conversion of a household the natural or even necessary way of establishing the cult in unfamiliar surroundings, but the household remained the soundest basis for the meeting of Christians.'

28. Cf. R. J. M. Kelvey, *The New Temple: The Church in the New Testament* (Oxford: Oxford University Press, 1969), and my article 'Cultic Language in Qumran and in the New Testament', *CBQ* 38 (1976), 159–79.

29. Cf. however E. Lohse, *Colossians and Philemon* (Hermeneia; Philadelphia: Fortress, 1971), 190: 'The lady of the house had to deal daily with the slaves. Therefore she had to give her opinion when the question of taking back a runaway slave was raised.' The tendency is clear. Apphia is reduced to a wife and mistress, although like the two men she is given a Christian characterization.

30. Cf. E. Käsemann, *An die Römer* (HNT 8a; Tübingen: Vandenhoeck & Ruprecht, 1973), 394, asserts that we are justified to count the couple among the most outstanding early Christian missionaries in the dispersion.

31. The writer of Codex D (second century) mentions the name of Prisca in second place in Acts 18:26. Not only does he make Aquila the subject of the sentence in 18:2 by writing 'Aquila with his wife Priscilla' but he also mentions Aquila three times (18:3, 7, 22) without referring to Priscilla.

32. Therefore A. v. Harnack, 'Probabilia über die Adresse und den Verfasser des Hebräerbriefes', *ZNW* 1 (1900), 16–41, suggests that she authored the Epistle to the Hebrews. It is significant that scholars always assume male authorship, although in most cases we do not know who wrote the NT books.

33. Cf. my 'The Apostleship of Women', 136 ff.

34. See Ellis, 'Paul and his Co-Workers', 445–51.

35. Cf. B. Bauer, 'Uxores Circumducere 1 Kor 9:53', *BZNF* 3 (1959), 94–102. E. Kaesemann suggests that the missionary couples follow the synoptic injunction that the apostles should go out 'two by two' (cf. Mk 6:7 par.). Cf. also the interpretation of Clement of Alexandria (Strom iii.6.53, 3f.), 'and took their wives with them not as women with whom they had marriage relations but as sisters, that they might be their fellow-ministers (*syndiakonous*) in dealing with housewives. It was through them that the Lord's teaching penetrated also the women's quarters without any scandal being aroused.' However, the text does not give any indication of encratite behaviour.

36. *The History of the Early Church* (London: Lutterworth Press, 1963), 146.

37. Cf. A Lemaire, 'From Services to Ministries: Diakonia in the First Two Centuries', *Concilium* 14 (1972), 35–49; K. H. Schelkle, 'Ministry and Ministers in the NT Church', *Concilium* 11 (1969), 5–11; A. Lemaire, 'The Ministries in the NT: Recent Research', *Biblical Theology Bulletin* 3 (1973), 133–66.

38. Cf. B. Reicke, '*prohistemi*', *Theological Dictionary of the New Testament* (*TDNT*), iv. 703: the verb as well as the substantive 'have the twofold sense of leadership and care'.

39. Cf. H. Gamble, *The Textual History of the Letter to the Romans* (Studies and Documents 42; Grand Rapids, Mich.: 1977), 87.

40. H. D. Betz, 'Spirit, Freedom and Law: Paul's Message to the Galatian Churches', *Svensk Exeg. Arsbok* 39 (1974), 145–60; M. Bouttier, 'Complexio Oppositorum: Sur les formules de l Cor xii. 13; Gal iii. 26–28; Col iii. 10.11', *NTS* 23 (1976), 1–19; Meeks, 'The Androgyne', 181.

41. Cf. A. Oepke, '*gyne*', *TDNT*, i. 777 n. 4. The prayer therefore expresses a commonly accepted cultural attitude toward women, and should not be used to denounce Judaism since we have rabbinic passages similar to Gal 3:28; cf. J. Leipoldt, *Jesus und die Frauen* (Leipzig: Quelle & Meyer, 1921), 14 f. For the critique of anti-Jewish tendencies in feminist theology cf. J. Plaskow, 'Christian Feminism and Anti-Judaism', *Cross Currents* 28/3 (1978).

42. This is maintained by W. Schmitthals, *Die Gnosis in Korinth* (FRLANT 66; Göttingen: Vandenhoeck & Ruprecht, 1956), 227 n. 1; cf. also Meeks, 'The Androgyne', 180 ff., and R. Scroggs, 'Paul and the Eschatological Woman: Revisited,' *JAAR* 42 (1974), 536. However these authors appear to identify gender roles with sexual-biological roles. Betz, 'Spirit, Freedom and Law', correctly stresses that here male and female societal cultural gender roles are abolished in the Christian community.

43. Cf. the Gospel of Thomas, the Gospel of Mary, and Pistis Sophia. See my analysis of gnostic perceptions and attitudes toward women, 'Word, Spirit, and Power: Women in Early Christian Communities', in R. R. Ruether and E. McLaughlin (eds.), *Women of Spirit* (New York: Simon & Schuster, 1979).

44. For the definition and distinction of sex and gender cf. A. Oakley, *Sex, Gender and Society* (New York: Harper, 1972), 158 ff.

45. Exegetes often understand the text as applying not to the Church but to the equality of souls, to eschatological equality, or to equality in heaven, or they maintain that the differences are only overcome sacramentally or spiritually *coram deo*. For a criticism of such an interpretation cf. K. Stendahl, *The Bible and the Role of Women* (FB 15; Philadelphia: Fortress, 1966), 32 ff.

46. Cf. B. L. Mack, *Logos und Sophio: Untersuchungen zur Weisheitstheologie im Hellenistischen Judentum* (SUNT 10; Göttingen: Vandenhoeck & Ruprecht, 1973); R. Marcus, 'On Biblical Hypostases of Wisdom', *HUCA* 23 (1950/51), 157–71.

47. B. A. Pearson, *The Pneumatikos-Psychikos Terminology in 1 Corinthians* (SBL Diss. 12; Missoula: Scholars Press, 1973), 37.

48. Cf. my 'Wisdom Mythology and the Christological Hymns of the New Testament', in R. Wilken (ed.), *Aspects of Wisdom in Judaism and Early Christianity* (Notre Dame: Indiana University Press, 1976), 17–41 (literature).

49. Cf. my 'Wisdom Mythology', 30 ff.; J. M. Reese, *Hellenistic Influences on the Book of Wisdom and its Consequences* (AB 41; Rome: Biblical Institute, 1970), 33–50.

50. Cf. Pearson, *Pneumatikos-Psychikos*, 82 ff.; Conzelmann, *1 Corinthians*, 58 ff.; id., 'Paul und die Weisheit', *NTS* 12 (1965/66), 231–4. Conzelmann, however, maintains that it is Paul and not the Corinthians who profess a Jewish–

Hellenistic wisdom theology. Cf. however B. A. Pearson, 'Hellenistic-Jewish Wisdom Speculation and Paul', in Wilken, *Aspects of Wisdom*, 43–66.

51. Cf. Wendland, *Die Briefe and die Korinther* (NTD 7; Göttingen: Vandenhoeck & Ruprecht, 1965), 80; Conzelmann, *1 Corinthians*, 182, points to a certain tension in chs. 11–14, because 11:2–16 already deals with behavior at divine worship, while a new topic is introduced only in 12:1. E. Kähler, *Die Frau in den Paulinischen Briefen* (Zürich: Gotthelf, 1960), 43 f., suggests that 10:32–11:2 are the introduction and headline to 11:3–16.

52. Conzelmann, *1 Corinthians*, suggests that 'this idea is better suited to interpolation than to Paul, and is suggested by it' (246). For the prophetic self-understanding of Paul, cf. however U. B. Müller, *Prophetie und Predigt im Neuen Testament* (StNT 10; Gütersloh: Mohn, 1975), 117–233.

53. On the concept of 'good order' cf. G. Dautzenberg, *Urchristliche Prophetie. Ihre Erforschung, ihre Voraussetzungen im Judentum und ihre Struktur im 1. Korinterbrief* (BWANT 104; Tübingen: Mohr, 1974), 278–84.

54. J. C. Hurd, Jr, *The Origin of 1 Corinthians* (New York: Seabury, 1965), 287: 'We have suggested that much of the "wisdom" and "knowledge" to which they clung had been given them by Paul himself . . . Here we meet a younger, more vigorous Paul, fired with enthusiasm in his new faith, less cautious in his theological statements than he later became, little conscious of the weaknesses of human nature.' Cf. also J. W. Drane, 'Tradition, Law and Ethics in Pauline Theology', *NovT* 16 (1974), 167–87, who points out the shift in Paul's theology in Gal. and 1 Cor.

55. Cf. G. Delling, *Paulus Stellung zu Frau und Ehe* (Stuttgart: Kohlhammer, 1931), 96–105. S. Lösch, 'Christliche Frauen in Korinth', *Theologische Quartalschrift* 127 (1947), 216–61; M. D. Hooker, 'Authority on Her Head: An Examination of 1 Cor 11: 10', *NTS* 10 (1963/4), 410–16; A. Joubert, 'Le voile des femmes', *NTS* 18 (1972), 419–30.

56. Cf. Lösch, 'Christliche Frauen', 240 ff.; J. B. Hurley, 'Did Paul Require Veils or the Silence of Women? A Consideration of 1 Cor 11:2–16 and 1 Cor 14:33b–36', *Westminster Theological Journal* 35 (1972/3), 190–220; W. J. Martin, '1 Cor 11:2:16: An Interpretation', in W. W. Gasque and R. R. Martin (eds.), *Apostolic History and the Gospel* (Grand Rapids: Eerdmans, 1970), 231–4; J. Murphy-O'Connor, *L'Existence chrétienne selon saint Paul* (LD 80; Paris: Cerf, 1974), 103–4 n. 37; A. Isaakson, *Marriage and Ministry in the New Temple* (ASNU 24; Lund: Gleerup, 1965), 165–86.

57. Tib. 1, 3, 29–32. For other cults cf. Lösch, 'Christliche Frauen'.

58. S. Kelly Heyob, *The Cult of Isis among Women in the Greco-Roman World* (Leiden: Brill, 1975), 60.

59. Ibid. 52.

60. Ibid. 105 f.; cf. also R. E. Witt, *Isis in the Graeco-Roman World* (Ithaca, NY: Cornell University Press, 1971).

61. W. C. Van Unnik, 'Les cheveux défaits des femmes baptisées', *VigChr* 1 (1947), 77–100.

62. Cf. H. L. Strack and P. Billerbeck, *Kommentar zum Neuen Testament aus Talmud und Midrasch*, iii (Munich: Beck, 1926), 428 f., for the hairstyle of Jewish women.

63. Cf. J. A. Fitzmyer, 'A Feature of Qumran Angelology and the Angels of 1 Cor 11:10', *NTS* 4 (1957/8), 48–58.

64. J. B. Schaller, 'Gen 1, 2 im antiken Judentum' (dissertation, Göttingen, 1961), points out that the series God–Adam–Eve is found in the targum translation of Gn 1:26 f. and 2:18. Therefore he argues that Paul enlarged this series by introducing Christ (188 f.).

65. H. Schlier, 'kephale', TDNT, iii. 679.

66. Cf. J. Jervell, Imago Dei: Gen 1, 26f im Spätjudentum, in der Gnosis und in den Paulinischen Briefen (FRLANT 76; Göttingen: Vandenhoeck & Ruprecht, 1960), 110, claims that 'the tendency of rabbinic theology is not only to deny image-of-God status to Eve . . . but also to every woman'.

67. Ibid. 301; cf. also 109. For the religious duties of women, cf. L. Swidler, Women in Judaism: The Status of Women in Formative Judaism (Metuchen: Scarecrow Press, 1976), 82 ff. The rabbinic evidence can only be used with great caution for the interpretation of Pauline texts, since the rabbinic passages are hard to date.

68. Cf. Gn r. 22(14d) in Strack and Billerbeck, Kommentar, iii. 440: man not without woman, woman not without man, neither of them without the Shekinah.

69. Cf. Conzelmann, 1 Corinthians, 190 esp. nn. 96 and 97.

70. Meeks, 'The Androgyne', 200: 'Paul seems primarily concerned to reassert the distinction between male and female and the inferiority of the woman to the man.' Similarly R. Scroggs, who claims that Paul intends to eliminate the inequality between the sexes but not the distinctions.

71. Cf. esp. the works of G. Dautzenberg and U. Müller. W. A. Meeks, ' "Since then You Would Need to Go Out of the World": Group Boundaries in Pauline Christianity' in Thomas J. Ryan (ed.), Critical History and Biblical Faith (Villanova: Villanova University Press, 1979), characterizes the Pauline church as 'an open sect, concerned not to offend "those outside" but attract them to its message and if possible to its membership'. However, it is questionable whether this describes the attitude of the Pauline church or of Paul himself.

72. Cf. Dautzenberg, 253–88.

73. Cf. esp. Scroggs, 'The Eschatological Woman', 295–7. Cf. also W. Schrage, 'Zur Frontstellung der Paulinischen Ehebewertung in 1 Kor 7:1–7', ZNW 67 (1976), 214–34 (literature).

74. K. Niederwimmer, Askese und Mysterium (FRLANT 113; Göttingen: Vandenhoeck & Ruprecht, 1975), 80–123.

75. Conzelmann, 1 Corinthians, 134; cf. also S. Schulz, 'Evangelium und Welt. Hauptprobleme einer Ethik des Neuen Testaments', in H. D. Betz and L. Schottroff, Neues Testament und Christliche Existenz (Tübingen: Mohr, 1973), 483–501.

76. Cf. Niederwimmer, Askese und Mysterium, 115.

77. J. E. Crouch, The Origin and Intention of the Colossian Haustafel (FRLANT 109; Göttingen: Vandenhoeck & Ruprecht, 1972), 138 ff.

78. Cf. my 'Interpreting Patriarchal Traditions', in Russel, The Liberating Word, 55–9.

79. For the impact of this development on the contemporary Church, cf. my 'Feminist Theology as a Critical Theology of Liberation', Theological Studies 36 (1975), 605–25; and my 'Feminist Spirituality, Christian Identity and Catholic Vision', NICM Journal 1 (1976), 20–34.

80. E. Pagels, 'Paul and Women: A Response to a Recent Discussion', JAAR 42 (1974), 547.

Part IV. Practice: And Her Works Shall Praise Her in the Gates

Women increasingly expect (if not experience) absolute equality with men in all areas of their lives, and for most women equality means being able to do precisely what men do. Organized religion is often an exception to this general rule. A religion may or may not promote equality between the sexes, but at any rate religious equality is rarely a matter of treating men and women identically. On the contrary, there are major Jewish and Christian denominations (Orthodox Judaism and the Catholic Church, for instance) that seek to reinforce differences between men and women. Even religious denominations for whom emphasizing gender differences is not a theological imperative may tacitly encourage them: men are elected to boards and councils while women teach in Sunday schools and visit the sick. Women who demand to be treated like men in other domains may seem happy to be treated differently in religious contexts but can the church and synagogue justify being out of step with Western society in this respect, and even if they can, how long will they be able to keep women on board?

Gender equality is more of an issue in Judaism than in Christianity. First, the question of permitted and prohibited action is central in a religion that privileges practice over doctrine. Second, Judaism's influence extends far beyond the place of worship, not merely into the kitchen and bedroom, but even into the courtroom should a divorce be required. (Despite Blu Greenberg's famous claim that where there is a rabbinic will there is a halakhic way, the problem of the 'chained wife', unable to demand a divorce and thus unable to remarry, has yet to be resolved.) Third, since the Jewish home is at least as important as the synagogue, women have in practice a crucial domain, albeit a private one, and this complicates the issue of gender equality. Women in egalitarian Jewish denominations often find it difficult to operate successfully in both spheres (who can cook and serve a traditional Friday night dinner whilst leading the synagogue service?). Encouraging a woman to operate in the public domain may compromise her activity in the

227

private one, and this may represent a loss for her and for Judaism. The question that many women are asking in other contexts—can we have everything?—is thus especially problematic in a Jewish context.

When it comes to the place of worship itself, the gap between Judaism and Christianity begins to narrow. Admittedly, Judaism, unlike the vast majority of Christian denominations, has the challenge of separate seating, and objects and areas that are off-limits for women. Christianity, meanwhile, has challenges arising from the maleness of Jesus. Setting aside the question of ordination or officiating in religious services, both Jewish and Christian women are affected by the language and symbolism of a traditional liturgy that may neither speak to them directly nor address their needs. Jewish liturgy caters for most eventualities (witnessing a natural disaster, seeing a rainbow), but there are no traditional services for women who want to mourn or celebrate women's lifecycle events. Some women have tried to invest new significance in the traditional celebration of Rosh Hodesh (the new moon), while others have dedicated themselves to inventing new liturgies and rituals. Still others have revised old liturgy—the Passover Haggadah, for instance—and developed complementary rituals. An unsympathetic Jewish man is supposed to have remarked that a woman on the Bima (platform for service leader) is like an orange on a Seder Plate (that is, entirely out of place). Jewish women around the world add an orange to the symbolic ritual foods at Passover as a response to this man and others like him, and in order to provoke a question amongst their guests about the appropriate role of women in organized Judaism.

Questions about women's roles in organized religion are important for all faith communities, as well as for the women who belong to them. Religious institutions have in the past relied on women for such activities as educating children, welfare, and maintaining places of worship. As more women work outside the home, fewer have time and energy to devote to these unpaid yet essential tasks. Women are redefining their roles within faith communities, and those communities must look for novel ways to ensure the gaps are filled.

DL

21   In Defense of the 'Daughters of Israel'

Blu Greenberg*

Female sexuality and fertility are naturally of central importance in a matrilineal religion preoccupied with descendants. For well over two thousand years, menstruation and related issues were the subject of a vast literature generated by Jewish men who necessarily wrote from the perspective of outsiders. In the twentieth century, Jewish women began to examine for themselves the laws of Niddah (purity). Yet, for different reasons, and with very different consequences, they too adopted the perspective of outsiders, and were inclined to view it as a system that enabled men to control women and encouraged them to disparage female bodily functions. Women who observed the laws of Niddah were, for these writers, unfortunate victims of an oppressive regime. Blu Greenberg, author of *How to Run a Traditional Jewish Household* (and the wife of an Orthodox rabbi), was a pioneer among women who wrote about Niddah explicitly and intentionally as an insider. This extract from her book is an excellent example of a genre of feminist literature that combines the theoretical with the experiential.   DL

A VERY PRIVATE AFFAIR

Several years ago, on a June evening, my husband and I left our children in the care of a baby-sitter and went out for two hours. I had told the baby-sitter and Moshe, the only child still awake at that hour, that we were going shopping. I knew that Moshe would be asleep by the time we returned, so there was no question of having to deal with the natural inquisitiveness of a six-year-old. I also knew that Patti, our baby-sitter, the teenage daughter of our Irish Catholic neighbors, was too well bred to inquire why I had come back from shopping with no packages but with a headful of long, wet hair.

It was not that I was ashamed to talk about mikveh, the ritual bath.

* Blu Greenberg, from 'In Defense of the "Daughters of Israel": Observations on Niddah and Mikveh', from *On Women and Judaism: A View from Tradition*. Copyright © 1981/ 1996 paperback, by The Jewish Publication Society. Used by permission.

But because the subject is so fraught with modesty and taboo, I would have preferred to avoid it. What I didn't anticipate upon our return was to find an old friend who had stopped by the house. Carol and I had been in graduate school together for four years. She knew a little about Jewish life; her grandparents had been Orthodox. Unlike some people of their liberal, intellectual background, Carol and her husband were not antagonistic toward Judaism. On the contrary, while they would have none of Shabbat, kashrut, synagogue life, or day-school education for themselves or their son, they were nevertheless quite respectful of our way of life.

Carol has an incredible mind. Anything she had ever read or heard was tucked away in some crevice of memory, to be recalled instantly at the proper moment. Somewhere in the past, maybe in her brief bout with Hebrew school fifteen years earlier, she had heard about mikveh. Thus, she was able to put it all together immediately—wet hair, street clothes, no packages—and come up with an answer. The moment the baby-sitter closed the door behind her, Carol blurted out, "Do you really practice *that*? Do you actually go to the ... the mikveh?"

For the first time in my life I had the feeling that someone was seeing me as some kind of aborigine disguised in twentieth-century garb. I found myself at a loss for words. It was a subject that lay very quiet and deep inside of me. I then had been married for ten years. No one had ever asked me why I observed the laws of niddah. (Niddah, it should be noted, has several meanings, depending on the context: the laws pertaining to niddah; the state of being sexually unavailable; that time of month that includes menstrual flow and after-period; a woman in a state of niddah.) I had never even asked myself the question or discussed it with my parents, sisters, or friends, not even with my husband, who observed the practice with me. In fact, the closest I had come to a discussion of the matter was when a high-school friend confided that her mother said she felt like a bride each month after going to the mikveh. It embarrassed me that a mother could make so suggestive and revealing a disclosure to a daughter, and for the rest of my impressionable teen years I could not look at that pious woman without a headful of immodest imaginings.

It wasn't that I didn't know the laws or the ancient and contemporary meanings attached to them. I had read many of the "little books" on the subject; they succeeded in neither frightening me nor inspiring me. Being a good "daughter of Israel"—the phrase is a euphemism for one who observes the laws of niddah and mikveh—it never occurred to me that I would do anything other than keep the particular practice. Just as my mother and mother-in-law went to some vague "meeting" once a month, there was no doubt that I too would carry on the chain of tradition. But like many such things, I took the whole matter of mikveh for granted. I had managed to appropriate intact its grand claims, but I had no sense of what positive meaning it had for me. Nor could I articulate what I was doing or thinking during those occasional times—and there were such—when it was a hardship or a nuisance for me to observe this mitzvah.

I think I mouthed some clichés to Carol and then quickly changed the subject. In time, Carol went on to become a well-known psychoanalyst, was divorced, remarried, and divorced again. The last I heard, she was making a fortune in private practice in Los Angeles and writing a book. I haven't seen her for fifteen years, but once a month, as I comb out my wet hair in the mikveh, I chuckle inwardly as her astounded expression passes before my eyes. Over the years, I have begun to sort out some of my feelings about this mitzvah, so powerful that it manages to control and make a statement about a human drive that everywhere else no longer seems to be subject to boundaries established by law, culture, or even family values.

The mikveh, as we all know, has come under attack by Jewish feminists, not-so-Jewish feminists, and not-so-feminist Jews. Carol didn't say so, but she probably thought to herself, "Mikveh. Ahah! 'Primitive blood taboo.' Outmoded and demeaning notions of 'unclean and impure'!" Perhaps some of these elements at one time or another were associated with the concept of niddah. Today they hold no weight, however, at least not for me nor, I believe, for most of the women who lovingly or reflexively take upon themselves the obligation. Besides, one just as easily could defend niddah in terms of its function in a prefeminist society. For example, niddah was intended to protect women's selves and sexuality; not bad, considering that society was oriented to the female serving the male, sexually and otherwise. Niddah also provided safeguards against women becoming mere sex objects; even when the law could not change social perceptions, at least it minimized those times when this attitude could be acted upon. Finally, the Talmud gives the most functional view of all, sexist though the language may seem today: "Because a man may become overly familiar with his wife, and thus repelled by her, the Torah said that she should be a niddah for seven clean days [following menses] so that she will be as beloved [to him after niddah] as on the day of her marriage" (Niddah 31b).

THE LAW AND ITS PRACTICE

The Bible lays down the initial principles of physical separation during menses:

When a woman has a discharge, her discharge being blood from her body, she shall remain in her impurity seven days; whoever touches her shall be unclean until evening. (Lev. 15:19)[1]

Do not come near a woman during her period of uncleanness to uncover her nakedness. (Lev. 18:19)[2]

If a man lies with a woman in her infirmity and uncovers her nakedness, he has laid bare her flow and she has exposed her blood flow; both of them shall be cut off from all the people. (Lev. 20:18)

In the rabbinic explication of biblical tradition, we find that the minimum niddah period increases from seven to twelve days[3]—that is, a five-day minimum allotted for the flow and seven days for the "whites," the additional days of separation.[4] (A word about the use of the term "whites": I do not like the term seven "clean" days, which all of the English sources employ, for it evokes its counterpart, "unclean." I therefore prefer "whites," which is the literal translation of the talmudic *levanim*, the white garments that women were required to wear during those seven days in order to facilitate the search for stains.) If the flow or the staining lasts longer than five days,[5] the seven-day "white" count begins after the last day of flow.[6] The whole cycle is completed with immersion.[7] This is known as *tevilah*. Afterward, a woman can resume sex until the next menstruation, some two and a half weeks later. The *tevilah* is also attended by numerous details. Unless there are extenuating circumstances, the immersion takes place in the evening, after dark, at the completion of the twelfth day.

As for the mikveh itself, there are numerous laws concerning the mikveh and its construction. In fact, a whole tractate of the Mishnah (Mikvaot) is devoted to the subject. Briefly, the mikveh must be nonporous, so that it has no object that can absorb *tum'ah* (impurities). It is to be constructed of two compartments: *bor ha-otzar* (the storage compartment) and *bor ha-tevilah* (the immersion basin that is drained each day). The word *mikveh* simply means a collection (of water). This must be stationary water, not flowing, as from a tap, and its sources must be natural—rain water, wells, natural ice, or ocean or lake water. As the ancient rabbis were of a practical nature, however, and since it would be difficult to collect all that water naturally, they legislated that only a certain percentage of these natural waters is required to constitute a kosher mikveh; the rest may be made up from regular tap or drawn water. A lake or ocean may be used for the purpose, although there is halakhic concern that out of fear of such waters the immersion will not be performed properly.

Since the destruction of the Second Temple, the mikveh has been used primarily for women, but there are other uses for it as well. Some men go to the mikveh to purify themselves before certain holidays, particularly Yom Kippur. Mikveh is also the final step in conversion to Judaism. Many traditional Jews also immerse their new utensils in the mikveh before using them. For these other purposes, the mikveh is used only during the day. You will never see a man about the mikveh at night. The men who accompany their wives to the mikveh—and this is often the case—sit in their cars parked down the street aways.

....

IN THE MIKVEH

....

If you have never been to a mikveh, this is what to expect. First you are asked whether you want a "private" or a "semiprivate." Private means that the mikveh basin (a small, deep pool) is in the same room where you bathe in a regular tub to prepare for the immersion; semiprivate and shower mean that you bathe or shower in your room but must go into an adjacent room to use the mikveh basin. Depending on the construction of the semiprivate, it can be like playing musical doors— all doors that lead to the mikveh basin are closed before your door is opened—so that you will have complete privacy while immersing. Before the bath, you brush your teeth, rinse your mouth, trim your nails, and remove all makeup, dentures, rings—anything that is not part of the body. After the bath, you rinse off in the shower, or just the latter if you have already bathed at home that evening. (This elaborate ritual of cleansing, incidentally, is further proof that the mikveh has nothing to do with personal hygiene or cleanliness.) You comb out your hair, which you have just shampooed, and wrap yourself in a white sheet or towel. Then you press the buzzer, which summons the "mikveh lady."

Mikveh ladies come in several varieties. I have been to a dozen different mikvehs over the last twenty years, and each mikveh lady has her own style. They are generally sensitive, devout women who are kind but not prying. They have a rather pleasant, quiet, businesslike manner that is exactly called for in so personal a situation. Occasionally, you will run across a mikveh lady who has some idiosyncracies, such as entering your room without knocking to see if you are ready, or one who will fight you over another sixteenth of an inch of your carefully trimmed fingernails, or even one who, without any warning whatsoever, will run a comb through your pubic hair while you stand there in total shock. In all fairness, however, these are the sum total of grievances I've heard concerning mikveh ladies over the years.

The mikveh lady checks to see if you have prepared yourself properly (trimmed nails, etc.). She looks you over to see if there are any loose hairs on your body, which she gently removes. Holding on to the side of the rail, you walk down a few steps to the bottom of the mikveh—the water is about shoulder height. With legs slightly apart, lips and eyes closed but not clenched tightly, arms spread a bit at your sides but not touching the side walls, you bend your knees in a crouching position and go completely under. If you have long hair you have to go a little deeper, so that every strand of hair will be under water. You don't have to stay under the water for even an extra second. All you have to do is immerse yourself completely and then come right up. If you've done it right (every bit of you below the water line) your mikveh lady will pronounce it "kosher."

Then, standing there in the water, you recite the blessing: *Barukh ata adonai eloheinu melekh ha-olam asher kideshanu be-mitzvotav ve-tzivanu al ha-tevilah* (Blessed are You O Lord, our God, King of the Universe, who has sanctified us by His commandments and commanded us concerning immersion). Other blessings are often added, the most common one being the *yehi ratzon*: "May it be Your will O Lord, our God and God of our fathers, that the Temple be speedily rebuilt in our time; give us our portion in Your Torah, so that we may serve You with awe as we did in days of old. And we shall offer to You the thanks offering of Judea and Jerusalem as was done in years gone by."[8] Many women cover their heads with a terry cloth, which the mikveh lady hands them, before saying the blessing. (It does seem rather incongruous, covering one's head in modesty and respect when all the rest of you is standing there stark naked. But that's how it is often done.)

After the blessings, you dip under two more times; each time, the mikveh lady pronounces it "kosher." Then you come up the steps, and she wraps a white sheet around you and leaves the room for you to dress. Before you leave, you pay a mikveh fee that ranges from three to ten dollars. (In no way does the fee cover the cost of running the mikveh, which is heavily subsidized by the community.)

A bride is brought to the mikveh a day or two before her wedding. There are some slight variations in custom, but the basic procedures are the same. Sephardim make a real celebration of the event, their equivalent to the bride's shower. Among Ashkenazim, it's pretty quiet, strictly a mother–daughter affair.

Most of the mikvehs today are quite pleasant places, especially the newer ones, built with the modern woman's tastes in mind. All mikvehs have hair dryers. Some even have beauticians and cosmeticians in attendance several evenings a week. The next stage will probably be whirlpools, saunas, and exercycles. And why not? It loosely fits the concept of *hiddur mitzvah*, the beautification of a mitzvah. No more the image of the mikveh for middle-aged rebbetzins only. I have seen women leaving the mikveh looking as if they had just stepped out of the pages of *Vogue*. Rabbi Akiba—who believed that women should use cosmetics and make themselves attractive (even during their menstrual period), so that they not become repulsive to their husbands— would have been proud!

THE HISTORICAL DEVELOPMENT OF THE LAWS OF NIDDAH

The laws of niddah provide us not only with an elaborate "how-to" but also with a fascinating lesson of the way in which Halakhah develops, for the precepts can be traced from the Bible, through the Mishnah, the Tosephta, the two Talmuds, and medieval and modern rabbinic literature.

The biblical commandment of separation during menses occurs in two different contexts: laws dealing with other forms of defilement, impurity, and death; and laws regulating forbidden sexual relations. Thus, at the outset, we encounter the two themes that are associated with niddah—themes that are reflected in Halakhah throughout history—sometimes intertwined, sometimes overshadowed, sometimes parallel.

As for the defilements and impurities mentioned in the Bible, these generally are related to death: contact with a dead body, loss of menstrual blood, loss of semen through nocturnal emission, or leprosy (all symbolic of the rampant forces of death taking over as the life-giving juices that nurture body tissue mysteriously cease). Purification through the living waters, then, symbolizes a renewal, a re-creation, a regeneration of the life forces.[9] As such, purification was considered a privilege, not a burden. To concretize this, there was a tangible communal reward: access to the sanctuary (and, later, the Temple), where one could bring a sacrifice and find oneself in the presence of God, who gives life. One who did not undergo a purification rite could not re-enter the sanctuary.

The second association is that of family purity. (In fact, the laws of niddah are known as *taharat ha-mishpahah*, the laws of family purity.) The ancient, eternal truth is that society will destroy itself if it lacks ethical sexual relationships. Although no explicit reason is given for forbidding relations during menses, clearly this falls into the category of curbing liaisons that are most open to exploitation or that are most typical of animal rather than human behavior: incest, sex with individuals who live under the same roof but who are not each other's partners, sex with animals. For these forbidden liaisons, a punishment of *karet* was meted—a cutting off of the soul of the transgressor from the community.

After the destruction of the Second Temple, the categories of *taharah* and *tum'ah* (pure and impure) become almost irrelevant to daily life. In Eretz Israel, certain practices were to be maintained because of the holiness of the land, but gradually even these died out. This does not mean that the rabbis of the Talmud ceased discussing these concepts and their practical implications; it does signify, however, that all other forms of *taharah* and *tum'ah* were essentially inoperative: vessels, tents, hands, liquids, etc. Thus, because there was no longer a Temple where purity had to be preserved, a person who came into contact with a dead body no longer had to undergo ritual immersion. The only vestige of this practice remaining today is the washing of hands after leaving a funeral parlor or cemetery. More germane to our concern, a man who had a bodily discharge no longer had to abstain from sex until he underwent purification. The only person still subject to purification rites is the menstruous woman.

Following the destruction of the Temple, the emphasis shifted from *tum'at niddah* (separation for reasons of defilement, impurity, pollution, and taboo) to *issur niddah* (proscription of a sexual relationship because it is forbidden by Jewish law). Still, the whole area of niddah never completely lost its association with impurity and defilement.[10] Indeed, the rabbis strengthened the "fence" around the original prohibition. Sometimes they built on one base, sometimes on the other, often connecting the two.

The talmudic discussion in Shabbat 13a is a perfect example. The pericope opens with an invitation to "come and see how purity has increased in Israel" (in rabbinic times). The scholars ask: may a niddah sleep in bed with her husband, each fully clothed, thus avoiding bodily contact? Shammai answers in the affirmative—they may sleep together fully clothed, for sleeping together (during the "white" days) is not prohibited, only intercourse. Hillel disagrees—and the law is according to Hillel.

In this discussion, several analogies are drawn as proofs: some evoke defilement, others the restrictions on proper sex relations. One is treated in this passage to a taste of Halakhah in process. The discussion takes place after the minimum day count was increased from seven days (biblical) to twelve (five menses plus seven "whites"); initially, only intercourse was forbidden during the seven "whites," but at some point in the rabbinic period, probably around the time of Hillel and Shammai (first century B.C.E.), the biblical taboo against any and all forms of bodily contact during menses was carried over to the seven "whites" as well. The elusive biblical concept, that impurity could be transmitted by contact by touching, was dropped from every other category, yet increased in the case of niddah.

Similarly, the biblical punishment for infraction of niddah was intensified, and *karet* was extended to include the seven "whites." As we read in Shabbat 13a–b:

[It is taught in the] Tanna de-be Eliyahu: It once happened that a certain scholar who had studied Bible and Mishnah and had unstintingly served scholars, died at middle age. His wife took his tefillin and carried them about in the synagogue and school houses and complained to them [the scholars]: "It is written in the Torah, 'For that is thy life and the length of the days' (Deut. 30:20). My husband, who read much Bible and studied much Mishnah and served scholars a great deal, why did he die at middle age?" No man could answer. On one occasion I [Eliyahu, the supposed author of the Tanna] was a guest at her house, and she related the whole story to me. I said to her: "My daughter, how was he to you in the days of your menstruation?" "God forbid," she replied, "he did not even touch me with his little finger." "And how was he in the days of your 'whites'?" "He ate with me, drank with me, and slept with me in bodily contact, and it did not occur to him to do otherwise." I said to her: "Blessed be the Omnipresent for slaying him, for He did not condone this behavior. Therefore, even though the man had much merit on account of his love for the Torah, God punished him, for lo, the Torah has said, 'And you shall not approach a woman as long as she is impure by her menses' (Lev. 18:19)."

The Mishnah refers to an institution that undoubtedly grew out of the defilement concept. *Bet ha-tum'ot* (special houses of uncleanness) were set aside so that women could be segregated during menses.[11] This isolation was not practiced in Babylonia during the mishnaic period, however.[12] As is written in Ketubbot 61a:

Rabbi Issac ben Hanania further stated in the name of Rav Huna: All kinds of work which a wife may perform for her husband, a menstruous woman may also perform, except for filling his cup, preparing his bed, washing his face, hands, and feet. Said Rabba: The prohibition for preparing his bed applied only in his presence. If done in his absence, it doesn't matter. With regard to filling his cup, Samuel's wife made a change [during her "whites"]; she served him with her left hand.

In other words, actions that were circumscribed biblically for reasons of defilement, such as touching the husband's bed, were now, in third-century Babylon, circumscribed for reasons of sexual arousal.

Variations showed up in attitudes as well as practice. The author of the following talmudic statement sounds a negative note: "If a menstruous woman passes between two [men] during the beginning of her menses, she will slay one of them; and if she is at the end of her menses, she will cause strife between them" (Pesahim 111a). Another talmudic passage (Niddah 31b) stresses the romantic element: a niddah is off limits so that she will be more desirable afterward.

And so it goes. The medieval literature largely emphasizes the pollution theme. The Zohar, with its almost palpable sense of purity and impurity in the world, is most explicit:

One who cohabits with a niddah drives the divine presence from the world. There is no stronger impurity in the world than that of niddah. Wherever they go, the divine presence is driven from before them. Furthermore, such a person brings evil sickness upon himself and upon the child born [from such a union]. . . . When a person draws near to a niddah, her impurity passes to him and resides in all of his limbs . . . for it is written: "and her impurity will be upon him" (Lev. 15:24). The seed which he brings forth at that time is imbued with the spirit of impurity and remains in a state of impurity throughout its existence, for its very creation and foundation stem from profound impurity, which is the strongest of all impurities. (Parshat Shmot)

We find a similar view in Nahmanides:

The glance of a menstruous woman poisons the air. . . . She is like a viper who kills with her glance. How much more harm will she bring to a man who sleeps with her? She is a pariah; men and women will distance themselves from her and she will sit alone and speak to no one. . . . The dust on which she walks is impure like the dust defiled by the bones of the dead. And the rabbis said: "Even her glance brings harm." (*Commentary on the Torah*, Lev. 12:14)

Maimonides, however, for all that he believed that women be kept under wraps, was of a different mind regarding isolation. The Babylonian tradition of setting women aside to prevent them from their normal household duties, was, in his eyes, inauthentic to rabbinic tradition; it smacked of sectarian extremism, perhaps even the most dreaded sectarianism of all, Karaism. Thus Maimonides permitted women to touch a garment, cook foods, and generally serve their husbands at all times (*Mishneh Torah*, Hilkhot Issurei Biah 11:6, 7, 15).

In medieval Spain, where Christianity stressed the sinfulness of sex and Islam played up the taboo, there arose some additional prohibitions in Jewish law. One in particular, the interdiction against a niddah entering a synagogue, was widely observed.

With the beginning of the modern period comes a new phenomenon, an attempt to provide a rationale for niddah in terms that would be more appealing to the enlightened mind. Thus, as Samson Raphael Hirsch writes, "in the proper marital relationship, husband and wife must live periodically as sister and brother. This tends to establish rather than curtail intimate family relationships, both morally and spiritually. And just as one gains entry to the holy sanctuary after purification, so one is able to resume sexual relations, which are also of a consecrated nature."[13]

In the contemporary literature on niddah, we see the dual influence. Some authorities stress impurity, defilement, punishment, danger, and various minute details, the neglect of which entails absolute infraction of the law; others emphasize married love, mutual respect, the holiness of sex, and the temptations that are involved when two people live in such close proximity.[14]

Often in contemporary literature these themes are meshed. Thus today, for example, strict observance of niddah means that there be absolutely no physical contact between husband and wife, that their beds be separated, that they do not hand any object to each other directly. One prominent halakhic authority states that even a baby is not to be handed directly (from husband to wife) during niddah, unless there is no other way. While it is possible to explain laws of this sort as safeguards against sexual arousal, they seem to be more evocative of biblical concepts of impurity, where, for example, a man who touches the chair or bed or clothing of one who is *tamei* (unclean) becomes unclean himself. Yet, there is also the other genre of prohibitions: a man should not gaze excessively upon his wife; a woman

239

should not sing in the presence of her husband. In other words, every-thing must be done to bank all the potential fires of passion.

ONE WOMAN'S CONTEMPORARY VIEW

Relatively few Jews observe the laws of niddah today, not the great mass of assimilated Jews who ignore mitzvot in general, nor Reform Jews who view niddah as a relic of rabbinic Judaism, nor Conservative Jews who default by silence, nor, for that matter, many Jews who con-sider themselves Orthodox. And yet, the laws of niddah and mikveh are considered *gufei ha-torah*, the essential laws of the Torah. Mikveh, for instance, takes precedence in communal efforts over building a synagogue or buying a Torah scroll. Moreover, observance of niddah is one of the three primary mitzvot of women, the other two being *nerot* (the kindling of candles) and *hallah* (taking off a portion of the bread dough and consecrating it) (Berakhot 20b). Why then has niddah fallen by and large into desuetude?

One explanation is that niddah is simply very difficult to keep. Of all the core mitzvot, it certainly makes the most rigorous demands. Sex is as powerful a drive as hunger, yet we have only five fast days a year compared with approximately one hundred fifty days of niddah. One not trained to observe the law would hardly consider it.

Some would say that niddah and mikveh have fallen afoul of brass plumbing, the arch symbol of modern civilization. Too many people confuse the laws of niddah with hygiene. Indeed, how often have I heard people say, "I can just as easily stay home and take a bath." This kind of thinking is due in part to an inadequate education on the subject, including the simple fact that one is required to take a bath *before* going to the mikveh. It is also probably due to the use of words like "clean" and "unclean," which might not have crept into Jewish tradition had women been part of the process of the rabbinic unfold-ing of the law during the last two thousand years. The Torah deals with concepts of spiritual purity and impurity that were amorphous and perhaps logically incomprehensible, even in Temple times. But once the Temple was destroyed and there was no longer a single physical locus of ultimate purity, the human mind transmuted these concepts into terms with which it could deal. Somehow, relative cleanliness became the code association.

A further fact that contributed to the growing disregard of niddah is that all throughout the medieval period the notion of taboo over-powered the element of *kedushah*, the holiness of the physical relation-ship. Of course, taboo and holiness are tied together intimately—that is, the setting up of limits so that what happens within them becomes very special. The preponderant focus, however, on what not to do during the niddah period—combined with little discussion or appreciation of what takes place during the time when sex is permis-sible—left the whole area quite vulnerable. Instead of giving post-niddah sex the green light, in the form of positive articulation, the laws, as they developed, continued to give sex the red light. This is seen most clearly in the *Shulhan Arukh*, which prescribes sex to be kept at a minimum. A certain prudishness was generated here, not to be con-fused with modesty. It is interesting to note that *onah* (the obligation of a husband to satisfy his wife sexually), an equally important concept in the Torah, has found little stress in Jewish tradition. Thus, as mod-ern men and women became increasingly disenchanted with taboos, niddah suffered accordingly. This falloff is unfortunate, for niddah and mikveh have great meaning today, in a woman's life and in the shared life of a man and woman who love each other.

Why do I observe niddah and mikveh? Because I am so com-manded, because it is a mitzvah ordained by the Torah. Were I not so commanded by Jewish law, I surely would not have invented such a rigorous routine. The flesh is weak and no lofty scheme imaginable could have made me tough enough to observe niddah. All of this is true for my husband as well, for neither of us could adhere to the practice unilaterally. Without a mutual understanding and acceptance of Halakhah, observance of niddah in marriage would be reduced to a test of wills each month.

Precisely because it is a mitzvah, it holds a certain sense of sweetness for me. As I go about my business at the mikveh, I often savor the knowledge that I am doing exactly as Jewish women have done for twenty or thirty centuries. It is a matter not only of keeping the chain going, but also one of self-definition: this is how my forebears defined themselves as Jewish women and as part of the community and this is how I define myself. It is the sense of community with them that pleases me. There is yet another aspect to observing a mitzvah for its own sake. The laws of niddah continually remind me that I am a Jew and niddah reinforces that deep inner contentment with a Jewish way of life.

Acceptance of the mitzvah, then, is the base; attendant sensations of "community," "Jewish womanhood," and "chain of tradition" are the embellishments. There is more to it than that, however. Niddah serves a whole range of functions in an interpersonal relationship, appropriate to its ebb and flow and to its different stages of growth.

In the early married stage, when passion and romance dominate, niddah allows, nay encourages, a man and woman to develop other techniques of communication. In the second stage, that of young children, tired mothers, and hardworking fathers, niddah is an arbitrarily imposed refresher period. Inasmuch as it regulates the off times, it synchronizes the on times. No law can program desire, but there is probably a better chance of the meshing of expectations among couples who observe niddah. In the third stage, as a woman approaches menopause, niddah and mikveh bring her to a monthly appreciation of her continuing ability to be fertile. One may wonder whether a woman who has faithfully observed mikveh all her life feels a heightened sense of loss at menopause.

Finally, in all of these stages, niddah generates a different sense of self for a woman, a feeling of self-autonomy. Some women can generate these feelings out of their own ego strength; for those to whom it is not innate or instinctive, niddah is a catalyst to this consciousness.

Some feminists have challenged the very concept of mikveh. Yet mikveh well could be the prototype of a woman's mitzvah. It is unique to woman; it makes a statement about woman as Jew; it builds human character. Thus we need not rationalize what has been wrong with mikveh but rather affirm what has been right and what is doable. Not everything concerning women that has withstood the test of time is good; not everything from biblical tradition has withstood the test of time. But in the cosmic order of things, mikveh seems to be an attempt to attach some measure of holiness to a primal urge. As it was passed on through countless generations, mikveh could not help take on certain nuances, some of them less honorable toward women. It falls to this generation of women, Jewish women with a new sense of self, to restore that element of holiness to our bodies, our selves.

Notes

1. 'Uncleanness' is a dreadful word, a poor translation and even poorer connotation of the Hebrew *tamei*. I could not find a single English Bible that used a different word, however. *Tamei* is more accurately understood as 'impure'—the reverse condition of *tahor* ('pure'); both words take on an entirely different meaning when considered in light of Temple access or worship, to which they are related. Part of the problem in this pericope is that the word *niddatah* (her state of being niddah) is translated as 'her impurity', so another word had

to be used for *tum'ah*. More properly, *niddatah* should have been translated as 'in the time of her flow (menses)' or 'in the time of her separation (distancing)'. Even where the concept of separation is used, some translators use the word 'banishment', based on Rashi's commentary of Lev. 15:19. See *Even Shoshan* and Jastrow dictionaries, s.v. niddah.

2. This verse seems to be the bridge phrase, interweaving the two themes, impurity and forbidden sexual relationships.

3. This is derived from the laws of a *zavah* (one who has a discharge), who must wait seven additional days after the discharge stops (Niddah 66a on Lev. 15:23).

4. There is a special dispensation for newlyweds: eleven days instead of twelve. The reason for this is that the loss of blood is probably from the breaking of the hymen and not from the womb. Since one could not know for sure, the rabbis set aside four days plus seven 'whites'. More logically, if it could be determined within four days that it is extrauterine blood (i.e., from the hymen), then why the seven 'whites' altogether? We know from other cases that it is only menstrual blood that made one a niddah; after a Caesarian birth there was no period of separation.

5. This is determined by a series of self-examinations. Staining is considered part of the flow period. In fact, there are more laws on staining than on any other aspect of niddah. Since the laws were so intricate, there were, by acclaim, certain rabbis in each generation who were specialists in the laws of niddah. Questions would be sent to them from great distances. The details were originally spelled out in Mishnah Niddah: finding color or size, determining whether it is part of the flow or part of seven additional days, where it originates (vagina or womb), the self-examination procedures, whose testimony counts, when are the tests properly done, etc.

6. Since it is not uncommon for a woman to stain for several days after the menstrual flow, this puts an extra burden on couples trying to observe the laws carefully. For women who have long menses (seven or eight days), it means a period of at least two weeks or more of abstention from sex.

7. Although the Bible doesn't describe the purification ritual for niddah (other than the passage of seven days), the rabbis taught that the same procedure used by men applied to women: immersion in living waters (Lev. 15:13).

8. I was never sure about the relevance of that particular prayer. The following, however, seems to suggest itself: niddah and mikveh are the only extant rituals of that period when *tum'ah and taharah* were taken with utmost gravity and when the Temple was the symbol of purity and closeness to God. Moreover, on the day following the immersion, the mendicant would bring two turtledoves to the sanctuary as sacrifice. This additional prayer symbolizes the longing for that time in our past or for messianic redemption of the future.

9. See Rachel Adler, 'Tumah and Taharah: Mikveh', in *The First Jewish Catalog*, ed. Richard Siegel, Michael Strassfeld, and Sharon Strassfeld (Philadelphia: Jewish Publication Society of America, 1973), 167–71.

10. The clearest indication of this was when the Mishnah was codified. Almost two hundred years after the destruction of the Second Temple, the tractate Niddah was classified not in Order Women but in Order Purification. It is also the only one of the twelve mishnayot in Order Purification that has a gemara explicating it.

11. Rashi and Bartenura explain this as rooms, not houses (Niddah 7:2).
12. Several centuries later, segregation was indeed practiced in Babylonia (*Mishneh Torah*, Hilkhot Issurei Bi'ah 11:6, 7, 15).
13. Cf. Samson Raphael Hirsch, *The Pentateuch* (London: I. Levy, 1962), ch. 15.
14. Some contemporary works of one kind or the other are Kalman Kahana, *Daughter of Israel: Laws of Family Purity* (New York: Feldheim, 1970); Norman Lamm, *The Hedge of Roses* (New York: Feldheim, 1968); Pinchas Stolper, *The Road to Responsible Jewish Adulthood* (New York: Union of Orthodox Jewish Congregations of America, 1967); Zev Schostak, *The Purity of the Family: Its Ideology and Its Laws* (New York: Feldheim, 1971).

22 Augustine on Marriage

Elizabeth Clark*

That marriage is 'a good thing' is now taken for granted by most Christian denominations, to the point of intimidating the unmarried, but it was not ever thus. Christians of the early centuries, following what they regarded as the unequivocal teaching of Paul and Jesus, thought it better to remain unmarried, a 'eunuch for the kingdom'. What 'good' then was marriage or, for that matter, sex? Augustine was an influential advocate of the thesis that reproduction was the primary justification for marriage. In this extract Elizabeth Clark shows how his position developed in the midst of controversies over the value of the body, and how close he came to developing a more 'companionate' view of marriage.

JMS

In the heat of the Pelagian controversy,[1] Augustine composed Book XIV of the *City of God*, the book that details the sin of the first couple in Eden and the idyllic life Adam and Eve would have enjoyed had the Fall not intervened. How, Augustine asks, could a male endowed with rationality and free will have been led astray by the "sly seductions" of Lucifer? With help from I Timothy 2: 14,[2] he argues that not Adam, but only Eve, the weaker element of that first "human society", was deceived. Then why did Adam fall, if he was not deceived? Because, Augustine asserts, he was faithful to a "social instinct": he refused to be separated from his "only companion".[3]

Embedded in Augustine's exegesis is a social view of marriage that he had evolved over twenty years or more. Had he developed its implications unswervingly, he would have arrived at a notion of marital friendship unique for his time and place. Yet Augustine's vision of companionate marriage was not just balanced, but often over-shadowed, by his emphasis upon the sexual and reproductive functions of marriage. His ambivalent conception of the "essence" of marriage, I shall argue, can be traced primarily to the necessities of theological controversy, for it was in the midst of controversies that he

---

* Extract from Elizabeth Clark, '"Adam's Only Companion": Augustine and the Early Christian Debate on Marriage', *Recherches Augustiniennes* 21 (1986).

formulated his marital ethic. His attempt to mediate between both orthodox and heretical asceticism on the one hand, and the later Pelagians' praise of lusty sexuality, on the other, contributed to his ambivalent assessment. Against the extreme ascetics, he taught that marriage was part of God's good plan for humankind, not a result of the "Fall" in Eden. Yet against Pelagian opponents, he insisted that all sexual intercourse bears the curse of our sinful condition, a curse that manifests itself in unruly lust. Even in the storm of the Pelagian debate, however, Augustine stressed the goodness of offspring. Indeed, so keenly did he stress the reproductive dimensions of marriage that his tentative exploration of a more companionate notion of marriage was to a great extent overshadowed. Only in a later era could his vision of companionate marriage be enlisted in campaigns for actual social change.[4]

To arrive at the sentiments expressed in Book XIV of the *City of God*, Augustine had travelled a long road. In his personal life, he had journeyed from years with his unnamed concubine and the joys of male friendship to the lonelier, more demanding ones as bishop of Hippo Regius. There had been a long road of religious controversy as well: before he arrived at his view of marriage expressed in Book XIV, he had mediated acrid debates on asceticism and had battled Manicheanism. In response to the excesses of the former and the errors of the latter, he had forged a more positive vision of marriage that centered on three marital "goods": offspring, fidelity, and the sacramental bond. (Augustine's pro-reproductive stance would guide the Catholic Church until the mid-twentieth century.)[5] With this revised understanding, he had equipped himself to face the Pelagian accusation that his theory of original sin rendered marriage and procreation damnable. In defending the goodness of intercourse for reproduction, Augustine failed to develop his social understanding of marriage as fully as he otherwise might. Although he did not abandon his view that the essence of marriage lay in something non-physical, it was more urgent for him to defend himself against Julian's charge that his theory of original sin undermined the goodness of reproduction.

In addition to the role played by theological controversy, two other factors contributed to Augustine's ambivalent assessment of the physical and non-physical elements of marriage. For one, Augustine's view of women-in-general, typical for his age, did little to advance his nascent argument about the possibility of friendship in marriage. Second, the ambivalence of Roman marriage law about the relative importance

of consensual and physical factors in marriage may also have contributed to Augustine's dilemma. Thus this paper explores the circumstances that prompted his theory of companionate marriage and those
that inhibited its realization.

The *Confessions* makes clear that in his youth, Augustine could not
reconcile the claims of friendship with sexual desire. He agreed with
classical authors that friendship was a union of souls, that a friend was
a "second self",[6] but in his own life, "the hell of lust" blackened that
lofty ideal all too soon.[7] In his adolescent estimation, a woman's love
could not make up for the death of his dearest male companion,[8] yet
he was nonetheless unable to live without it. Of his concubine, he
writes that he had chosen her for no particular reason but that his
"passions had settled on her," that their relationship was "a bargain
struck for lust".[9] His words sound callous, but less callous than
his reported reason for abandoning this faithful partner of perhaps
fifteen years in order to become engaged to a ten-year-old girl:[10] the
desire for a wife of high social and financial status who could help
advance his career.[11] Augustine and his male friends had hoped to
establish a commune in which a life of cultured *otium* could prevail,
but their utopian dreams foundered on the problem of what to do
with their women.[12] Only after his conversion to ascetic Christianity
did he find a brief substitute for his failed dream in his retreat to
Cassiciacum with male friends,[13] where he whiled away hours discussing the nature of God[14] and the soul.[15] The only feminine presence in
this paradise of male intellectuals was Augustine's widowed mother
Monica.[16]

Since the young Augustine tended to link women with the physical
realm, it is not surprising that his dramatic conversion in 386 A.D. was
a conversion *away* from women's sexuality, away from the ghosts of
his old mistresses, his *nugae nugarum* (aptly translated by Kenneth
Burke as "toys of toys"),[17] who whispered in his ear, "Will we never be
able to do this-and-that again?"[18] Conveniently, Augustine's youthful
prayer—"Grant me chastity, but not yet"[19]—was answered only many
years later, when Lady Continence gave him her decisive summons to
the ascetic life.[20] In the years before (and some may wonder about
those after), he denied that the blaze of friendship that "melts our
hearts and welds them into one"[21] was possible with a woman, least of
all with a woman with whom one slept.

Augustine's retreat from physical sexuality is also evident in the
exegetical writings of his post-conversion years. In his first extant
interpretation of the creation story composed in 388–389 A.D.,[22] *On*

Genesis Against the Manichees, Augustine so spiritualizes the tale that he nearly loses a flesh-and-blood couple. The reason for his spiritualizing exegesis is known: he wrote the treatise to answer Manichean accusations that the Old Testament contained gross anthropomorphisms.[23] Against this charge, Augustine employed the allegorical exegesis he had learned from Ambrose[24] to "rescue" the text. Thus he asserts that no physical creation took place in Genesis 1; the creation described therein consisted only of the "causal reasons." Bodily creation represented a second stage, arrived at only in Genesis 2.[25] If this was the case, how were we to explain the fact that God's command to "reproduce and multiply" stood in Genesis 1? According to Augustine, that command was for spiritual, not for physical, union. Fleshly union came about only after the Fall.[26] Thus the Old Latin text of Luke 20:34 was correct in holding that only the children of *this* (i.e., the fallen) world beget and are begotten.[27] This asexual interpretation of Genesis is still in evidence in 398, when he wrote Book XIII of the *Confessions*: there the words in Genesis 1:28 about reproduction are taken to mean the diverse thoughts and expressions produced by the fertile human mind.[28] This spiritualized, asexual reading of Genesis caused Augustine discomfort in his later years, after he had adopted an earthier interpretation of Edenic relations.[29]

In sum, Augustine's hard-won conversion and early writings portended a decidedly non-sexual interpretation of God's plan for the world. Events of the next decade, however, prompted him to moderate his teaching.

Two controversies of the late fourth century led Augustine to temper his early ascetic leanings. The first was the debate in the 390s between Jerome and Jovinian : surveying it in retrospect, Augustine concluded that Jerome had gone too far in his enthusiasm for ascetic renunciation. Although Augustine's mentor Ambrose had celebrated Christian virginity in general and that of Mary in particular,[30] his praise of virginity was not coupled with a relentless attack upon marriage, as was Jerome's. For Jerome, the only good of marriage was to produce virgins for the church.[31] He summons up the woes of marriage—screaming children, adulterous spouses, disobedient slaves, and the like—to deter young people from it.[32] He styles marriage the "vomit" to which no widow would wish to return. In tones of high satire, he mocks a young widow's desire for children: "Do you fear the extinction of the Furian line if you do not present your father with some little fellow to crawl upon his chest and drool down his neck?"[33]

Such vituperative lines prompted a rejoinder from a fellow ascetic,

Jovinian.[34] According to Jovinian, Christian baptism rendered all persons equal, whether they were married, widowed, or virginal; no tiers of merit existed to differentiate Christians on the basis of their ascetic practice.[35] Jerome's slander of marriage verged on a "Manichean" denial of the goodness of God's creation, in Jovinian's view.[36]

Against Jovinian's praise of marriage as a divine gift and his citation of Biblical passages proving that our holy forefathers had married,[37] Jerome argued that marriage occurred only after the Fall. God had created Adam and Eve as virgins,[38] and virgins they were presumably intended to stay. The command to "Reproduce and multiply" had in any event been replaced in the New Testament by the admonition, "Let those who have wives live as though they have none."[39] Jerome's argument was buttressed with some fanciful exegesis. In challenging Jovinian's use of I Timothy 2:15 (that women will be saved through childbearing if they raise their children in *sōphrosynē*) Jerome argues that the Greek word should be translated as *castitas*, and interprets it to mean that women who raise children for *virginity* can make up for their own lack of excellence through the virginal commitment of their children.[40] Turning to the animal kingdom for illustrations with which to devalue marriage, Jerome notes that it was only the *unclean* beasts who entered Noah's ark two by two.[41] Although Jerome protests that he is no "Manichean",[42] Christians in Rome were shocked by his violent language. His Roman friend Pammachius scooped copies of the *Adversus Jovinianum* off the market before more eyes fell upon them. For Pammachius' effort, Jerome expressed little gratitude.[43]

Eight years after Jerome's famous response to Jovinian, i.e., in 401, Augustine wrote *On the Good of Marriage* and *On Holy Virginity*,[44] in which (he later claimed) he tried to prove that Christian virginity could be praised without denigrating marriage.[45] He hints that "some" champions of Christian virginity (clearly Jerome) had so implicated marriage that they had lent plausibility to Jovinian's charge of "Manicheanism".[46] Unlike Jerome, Augustine praises marriage and reproduction as "goods".[47] He posits, quite tentatively, that Adam and Eve *could* have had sexual intercourse in Eden even if they had not sinned. Reproduction could be viewed as part of God's plan for the first couple even though they would not have aged or died[48] (thus Augustine precludes the explanation that the purpose of children is to fill up the ranks left empty by the deaths of the old). This new interpretation of Eden is not further developed in *On the Good of Marriage*,[49] but it was to re-emerge soon.

A few years later, Augustine advances the same view, now more definitively, in *On Genesis According to the Letter*.[50] By Book IX, he has moved far beyond his early spiritualized exegesis of Eden to postulate that the first couple would have had sexual relations leading to reproduction even if they had not sinned, although they would not have known the disrupting lust that sexual functioning today entails.[51] In Book IX, he speaks of procreation as woman's "purpose", necessary for the multiplication of the human race even at the world's beginnings.[52] These views he will explicate more fully about a decade later in the *City of God*. Thus Augustine, in tempering the extreme claims of the ascetic movement, champions the goodness of our sexual functions in their essential created state and the reproduction of the species that derives therefrom.

A second reason for Augustine's move away from his earlier sexual views lies in his battles against Manicheanism in the late 380s and 390s. That Augustine himself had been a Manichean for at least nine years[53] and that Christian ascetics were being slandered as "Manicheans"[54] rendered Augustine anxious to differentiate sharply his own views from those of the Manicheans. The Manichean deprecation of reproduction stemmed from their foundation myth: at the world's origin, the power of Light had been defeated by Darkness and entrapped in matter. Reproduction served only to dissipate particles of light further among matter and thus impede its collection and restoration to its heavenly home.[55] The lower ranks of Manicheans, the Auditors, to whom Augustine had belonged, were permitted to engage in sexual relations *if* contraceptive measures were taken to prevent the further entrapment of light in new bodies. That Augustine learned these techniques (a primitive form of the "rhythm" method[56] and perhaps *coitus interruptus*[57]) is suggested not just by his own testimony,[58] but also by the fact that he produced no other children during his long period as a Manichean, despite living with his concubine throughout the duration of his Manichean attachment.[59] The Manichean ethic was thus pro-contraceptive and anti-reproductive.

Augustine as a newly baptized Christian inverted the Manichean evaluation to champion a pro-reproductive and anti-contraceptive ethic. From his earliest anti-Manichean works, offspring stand as the central good of marriage.[60] Thus Augustine defends the polygamy of the patriarchs against Manichean attack, since (he claims) they were motivated solely by God's command to reproduce at the world's beginning, not by lust.[61] Since offspring are the central purpose of marriage, the use of contraceptive measures is now deemed tantamount to "adultery".[62] In this anti-Manichean context, Augustine develops his now infamous interpretation of Genesis 38: Augustine levels the story of Onan (who spilled his seed on the ground rather than impregnate his brother's wife, as levirate marriage demanded, and was slain by God for his sinful act) as a warning to Christian couples who practice contraception.[63] In his anti-Manichean writings, Augustine cleverly links the etymology of the word *matrimonium* with *mater*.[64] He also notes that the Roman marriage contract stipulates that children are the first "end" of marriage.[65] Thus it seems no accident that in the *Confessions*, written toward the end of Augustine's anti-Manichean literary activity, he champions the view that marriage is "for" children, and rues the fact that in his own youth he did not live in an honorable marriage that had children as its goal.[66]

In the second decade of the fifth century, Augustine's pro-reproductive schema was played out in yet a different way. In his anti-Pelagian writings from 412 A.D. on, Augustine argued that original sin led to the corruption of the sex act, although its result, offspring, were still blessed by God. The excitation of our sexual members is the constant reminder of that "injury" which entered the world with the Fall and was transmitted to all the descendants of Adam and Eve except Jesus.[67]

This view Augustine develops in Book XIV of the *City of God*. There he writes that if sin had not intervened, the sexual organs would have moved at the command of the will; no tussle between the will and lust would have occurred; tranquility would have prevailed in mind and body during the sexual act.[68] Moreover, no destruction of "virginal integrity" would have occurred and no labor pains would have accompanied childbirth.[69] Although Augustine admits that we cannot now experience the sexual act in this way,[70] his emphasis lies not on imaginary speculation but on the physicality of the intercourse that would have occurred. In Genesis 1:28, God commanded the first human into a genuinely physical relationship, not simply to "spiritual development",[71] as he earlier had posited.

In the treatises after the *City of God*, the goodness of conception and birth continues to be praised,[72] and marriage is extolled as God's institution.[73] But now Augustine must be on guard against Pelagian claims that his theory of original sin slandered God's created universe. Especially did he need to emphasize the goodness, indeed the primacy, of reproduction in his last works against Julian of Eclanum, for Julian did not hesitate to call Augustine's theory a throwback to the "Manichean" deprecation of the material world and childbearing.[74] Against this charge, Augustine incessantly repeats that reproduction is God's good gift; that even children of adulterers are a good work; that there would have been sexual union for reproduction even if no sin had occurred, albeit without pain or loss of "virginal integrity".[75] He concedes one further point to the Pelagians: possibly—but only possibly—*libido* could have been exercised in a sinless Eden, although there it would have acted in cooperation with the will, not against it.[76]

Thus from his early writings to his last treatise, Augustine was pushed by the demands of theological controversy to affirm the centrality of sexual reproduction. Yet this emphasis, so necessary for him to affirm against Jerome, the Manicheans, and the Pelagian attacks, was somewhat at variance with his more socially oriented ideal of marriage that he had also developed throughout the years. It, too, is present in his early works and in his later anti-Pelagian writings. It was this second, more social, view of male–female bonding that would later give impetus to theories of companionate marriage.

Notes

1. 418–19 A D: dating from Peter Brown, *Augustine of Hippo: A Biography* (Berkeley/Los Angeles: University of California Press, 1969), 284. Although the necessity of distinguishing the varying periods in which Augustine developed his sexual and marital ethic seems an obvious necessity to the historian, many theological treatments of the topic fail to make this distinction and hence are of diminished value for an historian (e.g. the series of six articles on Augustine's sexual teaching by Davide Covi in *Augustinus* 16 (1971), 17 (1972), 18 (1973), and 19 (1974)).
2. 'And Adam was not deceived, but the woman was deceived and became a transgressor.'
3. *De civitate Dei* XIV, 11 (*CCL* 48, 433): '. . . *ille autem ab unico noluit consortio dirimi* . . .' For an overview of the Augustinian texts emphasizing the social view of marriage, see A. Brucculeri, *Il pensiero sociale di S. Agostino*, 2nd edn. (Rome: Edizioni 'La Civiltà Cattolica', 1945), 145–63.
4. e.g. Milton's campaign for the legalization of divorce in seventeenth-century England; see *The Doctrine and Discipline of Divorce*, Book I.
5. On the three 'goods' of marriage, see *De bono coniugali* 24, 32 (*CSEL* 41, 227); *De sancta virginitate* 12, 12 (*CSEL* 41, 244–5); *De nuptiis et concupiscentia* I, 17, 19 (*CSEL*, 42, 231). The 1930 encyclical *Casti Connubii* is structured around Augustine's three 'goods' of marriage; the pro-reproductive stance is upheld in the prohibition against birth control. Only in the post-World War II addresses, such as *The Apostolate of the Midwife* (1951), is even the 'rhythm method' of contraception permitted.
6. *Confessiones* IV, 6, 11 (*CCL* 27, 45); see Horace, *Odes* I, 3, 8; Ovid, *Tristia* IV, 4–72 for similar sentiments. For problems various church fathers experienced over the claims of friendship, see Elizabeth A. Clark, *Jerome, Chrysostom, and*

Friends: Essays and Translations, Studies in Women and Religion 2 (New York: Edwin Mellen Press, 1979), 41–4, and references therein.

7. *Confessiones* III, 1, 1 (*CCL* 27, 27).

8. Ibid. IV, 7, 12 (*CCL* 27, 46).

9. Ibid. 2, 2 (*CCL* 27, 41).

10. Ibid. VI, 13, 23; 15, 25 (*CCL* 27, 89, 90): she was nearly two years too young to marry. See M. K. Hopkins, 'The Age of Roman Girls at Marriage', *Population Studies* 18 (1965), 309–27. Calculating a fifteen-year relationship of Augustine with his concubine, based on *Confessiones* VI, 11, 18 (*CCL* 27, 86), is Emile Schmitt, *Le Mariage chrétien dans l'œuvre de saint Augustin: Une théologie baptismale de la vie conjugale* (Paris: Études Augustiniennes, 1983), 26.

11. *Confessiones* VI, 11, 19 (*CCL* 27, 87); although cf. VI, 12, 22 (*CCL* 27, 88). Peter Brown wisely advises us to think that Augustine's relationship with his concubine crumbled 'not through "animal passion", but under the glacial weight of the late Roman caste system' (*Augustine and Sexuality* (Berkeley: Center for Hermeneutical Studies in Hellenistic and Modern Culture, 1983), 1–2). Brown's essay is a stimulating and sensitive treatment of the subject, a major advance on discussions found in older textbooks and monographs; the 'social' dimensions of Augustine's teaching on sexuality are explored in new ways.

12. *Confessiones* VI, 14, 24 (*CCL* 27, 89); cf. VI, 12, 21 (*CCL* 27, 87).

13. Ibid. IX, 3, 5–4, 12 (*CCL* 27, 135–40). From the *Confessions* we learn scarcely anything about this period of retreat; Augustine claims here that he must 'hasten on to tell of greater things' (cf. *Aeneid* VII, 45). The dialogues composed at Cassiciacum reveal more. See Brown, *Augustine*, 113–24, on the Cassiciacum period.

14. *Soliloquia* I (*PL* 32, 869–84).

15. *De quantitate animae* (*PL* 32, 1035–80).

16. *Confessiones* IX, 4, 8 (*CCL* 27, 137).

17. Kenneth Burke, *The Rhetoric of Religion: Studies in Logology* (Boston: Beacon Press, 1961), 114.

18. *Confessiones* VIII, 11, 26 (*CCL* 27, 129). For possible negative influences on Augustine's views of sexuality exerted by Virgil, see John J. O'Meara, 'Virgil and Saint Augustine: The Roman Background to Christian Sexuality', *Augustinus* 13 (1968), esp. 325–6.

19. *Confessiones* VIII, 7, 17 (*CCL* 27, 124).

20. Ibid. 11, 27 (*CCL* 27, 130).

21. Ibid. IV, 8, 13 (*CCL* 27, 47).

22. Dating in Brown, *Augustine*, 74.

23. *Rectractiones* I, 9, 1 (*CCL* 57, 30); cf. *De Genesi ad litteram* VIII, 2 (*CSEL* 28¹, 232). For the Manichean mockery that the 'image of God' might mean that God had nostrils, teeth, a beard, and internal organs, see *De Genesi contra Manichaeos* I, 17, 27 (*PL* 34, 186). For other Manichean complaints about Genesis and the Old Testament, see e.g. *Contra Faustum* IV, 1; VI, 1; X, 1; XXII, 1; 3; 5 (*PL* 42, 217, 227, 243, 401, 402, 403). Also see Gilles Pelland, *Cinq études d'Augustin sur le début de la Genèse* (Tournai: Desclée and Cie; Montréal: Bellarmin, 1972), 17–22.

24. See *Confessiones* V, 14, 24 (*CCL* 27, 71). On Ambrose's indebtedness to Philo and Basil of Caesarea for allegorical exegesis, see John J. Savage, 'Introduction', Saint Ambrose, *Hexameron. Paradise, and Cain and Abel*, Fathers of the

Church 42 (New York: Fathers of the Church, 1961), pp. vi–viii: F. Homes Dudden, *The Life and Times of St. Ambrose* (Oxford: Clarendon Press, 1935), ii. 680–1. For Augustine, see Michael Müller, *Die Lehre des hl. Augustinus von der Paradiesesehe und ihre Auswerkung in der Sexualethik des 12. und 13. Jahrhunderts bis Thomas von Aquin* (Regensburg: Friedrich Pustet, 1951), 9–32; Yves M.-J. Congar, 'Le theme de Dieu-Créateur et les explications de l'Hexameron dans la tradition chrétienne', in *L'Homme devant Dieu: Mélanges offerts au Père Henri de Lubar: Exégèse et patristique*, Théologie 56 (Lyon-Fourvière: Aubier, 1964), 189–215.

25. *De Genesi contra Manichaeos* II, 7, 9 (*PL* 34, 200–1); see Kari Elisabeth Borresen, *Subordination and Equivalence: The Nature and Role of Woman in Augustine and Thomas Aquinas*, trans. Charles H. Talbot (Washington, DC: University Press of America, 1981), 16, for further discussion.

26. *De Genesi contra Manichaeos* I, 19, 30 (*PL* 34, 187).

27. Ibid. Luke 20:34: '*Filii enim saeculi hujus generant et generantur . . .*' See Bernard Alves Pereira, *La Doctrine du mariage selon saint Augustin*, 2nd edn. (Paris: Gabriel Beauchesne, 1930), 10–11.

28. *Confessiones* XIII, 24, 37 (*CCL* 27, 264).

29. *Retractiones* I, 9, 2 (*CCL* 57, 30–1).

30. See Ambrose's treatises *De virginibus, De institutione virginis, Exhortatio virginitatis*, and *De virginitate* (*PL* 16, 197–244, 279–380). For Mary, see e.g. *De institutione virginis* 5, 35; 5, 37–9, 62 (*PL* 16, 328–9, 329–36). Ambrose on Mary's virginity *in partu*: Mary is the *hortus clausus* of Song of Songs 4:12 and the *porta clausa* of Ezekiel 44:1 ff. (*De institutione virginis* 9, 60–2; 8, 52 (*PL* 16, 335–336, 334)). On Ambrose's Mariology, see Charles W. Neumann, *The Virgin Birth in the Works of Saint Ambrose*, Paradosis 17 (Freiburg im Breisgau: Éditions Universitaires, 1962). For an overview of patristic Mariology, see G. Joussard, 'Marie à travers la patristique. Maternité divine, virginité, sainteté', in D'Hubert du Manoir (ed.), *Maria: Études sur la sainte vierge* (Paris: Beauchesne, 1949), 71–157.

31. *Ep.* 22, 20 (*CSEL* 54, 170).

32. See esp. Jerome's catalogue in *Adversus Jovinianum* I, 47 (*PL* 23, 288–91); also *Adversus Helvidium* 20 (*PL* 23, 214); *Ep.* 22, 22 (*CSEL* 54, 174–5).

33. *Ep.* 54, 4, 1–2 (*CSEL* 54, 469).

34. Jerome acknowledges Jovinian's asceticism, albeit grudgingly, in *Adversus Jovinianum* I, 40 (*PL* 23, 280). The point should be underscored: the debate could take place even among members of the ascetic camp. On Jovinian see Wilhelm Haller, *Iovinianus: Die Fragmente seiner Schriften, die Quellen zu seiner Geschichte, sein Leben und seine Lehre*, TU 17, 2 (Leipzig: J. C. Hinrichs, 1897); Ilona Opelt, *Hieronymus' Streitschriften* (Heidelberg: Carl Winter-Universitätsverlag, 1973), 37–53; John Gavin Nolan, *Jerome and Jovinian*, Catholic University of America, Studies in Sacred Theology, 2nd ser., 97 (Washington, DC: Catholic University of America Press, 1956).

35. *Adversus Jovinianum* I, 3 (*PL* 23, 224).

36. Ibid. 5 (*PL* 23, 227).

37. Ibid. (*PL* 23, 225–7).

38. Ibid. 4; 16 (*PL* 23, 225, 246).

39. Ibid. 16; 24 (*PL* 23, 246, 255), citing I Cor. 7:29.

40. Ibid. 27 (*PL* 23, 260).

41. Ibid. 16 (*PL* 23, 246): cf. *Ep.* 22, 19 (*CSEL* 54, 169–70).
42. *Adversus Jovinianum* I, 3 (*PL* 23, 223).
43. See Jerome, *Epp.* 48–9 (*CSEL* 54, 347–87); esp. 49, 2; 8; 9; 11; 14 (*CSEL* 54, 352–3, 361–3, 364, 365–6, 374–5).
44. Dating from Brown, *Augustine*, 184.
45. So he states in *Retractiones* II, 48 (= 22), 1 (*CCL* 57, 107–8).
46. Ibid.
47. *De bono coniugali* passim (*CSEL* 41, 187–231); *De sancta virginitate* 10, 9; 12, 12; 18, 18; 21, 21 (*CSEL* 41, 243, 244, 251, 254–5). In addition to works already cited on Augustine's marital ethic, see Emanuele Samek Lodovici, 'Sessualità, matrimonio e concupiscenza in Sant' Agostino', in R. Cantalamessa (ed.), *Etica sessuale e matrimonio nel cristianesimo delle origini*, Studia Patristica Mediolanensia 5 (Milan: Vita e Pensiero (Università Cattolica del Sacro Cuore), 1976), 212–72; François-Joseph Thonnard, 'La morale conjugale selon saint Augustin', *Revue des études augustiniennes* 15 (1969), 113–31.
48. *De bono coniugali* 2, 2 (*CSEL* 41, 188–90).
49. See above on his earlier view in *De Genesi contra Manichaeos*. That Augustine's new view may owe something to Jovinian, see Jerome, *Adversus Jovinianum* I, 29 (*PL* 23, 262), where Jerome implies that Jovinian held the view, and my argument in 'Heresy, Asceticism, Adam, and Eve: Interpretations of Genesis 1–3 in the Later Latin Fathers', in *Genesis 1–3 in the History of Exegesis: Intrigue in the Garden*, ed. Gregory Robbins (Toronto: Edwin Mellen Press, 1988); also in my *Ascetic Piety and Women's Faith: Essays in Late Ancient Christianity* (Toronto: Edwin Mellen Press, 1986).
50. As I have suggested elsewhere ('Heresy, Asceticism'), Augustine's report that he had 'recently' (*nuper*) written *De bono coniugali* (*De Genesi ad litteram* IX, 7 (*CSEL* 28¹, 276)) gives a clue to the dating of *De Genesi ad litteram*. Although *nuper* can cover variable amounts of time, probably we need not stretch it to mean more than eight or nine years at most. For example, in *De sancta virginitate*, 1, 1 (*CSEL* 41, 235) Augustine uses *nuper* to refer to the writing of *De bono coniugali*, which he had written in the very same year, 401 AD. Books X and XI of *De Genesi ad litteram* are usually dated to 412 AD or later, since they seem to involve discussion of Pelagian ideas: see P. Agaësse and A. Solignac, 'Introduction générale', in *La Genèse au sens littéral I–VII*, Œuvres de saint Augustin, 7 ser. (Paris: Desclée de Brouwer, 1972), t. 48, pp. 28–31; Joseph Mausbach, *Die Ethik des hl. Augustinus*, 2nd edn. (Freiburg im Breisgau: Herdersche Verlagshandlung, 1929), I, 319: Book IX dates to 410 AD.
51. *De Genesi ad litteram* IX, 3; 9; 10, 16–18 (*CSEL* 28¹, 271–2, 277–80). Although Augustine allows for the possibility of sexual functioning in a sinless Eden, he still retains the notion that Genesis 1 describes the creation of the 'casual reasons' and Genesis 2 the visible, physical creation: *De Genesi ad litteram* VI, 5; 6; 14; VII, 24; IX, 1 (*CSEL* 28¹, 175, 177–8, 189, 222–3, 268). For the change in Augustine's views, see Borresen, *Subordination*, 36–40 (although I think factors other than the Pelagian dispute led to Augustine's changed view on the possibility of sexual relations in a sinless Eden).
52. *De Genesi ad litteram* IX, 7 (*CSEL* 28¹, 275). See Pereira, *Doctrine*, 12–13.
53. *Confessiones* III, 11, 20; IV, I, 1. (*CCL* 27, 38, 40); *Contra epistolam fundamenti* 10 (*CSEL* 25¹, 206); *De moribus Manichaeorum* 68 (19) (*PL* 32, 1374): *De moribus ecclesiae catholicae* 18, 34 (*PL* 32, 1326). Pierre Courcelle (*Recherches*

sur les Confessions de Saint Augustin, 2nd edn. (Paris: E. de Boccard, 1968), 78) has argued for a Manichean period of at least ten years.

54. On Jovinian's charges of 'Manicheanism' directed against Ambrose and other ascetics, see Augustine, *De nuptiis* II, 15(5); 38 (23) (*CSEL* 42, 444–5, 458); *Contra Julianum* 1, 2, 4 (*PL* 44, 643).

55. For overviews of Manicheanism, see Hans Jonas, *The Gnostic Religion: The Message of the Alien God and the Beginnings of Christianity*, 2nd edn., rev. (Boston: Beacon Press, 1963), ch. 9; Henri-Charles Puech, *Le Manichéisme: Son fondateur—sa doctrine*, Musée Guimet, Bibliothèque de Diffusion 56 (Paris: Civilisations du Sud, 1949); Geo Widengren, *Mani and Manichaeism* (New York: Holt, Rinehart & Winston, 1963); L. J. R. Ort, *Mani: A Religio-Historical Description of his Personality*, Supplementa ad Numen, Altera Series 1 (Leiden: Brill, 1967); H. J. Polotsky, 'Manichäismus', *RE* Suppl. Bd. VI (1935), 240–71; C. Colpe, 'Mani-Manichäismus', *RGG*³ (1960), IV, 714–22. For a discussion of Augustine's relations with Manicheanism, see now Samuel N. C. Lieu, *Manichaeism in the Later Roman Empire and Medieval China: A Historical Survey* (Manchester: Manchester University Press, 1985), ch. 5.

56. *De moribus Manichaeorum* 18, 65 (*PL* 32, 1373). See John Noonan, *Contraception. A History of Its Treatment by the Catholic Theologians and Canonists* (New York: New American Library, 1967), 151–4. According to Soranus' *Gynecology* I, 10, 36, the woman's fertile period was thought to come at the end of menstruation.

57. So Noonan infers from *Contra Faustum* XXII, 30 (*CSEL* 25¹, 624): in intercourse, the Manicheans 'pour out their God by a shameful slip' (Noonan, *Contraception*, 153–4). Recall Augustine's interpretation of the sin of Onan as *coitus interruptus*; see below.

58. *De moribus Manichaeorum* 18, 65 (*PL* 32, 1373): the Manicheans advised Augustine to refrain from sexual relations during the woman's fertile period. Cf. *Confessiones* IV, 2, 2 (*CCL* 27, 41) (although we begrudge the birth of children, we love them after they arise) and *Contra Faustum* XX, 23 (*CSEL* 25¹, 567), on married Manichean Auditors who produce children, 'albeit they beget them against their will'.

59. On Augustine's early sex life, see *Confessiones* II, 2, 2; 4; III, I, 1; VI, 11, 20–15, 25; VIII, 7 (*CCL* 27, 18, 19, 27, 87–90). On a (probable) later reflection concerning his relationship with his concubine, see *De bono coniugali* 5, 5 (*CSEL* 41, 193–194). See n. 11 above.

60. *De moribus ecclesiae catholicae* 63 (30) (*PL* 32, 1336); cf. his later anti-Manichean treatise, *Contra Faustum* XXX, 6 (*CSEL* 25¹; 755).

61. Ibid. XXII, 31–2, 43, 45, 47–50, 81 (*CSEL* 25¹, 624–7, 635–6, 637, 639–44, 683). The theme is at the forefront in *De bono coniugali* 26–35 (*CSEL* 41, 221–30). Augustine rejects the Manichean tendency to pit the asceticism of some New Testament passages against the pro-reproductive views of the Old Testament: *Contra Adimantum* 3; 23 (*CSEL* 25¹, 118–22, 182); *Contra Secundinum* 21; 23 (*CSEL* 25², 938–9, 941); *Contra Faustum* XIV, 1 (*CSEL* 25¹, 401–4).

62. Ibid. XV, 7 (*CSEL* 25¹, 429–30); cf. *De moribus Manichaeorum* 65 (18) (*PL* 32, 1373).

63. *Contra Faustum* XXII, 84 (*CSEL* 25¹, 687); also later in *De adulterinis coniugiis* II, 12, 12 (*CSEL* 41, 396).

64. *Contra Faustum* XIX, 26 (*CSEL* 25¹, 529).

65. Ibid. XV, 7 (*CSEL* 25¹, 429); *De moribus Manichaeorum* 18 (*PL* 32, 1373).

Pereira (*Doctrine*, 45–50, 52–3) resolves the ambivalence of Augustine's teaching on marriage by distinguishing the 'end', 'goods', and 'essence' of marriage; his distinctions seem overly scholastic for Augustine, in my reading of the text. For references in Augustine to the reading of the *tabulae*, see Perera, *Doctrine*, 153, and Marcello Marin, '*Le tabulae matri moniales* in S. Agostino', *Siculorum Gymnasium* 29 (1976), 307–21, esp. 309–10.

66. *Confessiones* II, 2, 3–4; IV, 2, 2 (*CCL* 27, 18–19, 41).

67. *De peccatorum meritis et remissione* I, 57 (29); II, (4); 39 (25); III, 2(2) (*CSEL* 60, 56, 73, 111, 130); *De natura et gratia* 3, 3; 4, 4 (*CSEL* 60, 235–6); *De gratia Christi et de peccato originali* 43 (38)–45 (40) (*CSEL* 42, 200–3); *De perfectione iustitiae hominis* 18, 39; 21, 44 (*CSEL* 42, 40–1, 47–8). For Augustine's theory of original sin, now see Pier Franco Beatrice, *Tradux Peccati: alle fonti della dottrina agostiniana del peccato originale*, Studia Mediolanensia 8 (Milan: Vita e Pensiero (Università Cattolica del Sacro Cuore), 1978); Beatrice's argument that Augustine derived his theory from the Encratites through Messalian teaching (pp. 222–59) seems dubious. Also see Mausbach, *Ethik*, II, ch. 3.

68. *De civitate Dei* XIV, 23; 26 (*CCL* 48, 445–6, 449–50).

69. Ibid. 26 (*CCL* 48, 449); cf. *De gratia Christi et peccato originali* II, 40, 35–41, 36 (*CSEL* 42, 199).

70. *De civitate Dei* XIV, 23 (*CCL* 48, 445); cf. *De gratia Christi et peccato originali* II, 40, 35 (*CSEL* 42, 199).

71. *De civitate Dei* XIV, 21 (*CCL* 48, 443); cf. his spiritualized version in *De Genesi contra Manichaeos* I, 19, 30 (*PL* 34, 187).

72. e.g. *De nuptiis* I, 1; 6 (5)–8 (7); 23 (21); II, 14 (5); 19 (8); 20 (8); 42 (16); 53 (31) (*CSEL* 42, 212, 216–20, 236, 265–6, 271, 272–3, 295–6, 309–10).

73. e.g. *Contra duas epistolas Pelagianorum* I, 9 (5); 10 (5); II, 9(5); III, 25 (9); IV 9 (5) (*CSEL* 60, 430, 431, 469, 517–18, 529–30).

74. Ibid. 4 (2); 10 (5); (*CSEL* 60, 425, 431); *De nuptiis* II, 15 (5); 34 (9); 38 (23); 49 (29); 50 (29) (*CSEL* 42, 266–68, 288, 291–2, 304, 305); *Contra secundam Juliani responsionem opus imperfectum* I, 24; 115 (*CSEL* 85¹, 21, 132–3); and many other places.

75. *Contra Julianum* III, 15(7); 16 (7); 30 (16); IV, 12 (2); VI, 59 (19) (*PL* 44, 709, 710, 717–18, 742, 858).

76. *Contra duas epistolas* I, 10 (5); 31 (15); 35 (17) (*CSEL* 60, 341, 448, 451–2); *Opus imperfectum* I, 68, 5; II, 122; V, 14 (*CSEL* 88¹, 75, 253; *PL* 45, 1445); *Ep.* 6*, 5, I 7, 2 (*CSEL* 88, 34, 35–6). On the dating of the new *Ep.* 6*, see Marie-Françoise Berrouard, 'Les Lettres 6* et 19* de saint Augustin', *Revue des études augustiniennes* 27 (1981), 269–77, and Henry Chadwick, 'New Letters of St. Augustine', *Journal of Theological Studies* 34 (1983), 429.

23 The Trinity, Prayer and Sexuality

Sarah Coakley*

Christianity was, from its inception, as much a way of life as a set of beliefs. Sarah Coakley suggests here that attention to the practice of prayer, and a renewed perception of human beings as sexual beings, will enhance Christian understandings of trinitarian spirituality and human desire. In this extract she lays before us three theses on Trinity, prayer and sexuality.   JMS

I. The **first thesis** is this: *that the revival of a vibrant trinitarian conceptuality, an 'earthed' sense of the meaningfulness and truth of the Christian doctrine of the Trinity, most naturally arises out of a simultaneous renewal of commitment to prayer, and especially prayer of a relatively wordless kind.* I shall try to explain why I think this is so with special reference to Paul's discussion of the nature of Christian prayer in Romans 8 as 'sighs too deep for words' (Romans 8:26), instituted by the Holy Spirit; and how I think this Spirit-leading approach to the Trinity through prayer is the only experientially rooted one likely to provide some answer to the sceptical charge: why three 'persons' at all? Why believe in a trinitarian God in the first place?

So that will be my first thesis: the inextricability of renewed trinitarian conceptuality and the renewal of prayer practice, and I shall be arguing that Christian prayer practice is inherently trinitarian. In a way this is a belated riposte to the charge of the great German 'liberal' theologian, Friedrich Schleiermacher, that the Trinity can never be experienced, can never be, as he put it, 'direct to consciousness'. This I want to challenge.

II. The **second thesis** goes on from this, and is perhaps a little more surprising; it is that *the close analysis of such prayer, and its implicitly trinitarian structure, makes the confrontation of a particular range of fundamental issues about sexuality unavoidable.* (Note that I use 'sexuality' in a wider sense than is often employed in North America—

* Sarah Coakley, 'The Trinity, Prayer and Sexuality: A Neglected Nexus in the Fathers and Beyond', *Bulletin of the Centro Pro Unione* 58 (fall 2000).

not restricting it to actual genital sexual activity.) The unavoidability of this confrontation seems to me to arise from the profound, but messy, entanglement of our human sexual desires and our desire for God; and in any prayer of the sort in which we radically cede control to the Spirit there is an instant reminder of the close analogue between this ceding (to the trinitarian God) and the *ekstasis* of human sexual passion. Thus it is not a coincidence that intimate relationship is at the heart of both these matters. That the early Fathers were aware of this nexus of associations (between trinitarian conceptuality, prayer of a deep sort, and the—to them—dangerous connections with issues of sex and gender), I shall illustrate with a particular example from the third-century Alexandrian theologian, Origen. He was someone crucial in the early development of patristic trinitarianism, but whose doctrine of the Trinity is rarely discussed in relation to what he also writes about *eros*. What will emerge from this second thesis, I hope, is that no renewed trinitarian spirituality can *sidestep* these profound issues of the nature of sexual desire, issues which now so divisively exercise us in the Church's life, and are, in turn, of course, fundamentally connected with gender themes about women's roles, women's capacity for empowerment, and for professional equality.

In short, if I am right, then renewed prayer practice, enlivened trinitarian doctrine, and an honest confrontation of tough questions in the contemporary Church about issues of sexuality and gender constitute a thematic nexus. These three issues belong together, and can be shown with a bit of delicate archaeological digging beneath the polite edifice constructed by the standard history-of-doctrine textbooks, to have accompanied one another all along. Or so I shall argue.

III. My **third thesis**, then finally, is not so much a finished proposition, but a task in progress for us all. It is the task of *rethreading the strands of inherited tradition on these three matters in such a way that enacted sexual desire and desire for God are no longer seen in mutual enmity, as disjunctive alternatives, with the non-celibate woman or homosexual cast as the distractor from the divine goal.* Rather, I am seeking a renewed vision of divine desire (a trinitarian vision, I suggest) which may provide the guiding framework for a renewed theology of human sexuality—of godly sexual relations—rooted in, and analogously related to, trinitarian divine relations. In terms of the unfortunate polarities we face in contemporary Western culture between hedonism on the one hand and supposed 'repression' on the other, this very quest may appear 'subversive' of established ways of thinking. But again, I want to suggest, there are resources in the tradition for this task, even if one has to dig a bit.

I. THE TRINITY IN PRAYER PRACTICE

When we move to face the puzzling question of why perfect relationship in God was understood as triadic in the first place, I want to argue that an analysis of Christian prayer (especially relatively wordless contemplative or charismatic prayer) provides an acutely revealing matrix for explaining the origins of trinitarian reflection. Vital here is Paul's analysis of prayer in Romans 8, where he describes how, strictly speaking, we do not autonomously do the praying, for we do not even really know what to ask for; rather it is the 'Spirit' who prays in us to the ultimate source in God ('the Father',[1] or 'Abba') and does so with 'sighs too deep for words' transcending normal human rationality. Into that ceaseless divine dialogue between Spirit and 'Father' the Christian pray-er is thus caught up, and so transformed, becoming a co-heir with Christ and being fashioned into an extension of redeemed, incarnate life. Recall how Paul puts it:

> For all who are led by the Spirit of God are sons of God. For you did not receive a spirit of slavery to fall back into fear, but you have received a spirit of adoption. When we cry, 'Abba, Father!' it is that very Spirit bearing witness with our spirit that we are children of God, and if children, then heirs of God and joint heirs with Christ (Romans 8:14–17a). . . . Likewise the Spirit helps us in our weakness; for we do not know how to pray as we ought, but that very Spirit intercedes with sighs too deep for words. And God, who searches the heart, knows what is the mind of the Spirit, because the Spirit intercedes for the saints according to the will of God (Romans 8:26–27).

Now it is important to underscore that what is going on here is not three distinguishable types of 'experience' (in the sense of emotional tonality), each experience relating to a different point of identity— 'Father', 'Son', and 'Holy Spirit'. This in any case would prove to be a 'hunting of the snark' from the perspective of later developed orthodox trinitarianism, since the *homoousion* principle disallows that the different 'persons' should be experientially separate, or do different things. Rather, what is being described in Paul is *one* experience of an activity of prayer that is nonetheless ineluctably, though obscurely, triadic. It is *one* experience of God, but God as simultaneously (i) doing the praying in me, (ii) receiving that prayer, and (iii) in that exchange, consented to in me, inviting me into the Christic life of redeemed sonship. Or to put it another way: the 'Father' (so-called here) is both source and ultimate object of divine longing in us; the 'Spirit' is that irreducibly—though obscurely—distinct enabler and incorporator of that longing in creation—that which *makes* the creation divine; and the 'Son' is that divine and perfected creation, into whose life I, as pray-er, am caught up. In this sense, despite all the unclarity and doctrinal fuzziness of Romans 8, the prayer described here seems to be at least proto-trinitarian in its implications.

Now no one would suggest that most of our prayer, sweated out as it so often is in states of dryness and distraction, may clearly feel like this. But just occasionally, I submit (at least if we allow enough space in which we are not insistently setting the agenda—if we allow, that is, this precious *hiatus* for the Spirit), then we breathe the Spirit's breath in this way; we see briefly that this is, theologically speaking, the triadic structure of God's graced ways with us—what is always going on though we mostly cannot see it. As John of the Cross puts it in a lovely passage in *The Spiritual Canticle* (39.3.4), not coincidentally quoting Romans 8: 'the Holy Spirit raises the soul most sublimely with that His divine breath . . . that she may breathe in God the same breath of love that the Father breathes in the Son and the Son in the Father . . .'

The Spirit, on this view, note, is no redundant third, no hypostatized afterthought, no cooing 'feminine' adjunct to an established male household. Rather, experientially speaking, the Spirit is *primary*, just as Pentecost is primary for the church; and leaving noncluttered space for the Spirit is the absolute precondition for the unimpeded flowing of this divine exchange in us, the 'breathing of the divine breath', as John of the Cross puts it.

Now what we want to know next is this (and it brings us to our second thesis): What happened to exegesis of Romans 8 in the critical early patristic period? Why was it not the wellspring of the turbulent conciliar discussion of the Trinity? And why, as it seems from the standard textbooks, did the Spirit get properly attended to only third and last (in the later fourth century) in the development of trinitarian doctrine in the crucial early patristic period, when the equality of the rational Logos with the 'Father' was discussed and established so much earlier? Or was this really so? Was there perhaps a 'soft underbelly' history of the development of the doctrine of the Trinity which the textbooks have obscured, and in which the Spirit played a much more significant role from the outset?

II. THE TRINITY AND SEXUALITY

My answer to this last question, although it is a speculative answer, is 'Yes'. There *is* a 'soft underbelly' history of the early development of the doctrine of the Trinity which many of the Fathers themselves had reason to push to one side. What I suggest is that there is an alternative account of the genealogy of the doctrine which only becomes clear once we see the covert entanglement of this genealogy with questions of sex and gender.

What is striking, first, is how little Romans 8 gets used as a basis for trinitarian argument and reflection in the early period (with some important exceptions in Irenaeus, Origen, and then the later Athanasius).[2] My hypothesis is that this is because this Romans 8 approach, fertile as it was theologically, proved a little too hot to handle. Why?

What I suggest here is that, from the second century on, there were both politico-ecclesiastical *and* gender reasons for keeping this approach to the Trinity away from the centre stage in the public concil-iar discussions of the matter. For Paul's analysis of prayer in Romans 8 notably involves: (i) a certain loss of noetic control to the leading experiential force of the Spirit in the face of our weakness (8:26); (ii) an entry into a realm beyond words, beyond normal rationality or *logos* (ibid.); and (iii) the striking use of a (female) 'birth pangs' meta-phor to describe the yearning of creation for its 'glorious liberty' (8:22). After Montanism (the prophetic and rigorist sectarian move-ment of the second century, ultimately condemned by Rome), it is not hard to see why any or all of these features could look less that attract-ive to developing mainstream 'orthodoxy', at least as a first basis for trinitarian reflection. The danger of ecstatic prophecy, when loosed from the primary control of an extrinsic Logos, was one matter. This had all the drawbacks of an essentially sectarian manifestation of the faith. The releasing of 'wretched women', as Hippolytus reports of early Montanism,[3] into positions of authority and prominence, was a second one. But there was a third danger, with which I think the third-century theologian Origen is primarily concerned (much more than he is with Montanism); and that is the danger, in any form of prayer that deliberately gives away rational mastery to the Spirit, of possible confusion between loss of control to that Spirit and loss of *sexual* control.

Let me just describe to you briefly what Origen says about prayer, trinitarianism and sexuality—all together in one nexus of association—in his fascinating treatise on prayer, the *De Oratione*.[4]

I shall just draw attention to the following four features of this work, especially of its open sections, from which you will see how closely related they are to the themes I have just outlined:

(i) The work starts (I) with an insistence on the priority and primacy of the Holy Spirit in understanding the nature and purpose of prayer; and it stresses the capacity of the grace of God to take us beyond the 'worthless reasoning of mortals' to a sphere of unutterable mysteries (see 2 Cor 12), where 'spiritual prayer' occurs in the 'heart'. Already, then, there is the explicit willingness to allow that the Spirit—although from the start a 'fellow worker' with the Father and Son—escorts us to a realm beyond the normal constraints of human rationality, even though in Origen's case there is no suggestion that the Spirit finally undermines the significance of the rational sphere. (ii) Exegesis of Romans 8 is central to the argument from the start, and citations are reiterated more than once; it is through prayer, and being 'mingled with the Spirit', that we become 'partakers of the Word of God' (X.2). (iii) This form of prayer is repeatedly, and strikingly, compared to sexual intercourse and procreation. Thus, for instance, Origen writes: 'Just as it is not possible to beget children without a woman and without receiving the power that serves to beget children, so no one may obtain . . . requests . . . unless he/she has prayed with such and such a disposition' (VIII.1). The Old Testament figure of Hannah, on this view, becomes the supreme type of the pray-er who overcomes sterility through the Spirit (II.5, etc.). But finally (iv) (and this is where we see Origen putting the brakes on), an *absolute disjunction*, according to Origen, must be made between the sexual and procreative theme in its metaphorical force (as we would now call it), and in its normal human functioning. Thus Tatiana, the woman to whom (along with a man, Ambrose) this work is addressed, can be trusted with this approach only because she is 'most manly,' and has gone beyond 'womanish things'—in the 'manner of Sarah' (Genesis 18:11). And knowing how 'to pray as we ought' (Romans 8:26, see II.2) is paralleled with an appropriately 'passionless', 'deliberate,' and 'holy' performance of the 'mysteries of marriage,' lest 'Satan rejoice over you through lack of self control'. Unsurprisingly too, then, Origen's daring treatment of Romans 8 also occasions an immediate reminder (with reference to 1 Timothy 2 and 1 Corinthians 11), that women should always wear modest apparel and cover their heads at prayer, lest their distracting presence lead to the same loss of (male) sexual control.

263

Later in the text, too, Origen advises against praying at all in a room in which sexual intercourse has taken place (XXXI.4). The intrinsic connections between (deep) trinitarian prayer and sex, it seems, are too close, but also too dangerous.

For Origen, the answer to this closeness between trinitarianism, contemplative ascent and sexuality, and the concomitant danger of a sinful confusion of the areas, must lie in allowing only advanced contemplatives ('enoptics')—those who have also shed actual physical sexual relations—into the circle of those who may safely use the erotic language of the *Song of Songs* to describe Christ's intimate mystical embrace of us.[5] Hence erotic language becomes the (finally) indispensable mode of speaking of our intimacy with God, but only at the cost of renouncing the physical or fleshly expressions of sexuality. In other words, Origen, having charted the entanglement of deep trinitarian prayer and erotic thematization, steps back and wrenches them apart again. To pray in this deep trinitarian way can only be the preserve of the celibate or a 'manly' woman who is beyond the menopause.

But it is precisely here, with this dilemma exposed, that our third question presses, one to which I have no complete answer, but only some speculative suggestions in closing.

III. DIVINE AND HUMAN DESIRES

My third thesis is the call to rethread the strands of tradition on divine and human desires such that they are no longer set in fundamental enmity with one another, no longer failing in their alignment. For the fatal accompaniment of such a failure of alignment, as is all too clear in Origen (amongst others), is the implicit denigration of nonvirginal woman, or indeed any humanly desirable person, as a distractor for the contemplative from the divine goal.

What has the Trinity got to do with *this*? Let me just suggest two programmatic points in closing:

(i) The first is the hypothesis that unless we have some sense of the implications of the trinitarian God's proto-erotic desire for us, then we can hardly begin to get rightly ordered our own erotic desires at the human level. Put another way, *we need to turn Freud on his head.* Instead of thinking of 'God' language as really being about sex (Freud's reductive ploy), we need to understand sex as really about

God, and about the deep desire that we feel for God—the clue that is woven into our existence about the final and ultimate union that we seek. And it matters in this regard—or so I submit—that the God we desire is, in Godself, a desiring trinitarian God: the Spirit who longs for our response, who searches the hearts, and takes us to the divine source (the 'Father'), transforming us Christically as we are so taken.

In this connection there is a wonderfully suggestive passage in the fifth-century pseudo-Dionysius (*Divine Names*, IV) where Dionysius speaks of this divine *ekstasis* and yearning of God for creation catching up our human yearning into itself: 'This divine yearning', he writes, 'brings ecstasy so that the lover belongs not to self but to the beloved . . . This is why the great Paul, swept along by his yearning for God and seized of its ecstatic power, has these inspired words to say: "It is no longer I who live but Christ who lives in me". Paul was clearly a lover, and, as he says, he was beside himself for God.'[6]

Now it needs to be admitted that this passage of Dionysius' is not worked out explicitly in trinitarian terms, indeed it is open to the charge of being more influenced by neo-Platonic notions of emanation and effusion than by a strictly Christian conceptuality. But I want to suggest here that it is at least capable of trinitarian glossing, according to the model provided in undeveloped form in Romans 8, and discussed above. And on this basis I suggest that we need to have a vision of trinitarian divine *ekstasis* if we are even to begin to construct a decent theology of human sexual desire that is in analogous relationship to divine desire.

(ii) Thus secondly, and lastly: if human loves are indeed made with the imprint of the divine upon them—*vestigia* of God's ways—then they too, at their best, will bear the trinitarian mark. Here we have to take off where Augustine left us, at that crucial moment in the *De Trinitate*, at the end of book VIII, when he rejects finally the analogy of 'the lover, the loved one, and the love that binds', as inadequate to the Trinity because it is bound to bodies. 'Let us tread the flesh underfoot and mount up to the soul,' as he puts it (*De Trinitate* VIII 14). But sexual loves *are* bodily, and if they are also to be godly, then they too should mirror forth the trinitarian image. And what would that involve? Surely, at the very least, a fundamental respect each for the other, an equality of exchange, and the mutual *ekstasis* of attending on the other's desire as distinct, *as other*. This is the opposite of abuse, the opposite of distanced sexual control; it is, as the French feminist Luce Irigaray has written, with uncanny insight, itself intrinsically trinitarian; sexual love at its best is not 'egological', not even a 'duality in closeness', but a shared transcendence of two selves toward the other, within a 'shared space, a shared breath'. 'In this relation,' she writes, 'we are at least three ... you, me, and our creation of that ecstasy of ourself in us [*de nous en nous*] prior to any child'.[7] As each goes out to the other in mutual abandonment and attentiveness, so it becomes clear that a third is at play—the irreducibility of a 'shared transcendence'.

To speak thus of the trinitarian nature of sexual love at its best is a far remove from the grimy world of pornography and abuse from which Christian feminism has emerged to make its rightful protest. Unfortunately, no language of *eros* is safe from possible nefarious application; and hence the feminist hermeneutic of suspicion can never come to an end. Even these reflections on divine trinitarian *eros* could, I am well aware, be put to potentially dangerous and distorted applications.[8] In this regard, Origen's caution about putting the *Song of Songs* into the wrong hands looks less completely wrong-headed than we might have suggested earlier. We do indeed play with fire when we acknowledge the deep entanglement of sexual desire and desire for God.

Notes

1. I do not here address the vexed issue of whether a feminist theologian should, under any circumstances, call God 'Father'. In *God, Sexuality and the Self: An Essay 'On the Trinity'* (Cambridge: Cambridge University Press, forthcoming) I argue that in *inner-trinitarian* contexts there are theological reasons why it is difficult to insist on consistent substitutions for 'Father' language: 'creator', 'redeemer', and 'sanctifier', for instance, does not do the same theological *work* as 'Father', 'Son', and 'Holy Spirit'. In addition, the attempt to repress *all* 'Father' language out of liturgical usage may merely force paternal imagery underground, leaving it to continue its (often baleful) effects out of conscious sight. My solution is a multipronged one, including the use of deliberate illogical conjunction (maternal and paternal imagery combined) as a means of avoiding crass literalism in the attribution of parental characteristics; but I do not advocate the complete obliteration of 'Father' language, especially in the trinitarian context.

2. See e.g. Irenaeus, *Ad haer.*, 5.20.2; Origen, *De Oratione*, I.3–6 (see discussion below); Athanasius, *Ad Ser.* 1.6, 1.7, 1.19, 1.24, 1.25, 4.4. These passages are set in context in my article 'Why Three? Some Further Reflections on the Doctrine of the Trinity', in S. Coakley and D. A. Pailin (eds.), *The Making and Remaking of Christian Doctrine* (Oxford: Oxford University Press, 1993).

3. See Hippolytus, *Refutatio omnium haer*, 8.19; also discussed in 'Why Three?'

4. I use here the English translation of the *De Oratione* (and the section divisions) in R. A. Greer (ed.), *Origen* (New York: Paulist Press, 1979), 81–170.

5. Origen makes this point emphatically at the opening of his *Commentary on the*

Song of Songs (Prologue, I); see R. P. Lawson (trans.), *Origen: The Song of Songs Commentary and Homilies* (London: Longmans, Green & Co., 1957), 22–3.

6. Pseudo-Dionysius, *The Divine Names*, 4.13; see C. Luibheid (trans.), *Pseudo-Dionysius: The Complete Works* (London: SPCK, 1987), 82.

7. L. Irigaray, 'Questions to Emmanuel Lévinas', in M. Whitford (ed.), *The Irigaray Reader* (Oxford: Blackwell, 1991), 180.

8. The point about the *dangers* of some feminists' use of the 'erotic' as a positive and transformative category is well made in K. M. Sands, 'Uses of the Thea(o)-logian: Sex and Theodicy in Religious Feminism', *Journal of Feminist Studies in Religion* 8 (1992), 7–33.

24 Towards Inclusive Worship

Rachel Adler*

Jewish liturgy consists in large measure of biblical citations creatively interwoven with rabbinic texts. Even in non-Orthodox circles, liturgy is remarkably resistant to change; most Jews think their childhood melodies to particular prayers—let alone the words—were given on Sinai! Traditionally, there has been little scope for innovation or variety. Jewish services are repeated prayer by prayer, week after week, and regular 'davveners' (worshippers) find comfort and pleasure in familiarity. Not surprisingly, the unchanging nature of Jewish liturgy poses problems for many feminists. Events a woman might wish to share with her community are often overlooked, and an important task in recent years has been to find ways of marking them with new or reworked prayers and rituals. Another problem is the assumed maleness of both worshipper and worshipped (Hebrew is a gendered language). In this extract from her important book *Engendering Judaism*, Rachel Adler tackles the difficulties of anthropomorphism in God-language; should it be discarded as 'liturgical idolatry'? Adler offers a model that is helpful, though not without problems of its own, in the form of Reconstructionism, a Jewish movement that posits an impersonal God yet promotes prayer nonetheless.

DL

ENTER THEOLOGY

It is important, I think, to speak of theology when we are speaking about liturgy because theologies are implicit in the God-language we choose or reject. At the same time, God-language overflows the confines of particular theologies just as narratives overflow the boundaries of legal or normative systems. Both theologies and narratives lend themselves to be claimed, recast, recontextualized by other interpretive

---

* Rachel Adler, from *Engendering Judaism: An Inclusive Theology and Ethics*. Copyright ©
  1998 by The Jewish Publication Society. Used by permission.

communities. Moreover, theologies themselves are suspect when they are too complete, too clear, too coherent. Perhaps a God who hides (*el mistater*) and a correspondingly complex and elusive humanity are best reflected in the gaps—a riddling theology riddled with fissures. My theological discussion here will be mostly gaps, because I want to take up only one question and explore only one family of metaphors.

A central conflict underlying God-language controversies in feminist theologies, and indeed in all contemporary theologies, concerns whether or not personality is to be ascribed to God. Reconstructionist theology's response to this problem has shaped all contemporary conversation about this issue. The cornerstone of Reconstructionist theology is its assertion that God is an impersonal dynamic rather than a personality. But how can Judaism continue to link with its past without affirming a personal God? The founder of Reconstructionism, Mordecai Kaplan, understands God to be that power or process in the universe that supports human fulfillment.[1] Any language used to personalize or anthropomorphize God is merely a rhetorical device. However, the impersonality of God does not obviate prayer for Kaplan. Rather, he regards prayer as one of the most impressive ways Jewish civilization speaks to itself, perpetuating the mores and folkways that express its identity. Prayer serves a variety of useful social functions. It encourages group cohesion, instills moral values, offers uplifting spiritual and aesthetic experiences, and heightens awareness of the wonders of nature.[2]

Reconstructionists are therefore genuinely motivated to pray, and even to embrace Hebrew text and traditional liturgy, because these function to sustain identity and continuity. At the same time, as Richard Hirsh points out, traditional liturgy explicitly undermines Reconstructionist theology by addressing a supernatural being, using anthropomorphic imagery, and recounting improbable mythic events.[3]

Because they share some problems about how God is to be named and imaged, feminists and Reconstructionists have much to say to one another. Feminists fear the reifying power of particular images of God because, invariably, what is reified is God's masculinity. For Reconstructionists, in addition, the very attribution of personality to God is a reification. Hence, both feminist and Reconstructionist theologies are critical of the traditional language of transcendence. Reconstructionist suspicions of supernaturalism find their parallel in feminist charges that theologies of transcendence reject the human domain—the physical, the sensuous, the immanent—by relegating it to women.

The solution in some contemporary Reconstructionist theologies, notably that of Arthur Green, is to reconstruct spirituality by drawing a metaphoric language from mysticism.[4] The resulting theology is also profoundly attractive to some feminist theologians. Green identifies the quintessential spiritual experience as the mystical union with the divine. This fusion experience, dissolving boundaries that separate self, world, and God, can barely be articulated. Its most common anthropomorphic metaphor is sexual intercourse, but images connected with water, light, and fire abound as well.[5] Of course, the experience of merging is not confined to traditional religions. It can also be recognized in William James's "cosmic consciousness"[6] or the "oceanic feeling" that Romain Rolland described to Freud.[7] The universality of unitive mysticism, its appearance even among secularists or the "unchurched," is one of several features that make it harmonious with Reconstructionism. Although Green wishes to maintain personal address as a religious metaphor, some versions of unitive mysticism do not address God personally or depend on religious narratives that specify and concretize the ineffable. Unitive spirituality thus relieves the frigid rationalism of classical Reconstructionism without actually conflicting with it, since flexible boundaries between self and world are already a feature of Kaplanian theology.

Unitive spirituality also resolves some knotty theological and liturgical problems for feminists. Here is a spirituality in which metaphors of hierarchical relations are inapplicable and gender differentiation is irrelevant. Moreover, it is unnecessary to prove that anthropomorphism is inadequate. That has already been acknowledged, and alternatives are welcome. A feminist liturgist whose work embodies a distinctively feminist and implicitly Reconstructionist approach to unitive spirituality is Marcia Falk.[8] "My relationship to the divine," Falk says, "is about a loss of otherness, a merging, a breaking down of boundaries and a (momentary) release into the Wholeness."[9] The function of prayer for Falk is to evoke this experience.

Many feminist thinkers have revived interest in traditional images drawn from nature—God as rock, lion, or tree.[10] But these images have inspired Falk to create new images, often based upon phrases or concepts from earlier Judaisms, which imbue her prayer language with an uncannily traditional flavor. She explains:

I create and use new images—images such as *eyn ha-hayyim,* "well-spring or source of life," *nishmat kol khai,* "breath of all living things," and *nitzotzot ha-nefesh,* "sparks of the inner, unseen self"—to serve as fresh metaphors for Divinity. With these images and still others, composed of all the basic elements of creation—earth, water, wind and fire—I hope to help construct a theology of immanence that will both affirm the sanctity of the world and shatter the idolatrous reign of the lord/God/king.[11]

Falk's unique innovation is to incorporate this theology of immanence into the primary forms of Jewish liturgy. She has coined a *berakhah* formula that counters traditional theologies of transcendence by collapsing God into nature and community. What is revolutionary in Falk's blessing formula is that it replaces the rabbinically ordained formula *Barukh atah Adonai Eloheynu melekh ha-olam,* "Blessed are you, Adonai/Lord our God, king of the universe," whose essential components are known as *shem umalkhut,* "name and kingship."[12] In the classical formula, the divine name *Adonai,* Lord, stands in for YHVH, from the Hebrew root YHVH, Being, the name that is not pronounced, and God's kingship is acknowledged with the words "king of the universe." Falk begins her new blessing formula with *nevorekh,* "let us bless," instead of the traditional "Blessed are You." By addressing not God but the community, she evades the problem of having to address God as either masculine or feminine. One appellation she substitutes for *Adonai* is *eyn ha-hayyim,* "source [or spring] of life," echoing the imagery of many Psalms that praise God as a life giver or a water source. "My soul thirsts for you," the Psalmist says (Ps. 63). God "turns the rock into a pool of water, the flint into a fountain" (Ps. 114). Grammatically, like all Hebrew terms, the phrase *eyn ha-hayyim* has gender, but as an image it is gender neutral.

Falk's blessings have been criticized for rejecting the ancient and universal formula. Some find it unacceptable that God is not addressed directly. Others raise the halakhic objection that Falk's blessing does not acknowledge God's kingship. But even traditional blessings come in variant forms, not all of which obey the ex post facto rules established by the *Amoraim.*[13] Both the *Tefillah* and the wedding blessings, for instance, deviate from these rules. For Falk, because God is radically immanent, within us individually and communally, kingship would be an unsatisfactory metaphor even if its emphasis on hierarchy did not render it objectionable.[14] Her solution challenges those who would retain the ancient formula to ask what the rabbis meant by calling God a king and whether those are meanings we can either appropriate or reframe.

The larger question both Falk and the Reconstructionists raise is whether God should be imaged as an Other at all, since the imagery of otherness is particularly vulnerable to reification. In the traditional texts where it originates, it is largely masculine. Why continue to use imagery so easily abused? For me, the chief reason is that the otherness of God is compellingly real and infinitely precious. Eradicating otherness, breaking down all boundaries between self and other, self and God, God and world simultaneously eradicates relatedness. How is it possible to have a covenant without an Other? If God is not distinct from self and community, why use a theological language of partnership at all? Moreover, given how bitterly feminists have resisted being subsumed or swallowed up, how hard we have fought for integrity of selfhood, why embrace the experience of fusion in our spirituality? Opposite Falk's unitive spirituality, then, I would set a spirituality of otherness.

God's Otherness, God's difference from us, is what makes possible relationship and exchange. God's is the primary Otherness in a world where, as Emanuel Levinas teaches, self constantly raises its face to the other.[15] An other carried us in her belly, cut the cord that made us one, and embraced us as her other. An other fed us from her own body. Otherness is the mother of human language: because of the other, we are moved to speak. Others teach us and are taught by us. Others work and build the world with us. Others heal our loneliness. Others befriend us. Female or male, straight or gay, we seek the body of the other to cohabit, to be interpenetrated. Because God is Other, God creates a world filled with difference. Because God is Partner, all difference is filled with holy possibility.

Only if there is an Other can there be mirroring and reciprocity. Some of the tenderest rabbinic metaphors and stories describe how we see ourselves reflected in the responses of the other. In the first chapter of tractate Berakhot, a series of exegeses declare that God goes to synagogue, that God wears tefillin, and that God prays.

Rabbi Naḥman bar Yizthak asked Rabbi Ḥiyya bar Avin, "What is written in the tefillin of the Master of the Universe?" He replied, "Who is like your people Israel one unique nation in the world [*goy ehad ba-aretz*]" (1 Chron. 17:21) ... The Holy One said to Israel, You have made me the unique object of your love (*hativa*) in the world and I have made you the unique object of my love in the world. You have made me the unique object of your love in the world, as it says in Scripture, 'Hear O Israel, the Lord our God, the Lord is One' (Deut. 6:4). I have made you the unique object of my love in the world, as it says in Scripture, 'Who is like your people Israel one unique nation in the world' (1 Chron. 17:21)."[16]

In this passage, Israel's proclamation of God's Oneness and God's proclamation of Israel's oneness mirror one another. They are

reciprocal declarations of devotion. Neither is an ontological statement. They are testimonies to the way the other is experienced
relationally.

Mirroring and reciprocity reach across the boundaries of difference,
but do not dissolve it. God creates and upholds the distinctness of all
things one from another. The Psalmist depicts a God who not only
numbers the stars, but "calls each one by name" (Ps. 147:4). We matter
not only collectively, but also individually. Because we are utterly distinct from all others, we can make ourselves mysterious. We can hide,
leaving the Other to cry out, "*ayyeka*, Where are you?"[17] Or we can
make ourselves transparent to the Other, illuminate our mystery, allow
ourselves to be known.

The premise of relationship grounds metaphors in which we and
God are interdependent: friends, lovers, co-creators of the world.
Mutual commitments and shared projects bridge the boundary of
difference and open opportunities to redistribute power. When these
metaphors are woven into stories, they cease to be static ideals, because
relationships are filled with tensions and conflicts as well as harmonies
and coalescences. Friends may be insensitive, lovers may betray, co-
workers may clash. Relationship potentiates abandonment, violence,
enigma.

Sin, in the context of relationship, is not a transgression of an
abstract norm but an injury toward an Other rendered vulnerable by
his/her trust. *Teshuvah* is turning again to face the Other, not to annul
what has occurred, but to sew up the wounds and determine how to go
on. Relationships bear scars because they have memory. As memories
accumulate, they carry consequences that bind us. They retell how we
have come to be related in the way we are, but they also point us
toward what we must become, what we must recreate, what we must
repay. Without memory, there can be no covenants.

In a theology of relationship where there are flexible boundaries
between God and others, both unity with and separation from God
are possible. Imagine God as continually pregnant with, delivering,
rearing, and separating from the world, like a tree at once bearing
blossoms, unripe fruit, ripe fruit, and the stems and scars from fruit
that has fallen from the tree. The world is inside God, outside God,
part of God as in halakhah the unborn infant is "part of its mother's
body," and separate from God, as the emancipated child is separate
from a parent who still watches its story unfold, sometimes with pride,
sometimes with pain.[18]

METAPHORS OF POWER

To acknowledge God as Other than ourselves, as creator of the universe, as the covenant partner with whom we co-create a world of law, raises questions of power, authority, and responsibility. These are questions of particular moment in a feminist theology, because theologies can be used to enforce and validate distributions of power by gender, status, and class in the social world and to teach people to perceive themselves as helpless, incompetent, or irremediably flawed.[19] Metaphors of power and authority are particularly problematic if we believe they endorse absolutism or create castes, because, in democratic societies, we reject power distributions that disenfranchise people or that do not entitle them to equal respect.[20]

We need to ask ourselves whether disparities of power and authority are inherently oppressive or whether it is the abuse of these disparities that is unjust. I would like to suggest several categories of relationships that necessarily involve disparities but do not require disadvantaging or degrading the less powerful or less authoritative participant. These include relationships in which one participant with specialized competence helps the other to heal, to acquire learning or skill, or to gain self-understanding or spiritual illumination. Such relationships are ethical when recipients are made partners in the process and when the goal is to benefit and empower. Indeed, if the helper were to regard the recipient as passive and incompetent, it would make it impossible for the goal to be achieved.

Other relationships where disparities exist but need not degrade or infantilize are mentoring and parenting. Good mentors and good parents take pride in the developing powers of those in whom they have invested themselves and look forward eagerly to their full flowering. When maturation is complete, a generational boundary still remains in place between parent and child, mentor and disciple. They may respect each other deeply and yet not be peers. Obligations will still bind the guided and the guide to one another, but they will have come to share a language in which they can discuss how particular obligations fit into the overall pattern of what now are shared projects and values. Their history together invests the good mentor or parent with continuing influence and respect, without any presumption of incompetence on the part of the disciple or grown child.

Images of God as experienced helper show us to ourselves as attainers of competence. What they do not reflect are our limits, our gaps, our constraints, our regrets. We act, we make things happen, but things also happen to us. As storytellers together, we and God write our lives. God presents us with inevitabilities, with opportunities and con-straints. We present God with our choices and responses. Because of our power to choose, things also, as it were, happen to God. God as powerful Other, as the one who perceives beyond the bounded perspective, who permits into our stories elements we experience as disruptive, as agon-izing, is the lightning rod for our rage and fear, awe and dependency. To continue to affirm that we are in relationship with this God is not to affirm God-as-power or God-as-patterner in some abstract sense, but rather to assert that we as actors have moral weight: we matter to God. This does not necessarily require from us passive acceptance of God's will. Our indignation is an equally powerful act of trust: it presumes that our covenant partner can be held accountable in relationship.

Affirming God as Other, however, still leaves the problem of gender unresolved. Some who would grant that God reveals Godself to us as an Other argue that a more truthful language would purify itself of gendered imagery entirely, presenting the divine Other in neuter ter-minology. This is clearly impossible in Hebrew, which has no neuter gender. Even in English, however, objections arise. Used in reference to human roles and attributes, neuter language is more abstract and hence less emotionally charged. Vivid images and powerful feelings accompany the words *mother* or *father* but do not attend the word *parent*. Moreover, in a male-dominated society, neuter language is still assumed to refer to males. If the referent is female, it is customary to signify this difference through a modifier: "a woman rabbi," or "a woman judge." God can, of course, be compared to gender-free aspects of the creation, such as rocks, hills, wells, and fountains, but anthropomorphic imagery inevitably entails gender, because the human beings reflected in it are sexually differentiated creatures.

Should anthropomorphism then be discarded as a language of the-ology or prayer? Marcia Falk accuses it of facilitating "liturgical idolatry."

It is not just the exclusive maleness of our God-language that needs correc-tion, but its anthropocentrism in *all* its ramifications. For as long as we image divinity exclusively as a person, whether female or male, we tend to forget that human beings are not the sole, not even the "primary" life-bearing creatures on the planet. We allow our intelligence and our unique linguistic capabilities to deceive us into believing that we are "godlier" than the rest of creation.[21]

Yet I would argue that expunging anthropomorphism from the

language of prayer, even if it were possible, would be undesirable. We can still include the beautiful images of God as bird or rock or water. But these images alone are not sufficient to sustain relatedness. Anthropomorphism is necessary because stories are necessary. We know God from the stories we and God inhabit together. Stories are a human genre. For God to step into story with us, God must clothe Godself in metaphor, and especially in anthropomorphic metaphor, because the most powerful language for God's *engagement* with us is our human language of relationship.

We and God are characters in the foundational narratives that constitute the *nomos*, the universe of meaning in which we live as Jews, like the Exodus story, and in the interpretations, visions, biographies, and memories that augment them or transform them. Without stories, there is no Judaism, because without stories, there is neither the God of Israel nor Israel itself. We cannot talk about ourselves as a people without telling the stories of Egypt and Canaan, Babylon and Baghdad, Vilna and New York, stories of exile and return, of matriarchs, patriarchs, midwives, prophets, tricksters, scholars, martyrs, and rebels. We cannot talk about the God of Israel without talking about the creator, dweller in the thornbush, liberator, covenanter, nursing mother, adversary, voice in the whirlwind, scribe, judge, and exiled Shekhinah. Allegorizing the stories or abstracting them flattens all their meanings into a single layer, closes them off to further interpretation, surgically extracts their emotional content, censors all their ambivalences, contradictions, mysteries, and scandals. Only through stories can we glimpse the wildness of God, of infinite and untrammeled possibility, untamable within the confines of any systematic theology.

Story conveys the moral heft and heat that differentiates God as a living presence from the bodiless, passionless abstraction of the philosophers: *A story is a body for God*. The dilemma to which feminism points is not caused by the nature of stories but by a paucity of certain kinds of stories. Most of the stories transmitted to us clothe God in a male body. Only a few embedded metaphors ascribe to God feminine roles or attributes. That dilemma will not be solved by rejecting or dismissing stories but by telling more stories, clothing the nakedness of God as we become aware of it.

Investing God with bodies is admittedly a dangerous enterprise. How badly does God need bodies? In liturgy especially, I would maintain, very badly indeed. It is frequently suggested that because God is not literally male or female, the most appropriate God-language is neuter. But Hebrew has no neuter gender; all words must be grammatically masculine or feminine. There are, however, appellations and images that are *conceptually* gender neutral. Nevertheless, a God-language restricted to gender-free vocabulary presents difficulties. The Reconstructionist prayerbook *Kol Haneshama* attempts to mediate among the differing God-languages of feminism, classical Reconstructionism, and Reconstructionist mysticism by offering a wide range of translations, commentaries, and interpretive readings using feminine, masculine, and gender-neutral language.[22] In addition, *Kol Haneshama* offers both gender-neutral and grammatically feminine versions of the *berakhah* formula.[23] These options are located in the commentary, however. The Hebrew text uses the traditional masculine *berakhah* formula, although it translates *Adonai* in gender-free terms according to the theme of the prayer: "the Infinite," "Eternal One," "Compassionate One."

For a dedicated antisupernaturalist, however, the gender inclusiveness and gender neutrality of *Kol Haneshama* do not go far enough. Richard Hirsh would use English text to restate the themes of Hebrew prayers in nonpersonal and nonsupernatural terms.[24] Hirsh's solution illustrates the dangers of gender-free liturgy. Not only does it conceal the gendered nature of the Hebrew text, but in the process, it drains and deadens the language of prayer by translating the myths and metaphors of the original into moral and rational language. To use J. L. Austin's terminology, Hirsh replaces performative language with constantive language. Hirsh's treatment of the *Geulah* (Redemption) blessing of the *Tefillah* is a convincing demonstration. The Hebrew *berakhah*, "Blessed (masc.) are you (masc.) *Adonai* (masc.) Redeemer (masc.) of Israel," culminates a vivid account of the liberation from Egypt and the parting of the waters. Hirsh's restatement, "In moments of redemption, we become witnesses to and partners in the work of freedom," is a Kaplanian yawner.[25] As a liturgical statement, it replaces a performative with a moral observation. It makes no reference to the narrative it seeks to transvalue, and, hence, to the gendered nature of that narrative, and, by banishing imagery in favor of abstractions, disembodies both its subject matter and the liturgical community who are supposed to identify with the statement.

ADDRESSING GOD-SHE: A CONUNDRUM

Embracing a gendered God-language still leaves us with the question of what kinds of stories and metaphors can constitute a feminine body for God. To answer, one must ask, what does it mean to be a woman? Before feminism gave women voices, it was men who defined women. Philosophical definitions of women by male philosophers presupposed an essential feminine nature based upon women's biological characteristics that determines women's behavior, interests, and limits.[26]

In an early phase of contemporary feminism's development, many feminists enthusiastically embraced this idea of an essential feminine nature, although they rejected masculinist philosophical valuations of it. Instead, on the basis of women's shared biological characteristics and history of patriarchal oppression, they postulated a universal women's culture whose common experience transcended historical context, cultural difference, class, and politics. Biological processes were understood as universals whose meaning was not mediated by culture. The assumption was that, by menstruating, birthing, and nursing, middle-class white American women were having the same experience as Ndembu women in Zambian villages or nomadic Israelite women in ancient Canaan, experiences belonging to a timeless "women's culture."[27] The supporters of this cultural feminism catalogued and embraced indiscriminately a melange of feminine symbols and stories from world religions.[28] They used this cross-cultural stew of women's roles and functions both to discover options that differed from those in modern Western societies and to revalorize the traditional roles of mother and homemaker. Amid the clashes and diversities of pluralistic society, cultural feminists promoted a nostalgic vision of universal sisterhood.

For Jewish women, cultural feminism provided ways to affirm the holiness of bodies that do not have "the covenant sealed in our flesh,"[29] bodies that menstruate, bodies that lactate. Confronting a tradition from which women have seemed so absent, it was hard to know how to begin to generate a feminine language. Cultural feminism offered rich and readily accessible sources for feminine imagery. Moreover, because many of its images were archaic, they appeared superficially to be harmonious with traditional language. Some women looked particularly at the writings of Jung and his disciples because they seemed to offer a diverse and systematically organized feminine symbology. They searched out examples of these Jungian feminine images in classical midrashic texts and in Kabbalah and built upon them new rituals, new midrash, and new prayers. This influence is apparent in the liturgical and midrashic work of Lynn Gottlieb and in several alternative prayerbooks.[30] It is the philosophical bedrock upon which women's Rosh Ḥodesh rituals are constructed.[31]

For a variety of reasons, however, feminist philosophers are critical of essentialism. Essentialism conflates sexual differentiation, which is biological, with gender, which is socially constructed. It also ignores differences among cultures in the assignment of gender roles and the impact of sociohistorical contexts in shaping or changing them. Once we admit that gender roles and values attached to them are *constructed*, we also acknowledge that they are *contingent*. Then we must ask ourselves how we would wish to change them or whether we would wish to construct them at all.[32]

The extent to which biologically or culturally assigned roles could or should limit the roles and values women may embrace in the future is a matter of much debate. What is clear is that, because essentialist imagery reinforces gender stereotypes, it confines rather than throws open the significations of what it means to be a woman. Jungian accounts of the Feminine provide a prime illustration of how essentialism, while purporting to describe femininity, can enforce existing versions of it. Not only do Jungian accounts reify socially assigned gender roles and characteristics, representing them as innate sexual qualities, but they also uphold these descriptions as standards to which psychologically healthy women ought to conform.[33]

As feminist theory matures, bringing with it a more rigorous analysis of the category of gender, some of feminist Judaism's early attempts at feminine prayer language appear simplistic. It is no longer credible that a feminist Judaism can be achieved merely by including more moon and water imagery in our liturgies, by sitting in a circle, or by depicting God with essentialist imagery.[34] If we reject reducing human possibilities to the terms of gender constructs, essentialist God-language becomes doubly problematic. Depicting God-She exclusively as hushed, modest, helpful, and receptive: restricting femininity to images of parenting and domestic concern—the nursing mother, the nesting bird, the midwife, the busy *hausfrau*—limits both God and women.[35] If reductive or stereotyped imagery is inadequate to express human complexities, then how can it reflect a God who is, ultimately, beyond all human attempts at description? The issue here is not to censor out any experiences or activities of women as inappropriate to God-She, but to widen their diversity.

How, then, do we name God-She? Is it inauthentic to borrow language about goddesses from other religions?[36] Do we risk paganism by endowing God with a Canaanite goddess's title such as "Queen of

Heaven"?[37] In the Bible, God is called *el*, even though that is the name of the chief god of the Canaanite pantheon. Is gendered borrowing of names and titles somehow different from or worse than other borrowings? Specifically, is it blasphemous to feminize the generic term for God, changing *el* to *elah*, a term currently restricted to pagan deities? (My question is specifically about *elah*. The other feminine biblical term, *elilah*, is inherently contemptuous, for the doubled root letter forms a diminutive: an *elilah* is not a goddess but a female godlet.) Ellen Umansky, viewing *elah* as irrevocably idolatrous, warns that "the feminist theologian who [reclaims] the word *Elah* does so at the risk of breaking with the community of Israel."[38] Umansky's apprehension is puzzling. What kind of syncretism does she fear? There is no other deity in our social environment to whom the term *elah* commonly refers. *El* became identified with YHWH in ancient Judaism under far more dangerous conditions.

Feminine images and ascriptions from earlier Jewish traditions present a different set of problems. The ancient term Shekhinah is a prime example. Is it possible to extricate Shekhinah from the essentialist meanings with which it was endowed in Jewish mysticism? Plaskow embraces the term: "[T]he image of Shekhinah . . . like the term God itself, cuts across the layers of anthropomorphic and non-personal language. Addressed in myriad personal guises, the Shekhinah is also the presence of God in the place called the world and the one who rests in a unique way in the midst of community."[39] Frymer-Kensky objects that "Shekhinah has become almost the female deity, rather than a female facet of God. This presents the real danger that a message of God's duality will be delivered subliminally, in much the way that the maleness of God is currently conveyed."[40]

In place of *elah*, Ellen Umansky has recommended the abstract noun *elohut*, "Divinity," as a term untainted by past or present associations with idolatry.[41] But while *elohut*, like all nouns with the *-ut* ending, is grammatically feminine, its abstraction seems more suitable for metaphysics (or science or sociology) than for liturgy. In modern Hebrew, these abstract nouns abound in political and administrative discourse, which makes me fear that addressing *elohut* would feel like addressing the Israeli bureaucracy; one would anticipate the same level of responsiveness.

A new name current among some Jewish feminists is *Rahamema*, a feminine coinage from Hebrew *rahaman*, or Babylonian Aramaic *rahmana*, "merciful one."[42] Because the Hebrew word for mercy is derived from *rehem*, "womb," *Rahamema* represents a powerful melding of physicality and moral force. The name also has a punning, Joycean charm, combining the word for mercy with the intimate *ima*, "mama." At the same time, however, the term raises all the questions about essentialism. Frymer-Kensky asks, "Does using *rahamema* as a name reinforce the idea that mercy is a female quality? If so, does that give human males the right or the obligation to act without compassion?"[43] Yet given the long history of *rahaman* as a masculine appellation for God, it is difficult to see how the addition of a feminine equivalent would promote gender stereotyping.

One source of fresh and contemporary imagery that can be imported into theology and prayer can be found in literature created by Jewish women and men. I hesitate to call this literature secular, first, because I think the dichotomy between sacred and secular art is generally false, and second, because I believe that Jews, and Jewish women in particular, often turn to secular forms and contexts to articulate what are really Jewish concerns. If, as George Steiner argues, all art presupposes the presence of a transcendent Other whom the artist mirrors by creating moral universes, there is no secular art.[44] Art and prayer alike are acts of creation and of bearing witness, framed in revelatory metaphors.

In a special sense, however, many works by women poets in Hebrew and Yiddish cannot be considered secular. Poetry such as that by Zelda, Kadia Molodowsky, Malka Heifetz Tussman, and Leah Goldberg is engaged in a conversation with Jewish tradition. Like Rachel stealing the household gods, these poets steal the language of tradition, wresting it away from masculine theologies of spirit and transcendence and resituating it in embodied, sensuous, gendered experience. Some of these poems were originally conceived as acts of rebellion against a tradition that seemed to have no room for the perceptions and concerns of women or the riddles and ambiguities of modernity itself. It would be an act of *tikkun*, a mending of the shattered world, to make liturgies that could embrace these poems and say to them: "You can bring your stolen language home now."[45]

Notes

1. Mordecai Kaplan, *Judaism as a Civilization: Toward a Reconstruction of American Jewish Life* (New York: Schocken, 1967), 391–405.
2. Ibid. 343–9.
3. Richard Hirsh, 'Spirituality and the Language of Prayer', *Reconstructionist* 59 (spring 1994), 21–6.
4. Arthur Green, *Seek My Face, Speak My Name: A Contemporary Jewish Theology* (New York: Jason Aronson, 1992).

5. See, e.g., the discussion of Eastern and Western forms of unitary mysticism in Rudolf Otto, *Mysticism East and West*, trans. Bertha L. Bracey and Richenda C. Payne (New York: Macmillan, 1932).

6. William James, *Varieties of Religious Experience* (New York: New American Library, 1958), 306–7.

7. Sigmund Freud, *Civilization and Its Discontents*, vol. xxi of *The Standard Edition of the Complete Psychological Works of Sigmund Freud*, trans. and ed. James Strachey in collaboration with Anna Freud, assisted by Alix Strachey and Alan Tyson (London: Hogarth Press and the Institute of Psycho-Analysis, 1930), 72.

8. Falk's theology is in implicit agreement with contemporary Reconstructionism, as the Reconstructionist prayerbook's use of her work attests, but she does not identify herself as a Reconstructionist liturgist.

9. Personal communication from Marcia Falk, 26 July 1995.

10. e.g., Tikva Frymer-Kensky, 'On Feminine God-Talk', *Reconstructionist* 69 (spring 1994), 49.

11. Marcia Falk, 'Toward a Feminist Jewish Reconstruction of Monotheism', *Tikkun* 4 (July/Aug. 1989), 53–6. In the same issue, see Lawrence Hoffman, 'A Response to Marcia Falk', 56–7.

12. That a blessing must mention God's name is the opinion of Rav. That it must mention God's kingship is the opinion of R. Yoḥanan, B. Berakhot 12a, 40b. These are Amoraic dicta that postdate the invention of the blessing formula by several hundred years.

13. Ismar Elbogen, *Jewish Liturgy: A Comprehensive History*, trans. Raymond P. Scheindlin (Philadelphia and Jerusalen: Jewish Publication Society and Jewish Theological Seminary of America, 1993), 5–6. Lawrence A. Hoffman, 'Blessings and Their Translation in Current Jewish Liturgies', *Worship* 60 (1986), 136–8.

14. Falk, "Toward a Feminist Jewish Reconstruction of Monotheism", 153–6.

15. Emanuel Levinas, *Ethics and Infinity: Conversations with Philippe Nemo*, trans. Richard A. Cohen (Pittsburgh: Duquesne University Press, 1985). For a discussion of Levinas's metaphor of face, see Susan A. Handelman, *Fragments of Redemption: Jewish Thought and Literary Theory in Benjamin, Scholem, and Levinas* (Bloomington: Indiana University Press, 1991), 208–25.

16. B. Berakhot 6a.

17. Genesis 3:9.

18. A beautiful use of this metaphor of God as parent of grown offspring can be found in Margaret Wenig, "God is a Woman and She is Growing Older", *Reform Judaism* (fall 1992). A liturgical adaptation of this piece can be found in the Feminist Center Sliḥot Service of the American Jewish Congress, Los Angeles region, ed. Rachel Adler and Yaffa Weisman (unpublished).

19. Judith Plaskow, *Standing Again at Sinai* (San Francisco: Harper & Row, 1979), 128–34. Falk, 'Toward a Feminist Reconstruction of Monotheism', 53–6.

20. In Taylor's terminology, equal respect is a 'hypergood', Charles Taylor, *Sources of the Self: The Making of Modern Identity* (Cambridge, Mass.: Harvard University Press, 1989), 62–75.

21. Marcia Falk, 'Notes On Composing New Blessings', in *Weaving the Visions: New Patterns in Feminist Spirituality*, ed. Judith Plaskow and Carol P. Christ (San Francisco: Harper & Row, 1989), 132.

22. *Kol Haneshama* (Wyncote, Penn.: Reconstructionist Press, 1994).
23. These are listed in a section at the beginning of each service. See e.g. 5, 247.
24. Richard Hirsh, 'Spirituality and the Language of Prayer', 25.
25. Ibid. 24.
26. Linda Alcoff, 'Cultural Feminism versus Post-Structuralism: The Identity Crisis in Feminist Theory', *Signs* 13 (spring 1988), 405–36.
27. Social scientists make a distinction between sex, a biological condition, and gender, the social constructions upon sexual difference. Judith Butler argues convincingly that sex itself is in part socially constructed. Judith Butler, *Gender Trouble: Feminism and the Subversion of Identity* (New York: Routledge, 1990), esp. chs. 1 and 3.
28. An effective counterargument to this temptation to oversimplify gender symbolism is a nuanced and temperate account of the multivocality of gender symbols by Caroline Walker Bynum, 'Introduction: The Complexity of Symbols', in *Gender and Religion: On the Complexity of Symbols*, ed. Caroline Walker Bynum, Stevan Harrell, and Paula Richman (Boston: Beacon, 1986), 1–20.
29. 'Grace After Meals', in *Ha-Siddur Ha-Shalem*, trans. and annotated by Philip Birnbaum (New York: Hebrew Publishing Company, 1977), 762.
30. Lynn Gottlieb, 'Spring Cleaning Ritual on the Eve of Full Moon Nisan', in *On Being a Jewish Feminist*, ed. Susanna Heschel (New York: Schocken, 1983), 278–80. Margaret Wenig and Naomi Janowitz, *Siddur nashim* [unpublished]. *Siddur Birkat Shalom* (Somerville, Mass.: Havurat Shalom Siddur Project, 1992).
31. Sue Levi Elwell, 'Reclaiming Jewish Women's Oral Tradition? An Analysis of Rosh Hodesh', in *Women at Worship: Interpretations of North American Diversity*, ed. Marjorie Proctor-Smith and Janet Walton (Louisville, Ky.: Westminster/John Knox Press, 1993), 111–26.
32. To the question, 'Are there women?' poststructuralists answer 'no'. They 'attack the category and the concept of woman through problematizing subjectivity'. Alcoff, 'Cultural Feminism Versus Post-Structuralism', 407. Some political feminists have argued for the elimination of gender. Shulamith Firestone suggests the freeing of women from their reproductive biology through artificial reproductive technologies. *The Dialectic of Sex* (New York: Bantam, 1971), 205–42. Susan Moller Okin argues that to eliminate injustice in the family, it cannot be gender structured. *Justice, Gender and the Family* (New York: Basic Books, 1989), 3–24.
33. Theoretically, concepts such as animus–anima mitigate Jungian gender polarities and account for variation and complexity in human personalities. However, to see Jungian psychology's tendency to reinscribe gender stereotypes one need only open a book like M. Esther Harding, *Women's Mysteries, Ancient and Modern* (London: Rider, 1971).
34. Arthur Waskow, 'Feminist Judaism: The Restoration of the Moon', in *On Being a Jewish Feminist*, 261–72.
35. Virginia Ramey Mollenkott, *The Divine Feminine: Biblical Imagery of God as Female* (New York: Crossroads, 1984).
36. Gross recommends borrowing from Eastern religions. Rita M. Gross, 'Steps Toward Feminine Imagery of Deity in Jewish Theology', *Judaism* 30 (spring 1981).

37. Frymer-Kensky, 'On Feminine God-Talk', 50.
38. Ellen M. Umansky, 'Creating a Jewish Feminist Theology', in *Weaving the Visions*, 192.
39. Plaskow, *Standing Again at Sinai*, 165–6.
40. Frymer-Kensky, 'On Feminine God-Talk', 50.
41. Umansky, 'Creating a Jewish Feminist Theology', 191.
42. This name was coined by Miriam Bronstein and Shifra Lilith Klibansky Fielding in the early 1980s when they were students at Oberlin College. Both became members of Havurat Shalom in Boston. Bronstein participated in the Siddur Birkat Shalom project.
43. Frymer-Kensky, 'On Feminine God-Talk', 50–1.
44. George Steiner, *Real Presences* (Chicago: University of Chicago Press, 1989), 211–27.
45. This seems to be what Marcia Falk achieves in her interpretive *Amidah*, which is a mosaic of Jewish women's poetry. *Book of Blessings* (San Francisco: Harper & Row, 1996), 177–259.

Part V. Incarnation and Embodiment: The Word Became Flesh

Christianity, perhaps because of its contested origins as a sect within first-century Judaism, has always been more concerned than Judaism with doctrine. Despite its sour overtones to the modern ear (consider 'doctrinaire'), this word means simply 'teaching'. Christians were those who accepted certain teachings about Jesus: that he was the Messiah, that he rose from the dead, and that he was in a special way the Son of God. As early Christians hammered out their foundational beliefs, Christianity developed shared teachings on such matters as the Holy Spirit, the Trinity, salvation, and the inspiration of scripture. While the central core of Christian doctrine has remained relatively stable, its fringes are always contested and refined. Each theologian can shed a new light on accepted doctrines, and at times of upheaval even the most deeply settled doctrines have been challenged. The doctrines of Church and Eucharist were questioned during the Reformation, as were the doctrine of the inspiration of scripture in the nineteenth century and the doctrine of the Incarnation in the past two hundred years.

The doctrine of the Incarnation concerns the person and work of Christ. This includes the teaching that in Jesus of Nazareth, God became flesh and lived a human life—wholly and truly a human being and wholly and truly God. The doctrine of the Incarnation is Christianity's most signal departure from Judaism, and also the place at which the Christian God, Incarnate in Jesus of Nazareth, is literally male. Christology (broader teachings about the person and work of Christ) is a point of insuperable difficulty for some feminists. For others, no less jealous of their feminist credentials, this doctrine is the place where the full divine embrace of physicality and embodiment is evident in all its delights and pains. The pieces in this section have been chosen for thematic overlap on the one hand and, on the other, for their markedly divergent theological positions and conclusions. From post-Christian feminist (Daphne Hampson) to Orthodox Sister (Verna Harrison),

285

from Asian liberationist perspective (Sharon Bong) to philosopher of religion with an interest in queer theory (Grace Jantzen), we can see the impact of feminism across the theological enterprise and around the world.

JMS

25 Feminism and Christology

Daphne Hampson*

In this trenchant piece Daphne Hampson, a theist who is not a Christian, argues that there can be no Christology, which is genuinely a Christology, which is compatible with feminism. Christian feminists, she argues, either proclaim positions which cannot be held Christian, or, when Christian, involve the problem of Christ's non-inclusive gender and its consequences.   JMS

FEMINIST CHRISTOLOGIES

I shall now turn to the attempts by feminists of recent years to find a Christology which is at least not incompatible with their feminism. I shall suggest however that, through the very nature of Christology, there can be no Christology which is compatible with feminism.

There may be said to be three different types of Christology: 'high' Christologies, 'low' Christologies, and 'message' Christologies. A 'high' Christology is one which emphasizes Christ's divinity, a 'low' Christology his humanity, and a 'message' type Christology one which looks to his words rather than to the nature of his person. Feminists have advocated Christologies of all three types.

The problem in reconciling Christology with feminism is the very fact that, by definition, Christology speaks of Jesus as the Christ. However 'high' a Christology one may have, the divine nature of Christ is still bonded to the human nature of a human who was male. However 'low' a Christology, this human person, who is a man, is not simply human but his human nature is bonded to a divine nature. One might say that the feminist problem is that one cannot simply speak of the one nature without the other. Inescapably, if one is to have a Christology, one must bring the two natures together, and herein

---

* Daphne Hampson, excerpt from *Theology and Feminism* (Blackwell, 1990).

lies the problem. A 'message' Christology cannot simply consist in a message, a message which exists independently of the person who preached it. If it is to be a Christology, it must also concern Christ's person—whereupon all the problems which Christology entails are again present.

High Christologies

The advantage of a 'high' Christology would seem to be that there is less concentration on the maleness of Jesus, because less concentration on Jesus. If one thinks in terms of the 'cosmic Christ', or the second person of the trinity, one conceives of Christ as God rather than as a human. Moreover, in speaking, as one would tend to in a high Christology, of humanity as being summed up in Christ, or in saying that through the second person of the trinity humanity is taken into the Godhead, differences between humans may also be minimized. The problem is that this divine Christ is, in the second of his two natures, the human person Jesus, who is male. This tends to make Christ as God appear male.

A Christian feminist who has propounded what is clearly a 'high' Christology (though it may also be a 'low' one, for she wants to speak clearly of the humanity of Jesus) is Patricia Wilson-Kastner, in her book *Faith, Feminism and the Christ.*[7] Wilson-Kastner is an Episcopal priest and patristic scholar. Her theology is in effect a cosmology: through the Logos all was created; on the cross Christ gathers up our brokenness; his resurrection is proleptic (a making present through a prefiguration of what lies in the future) of the fact that alienation will in the end be overcome. Feminism likewise, she argues, is concerned for the overcoming of dualism and alienation. Hence we should '[understand] the significance of Christ as embodying values and ideals which also are sought for and valued by feminists'.[8] Trinitarianism too fits well with a feminist ethical position. '[Just as] feminism identifies interrelatedness and mutuality—equal, respectful, and nurturing relationships—as the basis of the world as it really is and as it ought to be, we can find no better understanding and image of the divine than that of the perfect and open relationships of love.'[9] Wilson-Kastner finds her 'high' Christology and her feminism to embody the same ideals.

Wilson-Kastner's emphasis is on what persons hold in common in their humanity. 'The unity of humanity is essential if humanity is to fulfill its vocation in creation. Any feminism which does not also begin with an assumption of one human race, composed of female and male, black, white, yellow, short, tall and so forth, each equally human and not bound by preconceived roles, is not compatible with the Christian faith.'[10] With this of course one may agree. I too have suggested that Christology should embrace a multiplicity. But for her the difference of sex is essentially of no more import than are differences of race. 'The division of persons into male and female is significant, but it is one category among many.'[11] That women are of the opposite sex to Christ should then, she believes, be of no great moment. The fact that she is basically thinking in terms of the resurrected, cosmic Christ again tends to minimize any distinction which there might be between a woman and Christ in regard to sex. Thus the question which confronts Christian feminists—how should they deal with the fact that the basic symbol of their religion is that of a male Christ—does not really impress her. Nor does she have a sense for the impact which the fact that Christ has been seen as male and as part of the Godhead has had on the relations of women and men in western culture. It is as though, for her, Christ is beyond sex. The question with which we are concerned is not tackled.

Furthermore, I think there is a problem for Christians today in thinking in terms of this non-gendered cosmic Christ which forms the key to her Christology (and I am sure I would have thought this at the time that I counted myself a Christian). Wilson-Kastner apparently makes no distinction between, on the one hand, a factual account of what is the case, and, on the other, a mythological symbolism. She moves (for example) between speaking of the crucifixion of Christ (fact) to the cosmic nature of Christ—which can hardly be said to be 'true' in the sense of an empirically known fact. She will frequently tell us that the fathers of the church, or the bible, state such things to be the case, as though that were the end of the matter. I do not doubt that people in an earlier age may well have thought in terms of the kind of cosmic world picture in terms of which she herself thinks. (It is difficult to tell how far theologians in the patristic period believed themselves to be, when they spoke of the cosmic Christ or the doctrine of the trinity, stretching language to its ultimate and speaking metaphorically. One like Gregory of Nyssa, an architect of the doctrine of the trinity, was deeply conscious that God was beyond all human description.) To simply state that the fathers or biblical authors believed something does not address the question as to whether they were right, or whether our picture of the world has not so much changed as to make theirs fantastic. In an age in which we have a keen sense for the difference between fact and symbol, Wilson-Kastner makes no distinction. For example, she takes the Nicaean expression of belief as literally true, speaking not simply of the Logos but of Jesus (*sic*) becoming incarnate. What can that mean?

Wilson-Kastner believes that Christianity proclaims (as indeed it may well) that alienation is overcome in Christ. Again, we may ask, is this a faith statement, or a statement of what is the case? Further, she argues from the fact that if one wills alienation to be overcome, that indeed it is overcome. 'There must be some reality that can heal the fragmentation of the world.'[12] Must there be? One could argue that brokenness and alienation are fundamental to the world. Though she has much to say of brokenness, my problem with her book is precisely that, through her swift movement to a triumphant conclusion, symbolized by the resurrection and the unity of humanity, she does not allow there genuinely to be brokenness.

I would then at any stage have found it difficult to believe in the cosmic Christ in whom, for her, lies the key to the solution to the world's affliction and the alienation of women. Evidently moves which for one person seem plausible are simply not moves which others can make. The debate is interesting, for it becomes evident that women who count themselves feminists may otherwise have a very different sense of reality.

Low Christologies

The advantage of a low Christology would seem to be that Jesus is considered to be just another human, one among us, our brother. Such a Christology stresses Christ's humanity rather than his divinity. The fact of Jesus' maleness then would seem to be of no more import than is his or her sexuality in the case of any other human being. It is not, in a low Christology, that we have a divine Christ who is male. The problem however is that were it simply to be said of Jesus that he was a human like any other who lived in history we should not have a Christology. A Christian position must necessarily hold of this human being Jesus that he existed (or exists) in relation to God as has no other. Either it must be said, in traditional terms, that, together with his human nature, he also had, in one person, a divine nature; or in some other way he must be held to be unique. But then we have present a male human being who, in some sense, is considered unique.

The problem with a low Christology becomes apparent through considering a liturgical situation. We have already said, that of a liturgy in which no mention was made of Christ, we might hold that it was meaningful, even theistic, but that it could not rightly be called Christian. In a Christian liturgy mention of Christ must necessarily be made, as is the case of no other human being. Indeed, through the fact that he is spoken of as though there present, something different is being said of Christ than of anyone else. No Christology can be so low that it overcomes the feminist difficulty by saying of Jesus that he was no different from every other human who has lived. A Christian position must necessarily have a *Christology*. The question is then posed as to whether one can reconcile that Christology with feminism. Indeed one might argue that talk of Jesus as our 'brother', emphasizing his humanity, makes Jesus more intrusively male than if one were casting him in the role of the cosmic Christ.

The difficulty a low Christology poses for feminists was brought home to me some years ago in attending a eucharistic liturgy, which I believe had been written by Carter Heyward, whose work I shall shortly mention. Only women were present and the service was orientated towards women. In place of a sermon there was a time of quiet in which women present spoke to the theme of 'creation', some from the perspective of giving birth. How jarring it seemed then that, at the consecration, reference had necessarily to be made to the man Jesus of Nazareth: he had to take centre stage. Not simply was he mentioned, as men may well have been in the prayers of intercession, but he was actively made present as lord of the situation. In such a liturgy it becomes apparent, in a way in which in a traditional liturgy, with a man celebrating, it does not, because there is not the same incongruity, that women are, at the very core of their religion, dependent on the male world.

Contrast the situation which pertains when a group of men celebrate the eucharist together, as has often been the case for example in a monastic setting. The central action revolves around persons of the same sex and figures of speech having the same gender reference as they themselves. Mention is made of a male Christ, God is conceived in male terms, and biblical readings doubtless largely concern the doings of men. Incidentally women may be mentioned, in prayers or as subsidiary figures in readings. How much more is the lack of symmetry between men and women apparent when one considers the fact that a congregation of nuns must invite an outsider, an outsider who, in many countries in the present Anglican and in the Roman Catholic context, has to be a man, to celebrate for them. If he does not arrive the action cannot proceed. Within the Christian context women must necessarily refer to, and exercise a dependence upon, the world of men, of a kind which men would not conceive of having in relation to the world of women.

Heyward, of whom I have just made mention, writes of Jesus as follows: 'Jesus matters only if he was fully, *and only*, human.' And further: he was 'a human person who knew and loved God'.[13] If this is all she thinks, she surely cannot be considered Christian. I too, as one who is not a Christian, might well say of him that he knew and loved God. Why then should she look in particular to Jesus? She writes: 'We cannot simply shift Jesus from centre-stage and replace him with humanity or God by wishing it were so.'[14] Why she should think this, apart from consideration of her own biographical context, is unclear. She, evidently, is Christocentric, while another (as I have always been) is theocentric. But I too would want to say that (as someone has expressed it) we see God through a Christ-shaped window: I have no doubt that, as a western person, my understanding of God has, in part at least, been shaped by the person who was Jesus of Nazareth. But again this does not make me a Christian. Heyward however shifts ground: 'I am hooked on Jesus. I could no more pretend that the Jesus-figure, *indeed the Jesus of the kerygma*, is unimportant to me than I could deny the significance of my parents and my past in the shaping of my future.'[15] The term *kerygma*, proclamation, is normally held to refer, in such a phrase as 'the Jesus of the kerygma', to the proclamation concerning Jesus; that is to say the proclamation of him as the resurrected one, as Lord and Saviour. To say this is very different from the assertion that he was simply human—and that is all. Jesus, in such a statement, is held to be unique, if only through the fact that this is the human of whom it must be said that God raised him. Heyward has a Christology (one close to the primitive Christology of the second chapter of Acts for example). If Jesus is our brother, he is a brother of a very special sort. But then the problem returns.

A 'Message' Christology

The advantage of a 'message' Christology would seem to be that, with the shift of concentration from the person of Christ to his message, we circumvent the problems which present themselves when the symbol of a male person is understood to be central to Christianity. Many feminists who are Christians are surely attracted to Christianity through the compelling nature of the person who was Jesus of

Nazareth and the power of his message, which resonates with their own beliefs and values.

A problem however presents itself similar to that which we have discussed when considering a 'low' Christology. To be concerned simply for Jesus' message, a message which anyone could have preached and which is now acknowledged quite independently of the person who preached it, is not to hold a Christian position. It is to hold a humanist position, to be one who, like Gandhi, finds Jesus' message striking. Compare such a position with the position that there is a kerygma to be preached about Jesus. An example of one who held this latter position is the existentialist theologian of the last generation Rudolf Bultmann. Bultmann, as I mentioned, never speaks in terms of a two-nature Christology of the type which arose in the Greek world. But Christ does for him have a uniqueness; and thus I count his position a Christian one. For Bultmann, the resurrection is not an event in our world (for resurrections he would hold, as I, do not occur in our world), but something of far greater magnitude, an eschatalogical event which represents the breaking in of another world order. It takes place in another dimension from our normal history, in God's history. Now the resurrection (an event of another order) is however the resurrection of the man who died (a normal event in our world). Thus Jesus is unique, for it is to be said of him as of none other that this is the man whom God raised, and his resurrection forms the turning-point of history. There is then, in Bultmann's theology, a necessary reference to the Christ event. (There are concomitant problems for the feminist.)

An interesting comparison here can be made with the position of Rosemary Ruether. Ruether's interest (as that also of Bultmann) is in Jesus' message, a message in her case held to concern the coming of the kingdom, the vindication of the poor and the creation of a just social order. The centre of her theology is the Christian vision. Women—who have been among the poorest of the poor—are primordially those who will be liberated. But how may this be said to be a Christology? If all she wants to speak of is a message and a vision then there is no reason to call this position Christian. Humanists too may have a vision, perhaps one which draws from Jesus Christ. Marxists have a vision, and Ruether is very much in tune with left-wing thought. There can be no incompatibility between being a feminist and taking on board the Christian vision. But to speak in terms of a vision involves no necessary reference to history, or to any particular person; one could make the vision one's own without knowing with whom it originated. If one simply wishes to speak of a social vision, one may without further ado drop any reference to the Christian 'myth', a myth which is so problematical for women. One need make no reference to a male human person who is proclaimed Lord. But to be Christian is not simply to preach Jesus' message. It is also to proclaim a message about Jesus—and therein for a feminist lie all the problems.

If one holds, of Christ, that he was, in whatever way, unique, then one is clearly a Christian. There arises the problem of reconciling a religion which has a unique Christ (who in his human nature is male) with feminism. But if Jesus of Nazareth is not thought to be unique, and the Christian story is just a myth, why, one must ask, should one who is a feminist choose to take up this particular myth when it is so male, and has central to it a male person who is held to be unique? Bultmann's is clearly a Christian position (and the problems arise for feminists). Ruether's, if she is not saying in any sense of Christ that he is unique, surely cannot be said so to be. In which case why not jettison this religion which has been so harmful to women?[16]

CONSERVATIVE CHRISTOLOGIES

I call 'conservative', for the purposes of the discussion in this chapter, Christologies which hold the maleness of Christ to be essential to his nature, and the fact that Christ was male to be central to Christianity. Conservatives do not essentially believe that the maleness of Christ in any way harms women. Women also have their place in God's creation. Indeed conservatives who are Catholics understand the feminine, as also the masculine, to be woven into a cosmic picture. The maleness of Christ may be said to form the linchpin of this picture.

Such an understanding of reality on the part of a Catholic conservative was well expressed by the Anglican bishop Graham Leonard, in his speech against the ordination of women to the General Synod of the Church of England in 1978.

I believe that the Scriptures speak of God as Father, that Christ was incarnate as a male, that he chose men to be his apostles ... not because of social conditioning, but because in the order of creation headship and authority is symbolically and fundamentally associated with maleness. For the same reason the highest vocation of any created being was given to a woman, Mary, as representative of mankind in our response to God because symbolically and fundamentally, the response of sacrificial giving is associated with femaleness. I do not believe it is merely the result of social conditioning that in the Scriptures, in the Jewish and Christian tradition, mankind and the Church is presented as feminine to God, to whom our response must be one of obedience in contrast to those religions in which the divine is regarded as contained within creation and is to be manipulated or cajoled in order to provide what man needs. For a woman to represent the Headship of Christ and the Divine Initiative would, *unless her feminine gifts were obscured or minimized,* evoke a different approach to God from those who worship. . . . As the American Protestant layman Thomas Howard has said 'Jews and Christians worship the God who has gone to vast and prolonged pains to disclose himself to us as he not she, as King and not Queen, and for Christians as Father not Mother, and who sent his Son not his daughter in his final unveiling of himself for our eyes. These are terrible mysteries and we have no warrant to tinker with them.'[17]

It is thus believed by Catholic conservatives to be no chance that the incarnation took place in a male human person. The Vatican declaration that women cannot be ordained to the priesthood states:

[The incarnation] cannot be disassociated from the economy of salvation; it is, indeed, in harmony with the entirety of God's plan. . . . For the salvation offered by God to men and women . . . took on, from the Old Testament Prophets onwards, the privileged form of a nuptial mystery: for God the Chosen People is seen as his ardently loved spouse. . . . Christ is the Bridegroom; the Church is his bride, whom he loves because he has gained her by his blood.[18]

Again, the Anglican V. A. Demant, arguing against the ordination of women, writes of the Christian religion: 'It is a Logos religion. And in so far as we can use gender imagery for these things the Logos is a masculine principle. . . . The Logos is the active, manifesting, creative-destructive, redemptive power of the godhead.'[19] Again, Hans Urs von Balthasar, at a later date the author of a statement officially sponsored by the Vatican in support of its declaration, describes Jesus' self-giving on the cross, re-enacted in the mass, in explicitly sexual terms.

In its origin [Christianity] presents to man and woman a glorious picture of sexual integrity: the Son of God who has become man and flesh, knowing from inside his Father's work and perfecting it in the total self-giving of himself, not only of his spiritual but precisely also of his physical powers, giving not only to one individual but to all. What else is his Eucharist but, at a higher level, an endless act of fruitful out-pouring of his whole flesh, such as a man can only achieve for a moment with a limited organ of his body?[20]

For Balthasar, Mary plays the 'female' part. She is 'the favoured place where God can, and wills to, be brought into the world'.[21]

It is within such a framework of thought that it is contended that a priest must necessarily be male. (It should be noted however that not every argument for the necessity of a male priesthood necessarily entails a complete picture of God's dispensation as embodying male and female principles. It may simply be said that it is just a 'fact' that Jesus was male, and that therefore priests should be.) The Vatican declaration puts forward, as one argument among others, a Christo-logical argument against the ordination of women. The context which it presumes is the Catholic teaching (found for example in Thomas Aquinas) that that which becomes the sign of the sacrament must be appropriate to that which it signifies. Thus in baptism water must be used; for extreme unction there must be the presence of a sick person. The declaration states: 'The whole sacramental economy is in fact based upon natural signs, on symbols imprinted upon the human psychology: "Sacramental signs", says Thomas Aquinas, "represent what they signify by natural resemblance".' It is then contended that: 'There would not be this "natural resemblance" which must exist between Christ and his minister if the role of Christ were not taken by a man. In such a case it would be difficult to see in the minister the image of Christ. For Christ himself was and remains a man.' The priest 'acts . . . *in persona Christi*, taking the role of Christ to the point of being his very image'.[22] The official commentary explains that the word 'persona' designated, in the ancient theatre, a part played using a particular mask: 'The priest takes the part of Christ, lending him his voice and gestures.' Thomas Aquinas says: ' "The priest enacts the image of Christ." ' The division of sex, it is said, goes much deeper than that for example of race and is fundamental to creation.[23]

Let us juxtapose this argument and that put forward by Norris, which I propounded in my discussion of patristic Christology: namely that Christ took on humanity, such that maleness is not of Christo-logical significance. Those who hold the position expressed in the declaration may in turn respond that indeed women are, as are men, 'in Christ'; the declaration speaks of Christ as the first-born of all humanity. Yet they may also say that they believe it to be of signifi-cance that the particular instance of humanity taken on by the second person of the trinity in the incarnation was a male human being. This, they say, was not chance, for maleness is intrinsic to the symbolism of God's initiative taken towards humankind in the act of redemption. If this is to be represented symbolically, the one who acts *in persona*

Christi must be male. I do not see that there is any counter argument to this. One should however perhaps comment on the fact that in this case sexual imagery has been understood to be fundamental to the act of salvation, and indeed to the action of the eucharist. It may be held to be doubtful that early Christians conceived of the eucharist in such terms. Was it not considered by them rather to be a celebratory meal, one which recalled the liberation from Egypt of the children of Israel and foreshadowed the banquet which should take place in the eschaton?

An interesting response to the Vatican's theology by one who is a Catholic is that of Christopher Kiesling. Kiesling argues that what constitutes the priest as the image of Christ is the character of orders, that is to say that the person is a priest. (A character, in Catholic Aristotelian theology, is a similitude or image impressed by another.) He comments: 'It is not a person's maleness which constitutes that person the representative image of Christ, but a person's having the sacerdotal character, the instrumental priestly power to perform those actions signifying the giving of divine gifts, a power deriving through ordination from Christ, *the* donor of God's grace.'[24] Thomas Aquinas indeed thinks that a woman cannot receive the character of ordination. But why? Because, as he believes, the state of woman is that of subjection: *quia mulier statum subjectionis habet*. Kiesling concludes: 'It does not appeaer that femaleness, femininity, womanhood *as such* is the barrier to woman's receiving holy orders, but femaleness *in a state of subjection*.'[25] Likewise Kari Børresen notes that (in this respect unlike Bonaventura) 'Thomas does not say expressly that a priest ought to belong to the male sex because Christ, whom he represents, became incarnate in this sex.'[26] Thomas' belief that woman's state is one of subjection derives, as we have seen, from the false biological presuppositions which he took from Aristotle. An indication as to what his position would logically have had to be, had he not held these false presuppositions, is evident from his discussion of the validity of baptism when administered by a woman. An initial objection which he poses is, interestingly, that it is not fitting that a woman should represent a father. He answers this objection however with the reply that, whereas in human generation a woman can only be the passive principle, in spiritual generation neither man nor woman function by virtue of their own powers, but only as instruments of the power of Christ. The baptism is valid.

However, the framers of the declaration have not quite been answered; for Thomas clearly thinks that God chooses certain things and persons to become sacramental signs because they provide the more suitable signification. Kiesling writes: 'We must take seriously . . . all the implications in the psychological and sociological realms of male priests to represent Christ.'[27] And Børresen concedes (of Thomas): 'His thought definitely is, that there should be conformity between the two kinds of instruments of Christ: His human nature and the priest.'[28] The Dominican Jerry Miller however has argued that the Vatican Declaration has 'misapplied [Thomas'] teaching on the issue of sign-value to support its argument from natural resemblance'. With Kiesling he argues that it is that femininity signifies inferiority to Thomas, and not femininity as such, which makes a woman unsuitable.[29]

A further line of argument which may be pursued against the declaration is that, according to Catholic theology, the power of orders lies in the soul, which is the same for both sexes, and not the body. Arguing against those who said that women could not be ordained, the Anglican theologian of the last generation Leonard Hodgson comments that to say 'that a woman is incapable of receiving the priestly or episcopal character involves saying that her sexual differentiation carries with it a deficiency in spiritual receptivity and power'.[30] Intriguingly, in his third proposition in *favour* of the argument that women can be priested, Thomas himself comments that orders lie in the soul, which is the same for both sexes, a point to which curiously (as George Tavard has pointed out) he makes no reply.[31] Thomas seems however to contradict himself in this matter, presupposing elsewhere that orders relate to the body, as when he writes: 'Since in matters pertaining to the soul woman does not differ from man as to the thing, . . . it follows that she can receive the gift of prophecy and the like, but not the sacrament of Orders.'[32]

The Vatican declaration furthermore expressly rules out the objection that, in the eucharist, it is the risen Christ who is represented; and that as such he has no sex. Referring to the biblical saying that in the resurrection men and women do not marry, the declaration comments that this does not mean that the distinction between man and woman is suppressed in the glorified state. (Such a position must, one would think, constitute the strongest provocation for feminists to conclude that maleness is, in Christianity, intrinsic to the Godhead no less!)

Conservative Protestant Christians may pursue what is a rather different Christology which issues in opposition to the ordination of women. Headship and authority are, it is said, properly vested in the male: thus Christ is head of the church, and hence also women should not exercise the authority involved in being in charge of a congregation. Such a line of argument is based primarily upon scripture, and does not necessarily involve a notion of there being male and female principles in the universe. In the case of some evangelical writers (though not Barth) it may also be said that male dominance is fundamental to creation and found in all known human societies. The evangelical Gordon Wenham pursues this line.[33] An interpretation of scripture is presupposed in which all verses must comport with one another. The scriptures are then read, from Genesis to Paul, as supporting male headship.

In response to this line of thought it may well be pointed out that the subordination of woman to man is depicted in scripture as having resulted from the fall. Subordination is, in the Genesis text, the punishment meted out to woman. It is of interest that it would seem to be the case that the Galatians verse, that in Christ 'there is neither Jew nor Greek, there is neither slave nor free, there is no male and female', makes direct reference to Genesis. (The parallelism of the three statements is interrupted by the different form of the third, and the particular words used for male and female, which are not those which one would expect, are the same as those which the Septuagint—the Greek translation of the Hebrew scriptures with which Paul would have been familiar—uses in the Genesis verse.)[34] If this is the case, then Paul is in effect saying that the subordination, which owes to the fall, is overcome in Christ, the second Adam. It is surely the redeemed order of creation, in which there is no subordination, rather than the fallen order, which should be symbolized in the ministry of the Christian church. If however a writer believes the creation of woman from man prior to the fall to imply subordination, then there is no answer possible.

Notes

1. I owe this point to John Riches ('The Case for the Ordination of Women to the Priesthood', unpublished paper given to the meeting of the Anglican Orthodox Joint Doctrinal Discussions, Athens, 1978 (London: Anglican Consultative Council AO/JDD 185), p. 34).
2. 'Interpreting the Doctrine of the Incarnation', in D. R. McDonald (ed.), *The Myth/Truth of God Incarnate* (Wilton, Conn.: Morehouse-Barlow, 1979), 80–1.
3. 'The Ordination of Women and the "Maleness" of Christ', *Anglican Theological Review*, Supplementary Series, 6 (June 1976), 69–80.
4. Unless it be said that maleness belongs to the essential character of priesthood, an argument which will be considered below.

5. The Constitution of the World Council of Churches, adopted at Amsterdam, 30 Aug. 1948 (W. A. Visser 't Hooft (ed.), *The First Assembly of the World Council of Churches*, vol. v, London: SCM Press, 1949, p. 197).

6. How different from e.g. Gregory of Nyssa, who writes that the three persons are as links in a chain, so that in the presence of one the others are immediately present; or from the patristic analogy of the Trinity as being like the moving pattern on a wall caused by the reflection of the sun's rays on water, so intimately are the three ways in which God is God one.

7. *Faith, Feminism and the Christ* (Philadelphia: Fortress Press, 1983).

8. Ibid. 92.

9. Ibid. 126.

10. Ibid. 60.

11. Ibid. 57.

12. Ibid. 52.

13. *The Redemption of God: A Theology of Mutual Relation* (Washington, DC: University Press of America, 1982), 31–2, emphasis mine.

14. Ibid.

15. Ibid. 196, emphasis mine.

16. For further discussion of Ruether's position in relation to Bultmann's see Daphne Hampson and Rosemary Ruether, 'Is There a Place for Feminists in a Christian Church?', *New Blackfriars* 68 (801) (Jan. 1987).

17. Speech to the General Synod of the Church of England, 8 Nov. 1978 (Church Literature Association for the Church Union, copy in the possession of the author).

18. *Inter Insigniores: Declaration on the Question of the Admission of Women to the Ministerial Priesthood*, 15 Oct. 1976, in L. Swidler and A. Swidler (eds.), *Women Priests: A Catholic Commentary on the Vatican Declaration* (New York: Paulist Press, 1977), 44.

19. 'Why the Christian Priesthood is Male', in *Women and Holy Orders: Report of the Archbishops' Commission*, appendix C (London: Church Information Office, 1966), 101.

20. 'The Christian and Chastity', in *Elucidations*, trans. J. Riches (London: SPCK, 1975), 150 (1971).

21. 'Welches Gewicht hat die ununterbrochene Tradition der Kirche bezüglich der Zuordnung des Priestertums an den Mann?', hg. von der deutschsprachigen Redaktion des 'Osservatore Romano', in *Die Sendung der Frau in der Kirche: Die Erklärung Inter insigniores der Kongregation für die Glaubenslehre mit Kommentar und theologischen Studien* (Verlag Butzon & Bercker Kevelaer), 57, my translation.

22. Swidler and Swidler, *Women Priests*, 43, 44, 43.

23. 'The Ordination of Women: Official Commentary from the Sacred Congregation for the Doctrine of the Faith on its declaration *Inter Insigniores*: "Women and the Priesthood" of 15th October 1976' (pamphlet) (London: Catholic Truth Society, undated).

24. 'Aquinas on Persons' Representation in Sacraments', in Swidler and Swidler, *Women Priests*, 254. It should be pointed out that we do not know what Thomas's opinion would have been in his maturity. The text in the *Summa*, added after his death, is taken word for word from the early *Commentary on the Sentences of Peter Lombard*.

25. 'Persons' Representation', 255.
26. *Subordination and Equivalence: The Nature and Role of Women in Augustine and Thomas Aquinas*, trans. C. H. Talbot (Washington, DC: University Press of America, 1981), 242.
27. 'Persons' Representation', 257.
28. K. E. Børresen, *Subordination and Equivalence: The Nature and Role of Women in Augustine and Thomas Aquinas*, trans. C. H. Talbot (Washington, DC: University Press of America, 1981), 242.
29. 'A Note on Aquinas and Ordination of Women', *New Blackfriars* 61 (719) (Apr. 1980), 190.
30. 'Theological Objections to the Admission of Women to Holy Orders' (pamphlet) (Anglican Group for the Ordination of Women, 1974), 8 (1967).
31. 'The Scholastic Doctrine', in Swidler and Swidler, *Women Priests*. ST, part III, supplement, qu. 39, art. 1, ad 1 obj.
32. Ibid. qu. 39, art. 1, ad 1 obj.
33. 'The Ordination of Women: Why is it so Divisive?', *Churchman* 92 (4) (1978), 310–19.
34. Cf. Krister Stendahl, 'The Bible and the Role of Women' (pamphlet) (Philadelphia: Fortress Press, Facet Books, Biblical Series 15, 1966), 32.

The Challenge of the Darker Sister

Jacquelyn Grant*

Black American feminists were amongst the first to challenge the hegemonic claims of white women to speak for all women. This was an important stage of maturation for feminism generally and for feminist theology in particular. Womanist theology arises from the experience of Black women in the United States. Jacquelyn Grant argues here that Jesus, as co-sufferer, retains a powerful place in Black spirituality. Christ 'found in the experiences of Black women, is a Black woman'.   JMS

....

THE USE OF THE BIBLE IN THE WOMANIST TRADITION

....

Theological investigation into the experiences of Christian Black women reveals that Black women considered the Bible to be a major source for religious validation in their lives. Though Black women's relationship with God preceded their introduction to the Bible, this Bible gave some content to their God-consciousness.[1] The source for Black women's understanding of God has been twofold: first, God's revelation directly to them, and secondly, God's revelation as witnessed in the Bible and as read and heard in the context of their experience. The understanding of God as creator, sustainer, comforter, and liberator took on life as they agonized over their pain, and celebrated the hope that as God delivered the Israelites, they would be delivered as well. The God of the Old and New Testament became real in the consciousness of oppressed Black women. Though they were politically impotent, they were able to appropriate certain themes of the Bible which spoke to their reality. For example, Jarena Lee, a nineteenth-century Black woman preacher in the African Methodist Episcopal Church, constantly emphasized the theme "Life

---

* Jacquelyn Grant, excerpt from *White Women's Christ and Black Women's Jesus: Feminist Christology and Womanist Response* (Scholars Press, 1989). Used by permission of the American Academy of Religion.

and Liberty" in her sermons which were always biblically based. This interplay of scripture and experience was exercised by many other Black women. An ex-slave woman revealed that when her experience negated certain oppressive interpretations of the Bible given by White preachers, she, through engaging the biblical message for herself, rejected them. Consequently, she also dismissed White preachers who distorted the message in order to maintain slavery. Her grandson, Howard Thurman, speaks of her use of the Bible in this way:

"During the days of slavery," she said, "the master's minister would occasionally hold services for the slaves. Always the white minister used as his text something from Paul. 'Slaves be obedient to them that are your masters . . ., as unto Christ.' Then he would go on to show how, if we were good and happy slaves, God would bless us. I promised my Maker that if I ever learned to read and if freedom ever came, I would not read that part of the Bible."[2]

What we see here is perhaps more than a mere rejection of a White preacher's interpretation of the Bible, but an exercise in internal critique of the Bible. The Bible must be read and interpreted in the light of Black women's own experience of oppression and God's revelation within that context. Womanists must, like Sojourner, "compare the teachings of the Bible with the witness" in them.[3]

To do Womanist Theology, then, we must read and hear the Bible and engage it within the context of our own experience. This is the only way that it can make sense to people who are oppressed. Black women of the past did not hesitate in doing this and we must do no less.

THE ROLE OF JESUS IN THE WOMANIST TRADITION

In the experiences of Black people, Jesus was "all things."[4] Chief among these, however, was the belief in Jesus as the divine co-sufferer, who empowers them in situations of oppression. For Christian Black women in the past, Jesus was their central frame of reference. They identified with Jesus because they believed that Jesus identified with them. As Jesus was persecuted and made to suffer undeservedly, so were they. His suffering culminated in the crucifixion. Their crucifixion included rape, and babies being sold. But Jesus' suffering was not the suffering of a mere human, for Jesus was understood to be God incarnate. As Harold Carter observed of Black prayers in general, there was no difference made between the persons of the trinity, Jesus, God, or the Holy Spirit. "All of these proper names for God were used interchangeably in prayer language. Thus, Jesus was the one who speaks the world into creation. He was the power behind the Church. . . ."[5]

Black women's affirmation of Jesus as God meant that White people were not God. One old slave woman clearly demonstrated this as she prayed:

Dear Massa Jesus, we all uns beg Ooner [you] come make us a call dis yere day. We is nutting but poor Etiopian women and people ain't tink much 'bout we. We ain't trust any of dem great high people for come to we church, but do' you is de one great Massa, great too much dan Massa Linkum, you ain't shame to care for we African people.[6]

This slave woman did not hesitate to identify her struggles and pain with those of Jesus. In fact, the common struggle made her know that Jesus would respond to her beck and call.

Come to we, dear Massa Jesus. De sun, he hot too much, de road am dat long and boggy [sandy] and we ain't got no buggy for send and fetch Ooner. But Massa, you 'member how you walked dat hard walk up Calvary and ain't weary but tink about we all dat way. We know you ain't weary for to come to we. We pick out de torns, de prickles, de brier, de backslidin' and de quarrel and de sin out of you path so dey shan't hurt Ooner pierce feet no more.[7]

As she is truly among the people at the bottom of humanity, she can make things comfortable for Jesus even though she may have nothing to give him—no water, no food—but she can give tears and love. She continues:

Come to we, dear Massa Jesus. We all uns ain't got no good cool water for give you when you thirsty. You know, Massa, de drought so long, and the well so low, ain't nutting but mud to drink. But we gwine to take de 'munion cup and fill it wid de tear of repentance, and love clean out of we heart. Dat all we hab to gib you, good Massa.[8]

For Black women, the role of Jesus unraveled as they encountered him in their experience as one who empowers the weak. In this vein, Jesus was such a central part of Sojourner Truth's life that all of her sermons made him the starting point. When asked by a preacher if the source of her preaching was the Bible, she responded "No honey, can't preach from de Bible—can't read a letter."[9] Then she explained; "When I preaches, I has jest one text to preach from, an' I always preaches from this one. My text is, 'When I found Jesus!' "[10] In this sermon Sojourner Truth recounts the events and struggles of her life from the time her parents were brought from Africa and sold "up an' down, an' hither an' yon . . ."[11] to the time that she met Jesus within the context of her struggles for dignity of Black people and women. Her encounter with Jesus brought such joy that she became over-whelmed with love and praise:

Praise, praise, praise to the Lord! An' I begun to feel such a love in my soul as I never felt before—love to all creatures. An' then, all of a sudden, it stopped, an' I said, Dar's de white folks that have abused you, an' beat you, an' abused your people—think o' them! But then there came another rush of love through my soul, an' I cried out loud—"Lord, I can love *even de white folks!*"[12]

This love was not a sentimental, passive love. It was a tough, active love that empowered her to fight more fiercely for the freedom of her people. For the rest of her life she continued speaking at abolition and women's rights gatherings, condemning the horrors of oppression.

THE SIGNIFICANCE OF JESUS IN THE WOMANIST TRADITION

More than anyone, Black theologians have captured the essence of the significance of Jesus in the lives of Black people which to an extent includes Black women. They all hold that the Jesus of history is important for understanding who he was and his significance for us today. By and large they have affirmed that this Jesus is the Christ, that is, God incarnate. They have argued that in the light of our experience, Jesus meant freedom.[13] They have maintained that Jesus means free-dom from the sociopsychological, psychocultural, economic and polit-ical oppression of Black people. In other words, Jesus is a political messiah.[14] "To free [humans] from bondage was Jesus' own definition of his ministry."[15] This meant that as Jesus identified with the lowly of his day, he now identifies with the lowly of this day, who in the American context are Black people. The identification is so real that Jesus Christ in fact becomes Black. It is important to note that Jesus' blackness is not a result of ideological distortion of a few Black thinkers, but a result of careful Christological investigation. Cone examines the sources of Christology and concludes that Jesus is Black because "Jesus was a Jew." He explains:

It is on the basis of the soteriological meaning of the particularity of his Jewishness that theology must affirm the christological significance of Jesus' present blackness. He *is* black because he was a Jew. The affirmation of the Black Christ can be understood when the significance of his past Jewishness is related dialectically to the significance of his present blackness. On the one hand, the Jewishness of Jesus located him in the context of the Exodus, thereby connecting his appearance in Palestine with God's liberation of oppressed Israelites from Egypt. Unless Jesus were truly from Jewish ancestry, it would make little theological sense to say that he is the fulfillment of God's covenant with Israel. But on the other hand, the blackness of Jesus brings out the soteriological meaning of his Jewishness for our contemporary situation when Jesus' person is understood in the context of the cross and resurrection.[16]

The condition of Black people today reflects the cross of Jesus. Yet the resurrection brings the hope that liberation from oppression is immanent. The resurrected Black Christ signifies this hope.

Cone further argues that this christological title, "The Black Christ", is not validated by its universality, but, in fact, by its particularity. Its significance lies in whether or not the christological title "points to God's universal will to liberate particular oppressed people from inhumanity."[17] These particular oppressed peoples to which Cone refers are characterized in Jesus' parable on the Last Judgment as "the least." "The least in America are literally and symbolically present in Black people."[18] This notion of "the least" is attractive because it descriptively locates the condition of Black women. "The least" are those people who have no water to give, but offer what they have, as the old slave woman cited above says in her prayer. Black women's experience in general is such a reality. Their tri-dimensional reality renders their particular situation a complex one. One could say that not only are they the oppressed of the oppressed, but their situation represents "the particular within the particular."

But is this just another situation that takes us deeper into the abyss of theological relativity? I would argue that it is not, because it is in the context of Black women's experience where the particular connects up with the universal. By this I mean that in each of the three dynamics of oppression, Black women share in the reality of a broader community. They share race suffering with Black men; with White women and other Third World women, they are victims of sexism; and with poor Blacks and Whites, and other Third World peoples, especially women, they are disproportionately poor. To speak of Black women's tri-dimensional reality, therefore, is not to speak of Black women exclusively, for there is an implied universality which connects them with others.

Likewise, with Jesus Christ, there was an implied universality which made him identify with others—the poor, the woman, the stranger. To affirm Jesus' solidarity with the "least of the people" is not an exercise in romanticized contentment with one's oppressed status in life. For as the Resurrection signified that there is more to life than the cross for Jesus Christ, for Black women it signifies that their tri-dimensional oppressive existence is not the end, but it merely represents the context in which a particular people struggle to experience hope and liberation. Jesus Christ thus represents a three-fold significance: first he identifies with the "little people," Black women, where they are; secondly, he affirms the basic humanity of these, "the least"; and thirdly, he inspires active hope in the struggle for resurrected, liberated existence.

To locate the Christ in Black people is a radical and necessary step, but an understanding of Black women's reality challenges us to go further. Christ among the least must also mean Christ in the community of Black women. William Eichelberger was able to recognize this as he further particularized the significance of the Blackness of Jesus by locating Christ in Black women's community. He was able to see Christ not only as Black male but also Black female.

God, in revealing Himself and His attributes from time to time in His creaturely existence, has exercised His freedom to formalize His appearance in a variety of ways. . . . God revealed Himself at a point in the past as Jesus the Christ a Black male. My reasons for affirming the Blackness of Jesus of Nazareth are much different from that of the white apologist. . . . God wanted to identify with that segment of mankind which had suffered most, and is still suffering. . . . I am constrained to believe that God in our times has updated His form of revelation to western society. It is my feeling that God is now manifesting Himself, and has been for over 450 years, in the form of the Black American Woman as mother, as wife, as nourisher, sustainer and preserver of life, the Suffering Servant who is despised and rejected by men, a personality of sorrow who is acquainted with grief. The Black Woman has borne our griefs and carried our sorrows. She has been wounded because of American white society's transgressions and bruised by white iniquities. It appears that she may be the instrumentality through whom God will make us whole.[19]

Granted, Eichelberger's categories for God and woman are very traditional. Nevertheless, the significance of his thought is that he was able to conceive of the Divine reality as other than a Black male messianic figure.

CHALLENGES FOR WOMANIST CHRISTOLOGY

Although I have argued that the White feminist analysis of theology and Christology is inadequate for salvific efficacy with respect to Black women, I do contend that it is not totally irrelevant to Black women's needs. I believe that Black women should take seriously the feminist analysis, but they should not allow themselves to be coopted on behalf of the agendas of White women, for as I have argued, they are often racist unintentionally or by intention.

The first challenge, therefore, is to Black women. Feminists have identified some problems associated with language and symbolism of the church, theology, and Christology. They have been able to show that exclusive masculine language and imagery are contributing factors undergirding the oppression of women.

In addressing the present day, womanists must investigate the relationship between the oppression of women and theological symbolism. Even though Black women have been able to transcend some of the oppressive tendencies of White male (and Black male) articulated theologies, careful study reveals that some traditional symbols are inadequate for us today. The Christ understood as the stranger, the outcast, the hungry, the weak, the poor, makes the traditional male Christ (Black and White) less significant. Even our sisters, the womanists of the past, though they exemplified no problems with the symbols themselves, they had some suspicions about the effects of a male image of the divine, for they did challenge the oppressive and distorted use of it in the church's theology. In so doing, they were able to move from a traditional oppressive Christology, with respect to women, to an egalitarian Christology. This kind of equalitarian Christology was operative in Jarena Lee's argument for the right of women to preach. She argued ". . . the Saviour died for the woman as well as for the man."[20] The crucifixion was for universal salvation, not just for male salvation or, as we may extend the argument to include, not just for White salvation. Because of this Christ came and died, no less for the woman as for the man, no less for Blacks as for Whites.

If the man may preach, because the Saviour died for him, why not the woman? Seeing he died for her also. Is he not a whole Saviour, instead of half one? as those who hold it wrong for a woman to preach, would seem to make it appear.[21]

Lee correctly perceives that there is an ontological issue at stake. If

Jesus Christ were a Saviour of men then it is true the maleness of Christ would be paramount.[22] But if Christ is a Saviour of all, then it is the humanity—the wholeness—of Christ which is significant. Sojourner was aware of the same tendency of some scholars and church leaders to link the maleness of Jesus and the sin of Eve with the status of women and she challenged this notion in her famed speech "Ain't I A Woman?"

Then that little man in black there, he says women can't have as much rights as men, 'cause Christ wasn't a woman! Where did your Christ come from? Where did your Christ come from? From God and a woman. Man had nothing to do with Him.

If the first woman God ever made was strong enough to turn the world upside down all alone, these women together ought to be able to turn it back, and get it right side up again! And now they is asking to do it, the men better let them.[23]

I would argue, as suggested by both Lee and Sojourner, that the significance of Christ is not his maleness, but his humanity. The most significant events of Jesus Christ were the life and ministry, the crucifixion, and the resurrection. The significance of these events, in one sense, is that in them the absolute becomes concrete. God becomes concrete not only in the man Jesus, for he was crucified, but in the lives of those who will accept the challenges of the risen Saviour the Christ.

For Lee, this meant that women could preach; for Sojourner, it meant that women could possibly save the world; for me, it means today, this Christ, found in the experiences of Black women, is a Black woman. The commitment to struggle, not only with symptoms (church structures, structures of society), as Black women have done, but with the causes (those beliefs which produce and re-inforce structures) yields deeper theological and christological questions having to do with images and symbolism. Christ challenges us to ask new questions demanded by the context in which we find ourselves.

The second challenge for Black women is that we must explore more deeply the question of what Christ means in a society in which class distinctions are increasing. If Christ is among "the least" then who are they? Because our foreparents were essentially poor by virtue of their race, there was no real need for them to address classism as a separate reality. Today, in light of the emerging Black middle class we must ask what is the impact of class upon our lives and the lives of other poor Black and Third World women and men.

Another way of addressing the class issue in the church is to recognize the fact that although our race/sex analyses may force us to realize that Blacks and women should share in the leadership of the church, the style of leadership and basic structures of the church virtually insure the continuation of a privileged class.

Contemporary Black women in taking seriously the Christ mandate to be among the least must insist that we address all three aspects of Black women's reality in our analyses. The challenge here for contemporary Black women is to begin to construct a serious analysis which addresses the structural nature of poverty. Black women must recognize that racism, sexism and classism each have lives of their own, and that no one form of oppression is eliminated with the destruction of any other. Though they are interrelated, they must all be addressed.

The third and final challenge for Black women is to do constructive Christology. This Christology must be a liberating one, for both the Black women's community and the larger Black community. A Christology which negates Black male humanity is still destructive to the Black community. We must, therefore, take seriously only the usable aspects of the past.

To be sure, as Black women receive these challenges, their very embodiment represents a challenge to White women. This embodiment (of racism, sexism and classism) says to White women that a wholistic analysis is a minimal requirement for wholistic theology. The task of Black women, then, is constructive.

As we organize in this constructive task, we are also challenged to adopt the critical stance of Sojourner with respect to the feminist analysis as reflected in her comment:

I know that it feel a kind o' hissin' and ticklin' like to see a colored woman get up and tell you about things, and woman's rights. We have all been thrown down so low that nobody thought we' ever get up again, but we have been long enough trodden now; we will come up again, and now I am here. . . .

. . . I wanted to tell you a mite about Woman's Rights, and so I came out and said so. I am sittin' among you to watch; and every once in a while I will come out and tell you what time of night it is.[24]

Notes

1. Cecil Wayne Cone, *Identity Crisis in Black Theology* (Nashville: African Methodist Episcopal Church, 1975), ch. 2.
2. Howard Thurman, *Jesus and the Disinherited* (Nashville: Abingdon Press, 1949), 30–1.

3. Olive Gilbert, *Sojourner Truth: Narrative and Book of Life* (1850 and 1875; repr. Chicago: Johnson Publishing Co., 1970), 83.
4. Harold A. Carter, *The Prayer Tradition of Black People* (Valley Forge: Judson Press, 1976). Carter, in referring to traditional Black prayer in general, states that Jesus was revealed as one who 'was all one needs!' (50).
5. Ibid.
6. Ibid. 49.
7. Ibid.
8. Ibid.
9. Gilbert, *Book of Life*, 118.
10. Ibid. 119.
11. Ibid.
12. Ibid. 122.
13. J. D. Roberts, *A Black Political Theology* (Philadelphia: Westminster Press, 1974), 138. See esp. ch. 5. See also Noel Erskine, *Decolonizing Theology: A Caribbean Perspective* (New York: Orbis Books, 1980), 125.
14. Roberts, *A Black Political Theology*, 133.
15. Albert Cleage, *The Black Messiah* (New York: Sheed & Ward, 1969), 92.
16. James Cone, *God of the Oppressed* (London: SPCK, 1977), 134.
17. Ibid. 135.
18. Ibid. 136.
19. William Eichelberger, 'Reflections on the Person and Personality of the Black Messiah', *Black Church* 2(1) (1972), 51–63.
20. Jarena Lee, *Religious Experiences and Journal of Mrs. Jarena Lee* (Philadelphia, 1849), 15–16.
21. Ibid. 16.
22. There is no evidence to suggest that Black women debated the significance of the maleness of Jesus. The fact is that Jesus Christ was a real crucial figure in their lives. Recent feminist scholarship has been important in showing the relation between the maleness of Christ and the oppression of women.
23. Truth, 'Ain't I A Woman', in M. Scheir (ed.), *Feminism: The Essential Historical Writings* (New York: Random House, 1972), 94.
24. Ibid. 96–8.

27 Jesus and Mary Magdalene

Teresa Okure*

In this essay, Nigerian New Testament scholar Teresa Okure makes rich use of both her African experience and her exegetical skills to explore the risen Christ's commission to Mary Magdalene—to declare the new family of God.

JMS

The appearance of the risen Jesus to Mary Magdalene in John 20:11–18 constitutes his first recorded appearance in John's gospel. It would seem that Jesus interrupted his journey of ascent to the Father (cf. 20:17a) in order to make this appearance before her. On this proto resurrection appearance, Jesus gave Mary a special commission: "Go and tell my brethren: I am ascending to my Father and your Father, to my God and your God" (v. 17b).

Unfortunately, when this appearance is recalled, what comes readily to mind is not this commission but Jesus' preamble to the commission: "Do not cling to me for I have not yet ascended to my Father" (v. 17a). This scene has been immortalized in the famous medieval painting entitled *Noli me tangere* (Do not touch me). In the painting Mary is shown in a kneeling position stretching out towards Jesus to touch him, while Jesus, standing withdrawn, prohibits her with a majestic gesture of the hand from coming near him. The impression created by this depiction of the scene, and later influenced by a puritanical culture, is that if Mary were to touch Jesus she would contaminate him with her human, specifically female, hands, and that Jesus now belonged to a new and divine sphere, different to that of Mary's. To touch him would be to commit a serious act of defilement, not only as a human being, but also as a woman; so interpreted since Jesus later invited Thomas to touch and feel him (20:27).[1]

* Teresa Okure, 'The Significance Today of Jesus' Commission to Mary Magdalene', *International Review of Mission*, Vol. LXXXI, No. 322.

But is this interpretation true to the evidence of the gospel itself? Was this the main point of Jesus' appearance to Mary Magdalene? What of the commission that he gave her in verse 17b? This study undertakes to re-examine the significance of this commission in its Johannine and New Testament contexts and to draw out its implications for us today in the work of evangelization, especially as we stand at the threshold of the third millennium, which is only eight years away. It will do this against the backdrop of modern understanding of mission generally and by John's gospel in particular.

MISSION IN JOHANNINE PERSPECTIVE

Generally mission is said to entail a sender, one sent, a commission (or the message), and in some cases, a reporting back to the sender of the task accomplished. But the Johannine approach to mission, as I have indicated elsewhere, requires that great emphasis be laid on the role and response of the audience for whose sake the mission is undertaken in the first place.[2] Second, John's gospel knows only of one mission, that of Jesus. All other missions are derivative of his and in function of it.[3] The purpose of his mission is to give life in all its fullness (John 10:10) or to empower those who believe to become the children of God (John 1:12–13).

One enters into this mission not primarily by being commissioned but by opening oneself to it, to receive its fruit, to be or to harvest from its fruit (John 4:34–38).[4] The discovery and experience of the new life in Jesus and in God then fills one with joy and moves one to share this joy with others. The author of I John states this very vividly, using three of the five senses:

That which was from the beginning, which we have heard; which we have seen with our own eyes and looked upon, and touched with our hands, the word who is life, this we declare to you . . . that you may share in our common life, that life which we share with the Father and with his Son Jesus Christ . . . that our common joy may be complete. (I John 1:1–4)

Entry into the mission of Jesus is rightly described as a witnessing to him, a confessing of him and the God who sent him, and an abiding in him. This constitutes the primary mode of participation in Jesus' mission. Without this primary participation, one cannot be commissioned or given a special mission.

Yet, ironically, over the years the understanding of mission has been restricted to its secondary sense, the commissioning. As a result, undue emphasis has been laid on the criteria for determining who was and who was not given a commission by Jesus. Arguments that hold that Jesus did not send women are based on this erroneous or one-sided conception of mission. The case of Mary Magdalene is no exception, even though long ago Augustine called her an "apostle of the apostles," based on the commission given her by Jesus (see John 20: 17–18). In the church, the commissioning has been tied to apostleship. This has been seen as the sole prerogative of men, since it is argued that Jesus did not choose women among his twelve apostles. Apostleship itself has been defined primarily in terms of governing, ruling and teaching. Women have been excluded from these activities, and divine intention has been cited to justify the practice (cf. I Tim. 2:11–12; I Cor. 14:33–36).

Finally, there has been a tendency in the past to equate mission with outreach to "pagans" in the third world. This has resulted in a complacency on the part of first-world Christians, a complacency that has led in many cases to the loss of faith itself among Christians in this first world. Though the picture is slowly changing, the effects of this past formation endure and will take a long time to eradicate. It is our hope that a re-examination of the commission to Mary Magdalene, of its importance in the life of the early Christian community, and of Mary's personal response to the mission of Jesus prior to her commissioning, will help to resolve some of these errors and move us to a more authentic understanding and practice of mission in the third millennium.

THE COMMISSION TO MARY MAGDALENE

On the first day of the week after the passion, death and burial of Jesus, Mary Magdalene went to the tomb "while it was still dark." This is Mary's second appearance in John's gospel. She is first mentioned among the women who stood at the foot of the cross (19:25). On neither occasion is she introduced, as are other characters in the gospel (cf. 11:1–2; 19: 38–39). One may conclude that she is so well known in the Johannine community or in the tradition generally that she needs no introduction. The story of Jesus' passion began with the key role of a woman—Mary of Bethany, who anointed him (John 12:1–8; cf. Matt. 26:6–13; Mark 14:3–9). That of his resurrection also begins with the unique role of a woman—Mary Magdalene. In the Synoptics, Mary visits the tomb in the company of other women to anoint the body of Jesus (cf. Matt. 28:1; Mark 16:1; Luke 24:10). Here in John she is portrayed alone even though the allusion to "we" in verse 2 implies that she was in the company of other women. Scholars see in this portrayal a fidelity to the oldest tradition, which made her the first witness of the empty tomb.

Finding the stone removed from the tomb, she ran to Peter and to the other disciple whom Jesus loved and reported in her grief: "They have taken away the Lord and we do not know where they have put him" (v. 2). Peter and the beloved disciple then set out to see for themselves. The beloved disciple outran Peter and reached the tomb first. When Peter arrived and entered the tomb to verify the evidence, the other disciple also went in: "He saw and believed" (v. 8). Both disciples then returned home forgetting Mary completely and leaving her to her own devices. It is as though she did not exist. Yet in the framework of the narrative, were it not for her, they would not have known in the first place that Jesus had risen from the dead (v. 9) nor would the beloved disciple have believed.

Mary's mission to the disciples thus started even before she encountered the risen Jesus himself. This mission arose out of her love for him. By it she surrendered her life entirely to him and became oblivious of everything else. This love drove her to visit the tomb in the dark hours of the morning at great risk to her own life while the men disciples were behind locked doors for fear of the Jews (20:19, 29; cf. 19:38). It kept her to the spot while the men returned home: "While the men returned, the weaker sex was fastened to the place by a stronger affection."[5]

As Mary continued to stand by the tomb weeping disconsolately, she too stooped down as the beloved disciple had done and peered into the tomb. This time she saw, not the linen cloths lying there as Peter and the other disciple had seen, but two angels in white, one at the head and the other at the feet where Jesus' body had lain. Their position, like that of the linen cloths in verse 7, is seen as indicating that the body had not been taken away. In the Synoptics, angels also appear to the women at the tomb, and they are frightened by it (Matt. 28:2–8; cf. Mark 16:5–8). Mary was too engrossed in her love and grief to be moved or alarmed by the sight of the angels. To their question, "Woman, why are you weeping?" she reiterated the cause of her grief, but this time on a more personal note: "They have taken *my* Lord away and *I* do not know where they have put him" (v. 13). Previously she had spoken of "the Lord" and "we," now it is "my Lord" and "I"; she is now on her own in her quest for Jesus.

Then, probably as the angels look over her shoulders or at the sound of Jesus' footsteps, she too turns round and sees Jesus standing there without recognizing him. Jesus in turn repeats the question of the angels: "Woman, why are you weeping?" adding, "Who are you looking for?" The Greek verb *zetein* (to seek, look or search for intensely) used here by Jesus has an evangelistic sense in the gospel. It is used, for instance, of the two disciples who follow Jesus as a result of the witness of John the Baptist that Jesus is the Lamb of God (John 1:38). The same word is used also to speak of God's seeking for true worshippers who will worship him in spirit and in truth (4:23–24). Mary's quest for Jesus is intense and from the heart. Her answer to Jesus' question is as bold and courageous as it is impossible for her to undertake: "Sir, if you have removed him, tell me where you have laid him and I will carry him away" (v. 15).

Strikingly, throughout all this narrative Mary never refers to the Lord's "body," as is done in other parts of the gospel (cf. 19:38, 40; 20:12), but always to "the Lord" and "him." It is as though for her Jesus never really died in the first place. This explains why she could weep and search passionately for what was no more than a corpse. In the Synoptics, the women go to anoint the body of Jesus since this was not possible on the burial day because of the Passover. But, according to John's gospel, the body had been properly anointed by Joseph of Arimathea and Nicodemus (19:38–42). Mary's concern, therefore, was not to prevent Jesus' body from being desecrated, especially as he had died a criminal's death; her love was too strong to accept that he could be dead and gone forever: "Love is strong as death" (Cant 8:6).

Marvelling at such a love, Jesus then calls Mary by name, perhaps with a shake of the head at her unabashed love. She in turn recognizes him, turns completely round to him and calls him "my master/ teacher" (*hrabbouni*). In her joy she holds on to him for dear life, hardly believing that he is alive. The entire scene recalls John 10:3–4. Jesus the Good Shepherd calls each sheep by name and they recognize and follow him. Mary is one of those sheep for whom Jesus laid down his life to take it up again, to the great delight of the Father (10:11, 17–18). In this regard, she is in every sense of the word the first fruit of Jesus' accomplished mission.

Mary called Jesus "my teacher." Some scholars hold that this title lacks the loftiness of the Easter faith, which refers to Jesus as Lord and God (cf. 20:28). From this it is concluded that Mary did not see in

Jesus anything more than she did before his death, hence hers was not yet an Easter faith.[6] This is an interesting conjecture. "My teacher" here is a term of endearment. For when she reports on the encounter she calls him "the Lord" (v. 18), using the technical Easter formula: "I have seen the Lord." The question is: What did he teach her on this occasion?

First, he taught her that she was important enough for him to interrupt his journey to the Father in order to let her know that he was still alive. This is shown by the particle "for" (*gar*) and the adverb "not yet" (*oupō*) in the statement: "Do not hold on to me thus, for I have not yet ascended [*anabebēka*] to my Father." The Johannine schema on the ascension is different from that of Luke, which allows a forty-day interval between the resurrection and the ascension.[7] Second, he taught her that he saw and valued her love and concern for him; and that he accepted this love and was moved by it.

The statement, *mē mou haptou* (v. 17a), popularly translated as "do not touch me," or worse still, "stop clinging to me,"[8] actually means "do not hold on to me" (for I have not yet ascended to my Father). The whole context makes this evident. Mary had believed all along that somebody had taken away the Lord. This concern is repeated three times (vv. 2, 12 and 15). Now that she had seen him, she was not going to take any chance of letting him go (cf. Cant 3:4).[9] She obviously then held on to him in such a way that he would not be wrenched from her grasp. Mary's action is a very natural one in the circumstances. It is done out of astonishment and delight. (The situation recalls that by Arrian where it is reported that Alexander received severe wounds in the chest from an arrow. His soldiers could not believe that he was alive. When he appeared among them recovered from the wound, they took hold (*haptomenoi*) of his hands, knees and clothing in delight and astonishment.)[10] If this is the situation, and the context supports this interpretation, then Jesus is not in any way rebuffing Mary. Quite the contrary; he gives her a message both for herself and the brethren to assure her that from now on both she and he and the other disciples are inseparable. This message constitutes the peak of his teaching on this occasion. What was this message? And how important was it to the early Christians?

The Message

Jesus sent Mary with a message to his disciples, while he, it is understood, would complete his ascent to the Father: "But go to my brethren

317

and tell them: I am now ascending to my Father and your Father, to my God and your God" (John 17b). We are so accustomed to the formality whereby Christians address one another as "dear brothers and sisters in Christ," especially in liturgical settings, that we miss the impact of this message and its newness at the time it was uttered. Scholars have remarked on the solemn tone of this commission.

This is registered by the repetition "my," "your" in the expression "my Father and your Father," "my God and your God." This solemnity underscores the importance of the commission. The rhythm of the statement: "my Father and your Father," "my God and your God," recalls that of Ruth to Noami (Ruth 1:16), where the former, the Moabitess, tells her Jewish mother-in-law that despite the differences of race between them, their lot is now so woven together that they cannot be separated: "Your people shall be my people and your God my God." As a result of this pact, which not even death or the grave could separate, Ruth became an ancestress of Jesus, listed in the Matthean genealogy (Matt. 1:5–6).

Prior to the resurrection, God's "fatherhood" (or parenthood), in John's gospel, was restricted to Jesus. At the last supper, Jesus gave the disciples the status of friends as opposed to slaves (John 15:15). On the cross, he further gave his mother to the beloved disciple to be his mother and the disciple to her to be her son (John 19:26–27). But now for the first time, the disciples are given to understand, through the message entrusted to Mary Magdalene, that they and Jesus now share the same parent or ground of being in God. They are in truth brothers and sisters of Jesus in God in much the same way as children relate who share the same father and mother. In other words, the message declares and proclaims the new status of the disciples after the resurrection: Only now does Jesus make his Father and God in the full sense the Father and God of his disciples. This declaration appears in this form only here in the whole NT tradition. It expands and fulfills the statement of Jesus in 14:6, that he is the only way to the Father.[11] Thus, while the repetition of "my/your" underscores the identity in the relationship between Jesus and the disciples in relation to God, it also pinpoints his uniqueness in this regard as the agent by which this relationship becomes possible.

Equally importantly, the statement declares that in Jesus believers now have a new relationship to one another. The "your" in the statement is plural (*hymon*). They relate to one another in Jesus as blood brothers and sisters relate to one another. Hence Jesus' relationship with his Father and with them now becomes the norm of their relationship with one another (cf. 13:1, 34–35; 15:9–14).

This interpretation finds a solid contextual backing in John's gospel and epistles, and in the rest of the NT. The prologue to the gospel declares that to all who believe in him Jesus gave the enabling power (*exousia*) to become the children of God; these were born not "of any human blood or by the will of any human being or father, but of God himself" (John 1:12–13). The Greek word *teknon* (child) used here in the plural "children" denotes the child in relation to its parents or grandparents. It differs from the other word for child (*pais*), which denotes other types of relationship of one human being to another, or emphasizes the age of the person concerned (cf. Mark 9:37; Luke 18:17; Matt. 18:3–4; John 4:49).[12] It also differs from "son" (*hyios*), which can also denote other types of relationship, though in John's gospel it designates Jesus' unique and untransferable relationship with the Father.[13]

In John 1:12–13 the status of believers as children of God is reinforced by the statement that they are born of God (*ek theou egennēthēsan*). This birth is brought about by Jesus' passion, death and resurrection. Jesus gave birth to believers on the cross (cf. 12:20; 16:21), through his pierced side whence blood and water gushed out as happens to a woman's womb when she gives birth to a child. The fathers of the church systematically saw in the piercing of Jesus' side and the outflow of water and blood the birth of the church. Water and blood signify the sacraments of baptism and the eucharist.[14] But the church is the gathering of the children of God, branches of the vine that is Jesus himself (15:1–8), the multifarious fish caught in his net (John 21:1–17). Hence the church cannot be born of Jesus unless individuals who make up the church are first born of him. Placed in the prologue, the statement in John 1:12–13 about the divine birth of believers stems from the message entrusted to Mary Magdalene by Jesus. It is written from this post-Easter perspective, and serves as evidence of the community's acceptance of her commission.

The importance of this message is reinforced in the dialogue with Nicodemus (John 3:1–21). One must be (*dei*) born of God if one is to have eternal life. This birth from God, Jesus explains, happens through his passion, death and resurrection (his *hypsēthēnai/doxasthēnai*, 3:14). Nicodemus' persistent misunderstanding of the nature of this birth and his insistence on its impossibility for a grown-up person only serve to underscore its reality. This birth is effected by the Spirit (3:5) whose coming depends on Christ's glorification (cf. 7:39; 14:16; 19:34;

20:22). As in John 1:12–13, this insight in the dialogue is influenced by the Easter message entrusted to Mary Magdalene. The Johannine community understood this birth to be real, not metaphorical. Hence the author of I John exclaims with a great sense of wonder:

> How great is the love that the Father has shown to us! We are called God's children, not only called, we really are . . . we are God's children, what we shall be has not yet been disclosed but we know that when he appears, we shall be like him. (I John 3:1–2)

The author then draws upon this relationship to exhort the believers to demonstrate their sonship and daughtership of God by loving one another as God and Jesus love them. It is only in this way that they can claim in truth to be children of God who is love (I John 3:16; 4:16).

Indeed, not only the Johannine corpus but the entire NT bears witness that after the resurrection the followers of Jesus regarded one another as brothers and sisters. Evidence of this is too numerous to be cited. There is hardly any book of the NT that does not corroborate this evidence (cf. Rom. 15:14; 1 Cor. 1:10, 11, 26; Gal. 1:2, 11; Eph. 6:21; Phil. 1:12; Col. 1:2; 1 Thess. 1:4; Heb. 2:11; Jas. 1:2; II Pet. 1:10; I John 2:9; Rev. 1:9; 22:9). But we may note in particular Romans 8:15–17, where Paul is thrilled that believers can now call God "Abba! Father!" based on the testimony of the Spirit that "we are children of God." In the Acts of the Apostles, believers consistently designate one another as brothers and sisters (cf. Acts 1:15; 6:3; 9:17, 30; 10:23; 12:17; 15:1, etc.). The striking point here is that this designation cuts across ethnic barriers and applies equally to persons of non-Jewish origin; whereas previously the term "brethren" (*adelphoi, andres adelphoi*), was reserved only for fellow Jews (cf. Acts 2:29, 39; 3:17, 22), that is, people of the same race and blood.

The instance in Revelations 22:9 is even more significant; the angel revealer is described as a "fellow servant" of the prophet in contradistinction to the rest of the believers who are designated as his "brothers and sisters." So pervasive is the NT evidence that one is led to conclude that the designation of believers as children of God or brothers and sisters of Jesus *before* the resurrection has been influenced by this post-Easter message entrusted to Mary Magdalene (cf. Matt. 23:8; 25:40). The point of this whole survey is to underscore that the NT understanding that believers are in the fullest sense children of God as are children of human parents is rooted in and derives from the Easter message entrusted to Mary Magdalene. Interestingly, in Matthew 28:10, it is to the women at the tomb that Jesus gave the commission to inform his "brethren" that he was going before them to Galilee. The message given to Mary in John 20:17 is here given to other women in a different form in the Synoptic tradition. This is the primary and foundational Easter message. Mary is, therefore, not simply an apostle of apostles; she was commissioned by the risen Jesus himself to bear and proclaim the message of messages to the disciples. This message, which concerns the significance of Jesus' resurrection for believers, their common parenthood in and brotherhood/sisterhood in Christ, sums up the entire purpose of Jesus' mission and God's work of salvation.

Mary Magdalene was not, therefore, primarily or even secondarily commissioned to tell the disciples that Jesus had risen from the dead. That was self-evident. She had seen him and would naturally have reported on that as did the disciples on the way to Emmaus and the other disciples (Luke 24:33–35). Rather her commission lay in the charge to proclaim the good news, which we have examined at length. In other words, Mary was not only the first to see the risen Lord; she was also the first to be commissioned by him to proclaim the Easter message concerning the new status of believers, that they are children of God and brothers and sisters to one another. All subsequent proclamation has this goal in view, to bring new members into this sonship and daughtership of God with its accompanying rights and duties (cf. I John 1:1–4; II Cor 5:18–20).

Mary's own report to the disciples corroborates this interpretation of the significance of her commission. She reported that she had seen the Lord and that "he had said these things to her" (John 20:18). Seeing the Lord was an important motif in the NT. But of itself it was not enough, except for catechetical and apologetic purposes (cf. I Cor 15:1–9). The emphasis on seeing the Lord lay in the authority it gave one to proclaim the good news, and to be an apostle. So Paul declares in I Corinthians 9:1; 15:8–9. Some, like the disciples on the way to Emmaus, saw the Lord but were not specifically commissioned; yet in their joy they ran to share the news with others. Mary had both. She saw the Lord and was commissioned by him to bear the foundational message of the resurrection to the community. Here was a proclamation in every sense of the word (*aggelousa*), not a mere story-telling.[15] This is all the more striking in an age and in a culture where the witness of women was regarded as null and void.

On the cross, Jesus entrusted his mother to the disciple whom he loved. From that day on the disciple took her into his own home, that is, he accepted her as his own mother. Following his example, the church has done so ever since. After his resurrection, Jesus, through the commission given to Mary Magdalene, also entrusted all believers into one another's keeping as his brothers and sisters in God. The NT evidence shows that the early Christians took this message seriously to heart and transformed it into a programme of action: they designated one another as brothers and sisters and forged a communitarian way of life to enable them to live out this new relationship. Thus they ensured that none of their brothers or sisters were ever in want (cf. Acts 2:43–46; 4:32–37). The Johannine community and Paul in particular emphasized the wonder of this new identity and urged their members to show that they are indeed children of God by loving one another as God loves them.

The insight that as Christians we are children of God, born to him/ her through baptism and the Holy Spirit and through the blood of Christ shed on the cross, is not new to us (I Cor 12:13). We have no difficulty in believing that God is our Father and Mother. But to what extent have we grasped the corresponding truth that in Christ we are in truth, not metaphorically, related to one another as are blood brothers and sisters? What challenges does this awareness hold for us today as people entrusted with this same Easter message for the third millennium? Let us attempt to answer these questions in the last part of this study.

THE SIGNIFICANCE OF MARY'S COMMISSION FOR TODAY

There is concern today to identify new emphases in mission as we move into the third millennium. In my view, this concern calls us first to re-examine our understanding of our common identity as Christians and to evaluate how we have lived this identity in the second millennium. In the light of the foundational Easter message entrusted to Mary Magdalene, we need to ask whether it is possible for us Christians to see ourselves as brothers and sisters in the way Jesus intended and as the early Christians understood and endeavoured to live it out.

To the Africans, it is not an impossibility for Christians of different races to regard one another as brothers and sisters, children of God. The love of one's family, extended family, clan and ethnic group constitutes a natural, cultural background for imparting and assimilating this message. It is a common saying in Africa that "blood is thicker than water." By this is meant that any relationship by blood takes precedence over all other types of relationship. This applies no matter how far down the line the blood may be. Indeed it is the blood of the ancestors and ancestresses who are always alive and who exercise a protective and watchful role within the community that unites peoples of the same family or ethnic group.

If this is true of human blood, should it not be more so of the blood of Christ, which has given birth and life to us all as children of God, and which continues to nourish us daily through the eucharist? But unfortunately the Christianity that the Africans inherited was riddled with divisions caused by the political quarrels of Europe. These divisions and their accompanying discriminations have deeply entrenched themselves into the psyche of most African Christians. In some parts of Nigeria, Christians of one denomination would rather side with Moslems in certain socio-political undertakings than with Christians of another denomination. Ecumenism remains for the most part no more than an academic exercise.

Second, in the African culture, it is possible for persons who are not in any way related by blood to forge a lasting bond of friendship that can be as thick as blood. Such friendships are sealed in some cultures by the letting out and mingling of the bood of the parties concerned.[16] Through this "covenant of blood" the parties see themselves not only as brothers or sisters, but as their other self. These practices and beliefs can be used as a solid cultural, hence natural background for transmitting the message of the resurrection given in the commission to Mary Magdalene.

The recognition of our common parentage in God carries with it an obligation to love all God's children as Jesus did, even to the point of breaking the bread of his life so that we may live. In the NT evidence, this is the only authentic way by which one can claim to know and represent God in the community and in the world. John 13:35 is the Christian identity card. To do otherwise is to demonstrate one's ignorance of God (1 John 3:16; 4:20–21).

Fidelity to our relationship to one another as brothers and sisters in Christ demands that we eschew all activities that smack of superiority and inferiority complexes. It also rules out all types of discrimination based on race, class and sex since it recognizes that we are all one person in Christ (Gal. 3:28). It leads us to "speak the truth in love" if a brother or sister errs, rather than deny them their fundamental human rights, deprive them of the freedom of theological speech, or treat them as inferiors in their own parents' house (cf. Heb. 23:22–24).

In the socio-economic and political spheres, the challenge of Mary

Magdalene's commission will move the so-called Christian countries of the west to care for their less fortunate sisters and brothers in the two-thirds world. This will be done out of a sense of duty, not of benevolence, the same duty that one has towards one's blood brothers and sisters, at least in the African context, to enhance their overall growth. The belittling relationship that often exists between donors and receivers should give place to a genuine sharing not only of goods but of technology and skills. The Christian culture is essentially one of sharing. It stands out against the modern one, which is based on accumulation rather than distribution of wealth. This also demands that a stop be put to all the covert and overt ways of exploiting the peoples of this two-thirds world.

More especially, the recognition that we are all brothers and sisters in Christ will help towards according to women their rightful place in church and society. In Africa nobody jokes with his sister or mother, women to whom one is related by blood. The wife and widow may be a different matter, because she is not related to the husband and the husband's family by blood. But whether wife or widow, as Christians we are all related to one another through the blood of Christ. In particular this will demand that the church listens to the witness of women to Christ today, that it takes seriously the commission that they alone can declare to be what they have received from Christ for the good of the community. Instead of citing arguments based on what "Jesus did not do" with regard to women, the church should listen with open ears and learn from what Jesus actually did when he sent a woman like Mary Magdalene to carry and proclaim the crucial or most significant message of his accomplished mission to the Christian community. The charge given to all the disciples in John 20:22–23 has been interpreted as admitting new members into this new relationship. It rests on and presupposes the commission to Mary Magdalene. Hers was the foundational commission.

This commission has to do essentially with life and relationships. The new approach to mission in the third millennium will need to focus its attention on ways of promoting genuine life and relationships between peoples and between them and God. It will not succeed in this undertaking if it continues to ignore the significant contributions of women who are by nature endowed by God to be covenanted with life, bearers and fosterers of life (cf. Gen. 3:20).[17]

CONCLUSION

This study has attempted to highlight that the risen Jesus entrusted to Mary Magdalene, a woman, the foundational message of the resurrection for the entire group of believers, namely, that they are now children of God hence brothers and sisters to him and to one another. The early Christians took this message seriously and evolved concrete ways of putting it into practice. They did this even though in their culture women's witness did not count. In the course of history the significance of this message was lost sight of or at best reduced to a mere formality of greeting in liturgical settings.

We noted, too, that Mary's involvement in the mission of Jesus lay first in her personal love and commitment to him. This love, which was stronger than death, made her a fitting bearer of this key Easter message, which is about love and lasting relationship between Christ and all his followers.

This analysis of the commission to Mary Magdalene challenges us today to re-examine our whole understanding of the concept of mission, our attitude towards and our relationship with one another as children of God, south–north, and east–west. It also challenges the church to take seriously the contributions of women in the missionary undertaking if it is to remain faithful to its mission in the third millennium. Today Jesus commissions all believers as he commissioned Mary Magdalene: "Go and tell the brethren: I am ascending to my Father and your Father, to my God and your God." Fidelity to him requires that we make this commission the heart and nerve centre of the work of evangelism in the third millennium.

Notes

1. See the discussion on this issue in R. E. Brown, *The Gospel According to John XIII–XXI*, AB 29A (New York: Doubleday, 1970), 1012–14; Pheme Perkins, 'The Gospel According to John', in *New Jerome Biblical Commentary* (London: Geoffrey Chapman, 1989), 983; Saint Augustine, 'Tractate CXXI, 1', in *Nicene and Post-Nicene Fathers*, first series, vol. VII (Edinburgh: T. & T. Clark, 1986), 437.
2. Cf. T. Okure, *The Johannine Approach to Mission: A Contextual Study of John 4:1–42*, WUNT 31/2 (Tübingen: Mohr/Siebeck, 1988), esp. 1–6, 39–49, 192–225.
3. Ibid., esp. 140–5.
4. Ibid. 145–64.

5. Augustine, 'Tractate cxx, 1', 436.

6. Cf. R. Schnackenburg, *The Gospel According to St John*, vol. iii (New York: Crossroad, 1982), 317; Brown, *The Gospel According to John*, 1010; Perkins, *The Gospel According to John*, 1983.

7. For a lengthy discussion on 'ascension' in John see e.g. Brown, *The Gospel According to John*, 1012–14; and Schnackenberg, *The Gospel According to John* 318–20.

8. Thus M. Zerwick and M. Grosvenor, *A Grammatical Analysis of the Greek New Testament* (Rome: Pontifical Biblical Institute, 1981), 345.

9. 'I found him whom my soul loves. I held him and would not let him go until I had brought him into my mother's house' (Cant. 3:4). The entire episode is in many ways evocative of this canticle.

10. Arrian, *Anab.*, 1.13.3; cited in Bauer, Arndt, and Gingrich, *Lexicon*, 7.

11. Cf. G. Shrenk, 'Pater', in *Theological Dictionary of the New Testament*, v. 958, 996.

12. Cf. Colin Brown (ed.), *The New International Dictionary of New Testament Theology*, vol. i (Exeter: Paternoster Press, 1978), 285–6.

13. Cf. Okure, *Johannine Approach*, 240, 249.

14. See e.g. John Chrysostom, 'Baptismal Instructions, 16–19', in *Ancient Christian Writers* (London: Longmans, Green, 1963), 61–2.

15. From the verb *aggello* (here aor. ptc. fem.) used for Mary's proclamation are derived the nouns *aggelos* (angel) and *aggelia* (good news, message). It is used in John 1:15 of the gospel itself and in I John 3:11 of the command to love the brethren. BAG (p. 7) applies it to the Easter message proclaimed by Mary. The noun *euaggelion* (gospel) comes from the same root.

16. Thus P. K. Sarpong observes: 'This is done, for example, in the northern part of Ghana. When such pacts of blood have been made, nothing can break the bond of fidelity between the two friends.' In a talk on 'Inculturation' given to the members of the Indigenous West African Religious Union (IWARU) at St Louis, Kumasi, 3 Jan. 1987; mimeographed, 7.

17. Cf T. Okure, 'Biblical Perspectives on Women: Eve, the Mother of All the Living, Gen. 3:20', in *Voices from the Third World* (Philippine Edition 8/2, 1985), 17–24, esp. 23; 'Women in the Bible', in *With Passion and Compassion: Third World Women Doing Theology*, ed. V. Fabella and M. A. Oduyoye (Maryknoll: Orbis, 1988), 51, 56–7.

28 The Breast of the Father

Verna E. F. Harrison*

Sister Nonna (Verna) Harrison has made over the years a quiet but influential contribution to the theology of her own Orthodox communion and to the study of early Christian thought. The early Greek theologians used biblical imagery in deliberately self-subverting ways to drive the faithful from idolatrous conceptions of God. Here Harrison speaks of the way Clement of Alexandria styles Christ both as the milk of the Father (who is in this case a nursing mother) and as a mother who gives birth to his people on the Cross. (Note that Teresa Okure's article draws these themes back into the text of the New Testament.)   JMS

As described in *Paedagogus* I, Clement's ideal human child combines symbolically masculine and feminine attributes.[1] So does his ideal parent, God. His language of child-rearing describes the relationships between human and divine persons, so the symbols naming both sides within this conceptual world are interrelated. Thus, God the Father and the Logos both function and act in fatherly and motherly ways toward their human children. In light of Clement's emphasis on divine transcendence and apophatic reserve, we must take care not to conclude from this use of masculine and feminine symbolism that he envisaged gender as present within the inmost being of God in God-self. But he uses such language in striking ways to describe some aspects of how the divine persons relate to humans, to which we will now turn.

In accord with the usage of the New Testament, he speaks of the divine parent known to Christians pre-eminently as Father. For Clement and other early Christians, God is present personally as the Father of Jesus Christ, and humans are called to approach this God through Christ with personal loyalty and attentiveness, having entered into a covenant relationship with him as adoptive children. To be sure, Clement's God is also the Creator whose Logos is the principle of rationality, order and virtue pervading the universe. But neither Father nor

* Verna E. F. Harrison, 'The Care-Banishing Breast of the Father: Feminine Images of the Divine in Clement of Alexandria's *Pedagogus* I', from *Studia Patristica*, Vol. XXXI.

Son is to be understood as an abstract principle or anonymous first cause serving as a blank screen upon which humans can project whatever metaphor they like. Thus, for Clement, in accordance with concrete Biblical revelation and ecclesial experience, God is known first of all as Father. He declares in *Paedagogus* I.17.1–2 that one's manner of recognizing him and relating to him precisely as Father is what defines one as authentically his child.

However, this relationship between human child and divine Father, including very importantly the mediation of Christ the Logos, becomes so deep, rich and all-encompassing that it includes all aspects of adult nurture and the corresponding childlike receptivity. This includes the care given children by the paedagogus and the teacher as well as the parents themselves. Thus other descriptions of divine parental and nurturing activity besides fatherhood including feminine ones are appropriate to express facets of this abundant nurturing love. Clement speaks of God caring for Israel as a maidservant, nurturing human children as male and female animals protect and care for their young, and watching over them like a mother eagle or a hen with her chicks.[2] In using feminine imagery he is not attempting to subsume and thereby extinguish the 'feminine divine' in his 'male god', as some of today's feminist scholars might suppose. He is affirming that the God who is known specifically and personally as the Father of Jesus Christ and his Son provide motherly as well as fatherly guidance and nurture to the faithful, that these dimensions of human interaction are somehow included in Christians' adoptive relationship with their God. This statement has important implications for spirituality as well as theology. It means that neither the Father nor the Son behaves toward humans in a narrowly or reductively 'male' way.

Clement's most stunning uses of feminine imagery for the divine occur in an extensive discussion of milk in *Paedagogus* I.34.3–I.52.1. Citing 1 Cor. 3.2, his Gnostic opponents have contrasted the solid food they claim to offer the mature with the milk the mainstream Church gives to mere children.[3] So in the context of Book I's appreciation of childhood he meditates on the glories of milk.[4] The idea of a return to Paradise is a subtext of his reflections on renewed childlikeness, so he equates milk with manna, the perfect food of the promised land, and the food of angels. Utilizing the concepts of current physiology, he argues that milk is made of the same material as blood and the human body itself. He concludes that it is really the same as solid food which is also transformed into body through digestion. However, he emphasizes that the milk God gives is the Body and Blood of Christ, the Eucharist, which is the food of children newly reborn in baptism. Clement's milk is ultimately Christ himself, who is life.

We will examine the central passage that links milk to the divine persons, *Paedagogus* I.41.1–I.43.4. Clement begins in §41 by saying that Christ's blood is like milk. After discussing the biology of breast feeding, he adds: 'This food, which is well adapted and appropriate to the child newly formed and born is a work of God the Nourisher (τροφέως) and Father of both those who are born and those who are reborn, as was the manna that poured down from heaven for the ancient Hebrews, the heavenly food of the angels'.[5] Thus God is the source of both earthly and spiritual milk, but Clement adds that the spiritual milk is better. He asserts that God the Father is effectively a better nurse than women are for their own children:

Women who are pregnant and become mothers are sources of milk, but the Lord Christ fruit of the Virgin, did not bless the breasts of women or consider them nurses [τροφεῖς], but when the loving and compassionate Father poured forth his Logos, then he himself became food for the prudent.[6]

The milk here is Christ. Clement contrasts his coming forth from a virgin with the milk coming from the breasts of ordinary mothers. As the context shows, the point here is that the biological processes of human procreation are wondrous works of God, but divine nourishment and nurture belong to an entirely different and higher level of reality. Mary's paradoxical fusion of virginity and mother-hood on the human level breaks the rules of biology. This symbol-izes a further paradox on the divine level. For Clement the gender distinction is linked to biological procreation, where fathers are not mothers or nurses.[7] But the divine Father utterly transcends human physiology, and in his activity he proves to be the greatest nurse of all.

Clement now comes to the heart of the discussion. He speaks of the Church as mother and again of Christ:

There is only one virgin become mother, as I love to call the Church. This mother alone does not have milk, since she alone does not become a woman; she is at once virgin and mother, uncontaminated as virgin, loving as mother, and she calls to herself her children and suckles them with holy milk, the Logos of little ones. Therefore she did not have milk, since the milk is the good and appropriate Child, the body of Christ. Thus she nourishes with the Logos the new people, which the Lord himself bore in the labor pains of the flesh, and which the Lord himself wrapped in swaddling clothes with precious blood. O the holy childbirths, O the holy swaddling clothes! The Logos is everything to the little one, at once father and mother and paedagogus and nourisher [τροφεύς]. 'Eat my flesh', he said, 'and drink my blood'. These are the foods appropriate to us that the Lord gives, he offers his flesh and pours out his blood. Nothing is lacking for the growth of the children.[8]

The curious statement that the Church is virgin and mother but 'does not become a woman' reflects a contrast sometimes made in Late Antiquity between the innocent virgin girl and the sexually active married woman. In Philo, for instance, 'virgin' and 'woman' are often contrasted as positively and negatively charged symbols of the feminine.[9] 'Mother', of course, is also positively charged. Here Clement ascribes two highly valued forms of femininity to the Church while denying her involvement in the ambivalent femininity of 'womanhood'.

The Church suckles her children with a milk that consists in the Logos, the Christ Child and the body of Christ. Interestingly, Clement sees the Lord as becoming a child like the faithful who are children so that through this likeness he is available to become united with them. Could this mean that for Clement he is actually present as Child in the Eucharist, which is more often thought by theologians to make present his crucified and/or risen body?

After this Clement's imagery shifts suddenly and dramatically. At first the Church is presented as nursing mother but is not herself the source of the milk she gives, which is the Logos. Now she appears as nurse but not herself mother. The mother is none other than Christ, who gives birth to the new Christian people 'in the labor pains of the flesh', that is in his passion and agony on the Cross. Christ's death has become his childbearing. He has transformed the destruction of life into an outpouring of new and eternal life. The gender reversal is the least part of this overawing paradox. As the ultimate loving mother, Christ gives his own life to and for his children in offering his body and pouring out his blood.[10]

Clement also depicts the Saviour tenderly wrapping his newborn babies in swaddling clothes. He combines in himself every aspect of the nurture, upbringing and education of his children and fulfills all the adult caregiving roles: 'father and mother and paedagogus and nourisher'. The last of these titles is τροφεύς, literally one who gives food, a title we have seen Clement ascribe to God the Father as well. Its feminine form means 'nurse'.

In §43, Clement suggests an alternative interpretation which continues the same themes but adds further astonishing feminine imagery of the divine:

The food, that is the Lord Jesus, that is the Logos of God, is spirit become flesh, sanctified heavenly flesh. The food is the milk of the Father, by which alone the little ones are nursed. And he, the beloved Logos, our nourisher, has poured out his own blood for us, saving humanity. We who have believed in God through him take refuge upon the 'care-banishing breast'[11] of the Father, the Logos. And he alone, as is natural, provides the milk of love to us little ones, and they alone are truly blessed who are suckled by this breast.[12]

Here, Christ's flesh and blood are the milk, the Logos is the breast, and the breast belongs to God the Father, who proves to be the ultimate source of the milk and thus the ultimate mother. For Clement, the Logos is the agent who manifests and enacts the Father's presence and work in the created world. The breast is the organ that conveys a mother's milk directly to the child. So this extraordinary metaphor of the mother and her breast, like the more familiar image of the mind and its speech, appropriately expresses in feminine language an important aspect of the relationship between the Father and his Logos. Clement is using feminine symbolism to describe the relationship between the divine persons themselves, though as so often in the ante-Nicene fathers it refers not so much to the immanent as to the economic Trinity, God active in the creation.[13]

Notes

1. §§ I.14.1–1.23.2; Henri-Irénée Marrou (ed.), *Clément d'Alexandrie: Le Péda-gogue*, Book I, Sources chrétiennes 70 (Paris, 1960), 134–52.
2. *Protrepticus* I.8.1 and X.91.3, Claude Mondésert (ed.), *Clément d'Alexandrie: Le Protreptique*, Sources chrétiennes 2 (Paris, 1949), 62, 159; *Paedagogos* I.21.2 and I.56.1, Marrou, *Clément d'Alexandrie*, 148, 210.
3. See Annewies van den Hoek, 'Milk and Honey in the Theology of Clement of Alexandria', in *Fides Sacramenti, Sacramentum Fidei: Studies in Honour of Pieter Smulders*, ed. Hans Jörg auf der Maur *et al.* (Assen, 1981), 27–39.
4. In *Stromata* V.62.2–4. Clement cites Hebrews 5:12–6:1 and compares milk unfavorably to solid food in much the same way as his opponents probably did, exhorting his audience to progress from childhood to spiritual perfection. However, he goes on in V.63.1–8 to make the opposite point, using milk imagery positively as in *Paedagogus* I. He cites the *Epistle of Barnabas* as encouraging the reader to move beyond simpler teaching and enter the good land flowing with milk and honey, and equates this good land with knowledge of the Father, eternal life and participation in the divine. In Clement's under-standing, these goals are identical with gnosis and its salvific consequences. Otto Stählin (ed.), *Clemens Alexandrinus, Zweiter Band. Stromata*, Books I–IV,

3rd edn., rev. Ludwig Früchtel, *Griechischen Christlichen Schriftsteller* 15 (Berlin, 1960), 368–9.

5. Marrou, *Clément d'Alexandrie*, 184–6.

6. Ibid. 186.

7. *Paedagogus* I.10.1–3; Marrou, *Clément d'Alexandrie*, 128; *Stromata* IV.58.2–IV.60.1; Stählin, *Clemens Alexandrinus*, 275.

8. Marrou, *Clément d'Alexandrie*, 186–8.

9. See Dorothy Sly, *Philo's Perception of Women* (Atlanta, Ga., 1990), 71–89; and my essay. 'The Allegorization of Gender: Plato and Philo on Spiritual Child-bearing', in *Asceticism*, ed. Vincent L. Wimbush and Richard Valantasis (Oxford, 1995), 520–34.

10. The image of Christ giving birth to us and then suckling us with his milk appears again in *Paedagogus* I.49.3–4.

11. Marrou, *Clément d'Alexandrie*, 189 n. 7, observes that this is a citation of Homer, *Iliad* XXII.83.

12. Marrou, *Clément d'Alexandrie*, 188–90.

13. The same imagery appears again in § 46: 'For Christ, food was to fulfill the Father's will [cf. John 4.32–4], but for us little ones the food is Christ himself; we drink the heavenly Logos as milk. . . . To the little ones who seek the Logos, the breasts of the father's love for humanity provide milk.' Ibid. 192–4.

29 Blood and Defilement

Janet Martin Soskice*

The Cross, with its blood, death, and sacrifice of a Son, is not an easy symbol for feminist theology, but can it be avoided? This selection explores the Christian symbolism of Cross, blood, and death in alignment with the symbolism of female blood, birth, and new life.

JMS

In her book *In the Beginning Was Love*, Julia Kristeva gives an account of her understanding of the psychoanalytic task and uses overtly theological language to do so.[1] Noting Freud's insistence that the foundation of his cure is "Our God Logos," she describes psychoanalysis as about making word and flesh meet—making the word become flesh in a discourse of love directed to an "impossible other." These comments are developed by means of a discussion of the Apostles' Creed. Kristeva, writing as an analyst, not a theologian, notes that in the Genesis narratives God creates by separating. Separation is the mark of God's presence: the separation of light and dark, heavens and earth, sea and dry land, male and female. And this dividing and separating reach a climax in the Christian story with the crucifixion, the desertion of Christ on the cross, and the cry of dereliction. (To add my own theological gloss, this is the separation of God from God.) Yet it is because one is deserted, Kristeva suggests, that one may achieve ecstasy in completion and reunion with the father, who, she adds, is "himself a substitution for the mother."[2]

A striking feature of Kristeva's psychoanalytic/philosophical reading is the suggestion that the symbolic weight of this Christian narrative is to reestablish fusion with the Other, who is both maternal and paternal. ("So God created man in his own image, in the image of God

* Janet Martin Soskice, excerpts from 'Blood and Defilement', from *The Convergence of Theology*, edited by Daniel Kendall, SJ, and Stephen T. Davis (Mahwah, NJ: Paulist Press, 2001). Used with permission of Paulist Press.

he created him, male and female he created them.") The theologian is bound to reflect that the cross is, by tradition, simultaneously the place of death and of birth, of abjection and the emergence of new life. Death and birth come together—an obvious scriptural reflection born out by the Eastern liturgies—yet, because commonplace, often stale and neglected.

We need to recall those ancient and venerable traditions in which the blood and water that flowed from Christ's side on the cross were taken as emblematic of human birth. Medieval religious art was often explicit in its representation of the crucifixion as childbirth. We see the church (*ecclesia*) being pulled from Christ's wounded side as Eve was pulled from Adam's. More commonly we see the blood flowing from the side of Christ into chalices borne by angels or flowing directly into the mouths of the faithful; this is, figuratively, the eucharistic blood on which believers feed, and by which feeding they become one with the body of Christ. While the iconography is familiar, we need to give weight to the overtly female nature of the imagery; the symbolic identification, that is, of the crucified Christ with the human female body, both in giving birth and in feeding. Caroline Walker Bynum has done much to bring this identification as it was made in medieval piety to our attention. The identification of women with the physicality of Christ was especially strong between the twelfth and fifteenth centuries. During this period in the West, women were thought by both men and women to be more physical creatures than men, and while frequently the basis for their disparagement, and even for misogyny, this greater physicality was also the way in which women were held to be closer to Christ, the physical side of God.[3]

The human body, or the concept of such, has a history. Ideas about the relationship of body and mind, of maleness and femaleness, conceptions of self and physical substance change. For instance, in the medieval period there was a sense in which everyone was thought to be male (since, following Aristotle, the female was a defective male) as well as female (since the soul is female to God). Sexual imagery, in its broadest sense, was both more pervasive and more fluid in Christian devotional writing than it has been in the modern period. A male mystic like Bernard of Clairvaux could understand himself in female images, as a bride to God and as a mother to his monks. F. Schleiermacher in the nineteenth century could wish he had been born a woman in order that he might know the world affectively (as he thought, according to romantic essentialism, women "naturally" did). Bernard in the twelfth century could affectively "be" female while not for a moment compromising his actual masculinity, for the gendered qualities associated with the two sexes were not rigidly attached to either.

The stylization of Jesus as mother in the medieval period has not only to do with psychological aspects of maternal nurturing, as modern treatments tend to be, but also with the physical side of what mothers do—bleed and feed. Bynum writes:

As all medievalists are by now aware, the body of Christ was sometimes depicted as female in medieval devotional texts—partly, of course, because *ecclesia*, Christ's body, was a female personification, partly because the tender, nurturing aspect of God's care for souls was regularly described as motherly. Both male and female mystics called Jesus "mother" in his eucharistic feeding of Christians with liquid exuded from his breast and in his bleeding on the Cross which gave birth to our hope of eternal life.[4]

Some of these devotions seem repugnant to the modern mind. Catherine of Siena is sometimes represented nursing at Christ's breast, sometimes as feeding at his side, blood and milk interchangeable.[5] These assumptions "associated female and flesh with the body of God. Not only was Christ enfleshed with flesh from a woman; his own flesh did womanly things; it bled, it bled food and it gave birth to new life."[6]

But this same nexus of imagery—blood, death, birth, food, milk—is of greater antiquity than Bynum indicates. John Chrysostom draws on it in his *Third Baptismal Instruction*, once again in connection with John 19:34:

But the symbols of baptism and mysteries (Eucharist) come from the side of Christ. It is from His side, therefore, that Christ formed His church, just as He formed Eve from the side of Adam . . .

Have you seen how Christ unites to Himself his bride? Have you seen with what food He nurtures us all? Just as a woman nurtures her offspring with her own blood and milk, so also Christ continuously nurtures with His own blood those whom He has begotten.[7]

Here the bridegroom feeds his spouse with his own blood and milk—a good example of what Paul Ricoeur calls the "mutual contamination" of metaphors, where the text deliberately violates a simple reading in order to frustrate an overly literalistic reading.

We can indeed take this imagery of blood and birth right back to the New Testament itself, to John 19 and elsewhere in the Johannine writings. Teresa Okure, in her essay entitled "The Significance Today of Jesus' Commission to Mary Magdalene" (see Chapter 27 above), draws our attention not so much to the fact of Christ's postresurrection commissioning a woman (often remarked), but rather to the specific nature of the commission (often overlooked). The Johannine Jesus says, "[G]o and tell my brothers and say to them, 'I am ascending to my Father and your Father, to my God and your God' " (Jn 20:17). This is the first time in John's Gospel that the disciples are told that the Father of Jesus is to be their Father too. At the Last Supper they are named as friends and not slaves, and now, with Mary's message, they are told "that they and Jesus now share the same parent . . . in God. They are in truth brothers and sisters of Jesus in God in much the same way as children related who share the same father and mother. . . . Only now does Jesus make his Father and God in the full sense the Father and God of his disciples."[8]

This revelation of the new family takes the reader back to the Prologue, where the believers are styled not only as children of God but as being born of God. It is such a birth Nicodemus is told he must have (Jn 3:1–21) to have eternal life.[9] This birth, Okure adds, has been "brought about by Jesus' passion, death and resurrection," and through his pierced side on the cross.

The commission to Mary Magdalene then tells primarily not of the resurrection but of the new family, the new kinship relations for the followers of Jesus. Jesus' words to Mary, "my God and your God," echo the words of Ruth to Naomi (Ruth 1:16), precisely at that juncture where the demands of patrilineage are put aside in favor of a family bound by faith.

Okure's conclusions are interesting in their own right and all the more so from an African New Testament scholar with a stated nearness to images of blood, kin, and birth, for she emphasizes that her own African understanding of such things make these Johannine associations resonant for her. The blood of kinship, she says, "is the blood of the ancestors and ancestresses who are always alive. . . . If this is true of human blood," she continues, "should it not be more so of the blood of Christ which has given birth and life to us all as children of God, and which continues to nourish us daily through the eucharist?"[10]

The symbolics of blood and the cross, it would seem, are by no means restricted to punitive and penal readings. Indeed other readings, notably that of blood, birth, and kin, are not only present within historical theology but may well afford better ways into the New Testament texts whose kinship patterns are nearer to those of medieval Europe than of the modern West. Birth as well as death is a type of sacrificial giving. As far as my original plea for flexibility goes, it should be apparent that the symbolic orderings of Christianity are neither obvious nor unchanging. Similarly it is by no means clear that Christ is always and everywhere in the symbolic order a "male" figure. There is abundant sense in seeing Christ as our mother, and his blood as the source of new life—indeed by doing so we recover a proud heritage of patristic theology.[11]

So blood is the source of life. But is it not also the case that in the Bible female blood is a source of impurity and defilement? As the Jewish scholar Leonie Archer has pointed out, Levitical purity laws affected women particularly. Rulings on the impurities caused by female blood (whether of menstruation, childbirth, or irregular flows) were part of an "all-pervasive blood taboo" that covered foods and sacrifice and effected separations of the sexes.[12] Although both sexes were affected by the laws concerning bodily emissions, in both Levitical law and the common Judaism of Jesus' time women were a far greater source of contagion than men. Women were impure after childbirth, and the impurity lasted longer if the child was female. The birth of a male child resulted in forty days of childbirth impurity, a daughter resulted in eighty. Whereas contact with semen resulted in impurity for one day, menstruants "were impure for a week, and anyone who touched a menstruant, her bed or chair was impure for a day."[13] Through many Christian centuries, and still in some quarters, menstruation and irregular bleeding were seen as defiling and as grounds for exclusion from eucharistic reception. How can one compare, as we did in the previous section, the blood of Christ to the blood of women?

The obvious point in the New Testament at which to explore the symbolism of female blood is the story of the healing of the woman with the hemorrhage (Mark 5:21–43; Matt 9:18–34; Luke 8:40–56), yet when discussed, curiously little is made of the major theme of impurity and defilement that runs through it. Contemporary preachers (and many commentators) are far more likely to focus on the healing that takes place and on the woman's faith. Even when the issue of female impurity is raised, the tendency of the typical Western Christian (and here I include the typical Western Christian feminist) is resolutely Marcionite. Even those who otherwise go out of their way to reach out to Jewish brothers and sisters quickly respond to this story by saying that the Jewish law of purity was a nonsense and that Jesus, being wise, knew this to be so. Yet, even apart from the offense to Jews, so easy and brutal a resolution is not acceptable in terms of modern New Testament scholarship. Jesus did not dismiss the law.

The modern Christian reader then seems stuck between the Scylla of misogyny and the Charybdis of anti-Judaism. New Testament critics deploy a number of strategies. Elisabeth Schüssler Fiorenza largely skirts the issue of impurity by focusing on the woman's illness, isolation, and inferred poverty (she "had spent all that she had"). Gerd Theissen and many others focus almost entirely on the woman's faith, drawing attention to the fact that the story of the woman with the hemorrhage is the only miracle story apart from that of the Stilling the Storm in which all three Synoptics talk about faith. In the woman's "unspoken confidence . . . that Jesus can absorb her disease without being endangered himself," says Theissen, we see "a faith which incorporates and transcends even the ambivalent and illegitimate."[14] But if we are to consider these stories not as simple observer reportage but as theologically motivated,[15] we must admit the possibility that the precise nature of the woman's illness is *not irrelevant*. The Gospel writers have, after all, gone out of their way in all three Synoptics, to identify her ailment as irregular bleeding. If this were irrelevant to the story, it would be more seemly to say simply that she had been ill for twelve years.

Jesus, you will remember, is on his way to heal Jairus' daughter when the woman with the flow touches his robes. The Synoptic accounts differ in details, but in all three the woman is immediately cured. In Mark and Luke Jesus asks who has touched him, and the woman comes before him "in fear and trembling." Jesus says to her, "Daughter, your faith has made you well; go in peace, and be healed of your disease" (Mark 5:34). Jesus calls the woman "daughter" in all three accounts.

We can ask questions in more than one theological register about such a story. One can and should, for instance, ask some "historical Jesus" questions: Was Jesus, in terms of contemporary Judaism, potentially defiled by her touch? Did this affect only Temple purity and, if so, what might this suggest about attitudes to Temple purity, and so on? But for the purposes of christological reflection, we can see the Gospels, too, as already theological constructions, perhaps already christological constructions, with deliberate symbolic and associative links.

Interpretations that, like Theissen's, put virtually the whole emphasis on the woman's faith are reductive. His own displays a hermeneutical disposition to see faith as the crucial explanatory motif in the miracle stories. The suggestion that the woman has an "unspoken confidence" that Jesus can absorb her disease without endangering himself does not explain adequately why the woman came "in fear and trembling" (Mark and Luke) when confronted. She is represented as believing she would be healed if she touched Jesus' garment, but as uncertain of the wider consequences.

One explanation sometimes given for her fear is that, apart from behaving presumptuously, she fears she will have defiled the teacher in touching him.[16] Difficulties attend this reading. Is it an insight into the woman's presumed psychology? Would the crowd have known of her ailment? And so on. Added to this, Charlotte Fonrobert has argued that, in the masoretic text, a *zavah* (a woman with an irregular or extended blood flow) *does not* transfer impurity by touching some-one.[17] These matters taken into consideration, it seems enough to say that the woman was in a state of impurity (which, if not culpable, is isolating) and also of disorder—unlike a normal flow, her blood was flowing to no purpose. Its flow precluded rather than foresaw the possibility of new life.

Theissen gives little weight to the placing of the story of the woman with the hemorrhage. But in all three Synoptics the story of the woman with the flow is contained within that of Jairus' daughter, not so obviously a story of faith. But what *more* might this placing suggest? Again, the commentaries are strangely silent. On the narrative level it seems that more than one feature links the two miracles. The woman has had the flow of blood for twelve years; the daughter of Jairus is twelve years old—the age at which Jewish girls were judged nubile. The woman with the flow is impure and infertile; Jesus risks defile-ment by entering a house that he is told contains a corpse and by touching the corpse/girl. The woman with the flow is made whole and (presumably) once again fertile by her healing and is called "daugh-ter"; the daughter of Jairus is declared not dead but "sleeping" and rises to enter womanly life. Both stories have elements of defilement and "death," and of fecundity and new life.

Apart from the exhortation to faith, another shared feature of the Synoptic stories of the Stilling of the Storm is the questions the dis-ciples ask: "Who then is this, that even the wind and the sea obey him?" The power to control the waves is, in the psalms, attributed to the Creator:

> Then they cried to the Lord in their trouble,
> and he brought them out of their distress;
> he made the storm be still,
> and the waves of the sea were hushed. (Ps 107:28–29)

In stilling the storm Jesus appears to participate in the creative power of God, as he does in the stories of the healing of the woman with the hemorrhage and of Jairus' daughter. In these, fertility, wholeness, and "peace" are restored, as befits one who is to fulfill the promises of Isaiah. In these stories Jesus displays a power over illness, infertility, and death emblematic of a new creation. To recapitulate, on this christological reading the story of the woman with the hemorrhage need have nothing to do with a dismissal by Jesus of Jewish purity laws. The woman has not necessarily transgressed in touching him, nor in milling with the crowd.[18] She is, however, isolated in her impurity and isolated in a different way by her infertility. It is possible then that the story does not dismiss purity laws or ignore them, but rather calls us back to the primal meaning of the Jewish laws surrounding blood and the flow of female blood. As Jewish women grow weary of pointing out, this "impurity" or "defilement" has nothing to do with sinfulness and a great deal to do with holiness—the holiness of birth and blood and life. The woman is in an excluded position by virtue of a bleeding that should betoken fertility but which in her case does not yield life.

Why might the Gospel writers wish to put these two female figures, the woman with the flow and Jairus' daughter, in symbolic alignment to Jesus? Early Christian legend and art identified the figure of the woman with the hemorrhage with the figure of St. Veronica, the historically shadowy figure whose cloth, on wiping the brow of Christ, was imprinted with the "true icon" (thus "veronica"). The blood of the flow is in this telling linked with the passion of Christ.[19] As the cloth of Christ's garment stopped the flow of the woman's blood, so Veronica's cloth stops the flow of Christ's blood. As the woman's flow of blood is stopped and her fertility restored (she is made fertile with faith), so Christ's flow of blood is turned from death to "new life." This ancient pairing of the woman with the flow with Veronica suggests an exegesis of the Synoptic story that is not concerned with "unclean female bodies," nor with dismissal of the Law.[20] Rather we are drawn back to the life-giving power of female blood—a power that the Jewish purity laws reflect and that this reading aligns with the blood shed on the cross. Once again, the blood of the Cross is mapped on the symbolics of the feminine.

The idiom of pollution lends itself to a complex algebra . . .[21]

Blood, indicating the impure, . . . inherits the propensity for murder of which man must cleanse himself. But blood, as a vital element, also refers to women, fertility, and the assurance of fecundation. It thus becomes a fascinating semantic crossroads, the propitious place for abjection *where death* and *femininity, murder* and *procreation, cessation of life* and *vitality* all come together. "But flesh with the life thereof, which is the blood thereof, shall ye not eat" (Genesis 9:4).[22]

Everyone who believes that Jesus is the Christ has been born of God, and everyone who loves the parent loves the child. By this we know that we love the children of God, when we love God and obey his commandments. . . . And his commandments are not burdensome, for whatever is born of God conquers the world. . . . Who is it that conquers the world but the one who believes that Jesus is the Son of God? This is the one who came by water and blood, Jesus Christ, not with the water only but with the water and the blood. (1 John 5:1–6)

   The symbolism of the New Testament texts is constantly disruptive. Leviticus prohibits the eating of blood, yet the central Christian rite involves drinking blood. In Leviticus childbirth is defiling, yet John's Gospel describes God as giving birth to the chosen. In Levitical terms a corpse radiates impurity, especially for priests. In Christianity the central icon of holiness, of the Great High Priest, is a dead man on the cross.[23] The symbolism of blood is deep within the texts of Christianity and does not abandon its Jewish ancestry or dismiss it; it is rather inexplicable without it. Blood is holy; it is the life of the animal. And if one claims to be fed on the blood of God? Furthermore, the subversion of symbols, the turning, for instance, from shame and exclusion to glory, does not mark a departure from Jewish hermeneutics but is in continuity with it. In the New Testament, as in the Hebrew Scriptures, symbolic orders are constantly challenged, broken open, and renewed. It is this inversion of our human expectations that keeps us open to what God might newly, freely choose to do.

Notes

1. Julia Kristeva, *In the Beginning Was Love: Psychoanalysis and Faith* (New York: Columbia University Press, 1987).
2. Ibid. 32.
3. Caroline Walker Bynum, 'The Female Body and Religious Practice in the Later Middle Ages', in *Fragmentation and Redemption* (New York: Zone Books, 1991), 181–238.
4. Ibid. 176.
5. We need recall that medieval biologists believed breast milk to be a transmuted form of the blood that nourished the fetus in the womb, which is not an unreasonable conjecture since in breast-feeding menstruation is suppressed (ibid. 182).
6. Ibid. 185.

7. John Chrysostom, *Baptismal Instructions*, ed. and trans. Paul Harkins, Ancient Christian Writers (New York: Paulist, 1963), 62. It is worth noting that Karl Rahner's successful doctoral thesis, after the rejection of *Geist in Welt*, was on the image of the birth of the Church from the side of Christ in patristic thought.

8. Teresa Okure, 'The Significance Today of Jesus' Commission to Mary Magdalene', *International Review of Mission* 81 (322) (Apr. 1992), 182.

9. Ibid. 183.

10. Ibid. 186.

11. Graham Leonard may have a point in saying that 'sacrificial giving is associated with femaleness'. Where his remarks are theologically suspect is in their symbolic alignment of this 'giving' with Mary/Church *over and against Christ*, and in his failure to see as clearly as did the medievals that the primary Christian locus of this giving must be Christ. All good Marian theology rests on this.

12. Leonie Archer, 'Bound by Blood: Circumcision and Menstrual Taboo', in *After Eve*, ed. Janet Martin Soskice (London: Marshall Pickering, 1990), 43.

13. E. P. Sanders, *Judaism* (London: SCM, 1992), 72. See also his *Jewish Law from Jesus to the Mishnah* (London: SCM, 1990), 142 ff.

14. Gerd Theissen, *Miracle Stories of the Early Christian Tradition* (Edinburgh: T. & T. Clark, 1983), 134.

15. That is, minimally, to say that the Gospel writers have chosen to describe this particular incident and have done so for a reason. I do not wish to imply, in saying that the Gospels are literary constructions, that they are therefore literary fictions. A history of the Second World War can be a literary construction without being a fiction.

16. Elisabeth Schüssler Fiorenza notes: 'this woman's predicament was not just incurable illness but also permanent uncleanness. She was not only unclean herself, but polluted everyone and everything with which she came into contact (Lev. 15:19–31)'. *In Memory of Her: A Feminist Theological Reconstruction of Christian Origins* (New York: Crossroad, 1983), 124. Another interpretation put forward is that Jesus' power heals her before any defilement takes place.

17. Charlotte Fonrobert, 'The Woman with a Blood-flow (Mark 5:24–34) Revisited: Menstrual Laws and Jewish Culture in Christian Feminist Hermeneutics', in *Early Christian Interpretation of the Scriptures of Israel*, ed. Craig A. Evans and James A. Sanders, *Journal for the Study of the New Testament* Supplement Series 148 (Sheffield: Sheffield Academic Press, 1997), 130–1.

18. Fonrobert is critical of M. Selvidge on this point. I take Fonrobert to have made a good case for saying that the story is not concerned with an 'abrogation of biblical traditions concerning menstruation and irregular discharges of blood' (p. 135), but believe she is on less solid ground in this article in suggesting that it is only important that the woman had a severe illness and that the nature of the illness is of no account. My suggestion is that the nature of the disorder is material to the narrative.

19. See Ewa Kurykuk, *Veronica and Her Cloth: History, Symbolism, and Structure of a 'True' Image* (Oxford: Blackwell, 1991), 7. See especially the introduction and chs. 5 and 6.

20. The idea that menstrual flow is in itself unclean in a repugnant (rather than ritual) sense Fonrobert sees as a distinctly Christian development and is, as

she notes, ambiguously inconsistent. If in Christ the law has been abolished, then the law can no longer be the reason why Christian women are enjoined not to 'approach the holy table' as they were in some traditions. Unlike the Jewish situation, that latter, distinctly Christian exclusion is, she suggests, the result of Western (and Greek) contempt for the body, especially the female body ('Woman with a Blood-flow', 137).

21. Mary Douglas, *Purity and Danger* (New York: Praeger, 1966), 9.
22. Julia Kristeva, 'The Semiotics of Biblical Abomination', in *Powers of Horror: An Essay on Abjection*, trans. Leon S. Roudiez (New York: Columbia University Press, 1982), 96.
23. See L. William Countryman, *Dirt, Greed and Sex* (Philadelphia: Fortress, 1988), and also a fascinating article by Timothy Radcliffe, OP, 'Christ in Hebrews: Cultic Irony', *New Blackfriars* 68 (Nov. 1987), 494–504.

30 Contours of a Queer Theology

Grace M. Jantzen*

Grace Jantzen writes as one for whom 'the straight rule' of Christendom has been not only the worst part of her personal past but also 'the best of it'. Abolishing the divine is not, for her, an option. She finds in the embodiment of Jesus possibilities for a theology of immanence and an aesthetics of difference, yet to be explored, in which the 'curved' is prized.   JMS

Or should that be, 'queer contours of theology'? My intention in this paper is certainly not an attempt to fix theological boundaries or positions, even if queer ones, or to generate a queer creed. Rather, I wish to begin an exploration of how queer thinking can be theologically creative, offering some suggestions towards a theology that gets rid of the straight and narrow boundaries of traditional christendom and is open to difference, fluidity, curvature.

From a queer perspective, christendom has often fared badly, and deservedly so. Christian churches, Christian theology, social policy informed by allegedly Christian values have banged the drum of heterosexual marriage and 'family values' until its monotonous beat has drowned out melodies of different ways of being. Indeed christendom is responsible not just for drum bashing but for a good deal of literal queer bashing, oppression and violence against any who openly reject the idea that its heterosexual agenda has come 'straight' from heaven. So it is no wonder that many who take up a queer orientation find ourselves at odds with the christendom that forms the history of the present in the west and forms also the personal history of many people, including many queer people, within it. I think it to be very important that that oppression and violence should be spelled out

* Grace M. Jantzen, 'Contours of a Queer Theology', *Literature and Theology* 15(3) (Sept. 2001). Copyright © Oxford University Press.

and acknowledged for what it is; and nothing I say in what follows should be read as minimising it.

But I have found myself wondering, 'And then what?' Like a child who knows there must be more to a story, I have turned round in my mind how this account of christendom and queer living might continue. But the script is not written. We will have to make it up as we go along. How the story continues is at least in part up to us. For many who have had the straight rule of christendom applied in hurtful and destructive ways, the answer is to slam the book shut altogether and have nothing more to do with this story. For some people that is surely a healthy response, not just 'understandable' in a condescending way, but a very good conclusion to the particular script they have been required to read.

But for me that will not do. Part of the reason is that christendom has not only been the worst of my personal past but also the best of it; and the need to deal with the former requires a reappropriation and transformation of the latter. I will not become a more flourishing person by cutting off my roots. A second reason is that, as I have argued elsewhere,[1] secularism is not a satisfactory alternative. The symbolic of western secularism is as sexist, racist and homophobic as the christendom that informs it, and by banishing the divine from the world has too often seen that world reduced to the quantitative calculus of a free market economy where targets and statistics measure supposedly commensurable goods.[2] Whether that is a necessary consequence of secularism is a moot point; in any case, it is surely as important to put secularism on trial as it is to evaluate christendom, and to find ways of thinking differently. A third reason, related to both of the above, is the lure of the divine. If the divine is understood (at least) as that which summons or stands for the best in us, or better than the best, understood therefore as fluidity and process rather than straight rigidity, what sort of queer theology does it imply? Can we do without it?

THE LESBIAN RULE

Architects have an instrument or gadget, so I understand, known as a Lesbian Rule. It is a flexible strip of metal, a device used for measuring curved or oddly shaped parts of a structure, where a straight, rigid rule would be clumsy or useless. Aristotle mentions it in the *Nichomachean*

Ethics, saying that it is a rule that 'adapts itself to the shape of the stone and is not rigid':[3] for him it is a simile for good ethical deliberation.[4] If we think of Greek columns, with their flutes and curves, it is easy to see that a rigid measuring device that works well for straight parts of the structure would be a nuisance for these queer shapes which give the columns their beauty.

This rule is called 'lesbian' because it came from the Island of Lesbos where the marble for the columns of Greek temples was quarried and shaped. It is sheer coincidence that this is also the Island of Sappho, whose name stands for a sexuality that does not conform to rigid heterosexual expectations. But I find the coincidence serendipitous. Too much theology has been quarried like chunks of limestone, with all odd angles and protrusions carefully chipped away so that the doctrines can be piled up, one fitting neatly on another, with square corners and straight sides, into a building of christendom within which the divine can be contained. What if we tried instead to build with a lesbian rule, with curves and flutes and rounded columns set far enough apart so there was plenty of room for the wind of the spirit to blow through? What if we released the divine—and ourselves—from the straight prisons and used instead a measurement of beauty in our theological constructions?

Another part of the appeal to me of the idea of a lesbian rule is that, though flexible, it is still a device for measurement. Not just anything goes. A pile of any old stones, curved or straight, is not a column nor a thing of beauty. Criteria are needed, even though not the straight criteria that set creed upon creed and consider any curves or queer angles an invitation for chipping away or bashing into conformity. But what criteria can there be? How do we measure the contours of a queer theology? Talk of criteria can all too easily be a way of taking up the rigid measurements after all, and before we know it we are back inside the confinements of straight and narrow christendom, business as usual. But if not that, then what?

DOCTRINES WITH A QUEER CURVE

I think that if we begin by valuing difference, fluidity, curvature; and questioning unity, rigidity, and uniformity, many of the doctrines of christendom become more open. I have taken some tentative steps in the exploration of these possibilities elsewhere,[5] and will offer only the briefest sketch here.

To begin at the beginning: the story of creation, as it is told in the first chapter of Genesis, is queer from the outset. Whatever else it might mean, surely it is the strongest possible mythological representation of difference, multiplicity, variety. All the infinite variety of plants and trees, insects, birds and animals are represented as designed by God and declared good. It is at the farthest possible remove from a doctrine valorising uniformity: it presents diversity as manifestation of the divine. If I were looking for theological underpinning for a manifesto of identity politics I would not start from here!

But what about a doctrine of incarnation? As it is often presented, it sounds like a story about divine child abuse: God the Almighty Father sends his son to earth from heaven to live in poverty and die a horrendous death as an atonement for sins of God's other children whom he cannot otherwise forgive. To suggest that the Son was a willing victim, and that all of this is a manifestation of divine love, makes the story, to my mind, even more gruesome. Violence is bad enough; but violence that involves collusion of the victim and calls itself love is the stuff of nightmares. If we would not tolerate it as a way for parents or teachers to treat children, why should it become acceptable when projected on to the divine?[6] This is of course a crude rendition, even a caricature, of traditional doctrine, but anyone who attempts a more sophisticated version will need to take very seriously indeed how easily it slips into a theological justification for child abuse.

Luce Irigaray, however, has suggested an alternative understanding of incarnation, an incarnation that is not one-off but diverse, queer in its contours. The idea that Jesus in his specificity of embodiment, context, and sexuality was divine, though he obviously did not encompass all embodiments, races, and sexualities, opens the way for thinking about other incarnations, 'the incarnation of all bodies (men's and women's) as potentially divine; nothing more nor less than each man and each woman being virtually gods'.[7] Since Jesus was one man, not all humanity, his incarnation—his being an embodiment of the divine—leaves room for other incarnations, other sexualities, other embodiments. Irigaray presses the point that this is our fundamental concern. 'God forces us to do nothing except *become*. The only task, the only obligation laid upon us is: to become divine men and women, to become perfectly, to refuse to allow parts of ourselves to shrivel and die that have the potential for growth and fulfilment.'[8] This is very queer incarnation, celebrating difference and fluidity, rejecting a monoculture of the mind.[9]

It is clear that such becoming divine cannot be a matter of being 'saved' from a wicked world or a sinful nature in order to escape from it to another world of bliss after we die and rid ourselves of our troublesome queer curves. Neither can we think of Jesus as a heroic Saviour who swoops out of heaven to rescue us. I suggest, however, that we might think instead of flourishing, becoming the best we can be. Flourishing, for a plant, can happen only when there is life and potential for growth from inside; it requires fresh air and nourishment but it does not require a rescue from outside, or a rejection of the world and its goodness. Nor do most plants grow straight and rigid. Their beauty is in their curves, their variety, the sheer abundance of difference. The metaphor of flourishing, of a vine and branches, of fruitfulness occurs often in biblical writings; but christendom has largely rejected it for a metaphor of salvation, replacing an emphasis on fulfilment and variety and goodness, with rescue from sin and evil to an immortality when once we have been freed from the restrictions of our bodies and specific contexts.[10]

Obviously in all this the concept of the divine is also changed. The one God of monotheism, the jealous Lord beside whom there can be no other, has been the coping stone of the rigid structure of straight christendom. The Name and Law of the Father has been the guarantor of orthodoxy, whether theological or psychoanalytic, and has served as the straight rule by which deviance is defined and found unacceptable. The lead that I am following from Irigaray, by contrast, construes the divine more in terms of process, of becoming, not as some developing ontological principle or being but as the energy of beauty and value within us and between us and beyond us. The divine is multiform, the horizon of our becoming. It does not construct the world from outside, as an absence to be overcome by a reason which masters the one truth. Rather, the divine is within us and between us, enabling our flourishing. Thus, as Irigaray puts it, we are not 'awaiting the god passively, but bringing the god of life through us',[11] embodied in all our differences in the projection and reclamation of ultimate value, becoming divine.[12]

I do not mean to imply that these crude representations of traditional doctrines are the best that can be said for them, nor that the queer curves I have suggested are the only ways in which they could be re-envisioned. My intention is only to open some possibilities for discussion for a theology that starts from a lesbian rule, rejecting the straight and narrow edifice of christendom as it has confined us, without reverting to a reductionist secularism. Rather than continue this discussion of doctrine, however, which after all starts from an orthodox rule and sees how it could be bent into queer shapes, I want now to return to the idea of the lesbian rule. In particular, I want to question the starting point of theological methodology, and contemplate the beauty of curves.

STRAIGHT TRUTH

Christendom has been much taken up with creeds, truth and orthodoxy. Theological attention is largely focused on issues of doctrinal truth; and the philosophy of religion, at least the Anglo-American analytic variety, is intensely preoccupied with evidences, proofs, and justified true beliefs. In this, christendom is mimicked by secularism, which is also much concerned with truth, often narrowly reduced to targets, quantification, and calculation. Now, it would be absurd to suggest that we could get along without evidence, beliefs and truth. In my opinion, however, a one-sided focus on truth, theological and otherwise, leads to (and springs from) a narrowing of life and a quest for rigid mastery. Indeed it distorts and falsifies the very truth it professes to exalt.

One way this can be seen is to consider who and what this emphasis on truth leaves out. At whose expense is this truth? In specific terms, the insistence on straight truth has largely privileged powerful white men and heterosexual normativity, at the expense of those—women, people of colour, every sort of 'deviant' from the straight and narrow norm—whom they can master with this construction of rationality and thus of humanity. Looking at it in another way, what this emphasis on truth leaves out is any focus on beauty. There is very little attempt to consider beauty in much theological writing in modernity, let alone to see how beauty might modify our conception of truth. No wonder so much theological writing—and even more so, philosophy of religion—is ugly, both in presentation and in consequence. Unrelieved straight rigid lines, whether of architecture or of thought, cannot build beautiful temples for the spirit.

We would (rightly) feel that we could not live with integrity if we did not care about truth. Isn't the same thing true of beauty? How can we flourish if we are content with ugliness? We live with light pollution and cannot see the stars. We live with noise pollution and cannot hear birdsong or insects or the breath of wind in pines: many of us would be hard pressed to identify a bird by its song or a deer by its bark if we did hear it. We live in cities that are crowded and dirty, where we seldom watch the dawn or the sunset, or wonder at the beauty of the world. We may feel that it is a pity, of course, a matter of regret that we try to remedy as best we can by holidays or weekends in the country, but we don't let it stop our lives and careers. Suppose we tried the same tactic in relation to truth: 'well, it's a pity, but I'll just have to live in untruth; I regret all these lies of course, but they are necessary for my career. I do try for truthfulness in my own home or at the weekends . . .' It is of course preposterous. A person evincing such an attitude would be immediately scorned—and feared. So how is beauty different?

Indeed, much of the world as it is organised by a free market economy effectively excludes many people from the beauty of nature, in part by actively destroying it through environmental degradation, and in part by making it an economic necessity that most people live in cities. Thus sensitivity to birdsong and wild flowers increasingly becomes a privilege of the wealthy. The beauty of art and music, too, is skewed to those with the leisure and education to develop an appreciation for them. If theologians do not protest against the belittling of the beauty of the world, how can we expect to be sensitive to the wonder of the divine?

Now, of course, it is important to recognise that 'beauty' is not a straightforward term. It has been defined in many ways; and what has counted as beauty is not unrelated to who has had the power to do the counting. A genealogy of beauty, moreover, would quickly reveal its convoluted entanglements with ideas of gender and of death. I think that such a genealogy would be a major contribution to a theology with queer contours. The idea that 'truth' is not as straightforward a notion as it might seem has preoccupied thinkers for several millennia, as they tried to develop epistemologies and logics that do justice to rationality. The complexity of beauty, surely, calls for at least as much attention; and I think that those who measure by a lesbian rule rather than in straight logical lines have an indispensable perspective to bring to bear upon it.

AN AESTHETICS OF THE SELF

Michel Foucault has reflected long on the task of self-formation in ways that are enlightening to such a queer perspective. Although he does not often explicitly discuss beauty, in his later writings especially he emphasises creativity: 'we have to create ourselves as a work of art'.[13] Rather than allow ourselves to be prefabricated in the power–knowledge relations that press for normalisation and conformity, we have the freedom to think differently, to be otherwise, to create ourselves according to our own queer styles. This freedom is not unlimited; no one could exist outside of a cultural and historical context and personal background that shapes our possibilities. Nevertheless, limited though it is, we have the power of resistance and creativity, the 'breath of life' that confronts and reshapes the history that claims a false hegemony.[14] Moreover, this freedom, this queer creativity, can be cultivated and enabled to flourish. As James Bernauer puts it in an important article, 'Foucault's ethics is an invitation to the practice of liberty, to struggle and transgression, which seeks to open possibilities for new relations to self and events in the world.'[15]

This invitation is open to all. But those of us who already take up queer positions have some extra practice in the creativity and the cost of an aesthetics of the self. We are learning how to dig deep into our best possibilities, and not to allow ourselves to become flat mirrors of our contexts, reflecting and reinforcing its self-perceptions. By deliberately adopting a lesbian rule, the mirror we hold up to our culture, religious and secular, is a mirror of curves and corners that reveals the multiple distortions of discursive and material reality.

It is hard to hold to these resistant and transgressive perspectives, hard not to let ourselves be fashioned again into straight contours. After all, we are the ones who are out of line. The big threat, often (and often internalised) is the threat of narcissism: if we are looking to develop an aesthetics of the self, a power of resistance and creativity in queer styles, is this not utter self-absorption? Isn't self-creation an ultimately unethical project?

But to bring the question into the open is already partly to answer it. What fear—*whose* fear—does this fear of self-creation bespeak? Clearly it is precisely those who most want conformity to the prefabricated straight lines of power–knowledge and their economic manifestations who will least welcome the reflections of a curved mirror. We can turn the question around: if self-creation is to be rejected, then who or what will create us, and by what rules? Why should they not rather be shown up for the restricting ugliness which they too often are?

We do not need to be afraid of self-creation. To try to realise our best possibilities, resistant to conformity to the taken-for-granted, is costly and takes perseverance, but is the way of freedom and beauty. We do not find it problematic that a beech tree or a sparrow should flourish from within itself, requiring only that its context give it requisite protection and nourishment: are we not to be trusted similarly to flourish as long as we are not put into straight jackets? An aesthetics of the self is the very opposite of flitting to and fro between desires and fancies; it is a steady work of self-creation that takes the measure of every queer curve and turn, but does so with a lesbian rule.

THE STONES CRY OUT

All this may seem a long way from a queer theology, but I suggest that it is not. Just as we are conditioned to look outside of ourselves and be conformed to the straight norms of the western symbolic, so, I suggest, it is taken for granted that theology must come from outside the world through revelatory words of truth. And just as we do not need to be afraid of self-creation, developing an aesthetic of the self from our own creative possibilities and resources of freedom, so, I suggest, we need not be afraid of encountering and learning to recognise the divine in the queer and wonderful beauty of the world. Indeed, unless we do so, we can hardly expect theological words to be anything more than straight and ugly verbiage.

Annie Dillard, an American author, tells a wonderful story of Larry, a man who lives alone with a stone that he is trying to teach to talk.[16] He covers it with a cloth, which he removes for its lessons several times a day. There is no particular expectation about what exactly the stone will say when it does at last speak; nor can this be counted on to happen anytime soon: it may well be the work of generations. Nevertheless Larry persists, though so far the stone keeps silent. In this the stone has made less progress than some other things in the natural world, which, even if they do not yet speak, already make some sounds: a fire crackles, wind sighs in branches, a stream gurgles along its course. All of these, Dillard suggests, have something to say if only they could be taught to speak.

For once upon a time they did speak; and often what they spoke of was the divine. There were holy wells, and groves of oak trees with sacred powers, and mountains and caves where the divine could be heard, and stones, too, not only small ones such as the one the recluse is working with but enormous boulders placed in circles and pointing to holy light. But all these have been silenced. God has been banished from the world. The water and fire and wind and stone no longer speak, are no longer sacramental.

Now we are no longer primitive; now the whole world seems not-holy. We have drained the light from the boughs in the sacred groves and snuffed it in the high places and along the banks of sacred streams. We as a people have moved from pantheism to pan-atheism. Silence is not our heritage but our destiny; we live where we want to live.[17]

The divine has been pushed out of the world into a heaven from which 'he' utters laws and words of straight truth, while the world itself has been deprived of the ability to speak.

So teaching a stone to talk could equally well be described as teaching ourselves to listen. One has to be in a queer place to be serious about listening to what a stone might say if it were allowed to speak from within itself rather than forced into silent square blocks. But what might we hear of the divine (and how radically might the world be changed for us) if we were in tune with the voice of its beauty? As Elizabeth Barrett Browning once wrote,

> Earth's crammed with heaven
> And every common bush afire with God:
> But only he who sees, takes off his shoes,
> The rest sit round it, and pluck blackberries . . .[18]

though nowadays many of us don't even bother about the black-berries, but prefer the straight and sterile aisles of a supermarket to the thorny brambles of the common bush.

CONTOURS OF A QUEER THEOLOGY

But what might we hear if we had learned to understand what the stone says, learned to recognise the divine in the hedgerows? Surely this would be highly unorthodox, a very queer theology indeed, would it not? Yes, I think it well might be—and about time too! What its content is will only emerge as the stone has many more lessons in elocution, and as we learn more readily to stop and turn aside and see the flaming bushes and remove our shoes. But though its substance cannot be prejudged, I think it possible to suggest some of the contours of a queer theology.

First, I think that a queer theology is one that privileges immanence, indeed one that treats transcendence not as other *than* this world but rather as other than a secular reduction *of* this world. If we do not turn aside to see the bush ablaze it is unlikely that we will properly hear the words of the divine; rather than burn in our souls, they will be turned all too quickly into the Law of the Father. Unless the divine can be encountered in grass and rain, in the beauty and terror of the world, the idea that bread and wine could be sacramental is mockery. As an aesthetics of the self is an effort to enable flourishing from within, not by some superimposed rigid frame, so a theological aesthetics looks to the splendour within the world rather than consigning the world to the satisfaction of a greed for commodities.

Second, and closely related, I think that the contours of a queer theology will be fashioned by beauty as much as by truth and goodness. I hardly yet know what this may come to: a genealogy of beauty has yet to be written, and its connections with gender and power explored. The frequency with which the beautiful is identified with the feminine in modernity (and then quickly denigrated to mere prettiness), while the sublime is masculine and transcendent, gives some hints towards the direction of work involved. The ugliness of much theology—in its style, in its content, in its effects—is long overdue for displacement.

Finally, the contours of a queer theology must surely be measured by a lesbian rule: it must welcome multiple shapes and curves and differences rather than look for a rigid monolithic structure. Quite what happens when we have the courage to give up the idea of one truth straight from heaven remains to be seen. Certainly building a theology from within, enabling our queer shapes to emerge and flourish, is no easy option: it is sustained reflective work that is both costly and liberatory, the very opposite of careless relativism. It involves living always with the question: what do you long for most of all, and what are you doing to prevent it?

Notes

1. 'Before the Rooster Crows: John Locke, Margaret Fell, and the Betrayal of Knowledge in Modernity', *Literature and Theology* 15(1) (Mar. 2001), 1–24;

see also *Becoming Divine: Towards a Feminist Philosophy of Religion* (Manchester: Manchester University Press, and Bloomington: Indiana University Press, 1998).

2. For a strong argument against commensurability see M. Nussbaum, 'Plato on Commensurability and Desire', in her *Love's Knowledge: Essays on Philosophy and Literature* (Oxford: Oxford University Press, 1990), 106–24. Nussbaum does not extend her argument to a critique of secularism.

3. Aristotle, *Nichomachean Ethics* V. 10, 1137b, in R. McKeon (ed.), *The Basic Works of Aristotle* (New York: Random House, 1941), 1020.

4. For a discussion of this see M. Nussbaum, 'The Discernment of Perception: An Aristotelian Conception of Private and Public Rationality', in *Love's Knowledge*, 70–2.

5. See 'Off the Straight and Narrow: Towards a Lesbian Theology', *Theology and Sexuality* 3 (autumn 1995); see also *Becoming Divine*.

6. See further R. N. Brock, 'And a Little Child Will Lead Us: Christology and Child Abuse', in J. C. Brown and C. R. Bohn (eds.), *Christianity, Patriarchy and Abuse: A Feminist Critique* (New York: Pilgrim Press, 1989).

7. L. Irigaray, 'Equal to Whom?', trans. R. L. Mazzola, *Differences* 1(2) (1989), 64.

8. L. Irigaray, 'Divine Women', in her *Sexes and Genealogies*, trans. G. C. Gill (New York: Columbia University Press, 1993), 68.

9. For further discussion see my *Becoming Divine*, ch. 1.

10. See further ibid., ch. 7.

11. Irigaray, 'Divine Women', 63.

12. *Becoming Divine*, ch. 11.

13. M. Foucault, 'On the Genealogy of Ethics', in H. L. Dreyfus and P. Rabinow, *Michel Foucault: Beyond Structuralism and Hermeneutics*, 2nd edn. (Chicago: Chicago University Press, 1983), 237.

14. M. Foucault, 'Is it Useless to Revolt?', *Philosophy and Social Criticism* 8 (spring 1981), 8.

15. J. Bernauer and M. Mahon, 'The Ethics of Michel Foucault', in G. Gutting (ed.), *The Cambridge Companion to Foucault* (Cambridge: Cambridge University Press, 1994), 54.

16. A. Dillard, *Teaching a Stone to Talk: Expeditions and Encounters* (London: Picador, 1984), 67–76.

17. Ibid. 69.

18. E. Barrett Browning. *Aurora Leigh* VII. 821–4 (London: Penguin, 1995), 232.

31 The Suffering Christ and the Asian Body

Sharon A. Bong*

Sharon Bong identifies speaking from the vantage point of the poor as a hallmark of Two-Thirds world theology, yet asks how can we speak about the bodies of the poor and suffering without words becoming 'just words'? This problem is particularly fraught in relation to poor women. It is all too easy to reduce 'the poor woman' to a theological trope, a Christian 'superwoman' of suffering, and in so doing neglect the diversity, delight, hope, and healing present amongst even the poorest of the poor. The embodied Christ, Bong emphasizes, both suffers and is resurrected.   JMS

A theology that matters is one that is embodied. That Asian Christian theology is 'body language, heart semantics or soul-syntax' reclaims the body and its corporeality in theologizing from the lived experiences of the grassroots and in particular, women.[1] It is premised on the historical and material conditions of specific Asian communities and articulated from their positions of marginality *and* agency. And it effects the following doctrinal transgressions. It is firstly an antithesis to the denigration of the body fed by the church's tacit valorization of asceticism and residual misogyny of the (male) spirit/(female) body duality. Secondly, it digests the humanization of God in the body of Christ that suffers, resists and heals and in so doing, eschews a Godhead that is disembodied. And thirdly, it rejects the exegetic 'violence of abstraction'[2] by foregrounding faith and praxis towards the realization of a local/global community that is more equitable, just and sustainable from within the church and beyond.

In contrast, from my personal standpoint as an Asian-Malaysian Catholic feminist, the platter of doctrinal interpretation of the 'economy of "signs"' served on women's bodies, sexuality and roles has

---

* Sharon A. Bong, 'Suffering, Resisting, Healing: An Asian View of the Body', *Concilium* (2002/2).

become not only unsavoury but also distasteful.[3] Women are equal but different within the equation of the complementarity of the sexes. Secondly, women are divested of the capacity to act 'in persona Christi' (imaging Christ) notwithstanding their 'feminine genius'. This essential lack inherent in the ontology of woman, her very being, affords the irrefutable and therefore irreversible rationale to women's exclusion from priestly ordination.[4] And thirdly, extolling the virtue of 'heroic love' of women who refuse to abort a foetus resulting from 'the injustice of rape'[5] evinces the 'violence of abstraction' of a theology disconnected from the signs of the times. Its maturity date for those who inhabit and negotiate their bodies and sexualities within the intersection of gender, race, caste, class, cultures and religions, has long expired.

Bodies that suffer, bodies that resist and bodies that heal constitute the life-blood, sinew and fibre of Christian theologies from Asia. In this article, with 'an economy' of words, I reflect on the centrality and limits of theologizing on the materiality of bodies that are pathologized (bodies that suffer), politicized (bodies that resist) and spiritualized (bodies that heal).

BODIES THAT SUFFER

Imaging a suffering Christ is literalized in women (and men) who are dehumanized. An embodied theology in faithful allegiance to Christ's preferential option and actualization of scarred bodies confers hermeneutical privilege on the biblical poor. It does so in recognition of the lived realities of Asian women (and men) who are pinioned by structural and systemic violence in the form of gender, racial, caste, class, cultural and religious oppressions.

The bodies that suffer are thus those who know (suffering) as opposed to the primacy of historically laudable mediators of knowledge, translators of experience and codifiers of faith. And they are mothers, wives, daughters, sisters who are victims and survivors of familial violence in the form of female infanticide, incest, dowry deaths, honour killings, domestic violence (which includes marital rape); communal and military violence in the mass rape of women from ethnic minorities, outcast (i.e. Dalit of India) or indigenous communities; state violence manifest in rape, torture, summary executions and forced relocation, labour and deportation of women in

situations of armed conflict; and global violence through the traffick-
ing of women and girls and inhumane treatment of migrant and sex
workers and disenfranchised sexual minorities. They are the 12,612
dowry deaths recorded across India in 1998–9 where new brides were
starved, beaten, tortured, imprisoned at home and/or doused with
paraffin and set alight by their husbands or mothers-in-law because
their families failed to make 'adequate' dowry payments to the
husband's family.[6]

It is women's bodies constructed as repositories and markers of
ethnic, cultural and religious boundaries that result in women's
greater vulnerability to racism, racial and ethnic discrimination, xenophobia and related intolerance which not only affect women in different ways and degrees from men but also exacerbate gender-based
violence.[7] It is the 168 Indonesian women and girls of mostly Chinese
descent who were gang raped in the streets and raped in front of their
families during the mid-May 1998 Jakarta riots.[8]

It is the appropriation of women's bodies as a site of contestation
between fundamentalism and feminism: where women's bodies in the
former ideology serve as retainers of pristine and immutable identity
and in the latter, as breeding ground for polluting subversive change.
The scene is the 1994 Cairo International Conference on Population
and Development (ICPD); the script, 'replete with death threats from
militant Egyptian Muslim groups, eschatological rhetoric from the
Vatican' amid the dissonant chorus of women's health, rights and
empowerment; and the 'prop', women's bodies, their sexuality and
their roles in family and society.[9]

It is the inscription of women's bodies as a lesser body that is the
foundational premise of son preference endemic in Asian cultures and
contentiously, in the church. This predisposes a girl-child to a life of
gender-based violence, in particular early marriage (including child
marriage) and sexual exploitation and a life of deprivation in terms of
adequate access to food, health, education and love. It is nearly one
seventh of Chinese baby girls missing— for every 100 girls registered
at birth, there are 118 little boys—as a result of female infanticide (or
baby dumping) and prenatal sex selection (illegal, selective abortion)
as extensions of son preference.[10]

The democratization of Asian theology reinstates the primacy of
bodies that suffer into the body of the canon. Hermeneutical privilege
is thus accorded to them and the 'community becomes the theologian'.[11] They thereby serve as the pulse of Asian theologies of
liberation for they liberate theology from its doctrinal abstractions,

hegemony and disconnectedness. To illustrate the centrality of the oppressed as the foundational basis of theologies from Asia, 'Dalit theology' or 'No people's theology' embraces the 'no-humanness' of *dalits* (pariah of Indian society) as symptomatic of the negation of their humanity, yet strives to realize their 'full divinity' as created in God's image (*Imago Dei*).[12] In so doing, theologies premised on bodies that suffer call for the 'primacy of anthropological element over the ecclesiastical', 'utopian over the factual', 'critical over the dogmatic', 'social over the personal' and 'orthopraxis over orthodoxy'.[13]

Theologizing from the vantage point of the marginalized does not detract from but essentially concretizes Christ's preferential option for the poor: where one's compassion and interconnectedness with those who are more dispirited is the hallmark of Two-Thirds world women and men *doing* theology. It stretches the limits of Christianity as an eschatological faith premised on the potential and obligation of human agency to evince a better tomorrow today: to approximate a heaven on earth. This conviction then materializes into a catalytic spirit that embraces solidarity with the marginalized and culminates in an 'eruption from below'.[14] In profoundly identifying with the poor, in being a servant to the poor, in conferring upon the poor the dignity of self-determination, theologians reinstate the plural and radical voice of the marginalized of Asia as the cornerstone of theologies of, for and by Asians.

However, eschewing an exegetic 'violence of abstraction' runs the risk of pathologizing bodies that suffer: of inscribing Asian bodies, particularly Asian women's bodies, as weak, infirmed and violated. On one level, the inferiorization, subjugation and victimization of women and the girl-child from birth to grave substantiate bodies that suffer as knowing subjects of theological discourse as argued above. But hermeneutical and political privileging of bodies that suffer is also problematized. For instance, the 'theology of "the poor woman" in Asia' has its discursive limits as Wong Wai Ching deconstructs the monolithic categorization of 'the poor woman' as a metonym for human suffering. Within the economy of a nationalistic rhetoric and strategy that dichotomizes the colonized Asian against the Western imperialist, women's individuated historical and political agency is often subsumed. Women's bodies are on the one hand homogenously constructed as victimized to justify colonial intervention in the form of civilizing missions; on the other hand, they are propped up as barometers of national essence to preserve tradition and to fortify resistance. Within a postcolonial identity politics, she is thus doubly colonized: denigrated as 'poor woman' and idealized as 'superwoman'.[15]

BODIES THAT RESIST

Theologizing therefore begins with an awareness of the pitfalls of pathologizing and its attendant risks of romanticizing and appropriating the narratives of subjugated positions. It follows through with a conviction that foregrounding bodies that suffer as the foundational premise of theology would potentially illuminate the underlying causes of structural and systemic sin towards the realization of a transformative vision of the world. Solidarity with the oppressed and substantiation of our collective and reciprocal self-worth and determination thus serve as prerequisites to the authentication of embodied theologies from Asia.

As such, hermeneutical subjects or bodies that know are also bodies that resist. In breaking the silence on sexuality, they generate new ways of seeing which are grounded, specific and critical. It is those who challenge homophobia and heterosexism in negotiating sexuality from a human rights perspective:[16] whereby women—as affirmed in the *Beijing Platform For Action*, the international blueprint of women's human rights—are 'to have control over and decide freely and responsibly on matters related to their sexuality, including sexual and reproductive health, free of coercion, discrimination and violence'.[17] It is those who recognize that empowering women does not disempower men in stemming the HIV/AIDS pandemic in Asia: that more gender-equitable relationships significantly reduce the risk of vulnerability of *both* women and men to HIV infection.[18] It is those who redefine virginity on their own terms in embracing chastity of mind, body and spirit and those who reject the construct of virginity as proof of a woman's marriageable worth.[19] It is those who demystify the regulation of women's sexuality and representation as 'ornamented surface' for the gratification of male pleasure and gaze.[20] And it is the 80 comfort women who broke the silence of their victimization in a mock tribunal on Japan's World War II enslavement of at least 200,000 women in military brothels in occupied territories in South East Asia and East Asia.[21]

It is the bodies that resist seamless categorizations within the plurality and proliferation of identities embroiled in multi-ethnic, multi-cultural and multi-religious contexts in Asia compounded by the disparity between the have and have-nots therein. It is the implausibility and indecency of ranking hierarchically suffering and resistant bodies. It is Vietnamese women opting for cosmetic surgery in pursuit of the idealization of Western standards of beauty to embellish their Asian features *and* Bangladeshi women who receive reconstructive surgery as survivors of acid attacks to refigure physical but not emotional scars.[22] It is not de-sexualizing the grassroots as bodies that suffer and bodies that resist in agitating for structural change within the church and society. It is avoiding the violent othering of the Other in embracing gay, lesbian, bisexual, trans-sexual, trans-gendered and other disinherited bodies as well as the single, widowed and childless as deviations from normative heterosexual and (re)productive relations. It is recognizing that the bodies that do not have enough to eat, bodies that overeat and bodies that refuse to eat rest on the same continuum of need. It is coming to terms with the inequitable distribution of the world's resources that accounts for hunger and obesity as corollary eating disorders. And it is being aware that voluntary starvation is paradoxically a protest against the construction of women's bodies and regulation of women's sexualities as well as an eroticization of thinness as a beauty myth that is internally inflicted.

BODIES THAT HEAL

In 'an epistemology of the broken body', the restoration of bodies that suffer and bodies that resist becomes the dialectical site of redemption, for as Chung Hyun Kyung contends, 'to be human is to suffer and resist' and 'to be human is to be created in God's image'.[23] For Asians where the spirit is corporeal and the body (and sexuality) sacred, by inference, the body is the spirit. The configuration of the human person as both body *and* spirit reinstates not only their human agency but also human worth and in repositioning the spirit as corporeal and the body as sacred, Asian theologians depart from doctrinal eschatology that maintains the inferiorization of material and sexualized bodies.

The benchmark of Christianity in Asia is as such, its insistence on praxis—faith translated as compassionate identification and solidarity with the marginalized. The Asian sense of ecclesiastical mission as premised on the 'epistemology of the broken body'—alluding simultaneously to the crucifixion of Christ as/and bodies that suffer, resist and heal—attests to the concretization of a transformative faith that witnesses the transition from '*anthropocentrism to life-centrism*' and the adoption of 'voluntary [spiritual] poverty' in dialectical opposition to 'forced [material] poverty'.[24] Embodied theologies thus problematize dualisms such as mind/body, spirit/matter, abstract/concrete, objective/subjective, theory/praxis, universal/particular, observer/observed and male/female.

For Asian theologies, the representation of God in the anthropomorphic Christ is both transcendent *and* immanent. God therefore is not immutable and dispassionate but is embodied in and through the oppressed. The phenomenon of a '*christological transformation*' is exacted through the use of 'religio-political symbols' to encapsulate unique images of Christ concordant with the experiences of Asian peoples.[25] The postcolonial portrayal of Jesus as 'liberator, revolutionary and political martyr' mirrors the political martyrdom of Filipino women in their relentless crusade for social transformation: that they 'do not merely accompany Christ to Calvary as spectators [but also] carry the cross with him and undergo his passion in an act of identification with his suffering' and in so doing, resurrect 'the *Bagong Kristo* (the New Christ)' that resides within them.[26] Through a 'christology from below'[27] God is thus transmuted and humanized. Knowledge of God as omniscient, omnipresent and omnipotent is arbitrated through the agency of the suffering and resistant and God the Signifier thus becomes known, present and empowering.

An emerging Asian spirituality of, for and by Asian people is fundamentally a theology that necessitates the politics of difference and the politics of identity premised on the socially determinate lives of its knowing subjects—the bodies that suffer, resist and are healed. A theology that matters is a theology that is embodied. And a theology that is embodied is sound theology. The spirituality of Asian people affords a site of theological inquiry to the question of praxis or committed action. The politicization of spirituality and the spiritualization of politics endemic in Asian theologizing prophetically herald the eschatological promise of begetting a heaven on earth. It is the realization of an equitable, just and sustainable global/local community from within the church and beyond. It is in the context of Asia, ceasing to wonder at the extent to which favouring sons and neglecting daughters, is sanctioned by the 'economy of "signs"' of the body of the church.

Notes

1. C. S. Song, quoted in Charles Elliott, *Sword and Spirit* (London, 1989), 42.
2. Chung Hyun Kyung, *Struggle to be the Sun Again: Introducing Asian Women's Theology* (London, 1990), 101.
3. 'Pope John Paul II's Letter to Women' issued (10 July 1995) to address the Fourth United Nations World Conference on Women, Beijing (para. 11) at: http://www.womenpriests.org/church/Beijing.htm
4. Sally M. Vance-Trembath, 'John Paul II's *Ut Unum Sint* and Conversation With Women', *Theological Studies* 60 (1999), 103.
5. 'Letter to Women' (n. 3), para. 5.
6. BBC News, 'Jail Crisis for Dowry Crimes', 1 June 2000 at: http://news.bbc. co.uk/hi/english/south_asia/newsid_772000/772896.stm
7. The Asia-Pacific NGO (non-governmental organization) Position Paper prepared for the 45th Session of the UN Commission on Status of Women (CSW), New York, 6–16 Mar. 2001, as well as the recent World Conference Against Racism, Racial Discrimination, Xenophobia and Related Intolerance (WCAR), Durban, South Africa, 31 Aug.–7 Sept. 2001. It was originally drafted by the Asia Pacific Forum on Women, Law and Development (APWLD), based in Chiangmai, Thailand, in consultation with women's NGOs and other grassroots organizations in the Asia-Pacific at: http://194.78.216.158/whrnet3/wcar/key_docs/intersection.htm
8. *New Straits Times Press* (Kuala Lumpur, Malaysia), 18 Aug. 1998, 20.
9. Lynn P. Freedman, 'The Challenge of Fundamentalisms', *Reproductive Health Matters* 8 (Nov. 1996), 56.
10. BBC News, 'China's Unwanted Girls', 23 Aug. 2001 at: http://news. bbc.co.uk/hi/english/world/asia-pacific/newsid_1506000/1506469.stm
11. Chung, *Struggle to be the Sun Again*, 103.
12. Arvind P. Nirmal, 'Toward a Christian Dalit Theology', in *Frontiers in Asian Christian Theology: Emerging Trends*, ed. R. S. Sugirtharajah (New York, 1994), 40, 34.
13. Alfred T. Hennelly, *Liberation Theology: A Documentary History* (New York, 1990), 160–1.
14. Jojo M. Fung SJ, *Shoes-Off Barefoot We Walk: A Theology of Shoes-Off* (Kuala Lumpur, 1992), 79.
15. Wong Wai Ching, 'Negotiating for a Postcolonial Identity: Theology of "the Poor Woman" in Asia', *Journal of Feminist Studies in Religion* 16(2) (fall 2000), 9.
16. beng hui, 'Time's Up! Moving Sexuality Rights in Malaysia into the New Millennium', *Women in Action*, 1999 at: http://www.isiswomen.org/wia/wia199/sex00006.html
17. United Nations, *The Beijing Declaration and the Platform For Action, Fourth World Conference on Women, Beijing, China 4–15 September 1995*, para. 96.
18. Geeta Rao Gupta, 'Gender, Sexuality and HIV/AIDS: The What, the Why, and the How', Plenary Address, XIIth International AIDS Conference, Durban, South Africa, 12 July 2000.
19. Celeste Cinco, 'Virginity in the 90s: Young Filipinas Face up to Contending Pressures [of] Virginity', *Women in Action*, 1999 at: http://www.isiswomen.org/wia/wia199/sex00008.html

20. Young-Hee Shim, 'Gender and Body Politics in Korea: Focusing on the Making of the Feminine Body', *Asian Women* 6 (June 1998), 23.
21. *New York Times*, 'Mock Tribunal for Sex Slaves Opens', Dec. 2000 at: http://194.78.216.158/whrnet3/tribunal/press/sex_slaves.htm
22. BBC News, 'Vietnam: West is Best for Beauty', 11 Jan. 1999 at: http://news.bbc.co.uk/hi/english/world/asia-pacific/newsid_250000/250630.stm and 'Joyous Homecoming for Acid Attack Victims', 22 July 1999 at: http://news. bbc-.co.uk/hi/english/world/south_asia/newsid_401000/401993.stm
23. Chung, *Struggle to be the Sun Again*, 39, 47.
24. Ibid. 42–3.
25. Ibid. 62.
26. Ibid. 63–4. Wong Wai Ching cautions that such postcolonial discourse, which polarizes Western imperialist/Asian colonized in politicizing Christ's salvific mission, runs the risk of 'normalization and routinization of one kind of women's experience—that is, as victims of foreign and home exploitation—and one form of women's agency—that is, as national-liberation combatants'. 'Negotiating for a Postcolonial Identity', 21.
27. Chung, *Struggle to be the Sun Again*, 60.

Further Reading

Here follows a select bibliography of edited collections on feminism and theology. We hope it will help readers to extend discussions begun in this volume, as well as suggesting sources for approaches and issues we have not been able to address.

Sources: In the Beginning God . . .

ADAMS, CAROL J. (ed.), *Ecofeminism and the Sacred* (New York: Continuum, 1993).

CHRIST, CAROL P., and PLASKOW, JUDITH (eds.), *Womanspirit Rising: A Feminist Reader in Religion* (San Francisco: Harper & Row, 1979; repr. 1992).

CLARK, ELIZABETH A., RICHARDSON, HERBERT, BOWER, GARY, and STYERS, RANDALL (eds.), *Women and Religion: The Original Sourcebook of Women in Christian Thought* (San Francisco: Harper & Row, 1996).

ISHERWOOD, LISA, and McEWAN, DOROTHEA (eds.), *An A to Z of Feminist Theology* (Sheffield: Sheffield Academic Press, 1996).

JUSCHKA, DARLENE M. (ed.), *Feminism in the Study of Religion: A Reader* (New York: Continuum, 2001).

KING, URSULA (ed.), *Feminist Theology from the Third World: A Reader* (London: SPCK, 1994).

LOADES, ANN (ed.), *Feminist Theology: A Reader* (London: SPCK, 1990).

PARSONS, SUSAN FRANK (ed.), *The Cambridge Companion to Feminist Theology* (Cambridge: Cambridge University Press, 2002).

RUETHER, ROSEMARY RADFORD (ed.), *Womanguides: Readings Toward a Feminist Theology* (Boston: Beacon Press, 1996).

—— (ed.), *Women Healing Earth: Third World Women on Ecology, Feminism, and Religion* (London: SCM Press, 1996).

RUSSELL, LETTY M., and CLARKSON, J. SHANNON (eds.), *Dictionary of Feminist Theologies* (London: Mowbray, 1996).

Identity: Who Do You Say I Am?

AQUINO, MARIA PILAR, MACHADO, DAISY L., and RODRÍGUEZ, JEANNETTE (eds.), *A Reader in Latina Feminist Theology: Religion and Justice* (Austin: University of Texas Press, 2002).

CARR, ANNE E., and SCHÜSSLER FIORENZA, ELISABETH (eds.), *The Special Nature of Women?* Concilium 1991/6 (Philadelphia: Trinity Press International, 1991).

CHOPP, REBECCA S., and GREEVE DAVANEY, SHEILA (eds.), *Horizons in*

Feminist Theology: Identity, Tradition, and Norms (Minneapolis: Fortress Press, 1997).

DAVIDMAN, LYNN, and TENENBAUM, SHELLY (eds.), *Feminist Perspectives on Jewish Studies* (New Haven: Yale University Press, 1996).

HESCHEL, SUSANNAH (ed.), *On Being a Jewish Feminist* (New York: Schocken, 1995)

KING, URSULA (ed.), *Feminist Theology from the Third World: A Reader* (London: SPCK, 1994).

IRIGARAY, LUCE, and WHITFORD, MARGARET (eds.), *The Irigaray Reader* (Oxford: Blackwell, 1991).

KIM, C. W., ST VILLE, MAGGIE, and SIMONAITIS, SUSAN M. (eds.), *Transfigurations: Theology and the French Feminists* (Minneapolis: Fortress Press, 1993).

PESKOWITZ, MIRIAM, and LEVITT, LAURA, *Judaism since Gender* (New York: Routledge, 1997).

RUSSELL, LETTY M., GENEVA CANNON, KATIE, and ISASI-DIAZ, ADA MARÍA (eds.), *Inheriting Our Mothers' Gardens: Feminist Theology in Third World Perspective* (San Francisco: Westminster John Knox Press, 1991).

RUTTENBERG, DANYA, and HESCHEL, SUSANNAH (eds.), *Yentl's Revenge: The Next Wave of Jewish Feminism* (Seattle: Seal Press, 2001).

SANDER, CHERYL J. (ed.), *Living the Intersection: Womanism and Afrocentrism in Theology* (Minneapolis: Fortress Press, 1995).

SCHÜSSLER FIORENZA, ELISABETH (ed.), *The Power of Naming: A Concilium Reader in Feminist Liberation Theology* (Maryknoll, NY: Orbis, 1996).

Sacred Texts: Your Word is a Lamp to My Feet

BACH, ALICE (ed.), *Women in the Hebrew Bible: A Reader* (New York: Routledge, 1999).

BRENNER, ATHALYA, and FONTAINE, CAROLE (eds.), *A Feminist Companion to Reading the Bible: Approaches, Methods and Strategies* (Sheffield: Sheffield Academic Press, 1997).

BUCHMANN, CHRISTINA, and SPIEGEL, CELINA (eds.), *Out of the Garden: Women Writers on the Bible* (New York: Fawcett Columbine, 1995).

KWOK, PUI-LAN, and SCHÜSSLER FIORENZA, ELISABETH (eds.), *Women's Sacred Scriptures*, Concilium 1998/3 (Maryknoll, NY: Orbis, 1998).

RUSSELL, LETTY M., *Feminist Interpretation of the Bible* (Philadelphia: Westminster Press, 1985).

SCHOTTROFF, LUISE, SCHROER, SILVIA, and WACKER, MARIE-THERES (eds.), trans. Barbara and Martin Rumscheidt, *Interpretation: The Bible in Women's Perspective* (Minneapolis: Fortress Press, 1998).

SCHÜSSLER FIORENZA, ELISABETH, BROCK, ANN, and MATTHEWS, SHELLY (eds.), *Searching the Scriptures* (London: SCM Press, 1994).

WASHINGTON, HAROLD E., LOCHRIE GRAHAM, SUSAN, and THIMMES,

PAMELA (eds.), *Escaping Eden: New Feminist Perspectives on the Bible* (Sheffield: Sheffield Academic Press, 1998).

Practice: And Her Works Shall Praise Her in the Gates

BERGER, TERESA (ed.), *Dissident Daughters: Feminist Liturgies in Global Context* (San Francisco: Westminster John Knox Press, 2002).

CAHILL, LISA SOWLE, and MIETH, DIETMAR (eds.), *The Family*, Concilium 1994/5 (London: SCM Press, 1995).

CARR, ANNE E., SCHÜSSLER FIORENZA, ELISABETH, and HILLYER, PHILIP (eds.), *Motherhood: Experience, Institution, Theology*, Concilium 206 (Edinburgh: T. & T. Clark, 1989).

CARR, ANNE E., and STEWART VAN LEEUWEN, MARY (eds.), *Religion, Feminism, and the Family* (Louisville, Ky.: Westminster John Knox Press, 1996).

DALY, LOIS K., LOVIN, ROBIN W., and SCHWEIKER, WILLIAM (eds.), *Feminist Theological Ethics: A Reader* (Louisville, Ky.: Westminster John Knox Press, 1994).

JOY, MORNY, O'GRADY, KATHLEEN, and POXON, JUDITH L. (eds.), *French Feminists on Religion: A Reader* (London: Routledge, 2001).

PLASKOW, JUDITH, and CHRIST, CAROL P. (eds.), *Weaving the Visions: New Patterns in Feminist Spirituality* (San Francisco: Harper & Row, 1989).

ROTHSCHILD, SYLVIA, and SHERIDAN, SYBIL (eds.), *Taking Up the Timbrel: The Challenge of Creating Ritual for Jewish Women Today* (London: SCM Press, 2000).

SCHÜSSLER FIORENZA, ELISABETH, COLLINS, MARY, and LEFÉBURE, MARCUS (eds.), *Women: Invisible in Theology and Church*, Concilium 182 (Edinburgh: T. & T. Clark, 1985).

Incarnation and Embodiment: The Word Became Flesh

BYNUM, CAROLINE WALKER, HARRELL, STEVEN, and RICHMAN, PAULA (eds.), *Gender and Religion: On the Complexity of Symbols* (Boston: Beacon Press, 1986).

COAKLEY, SARAH, *Religion and the Body* (Cambridge: Cambridge University Press, 1997).

DAVIES, JON, and LOUGHLIN, GERARD (eds.), *Sex These Days: Essays on Theology, Sexuality and Society*, Studies in Theology and Sexuality 1 (Sheffield: Sheffield Academic Press, 1997).

FABELLA, VIRGINIA, and ODUYOYE, MERCY AMBA (eds.), *With Passion and Compassion: Third World Women Doing Theology* (Maryknoll, NY: Orbis, 1988).

HAMPSON, DAPHNE (ed.), *Swallowing a Fishbone? Feminist Theologians Debate Christianity* (London: SPCK, 1996).

ISHERWOOD, LISA, and STUART, ELIZABETH (eds.), *Introducing Body Theology* (Sheffield: Sheffield Academic Press, 2000).

KRISTEVA, JULIA, and MOI, TORIL (eds.), *The Kristeva Reader* (New York: Columbia University Press, 1986).

LaCugna, Catherine Mowry (ed.), *Freeing Theology: The Essentials of Theology in Feminist Perspective* (New York: HarperCollins, 1993).

Oduyoye, Mercy Amba, and Kanyoro, Musimbi (eds.), *The Will to Arise: Women, Tradition and the Church in Africa* (Maryknoll, NY: Orbis, 1992).

Russell, Letty M., Farley, Margaret A., and Jones, Serene (eds.), *Liberating Eschatology: Essays in Honor of Letty M. Russell* (Louisville, Ky.: Westminster John Knox Press, 1999).

Townes, Emilie M. (ed.), *A Troubling in My Soul: Womanist Perspectives on Evil and Suffering*, Bishop Henry Mcneal Turner Studies in North American Black Religion 8 (Maryknoll, NY: Orbis, 1993).

Index